OFFICE INTERIORS
& BUSINESS BUILDINGS

LINKS

OFFICE INTERIORS & BUSINESS BUILDINGS

Author: Carles Broto

Editorial coordination: Jacobo Krauel

Graphic design & production: Roberto Bottura, architect

Collaborator: Oriol Vallés, graphic designer

Text: Contributed by the architects, edited by Jay Noden & William George

© **LINKSBOOKS**

Jonqueres, 10, 1-5

08003 Barcelona, Spain

Tel.: +34-93-301-21-99

Fax: +34-93-301-00-21

info@linksbooks.net

www.linksbooks.net

© This is a collective work. In accordance with Intellectual Property Law "collective works" are NOT necessarily those produced by more than one author. They have been created by the initiative and coordination of one person who edits and distributes them under his/her name. A collective work constitutes a collection of contributions from different authors whose personal contributions form part of a creation, without it being possible to separately attribute rights over the work as a whole.

© All rights reserved. No part of this book may be used or reproduced in any manner whatsoever without written permission except in the case of brief quotations embodied in critical articles and reviews.

OFFICE INTERIORS
& BUSINESS BUILDINGS

LINKS

INDEX

008 Studio O+A
Facebook Headquarters

016 John Friedman Alice Kimm Architects
GALCIT (Graduate Aerospace Labs, Caltech)

028 Caterina Tiazzoldi
Toolbox. Torino Office Lab & Co-working

038 Bosch & Fjord
LEGO Offices

046 RA-DA
Bugaboo Headquarters

054 KDa
TBWA \ HAKUHODO HQ

064 Rottet Studio
Artis Capital

072 Studio Ramin Visch
Office Dupon

082 chadbourne + doss architects
HTC Office

092 arquitectura x
Ruales Izurieta Publicidad

100 HASSELL
ANZ Learning Centre

110 BVN Architecture
Goods Shed North

120 Jump Studios
Engine offices

128 Sinato
Yuras

136 Lemaymichaud
Lemaymichaud Offices

148 aplus arquitectes associats
Promobuilding Group

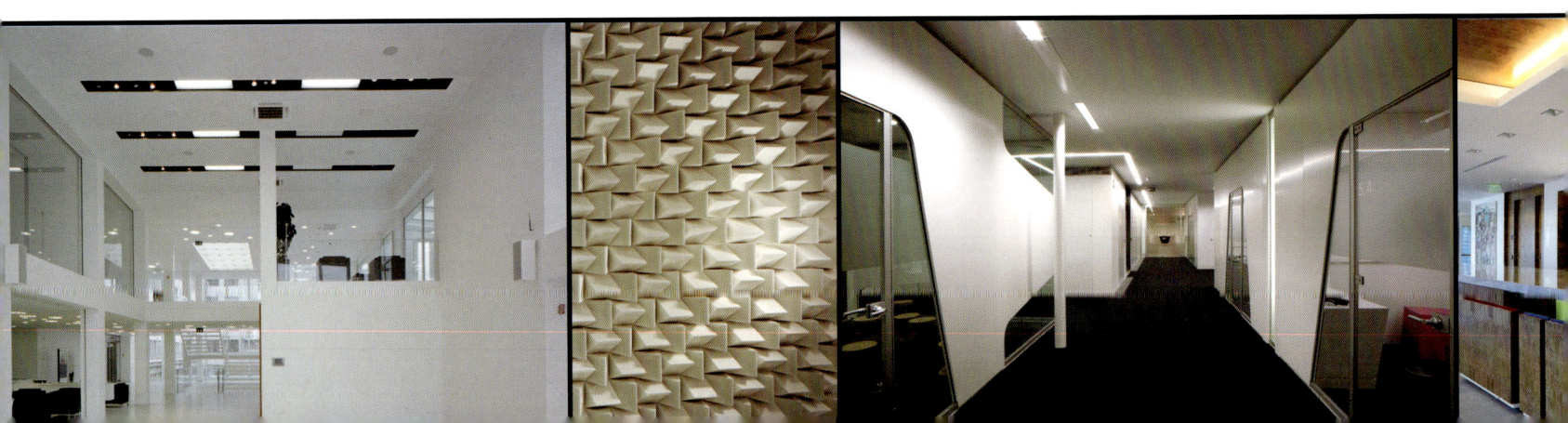

158 Maurice Mentjens PostPanic Office space	**228** El Dorado Architects Hodgdon Powder Company
168 i29 l interior architects Herengracht Office	**238** CL3 K-Boxing Headquarter
178 eins:eins architekten Syzygy agency	**248** Giorgio Borruso Design Fornari Group Headquarters
184 DEGW Ericsson Telecomunicazioni	**256** Featherstone Young Architects Wieden + Kennedy London
194 HASSELL dtac House	**264** Dive Architects Electric Works
204 RA-DA 72andsunny	**274** HASSELL National Foods
212 xarchitekten Ecomplexx Office	**282** Camenzind Evolution Google Zurich
218 Studio Ramin Visch Ogilvy Offices	**292** Clive Wilkinson Architects The Disney Store Headquarters

INTRODUCTION

The work environment, as a space for professional and interpersonal exchange, has undergone dramatic changes in recent years. The continuing swift pace of developments in communication technology, with a new, more timeless, ubiquitous and portable handling of information, has greatly contributed to these changes. Gone are the bulky filing cabinets and expansive tables of yesteryear, with work surfaces having been reduced to the size of a computer. Tele-work and video-conferencing are further indications of this omnipresence.

At the same time, however, there is an ever-increasing trend towards sustainability in architecture, as evidenced by energy-saving measures, alternative energy sources and the use of new materials.

These, and a host of additional concerns particular to office design, greet the architect and interior designers when drawing up the plans for a new workspace. The company's corporate identity, for example, must be somehow translated into the volumes of the interior spaces, as well as infusing the building as a whole. The modern office also requires versatility and dynamism – it must be flexible enough to quickly adapt to a range of uses. It must be aesthetically pleasing and should encourage interpersonal communication amongst employees, whilst significantly lessening outdated hierarchical barriers. In short, this is a concise yet wide-ranging volume, bringing together examples of renovated spaces as well as entirely new ground plans – proposals which comprise an invaluable source of inspiration and a concentrated study of the challenges involved in creating new workspaces.

Studio O+A

Facebook Headquarters

Palo Alto, California, USA   Photographs: contributed by Studio O+A

In 2009, employees of Facebook moved to new headquarters that facilitate interaction and connection, reflecting the company's mission as a social networking website provider. Formerly a laboratory facility for a high-tech manufacturer, the 13,935 sqm structure at Palo Alto's Stanford Research Park brings together more than 700 employees originally scattered throughout 10 locations in and around downtown Palo Alto.

The design of the space relied heavily on input from the users, appropriate for a flatly structured company that weighs every employee's opinion equally. O+A designers interviewed employees about what they wanted from their new headquarters. The Facebook platform was used to conduct company-wide polls about design decisions, post construction photos and updates, and keep everyone informed of the thought processes behind the project.

Because the new facility houses employees coming from various locations, the company wanted to maintain each division's distinct identity. The design takes its inspiration from the patchwork nature of Facebook users and employees, bringing together seemingly disparate elements to form a cohesive pattern and using color and interior spacing to create neighborhoods within the open plan space. The company's executives sit in central areas, accessible to all employees. Large lounges and open spaces provide venues for the community to come together. A kitchen and café continue Facebook's tradition of providing gourmet meals to staff at all hours, while drinks and snacks are available at micro-kitchens throughout the headquarters.

Reflecting employees' desire for green headquarters, the facility is the first commercial project completed under Palo Alto's 2008 Green Building Ordinance, making extensive use of existing architectural features, recycling millwork from the original lab, and 're-purposing' industrial components for post-industrial use. Other sustainable features include high recycled-content carpet and energy-efficient lighting.

The design goal for the new facility was to maintain the history and raw aesthetic of the building and create a fun dynamic appropriate for the company's youthful staff. Many walls and spaces are left unfinished: employees are encouraged to write on the walls, add artwork, and move furniture as needed, allowing the building to evolve continuously.

Architecture:
Studio O+A
Floor area:
150,000 sqft (13,935 sqm)

The design of the space relied heavily on input from the users, appropriate for a flatly structured company that weights every employee's opinion equally.

Referencing the industrial aesthetic of the building, a felt canopy spreads up one wall and onto the ceiling, defining a central meeting area that can double as an impromptu auditorium. Mounted on threaded rods of varying length to achieve an undulating effect, the canopy absorbs sound and is penetrated at intervals by overhead lighting.

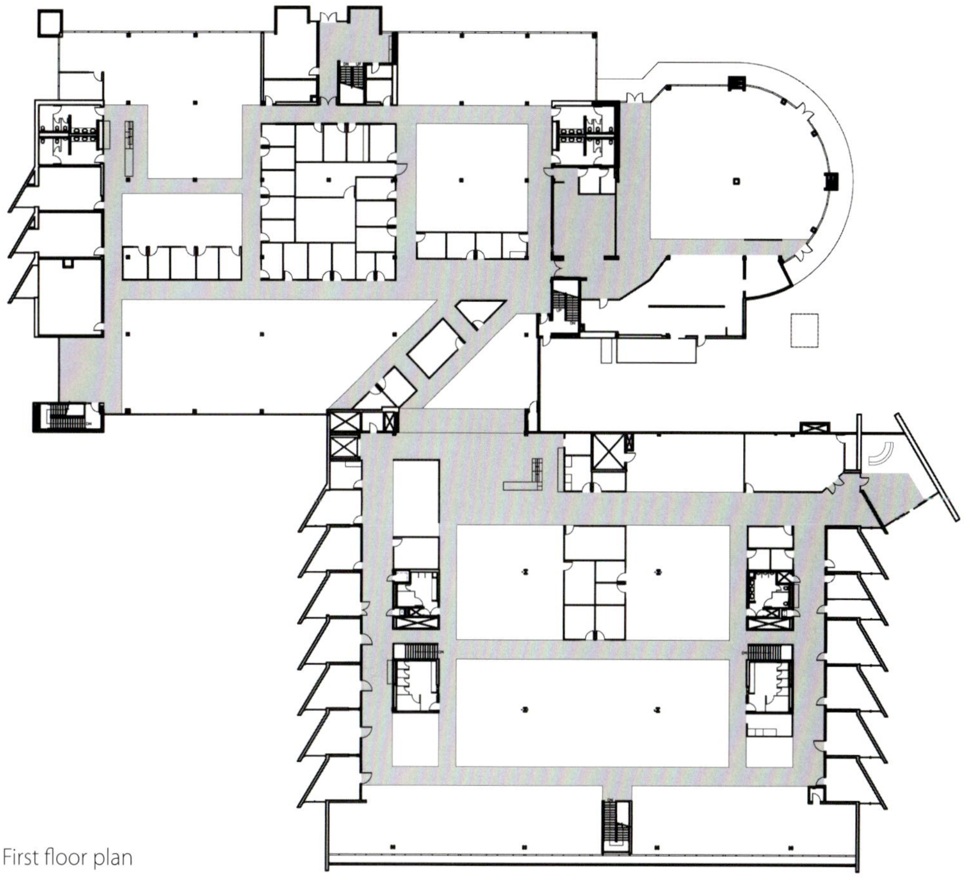

First floor plan

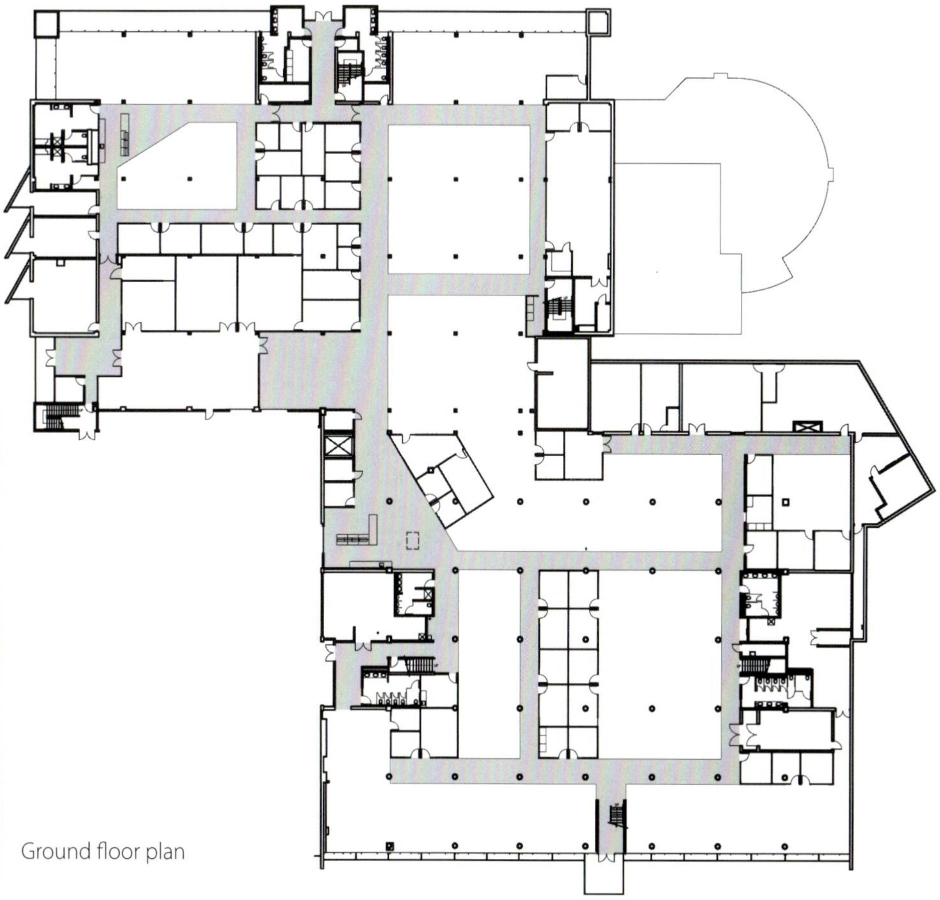

Ground floor plan

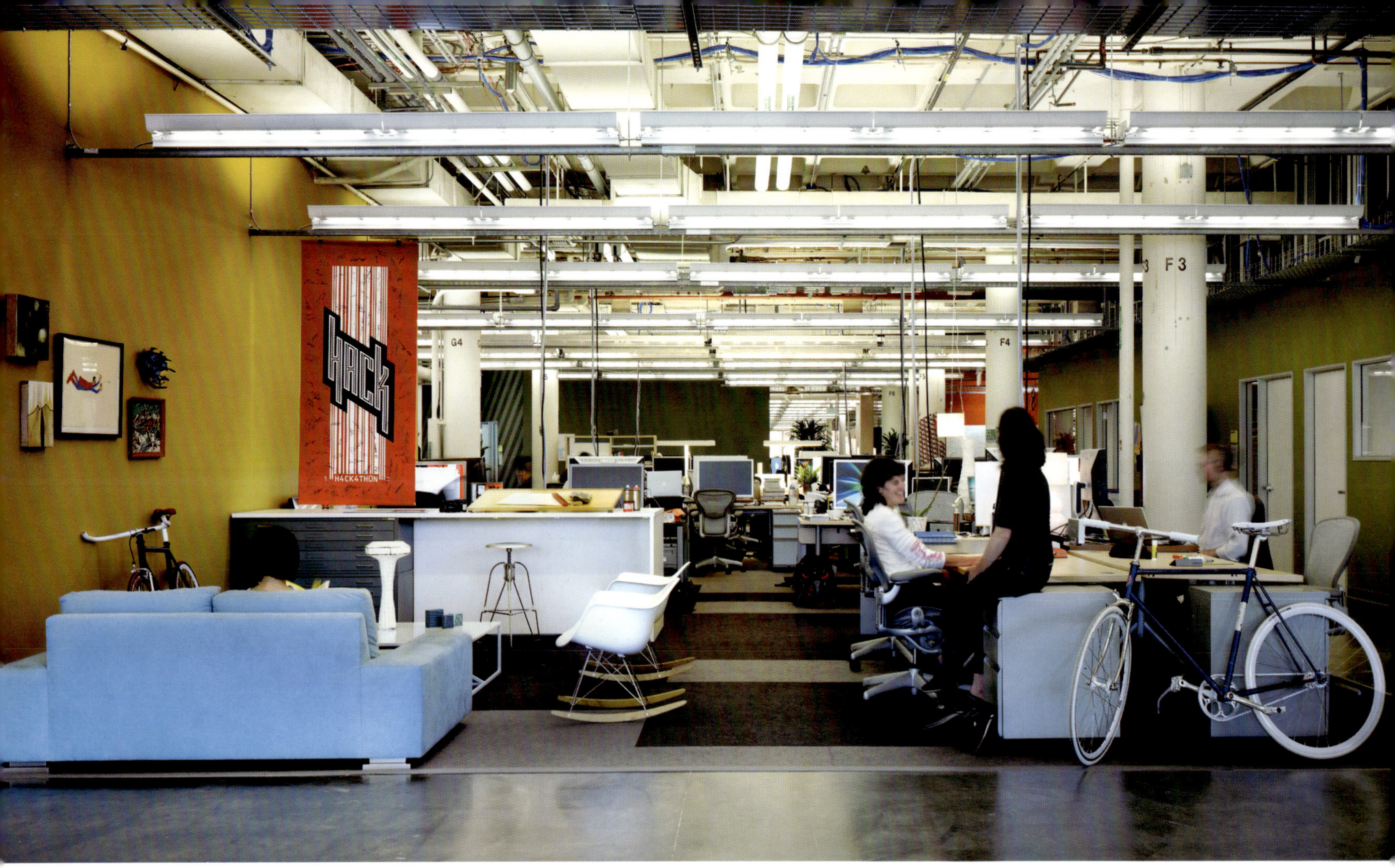
HACK
F3

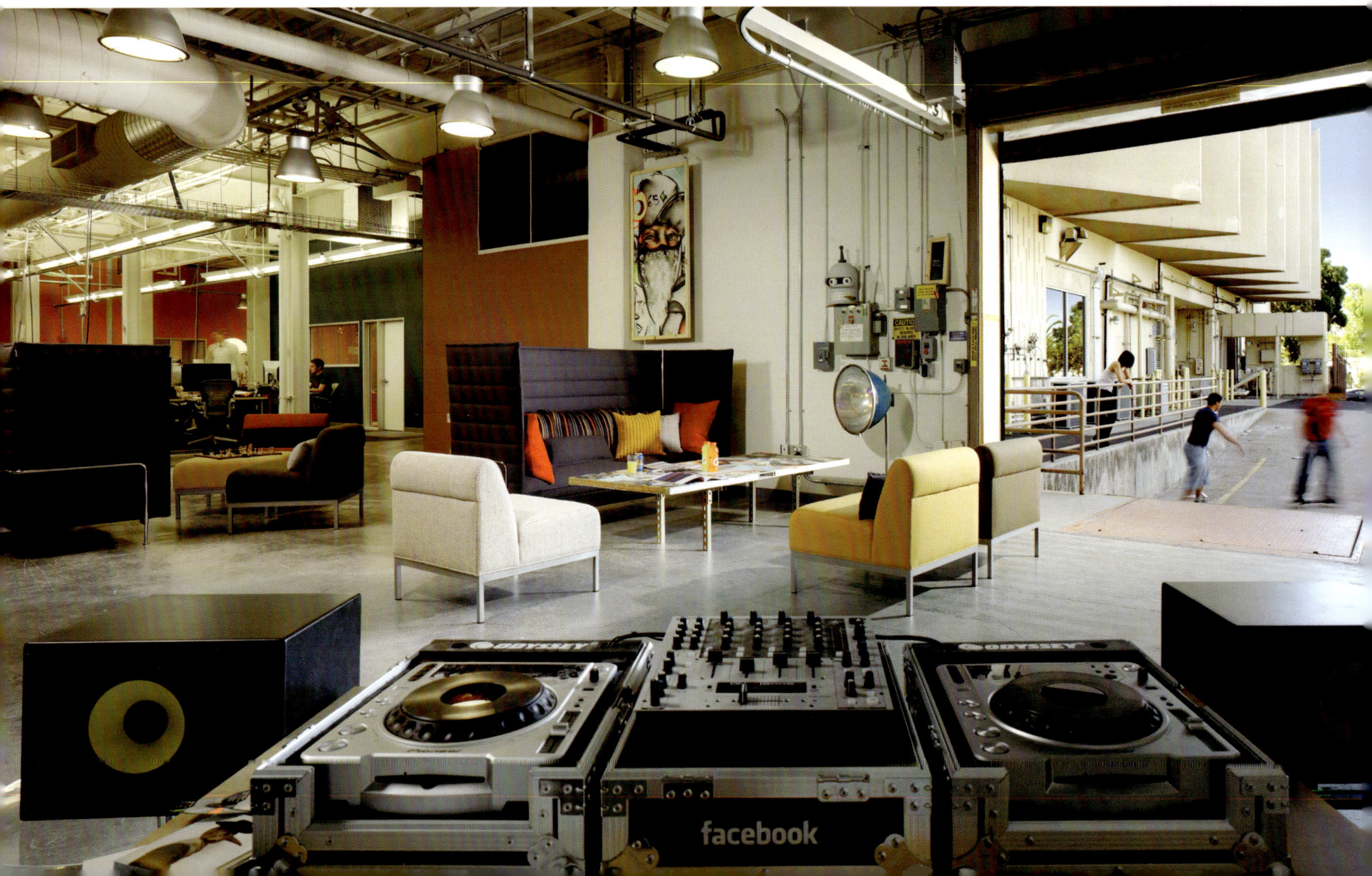
ODYSSEY
ODYSSEY
facebook

A bright orange industrial crane, left over from the building's previous user, was repurposed by San Francisco sculptor Oliver DiCicco to support a table surface from its heavyweight hoist, offering maximum maneuverability.

John Friedman Alice Kimm Architects

GALCIT (Graduate Aerospace Labs, Caltech)

Pasadena, California, USA   Photographs: Benny Chan/Fotoworks

When the architects were asked by the Graduate Aerospace Laboratories at the California Institute of Technology (GALCIT), well-known for pioneering important advances in aeronautics and space exploration, to transform their outdated facilities in Caltech's Guggenheim Building into a dynamic work environment, they were delighted. The client wanted the space to reflect the innovative research being performed by the department's teachers and students. In reworking the 33,000 sq ft (3065 sqm) building designed by Bertrand Goodhue, the following goals were envisaged:

1. Find formal and spatial analogies for GALCIT's research, and create an environment that reflects its innovation and breadth.
2. Provide a strong new identity for GALCIT to enter a new era, enabling it to attract a new kind of student with new expectations about collaborative work.
3. Maximize transparency throughout, promoting the creative exchange of ideas.
4. Celebrate the program's history as well as the current research underway there.

These objectives involved exploring a wide range of digital design and construction tools, many utilized in GALCIT's own research, which successfully expressed the institution's spirit of invention. The program included a new lobby; new laboratories for teaching and experimental research; new exhibition areas; and new conference, office, and interactive spaces, configured to give GALCIT the strong, dynamic branding they desired to attract the world's best scientists, engineers, and students. Given the variety of topics that the GALCIT faculty and students research, pinpointing a formal starting point was a challenge. Aerospace engineering includes everything from the way blood cells flow to rocket science, or a new Mars Rover vehicle in collaboration with a group from NASA. How to be inclusive? Ultimately the formal language derived from the notion of FLOW. Almost all GALCIT research involves flow – understanding how solids, liquids, and gases behave under differential pressures. As a result, the existing building became a metaphorical wind tunnel a neutral container into which new ceilings and wrappers could be inserted. The resultant flow patterns became the basis of new spatial relationships and definitions.

Architecture:
John Friedman Alice Kimm Architects, (JFAK)
Project architect:
Claudia Kessner
Project team:
Robert McFadden,
Garrett Belmont,
Brendan Beachler
Engineers:
TMAD Taylor & Gaines (Structural),
MEDG Consulting Engineers
(Mechanical and plumbing),
Pacific Engineers Group (Electrical)
Consultants:
Lighting:
Allan Leibow, Light Vision;
Jack Lue, Fire Ltd.
Graphics:
Patricia Kovic and Maureen Nishikawa
General contractor:
Del Amo Construction:
Mitch Hudson (Partner, Project Manager),
Kevin Cooper (Project Superintendent)

The building lobby is a central venue for interactive dialogue used for public events and gives GALCIT its new identity. Its suspended plastic ceiling flows in front of the entrance. The ceiling's topography is formed in reaction to light sources above; each source "pulls" at the ceiling's surface, creating a dimple. The ends of the ceiling terminate at doors into the Laboratory of Large Space Structures.

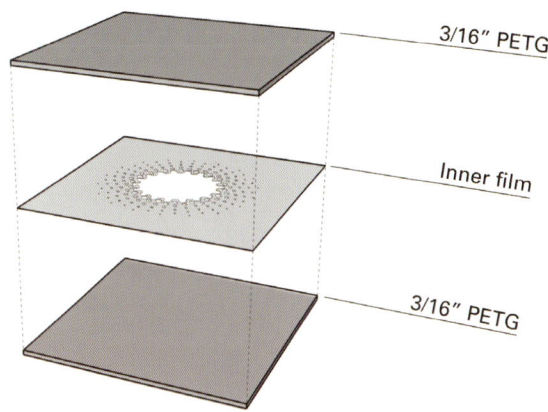

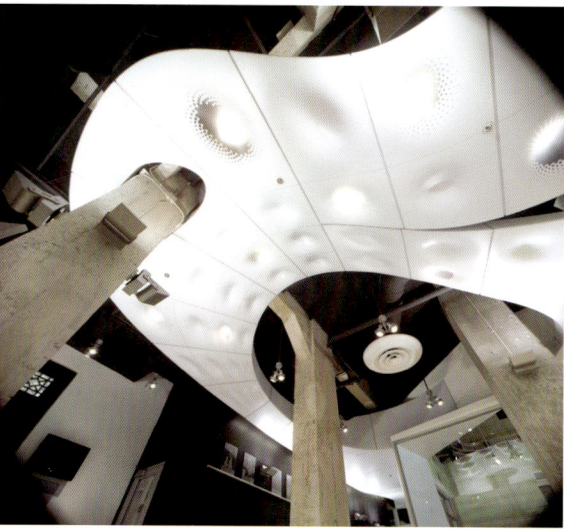

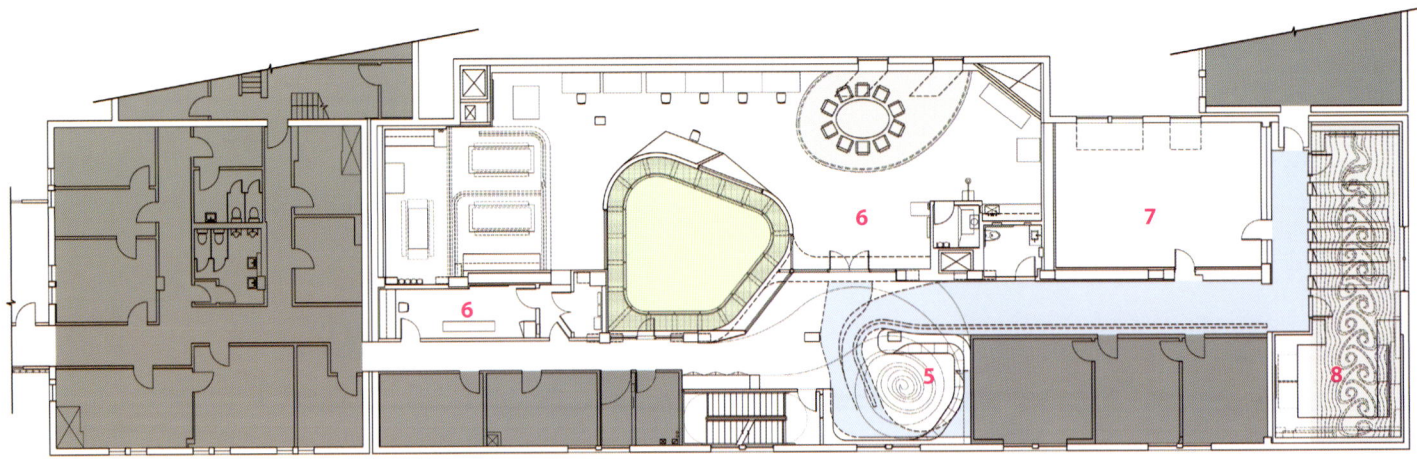

Second floor plan

1. Lobby
2. Laboratory of large space structures double height space
3. Laboratory of large space structures
4. Laboratory of large structures museum
5. Interactive lounge
6. Cann laboratory of experimental innovation classroom
7. Classroom
8. Karman conference room and GALCIT archives
9. Puckett display hall
10. Puckett conference room
11. Puckett computational laboratory
12. Faculty office
13. New laboratory (unassigned)
14. Visiting faculty and doctoral candidates office
15. Interactive study area

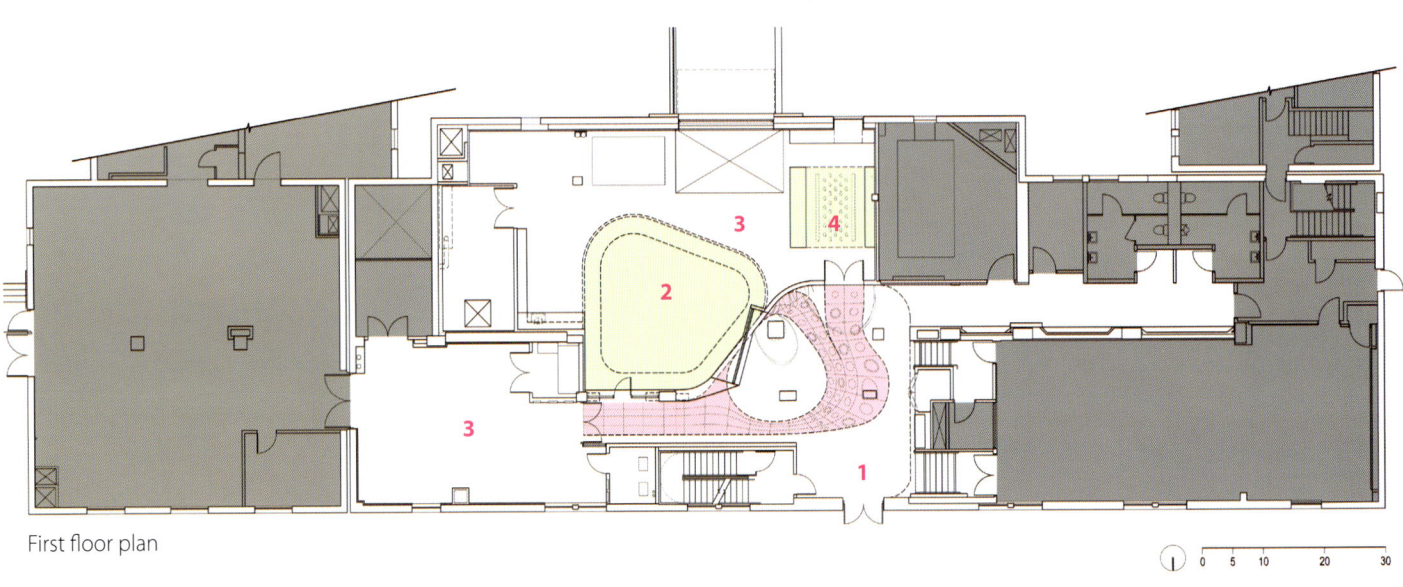

First floor plan

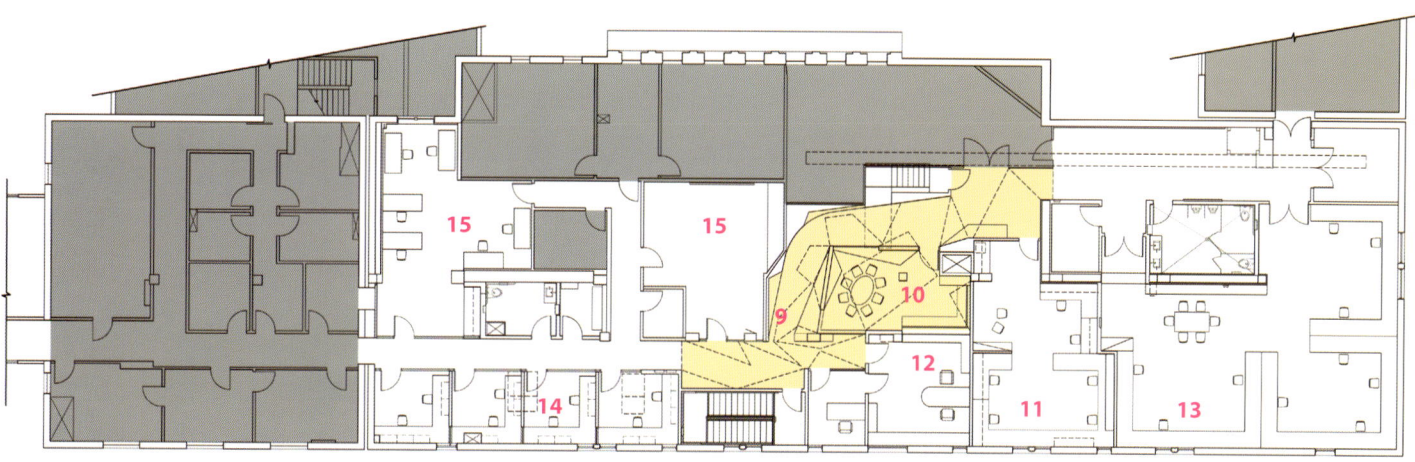

Third floor plan

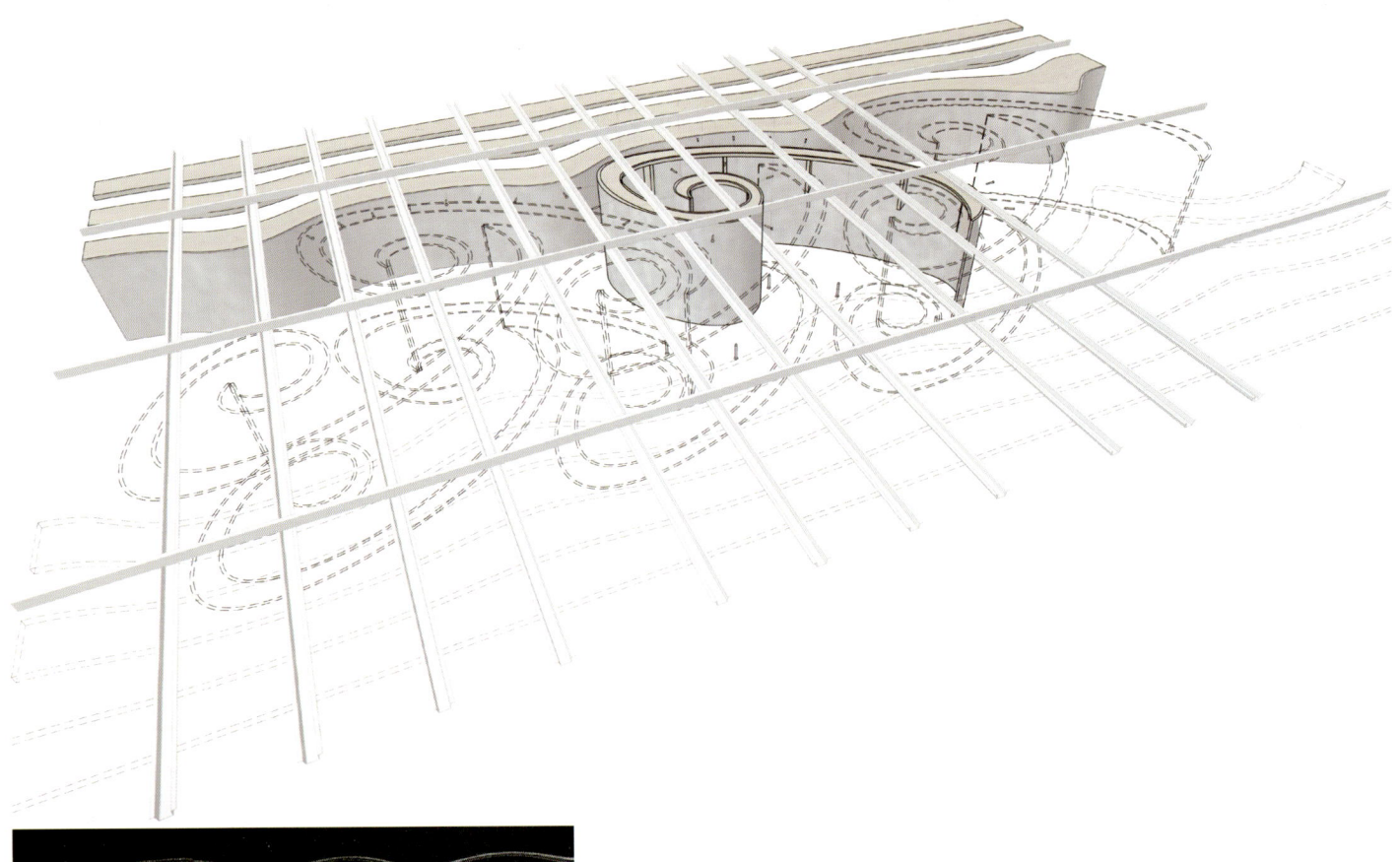

Above: ceiling construction study
Left: GALCIT research image: 'von Karman Vortex' showing the asymmetrical flow due to changes in pressure distribution.

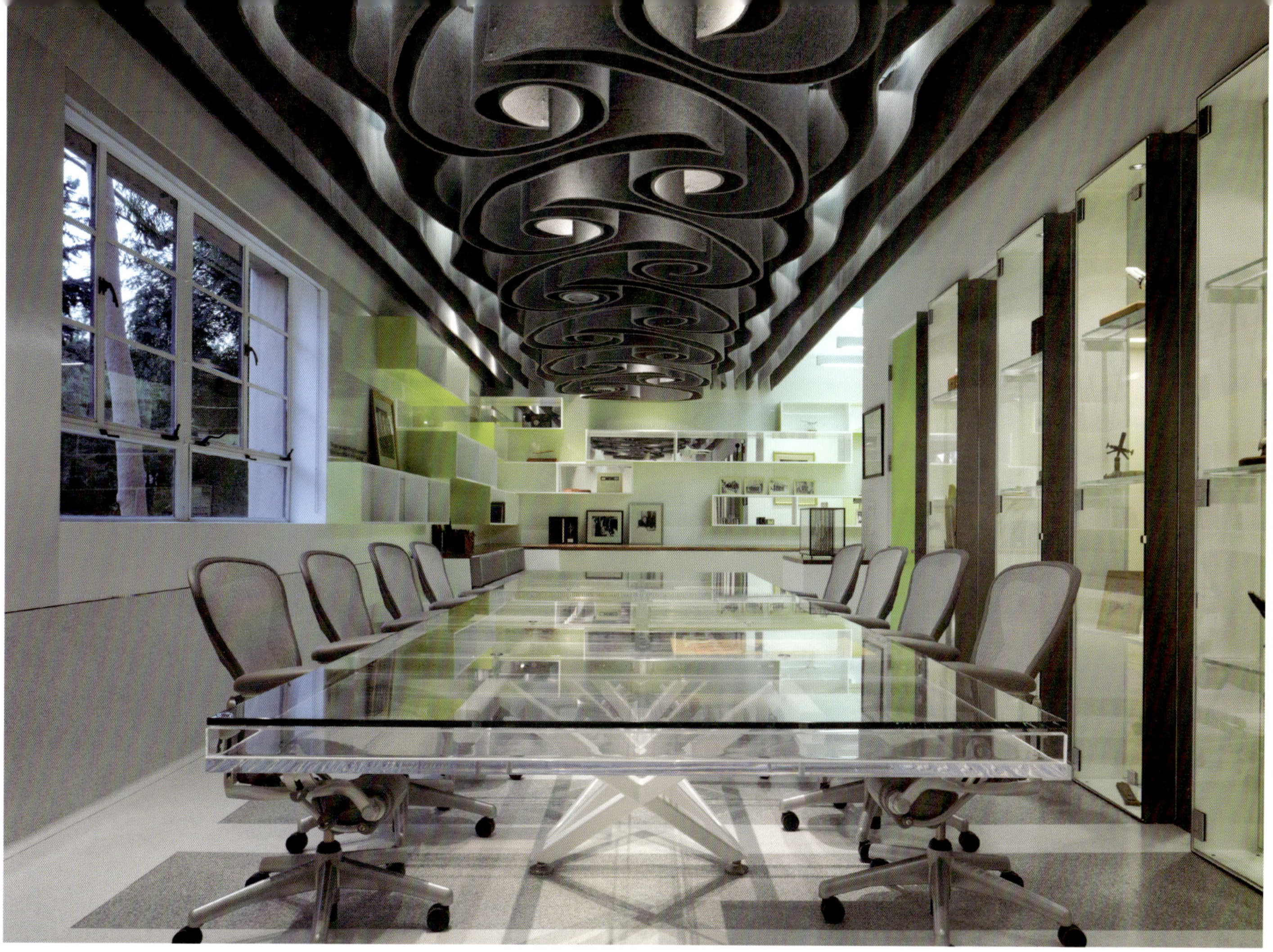

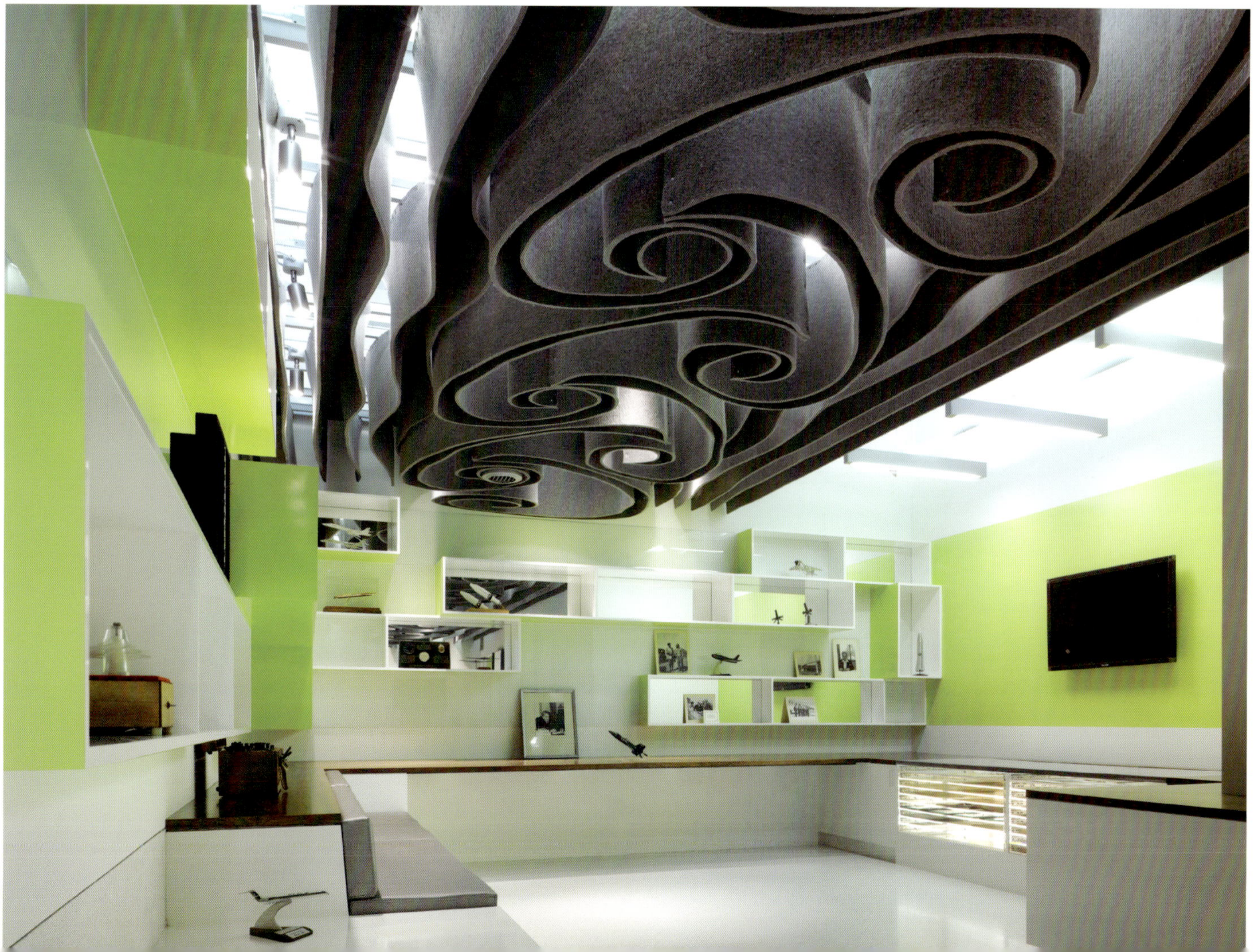

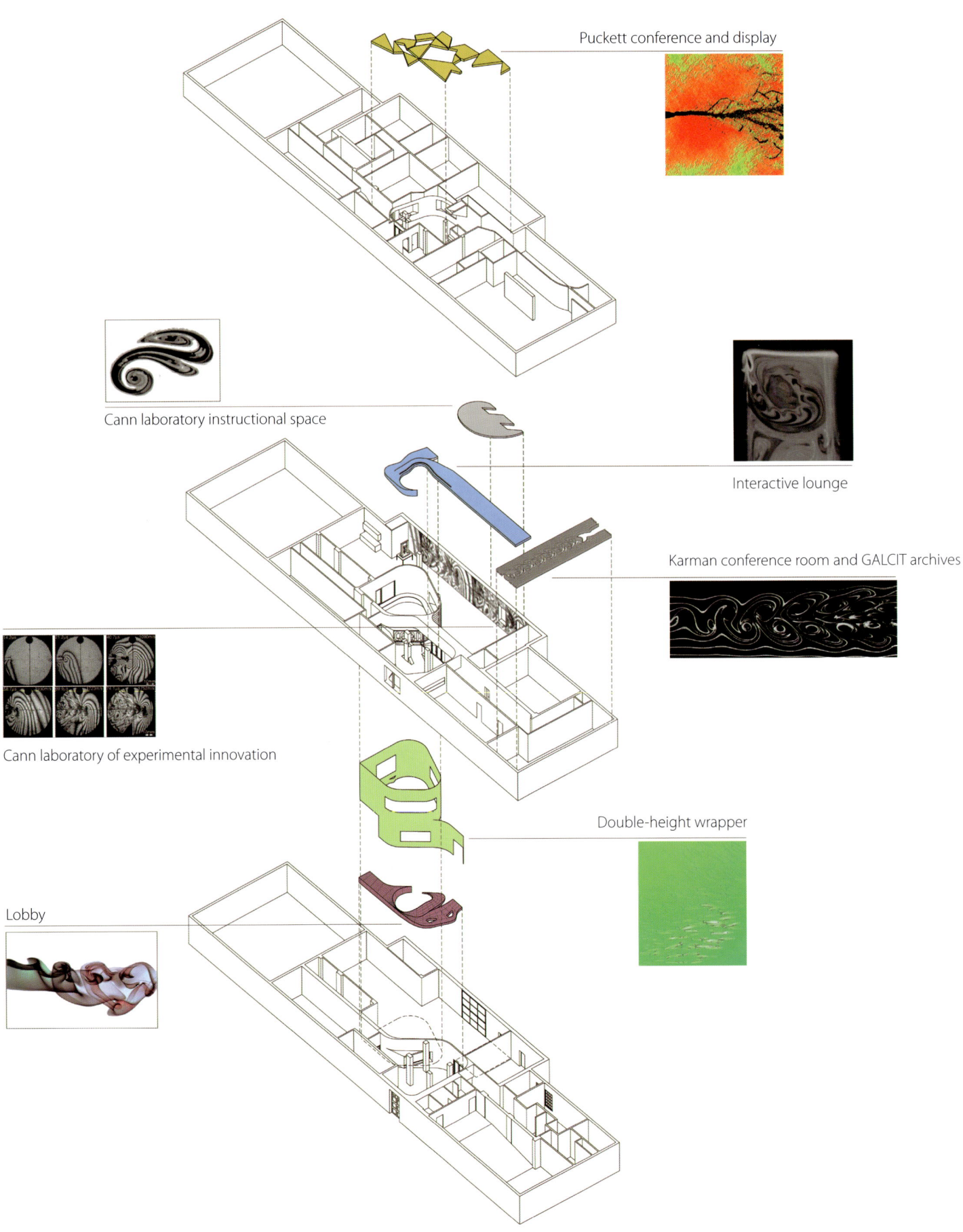

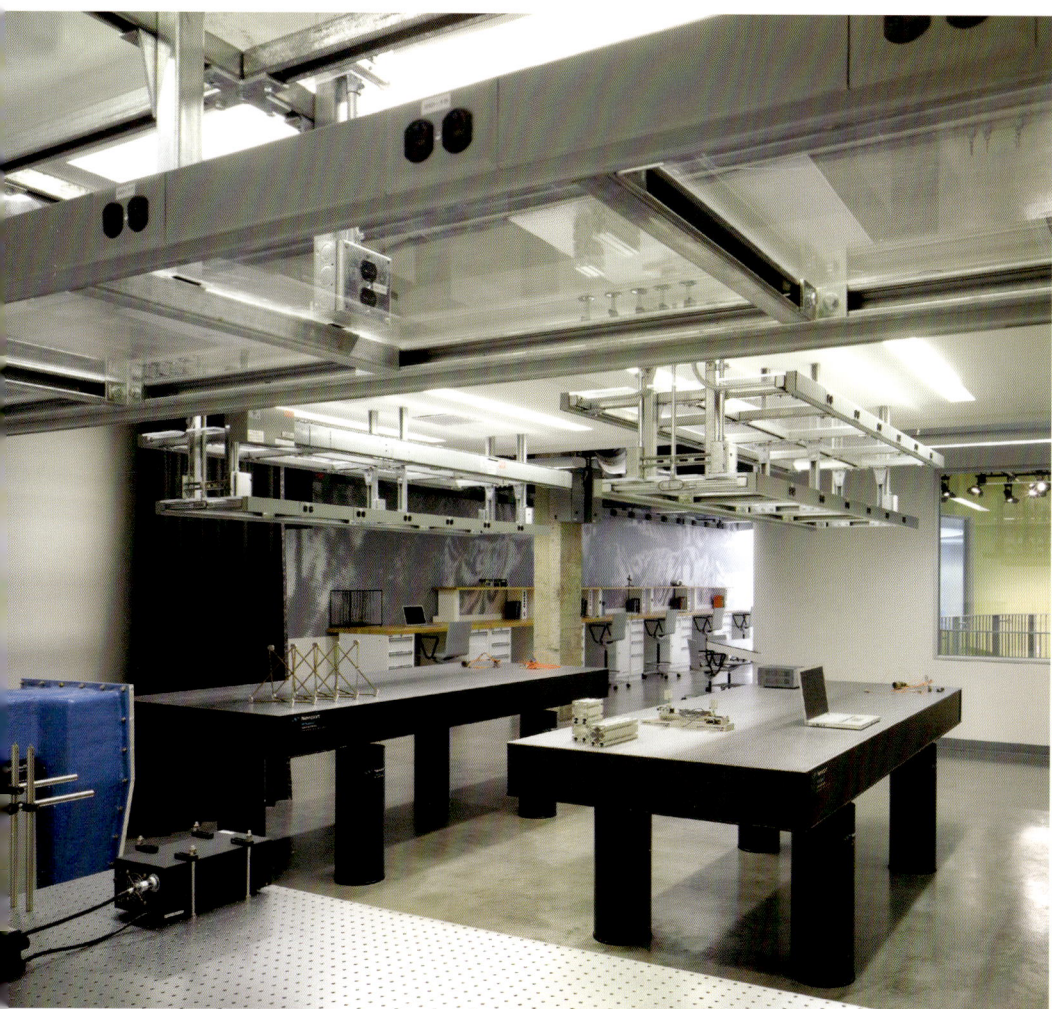

Caterina Tiazzoldi

Toolbox. Torino Office Lab & Co-working

Torino, Italy   **Photographs:** Sebastiano Pellion di Persano, Heléne Cany

Toolbox is a professional incubator realised in an industrial building in the city of Torino. The project is intended to meet the needs of a city in a phase of substantial transformation.

At a time when, with a laptop and a Wi-Fi connection, it is possible to work from anywhere, the question is, what professional space is needed? How is it possible to design a space combining users' plurality with the coherence of the whole design? How is it possible to mediate between a need for socialisation and privacy, between relaxation and concentration?

From a functional point of view, the project consists of the creation of an open space with 44 individual workstations combined with other services and activities. The goal has been to keep the modular concrete structure unaltered.

The main span of the building has been divided lengthwise by a series of 'filter volumes' used as technical spaces for storing lockers and equipment. On one side there is the co-working space, on the other side the corridors and the functional 'box' containing shared facilities such as meeting rooms, print rooms, informal meeting spaces, mailboxes, a patio and a kitchen.

From the perspective of the design process, the goal was to mediate between the plurality of users' needs and the coherence of the design. The variety of solutions is obtained by use of a unique design rule. A set of initially identical volumes acquires specialisation or differentiation through the use of different materials - cork, rubber or polished paint - according to the programmatic function hosted in the box. The specialisation of a generic volume occurs in accordance with a specialisation generated by acoustic, thermal, and visual requirements.

The goal was to convey a harmonious coexistence of different worlds and cultural references. The principle of variation and transformation of a unique element was also pursued in other parts of the project by differentiating the colours of natural rubber floors in the meeting rooms, sound insulation coating alternating with small telephone pods and finally by varying the sizes, colours and levels of transparency of the bubbles that form the external texture of the box-bar.

Concept:
Aurelio Balestra,
Caterina Tiazzoldi,
Giulio Milanese
Designer:
Caterina Tiazzoldi
Design team:
A. Balzano, T. Branquinho,
H. Cany, C. Caramassi, L. Croce,
M. Fassino, M. Pianosi

© Sebastiano Pellion di Persano ▶

© Sebastiano Pellion di Persano

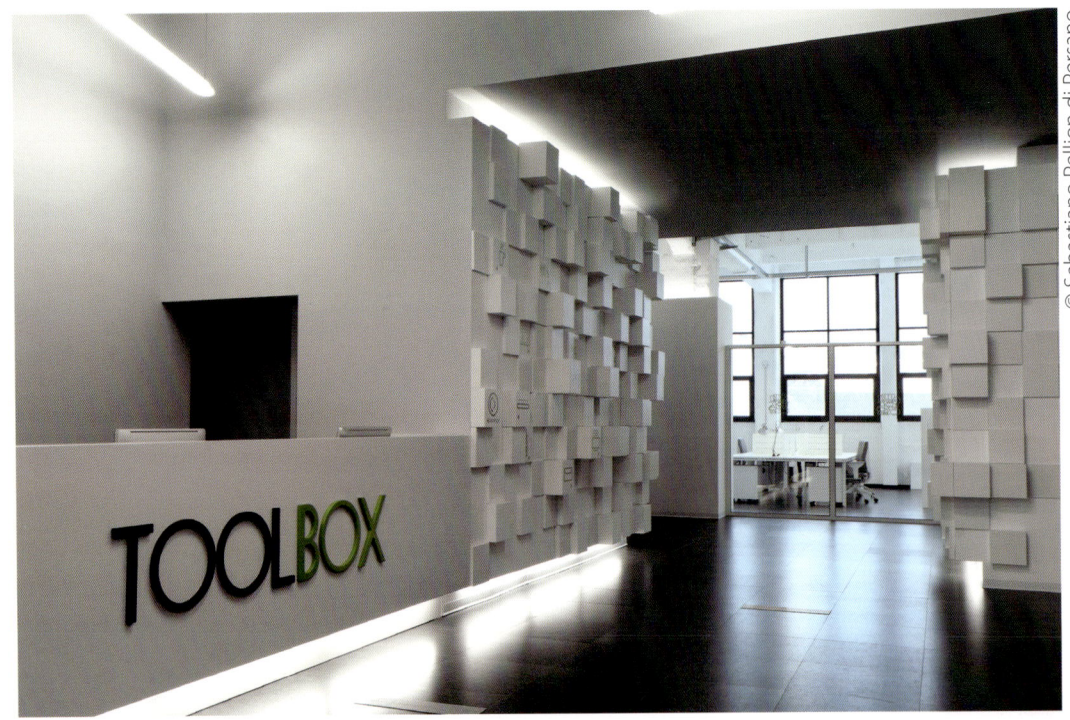

The design concept uses a very few items in endless variations, a single system developing an infinite range of possibilities to respond to the plurality of users' needs.

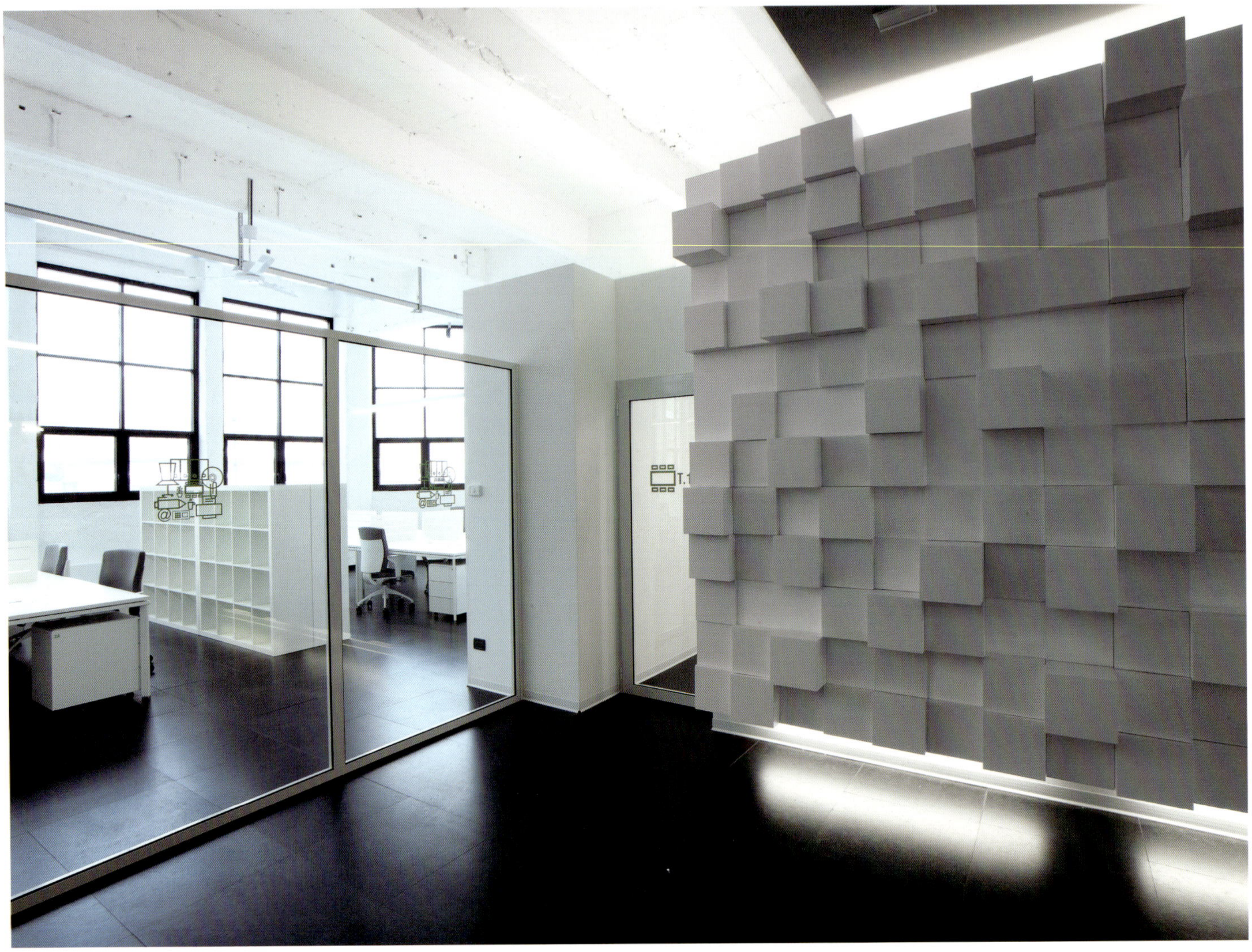

© Sebastiano Pellion di Persano

FLOOR PLAN

1. Entrance
2. Reception
3. Informal meetings
4. Bar
5. Lounge / relax area
6. Printing rooms
7. Meeting rooms
8. Co-working
9. Bathroom
10. Pod for private phone calls
11. Patio
12. Kitchen

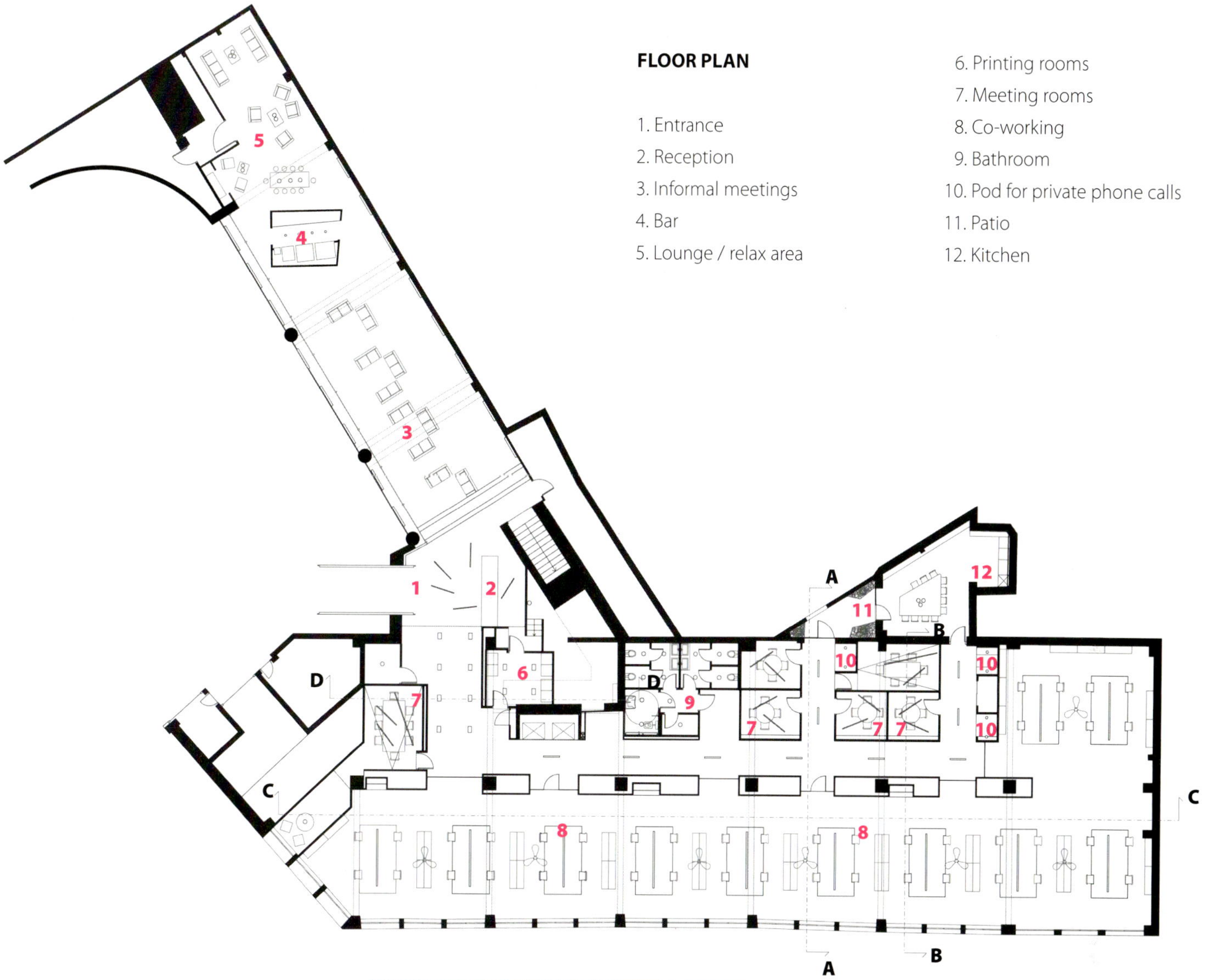

The walls of the entrance were made with 500 variations of one single white box.

© Heléné Cany

© Sebastiano Pellion di Persano

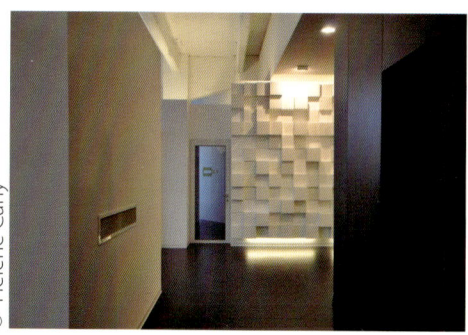

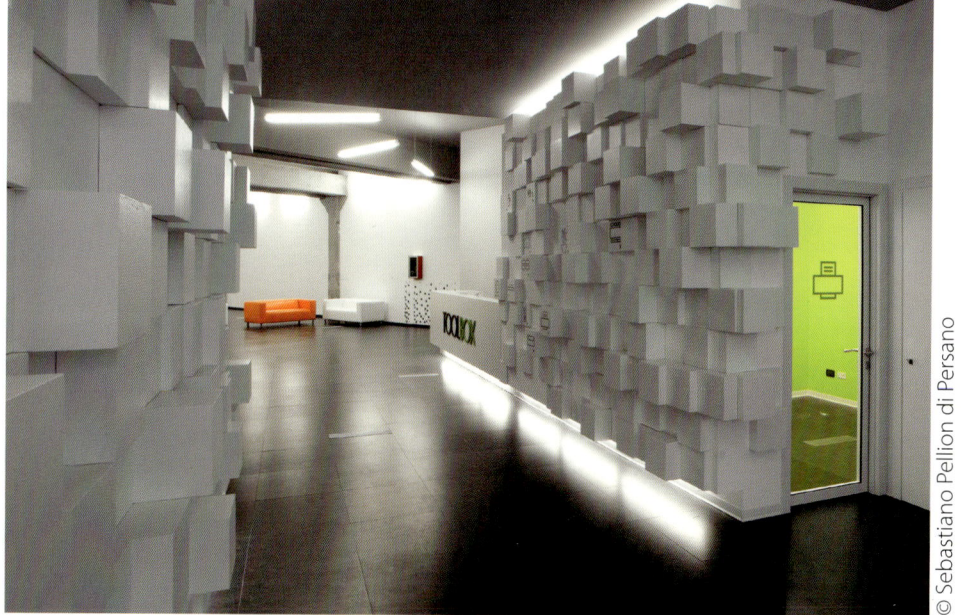

The principle of endless variations was applied in the management of space oriented towards sustainable flexibility, a flexibility which is not based on the transformation of physical space but on a variety of uses obtained through the use of a few combinatorial functions (co-working, meeting rooms, kitchen, patio, parking).

The overall design was obtained with parametric software generating endless configurations from a single digital model. Similarly, conditioning grids were obtained from a single parametric model that recalculates the size and position of the holes based on the exchange of air required in each environment.

© Sebastiano Pellion di Persano

© Heléné Cany

CONSISTENCY AND PLURALITY RECEIVED FROM VARIATIONS OF A RULE

VARIABLE PARAMETERS

parameter			
diameter	40 cm	17 cm	10 cm
colour	white	PANTONE solid coated 384 C	PANTONE solid coated 382 C
transparency	70%	50%	20%
position	change of coordinates of the bubbles on the axles X and Y		

CONFIGURATIONS

33

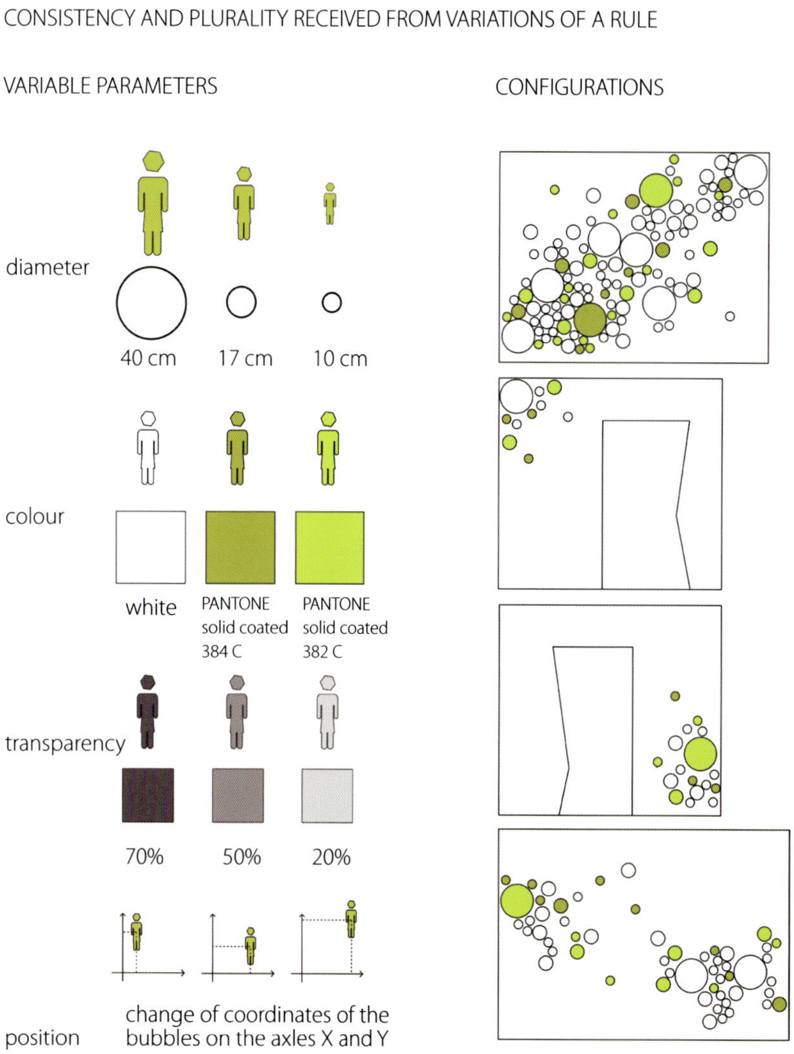

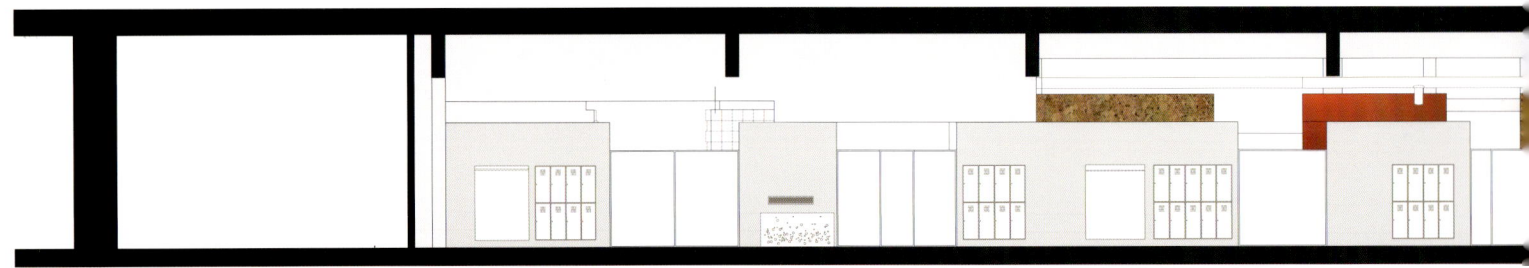

Section AA

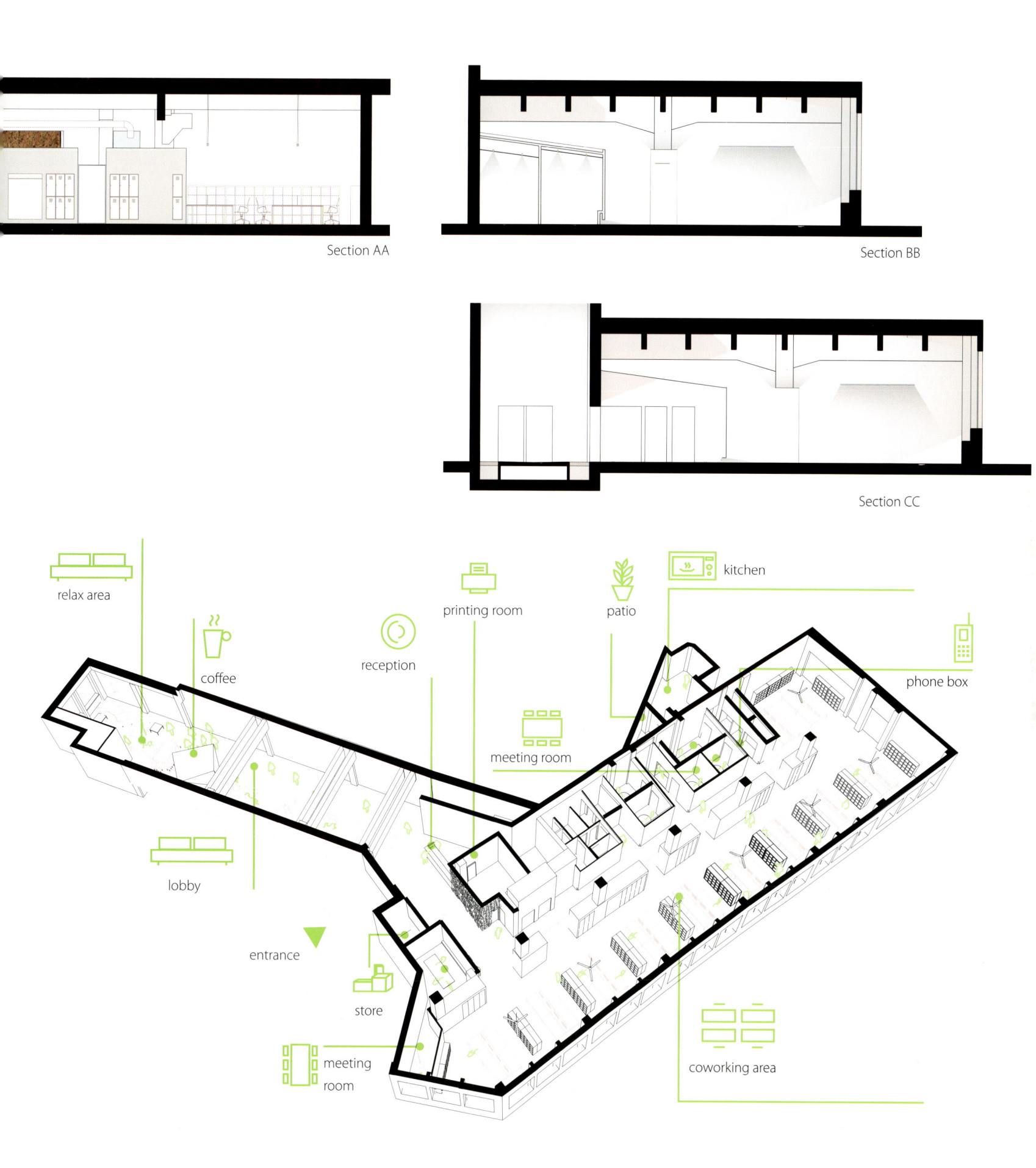

Section BB

Section CC

- relax area
- coffee
- reception
- printing room
- patio
- kitchen
- phone box
- meeting room
- lobby
- entrance
- store
- meeting room
- coworking area

35

Thanks to its unique features, Toolbox is an urban concept that draws its strength from the complexity, variety, and changeability of the contemporary city.

© Sebastiano Pellion di Persano

© Heléné Cany

© Sebastiano Pellion di Persano

Bosch & Fjord

LEGO Offices

Copenhagen, Denmark **Photographs: A Anders Sune Berg, Bosch & Fjord**

LEGO Group in Billund, Denmark, is a creative, multinational work place. By inviting Bosch & Fjord to design their development department LEGO acquired an interior that mirrors its corporate values. Cooperation and knowledge-sharing is not just something that happens between the people who work there; it is also visible in the interior design of the development department, where Bosch & Fjord designed a series of meeting rooms, a reception and cafe area, as well as several project rooms in order to inspire and challenge the employees and increase the ongoing development process at LEGO Group's development department.

Innovation begins at the entrance to LEGO Group's development department. The visitor steps directly into a dynamic reception area where the reception desk is part of a cafe area that welcomes visitors, and where employees are having coffee, informal meetings or lunch. It is a very lively and dynamic place, buzzing with activities and people. The cafe is divided into three areas, each with its own character and functionality, inviting different types of meetings and gatherings. There is the 'Dining Area' with a long black common table and a book case; the 'Cafe' area with white furniture and shadow decoration in the windows; and the 'Lounge' with long, red benches, white tables and wall paper with an organic design. The reception desk is part of a huge organically shaped high table winding through the room on the green floor, which acts as a reception counter, a buffet and a dining table. The table places the receptionist on eye level with the visitors, thus creating a direct and engaging reception situation to make people feel welcome.

In LEGO Group's development department, Bosch & Fjord also designed 13 meeting rooms, each with its own unique identity. There are rooms for all kinds of meetings: large and small; long and short; development and brainstorming meetings; confidential and intimate; formal business meetings, etc. The design and the creative solutions stimulate more than just the work processes. The employees are personally challenged and motivated, which in turn contributes to a healthy and comfortable working environment and boosts the ongoing development process within the company.

Architecture:
Bosch & Fjord

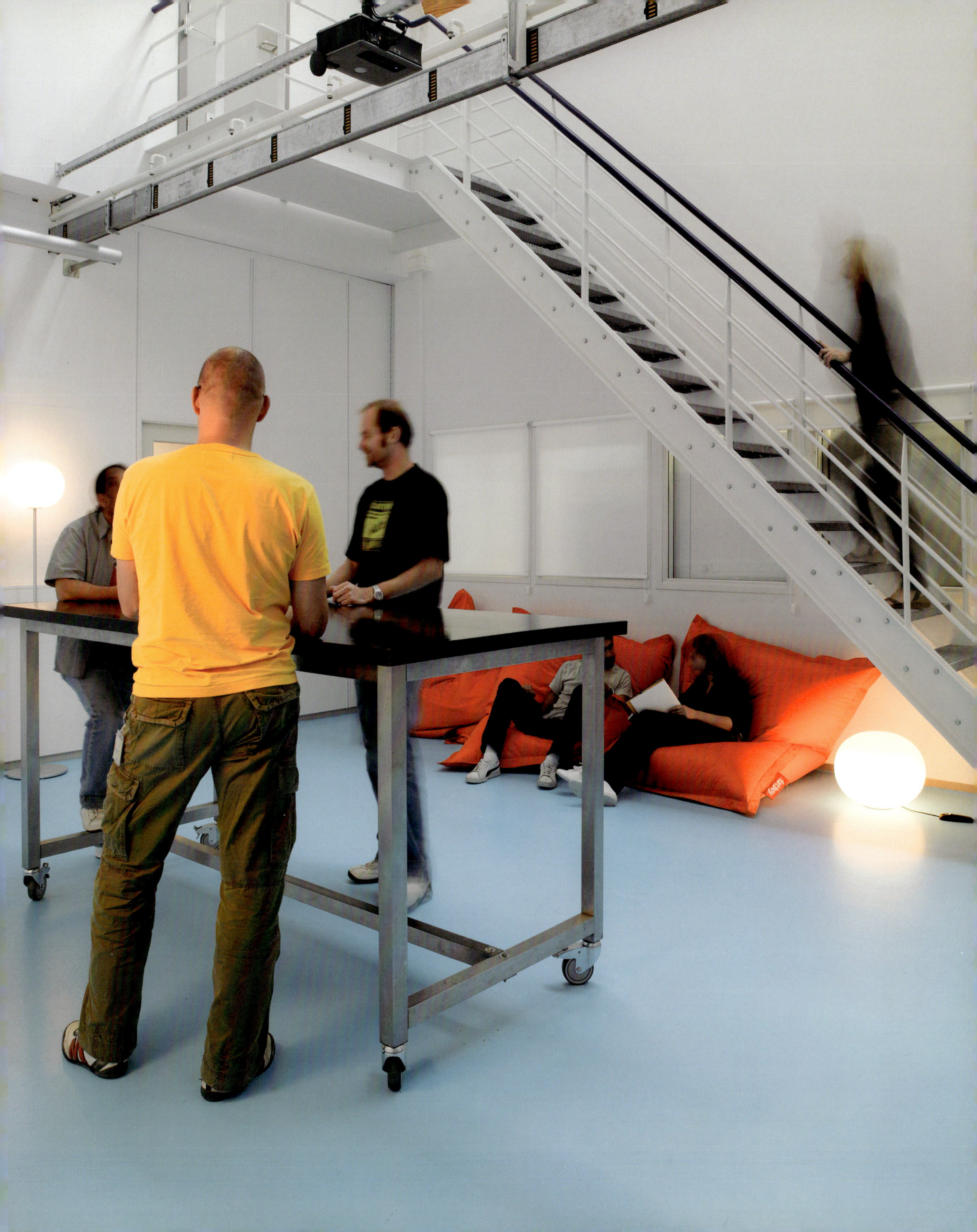

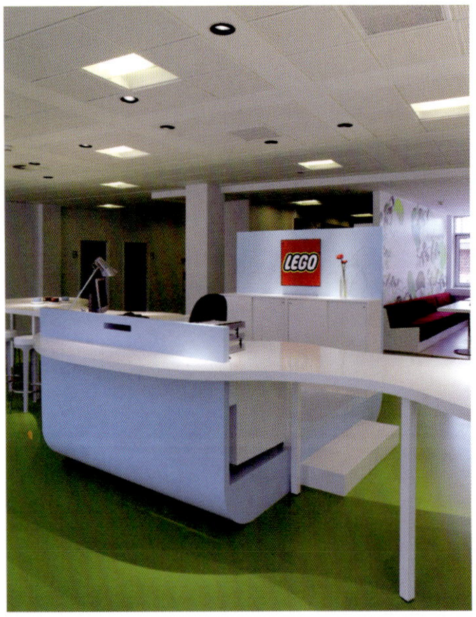

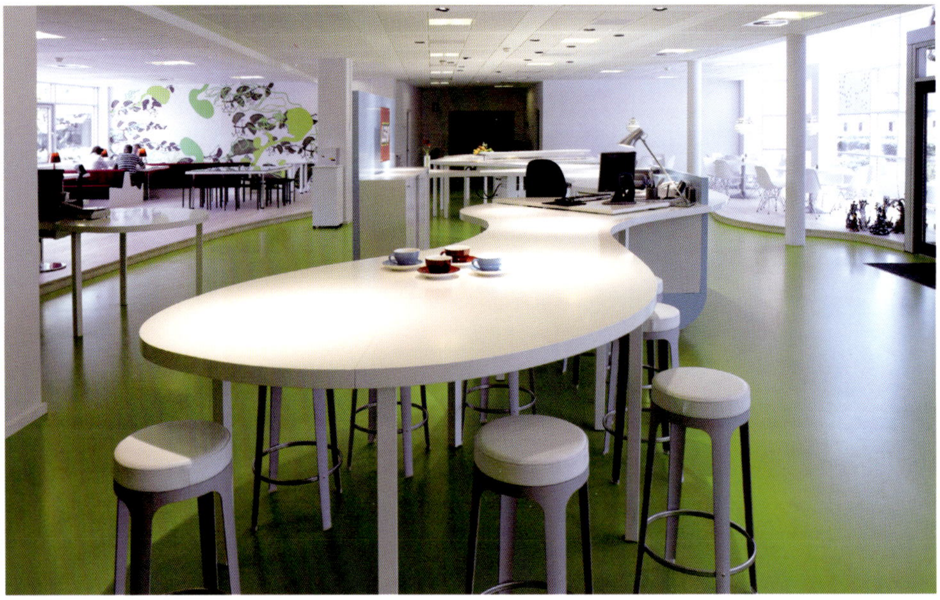

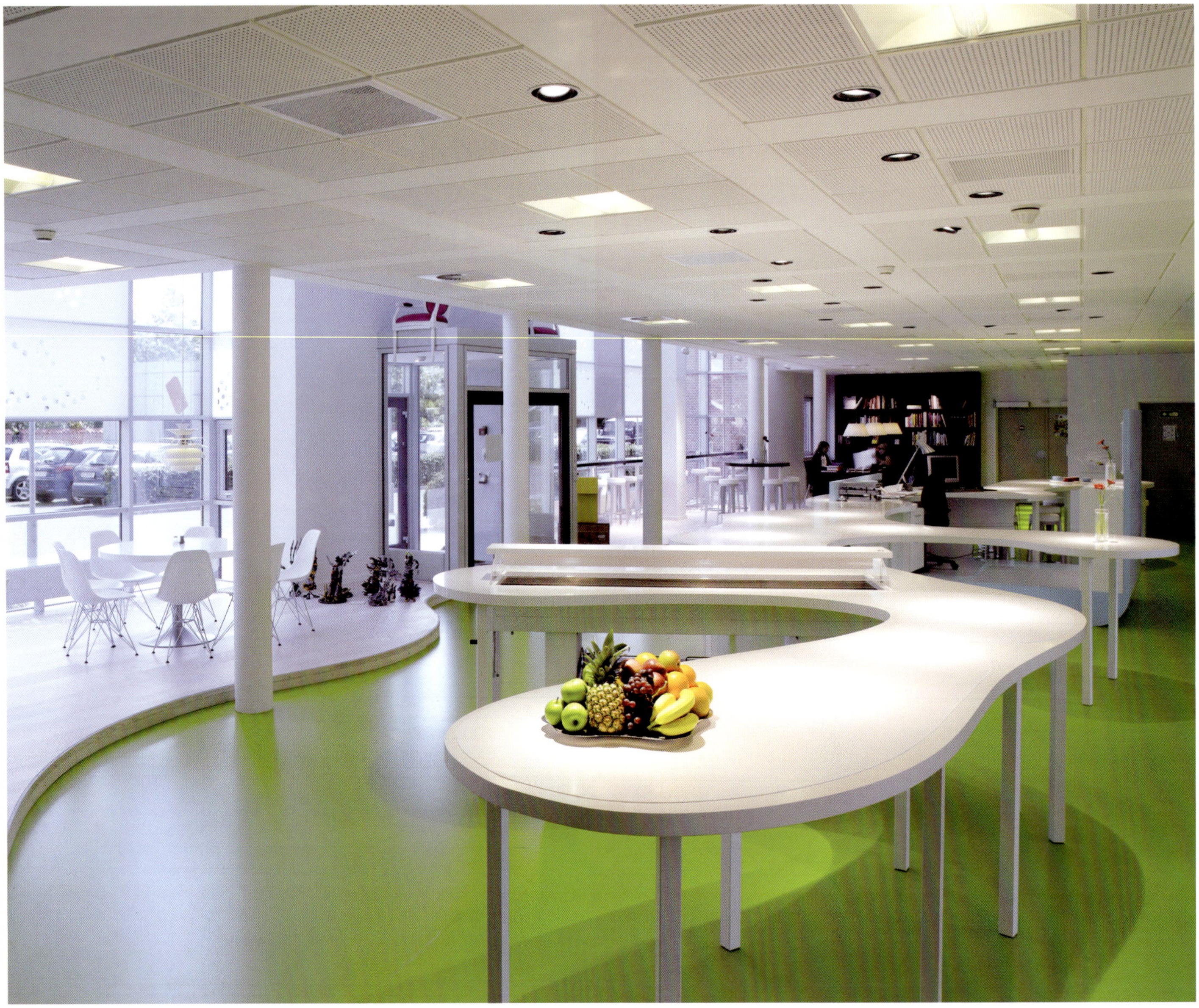

Floor plan

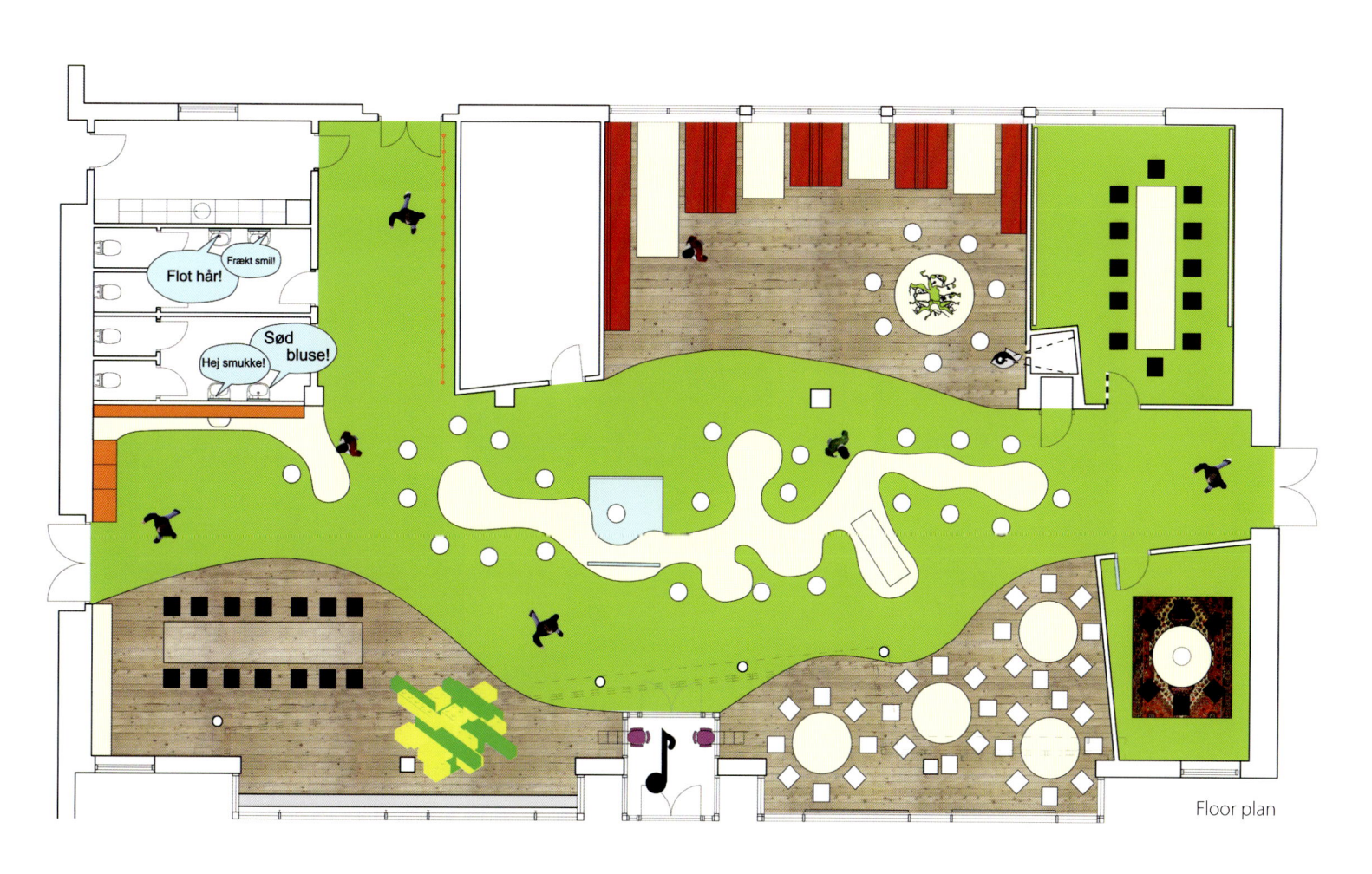

41

In LEGO Group's development department, Bosch & Fjord also designed 13 meeting rooms, each with its own unique identity.

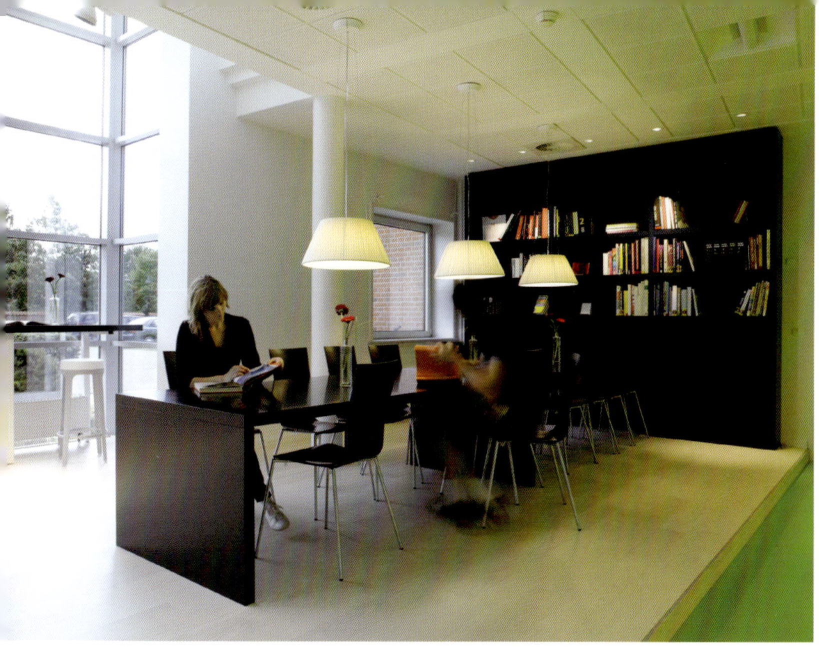
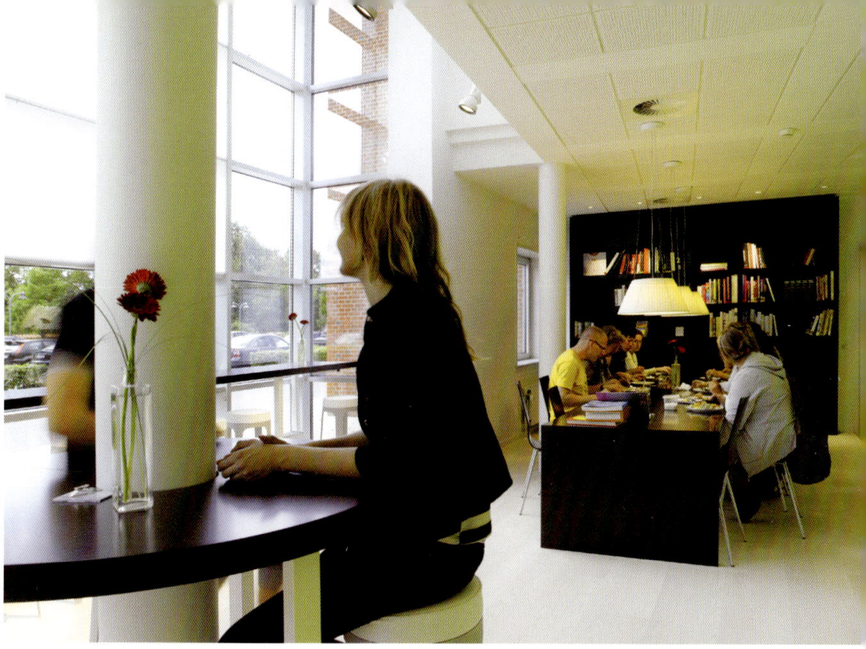
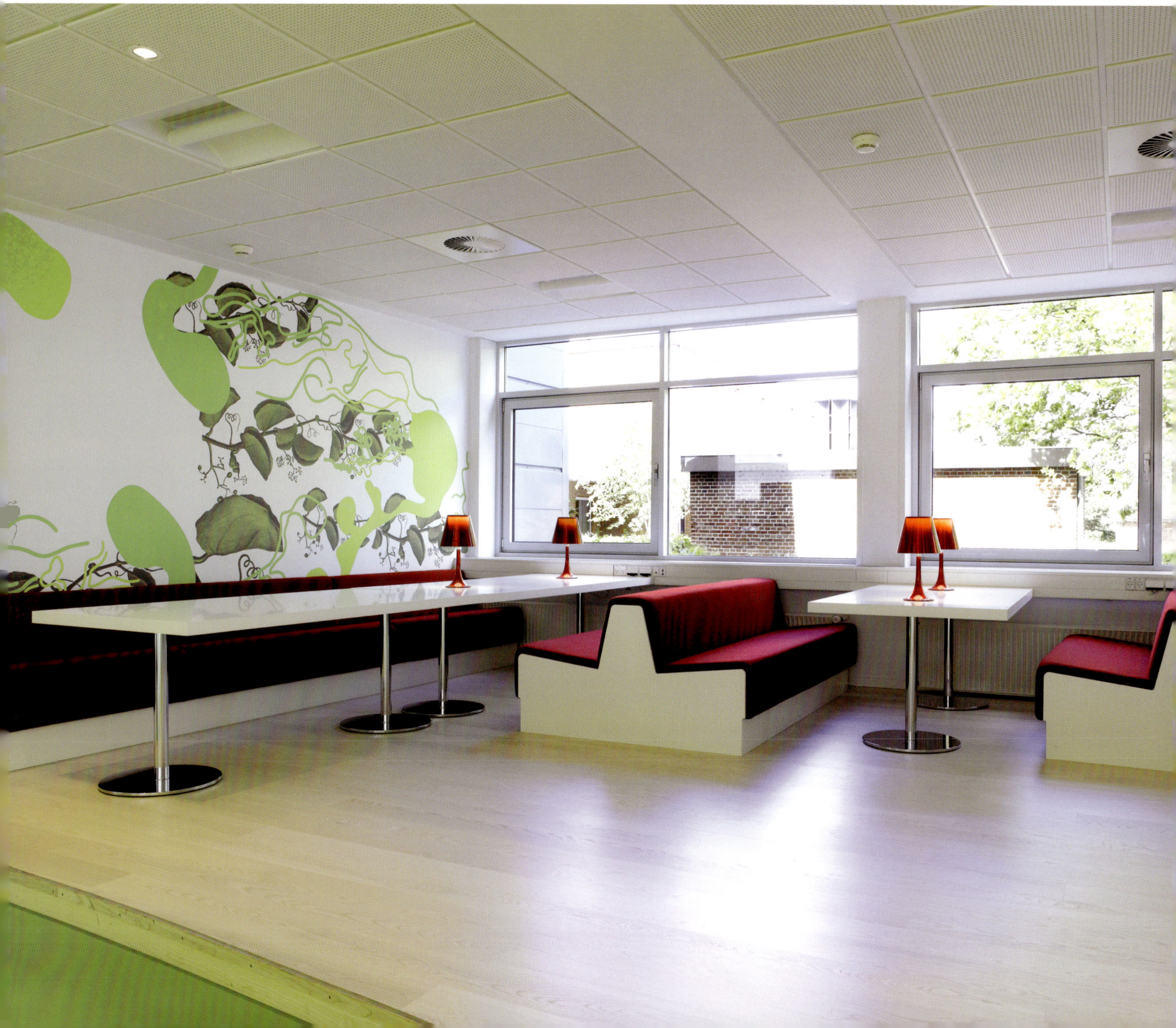

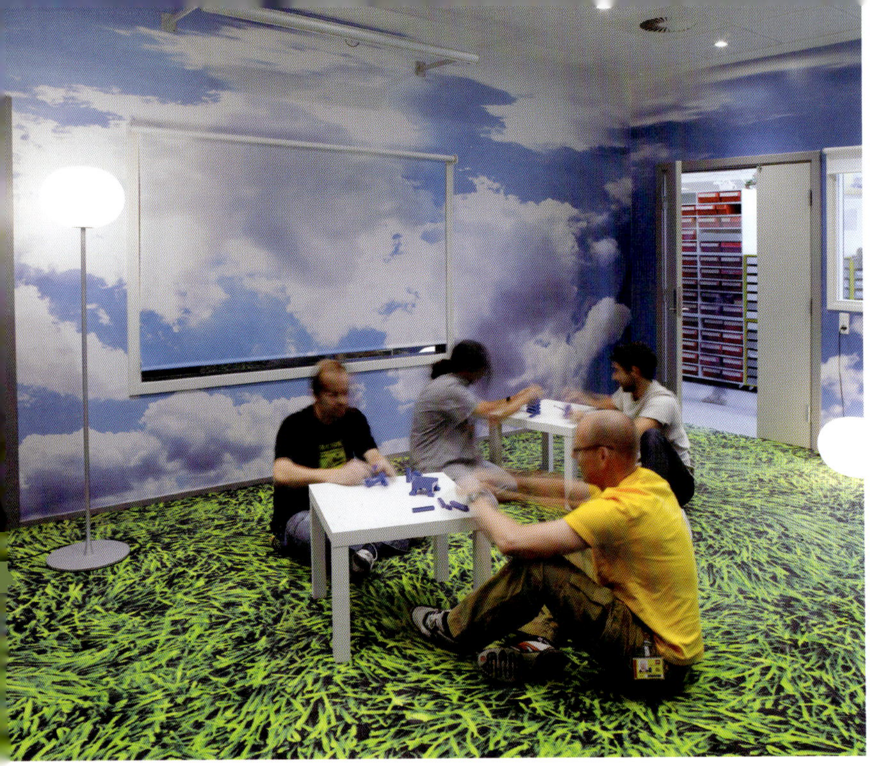
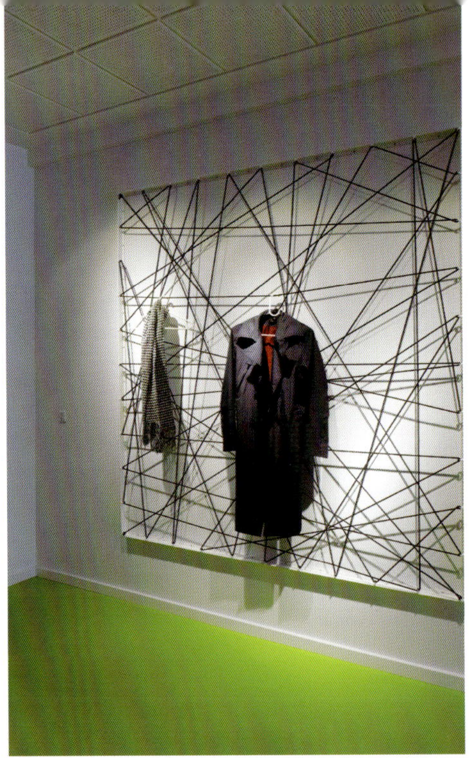
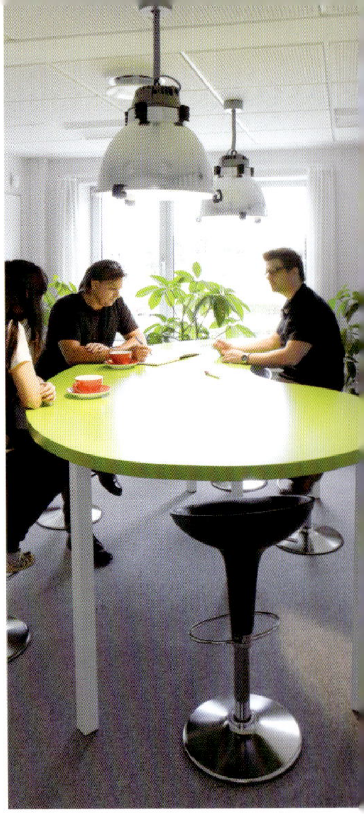
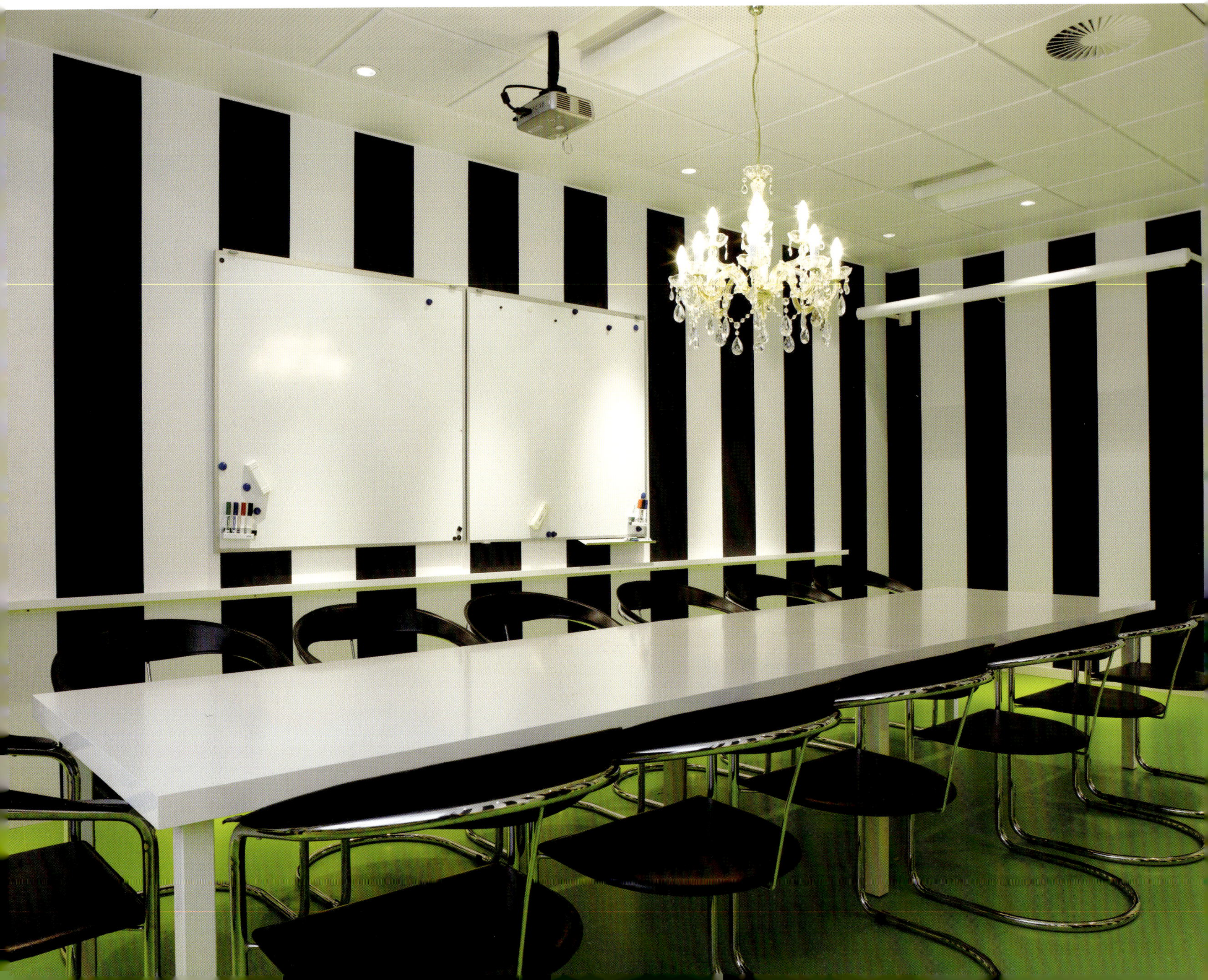

There are rooms for all kinds of meetings: large and small; long and short; development and brainstorming meetings; confidential and intimate; formal business meetings, etc. The design and the creative solutions stimulate more than just the work processes.

RA-DA

Bugaboo Headquarters

El Segundo, California, USA   Photographs: Ralf Strathmann

Bugaboo is a Dutch mobility company based in Amsterdam with offices around the globe, founded in 1999 by designer Max Barenbrug and physician Eduard Zanen, whose passion for innovation results in products that inspire people to get out and explore the world. Bugaboo means mobility. When the architects first met the clients, their US West Coast headquarters was located in a cramped building in an industrial area just south of Los Angeles. They were using a trailer parked in their parking lot as a conference room, were sharing desks and had their products strewn throughout the office for reference as they worked. It was clear right away that they were in desperate need of more space, more order within their space and a place for all the products and equipment they needed for the office to function on a daily basis. They had found a large wooden-trussed warehouse building in El Segundo that included a small retail front that would soon be their first retail store in America. RA-DA architects decided to approach the design from a practical and minimal perspective. The Bugaboo "strollers" are characterized by a simple no-fuss form and an intentional use of color. It was decided to use the work-area as a backdrop to the product so that the strollers would be the primary elements activating the space. This was achieved by keeping the layout simple and making most of the space white: white floors, white desks, white light fixtures, mimicking a photographer's product backdrop. The strollers are set on platforms that bookend each row of desks, for easy viewing and reference. Rather than separating the departments, the desks were organized around internally-lit, partial height walls so that employees would have some sense of privacy, but also be able to have visual access throughout the entire office and communicate readily with other departments.

Architecture:
RA-DA
Project architect:
Rania Alomar
Architecture project team:
Rania Alomar, Design Principal
Carolyn Telgard, Senior Designer
Jesse Madrid, Designer
Area:
9,000 sqft (836 sqm)

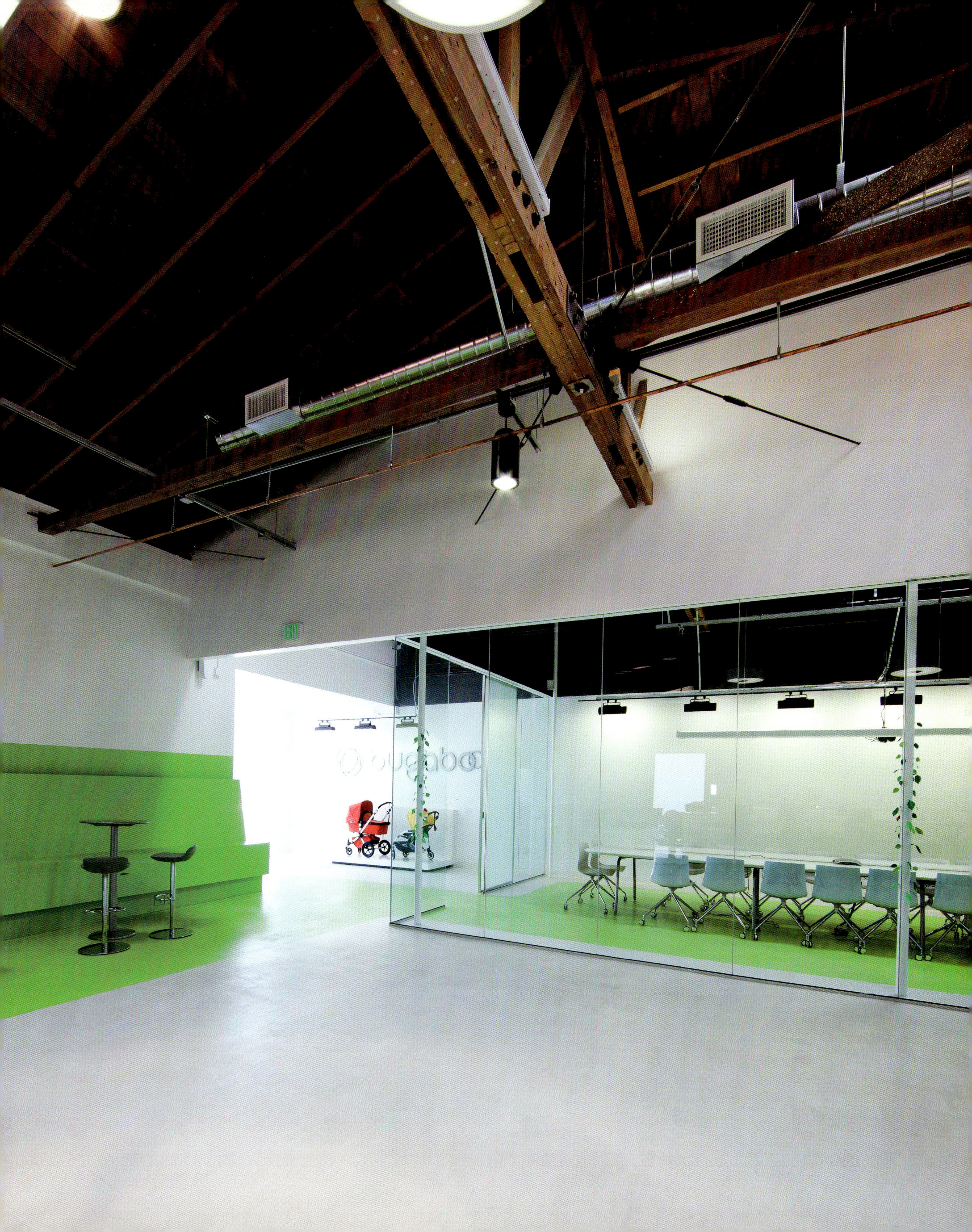

The retail space takes a more defined approach. Although maintaining the idea of a white backdrop to the colorful products, the forms here are more distinctive. The walls are built out to enclose smooth white cavities that hold the products and provide opportunities for Bugaboo's vivid graphics to be displayed. The floor and ceiling are darker in color which allows the walls to stand out and helps to draw attention to the products.

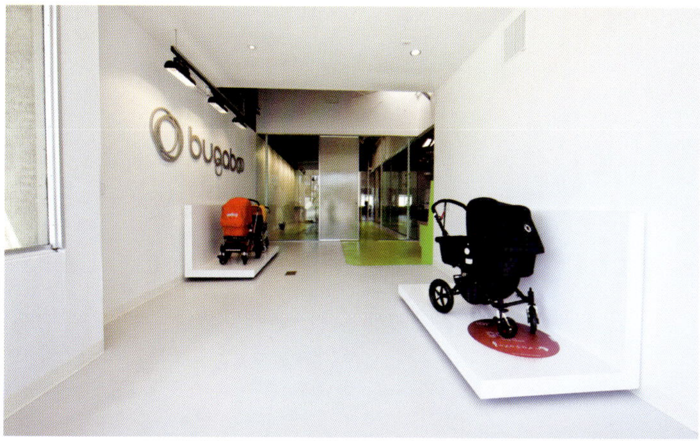
bugaboo
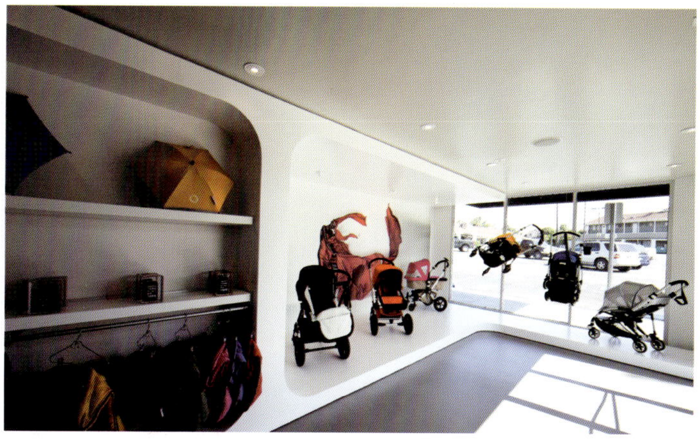
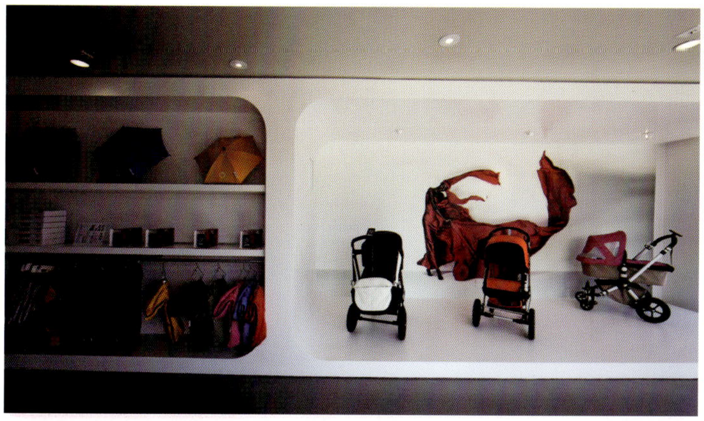
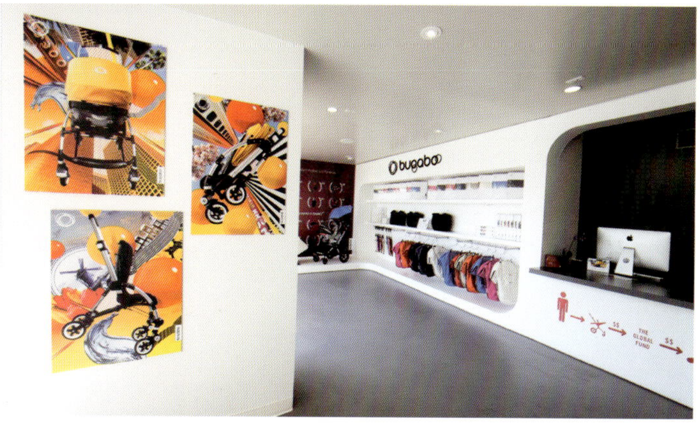
bugaboo
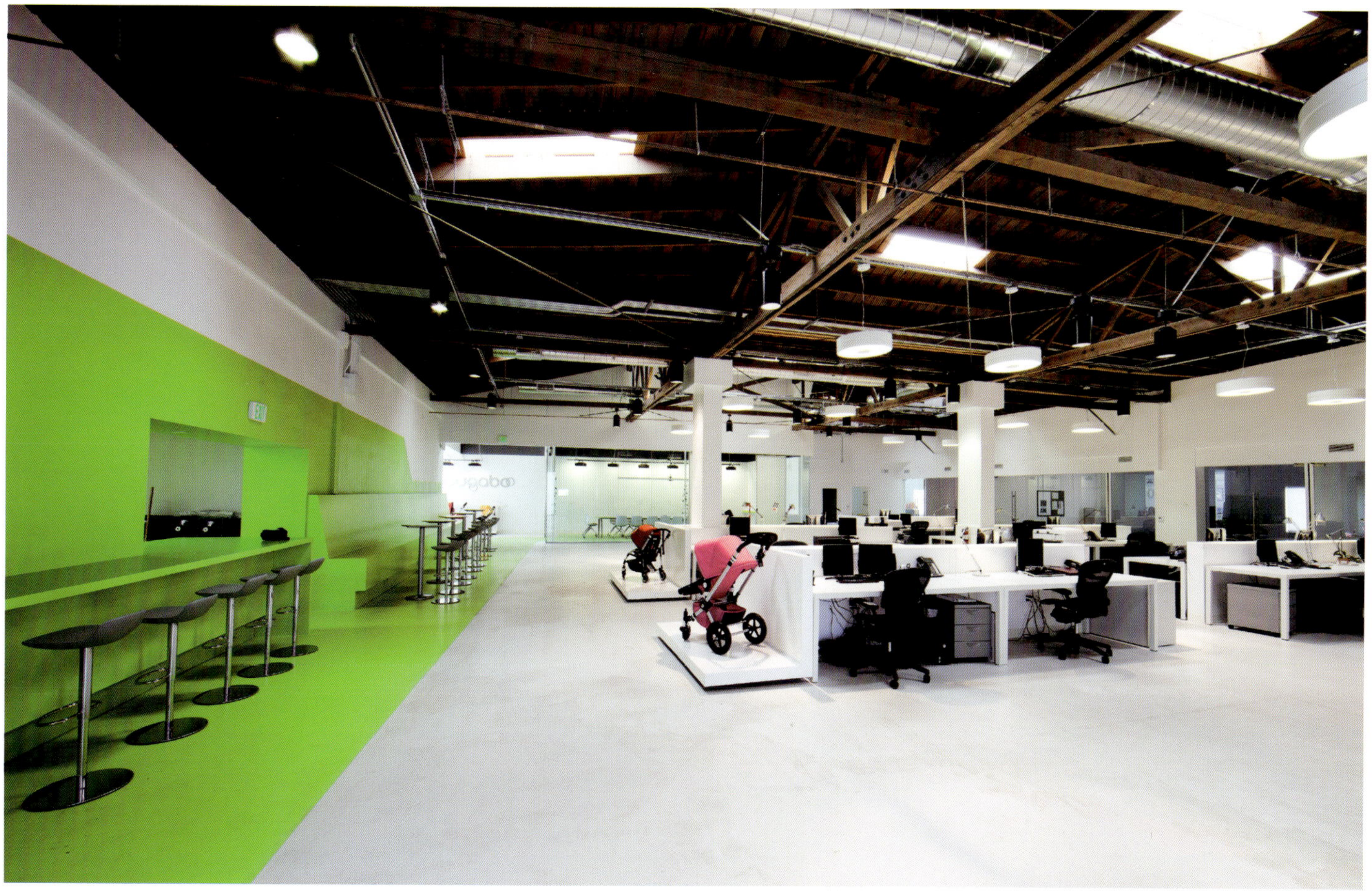
bugaboo

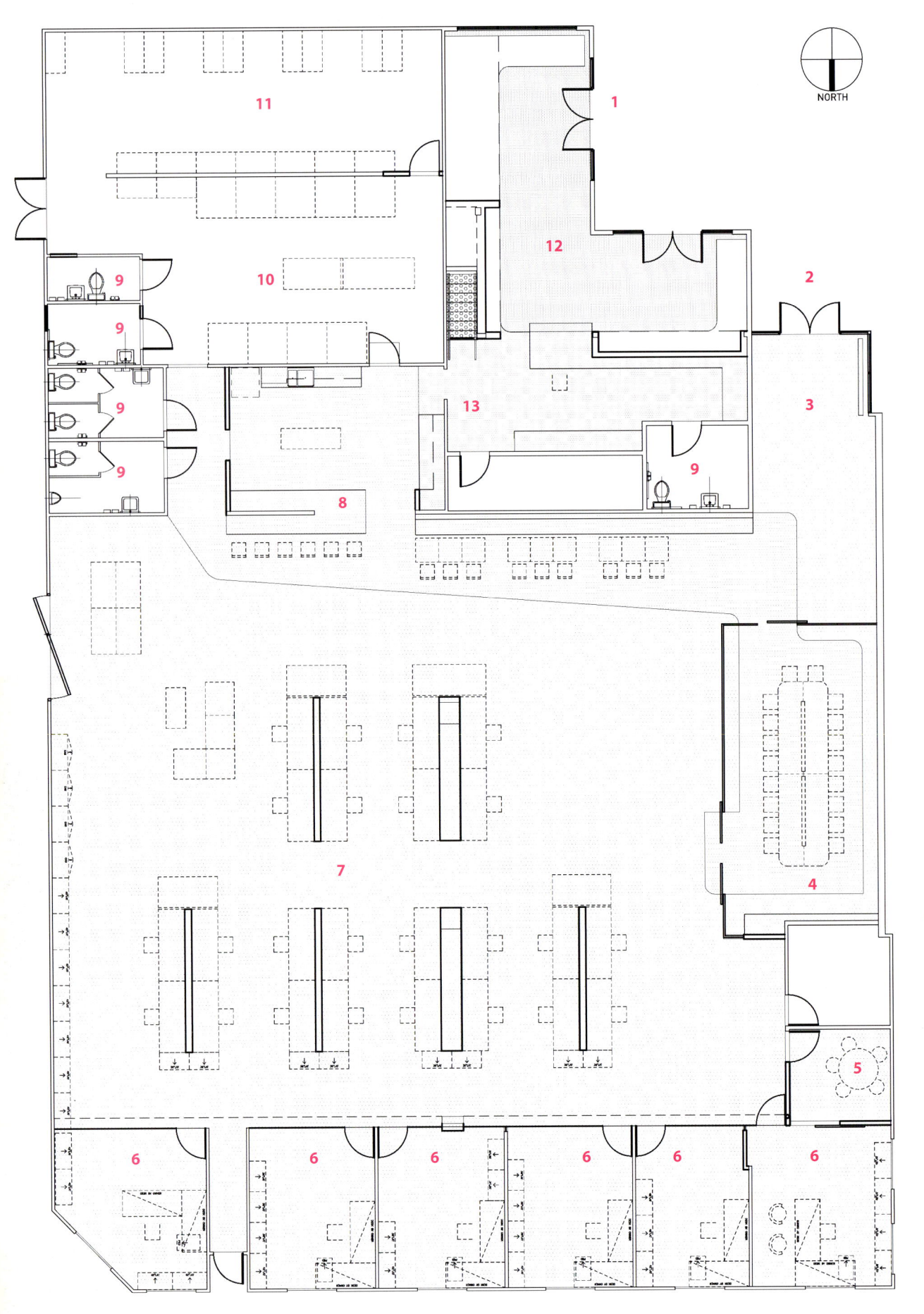

FLOOR PLAN

1. Entrance - retail / showroom
2. Entrance - office/workspace
3. Lobby and reception
4. Conference room
5. Small meeting room
6. Office
7. Main workspace
8. Café / bar
9. Restroom
10. Outlet center
11. Storage
12. Showroom
13. Stairs

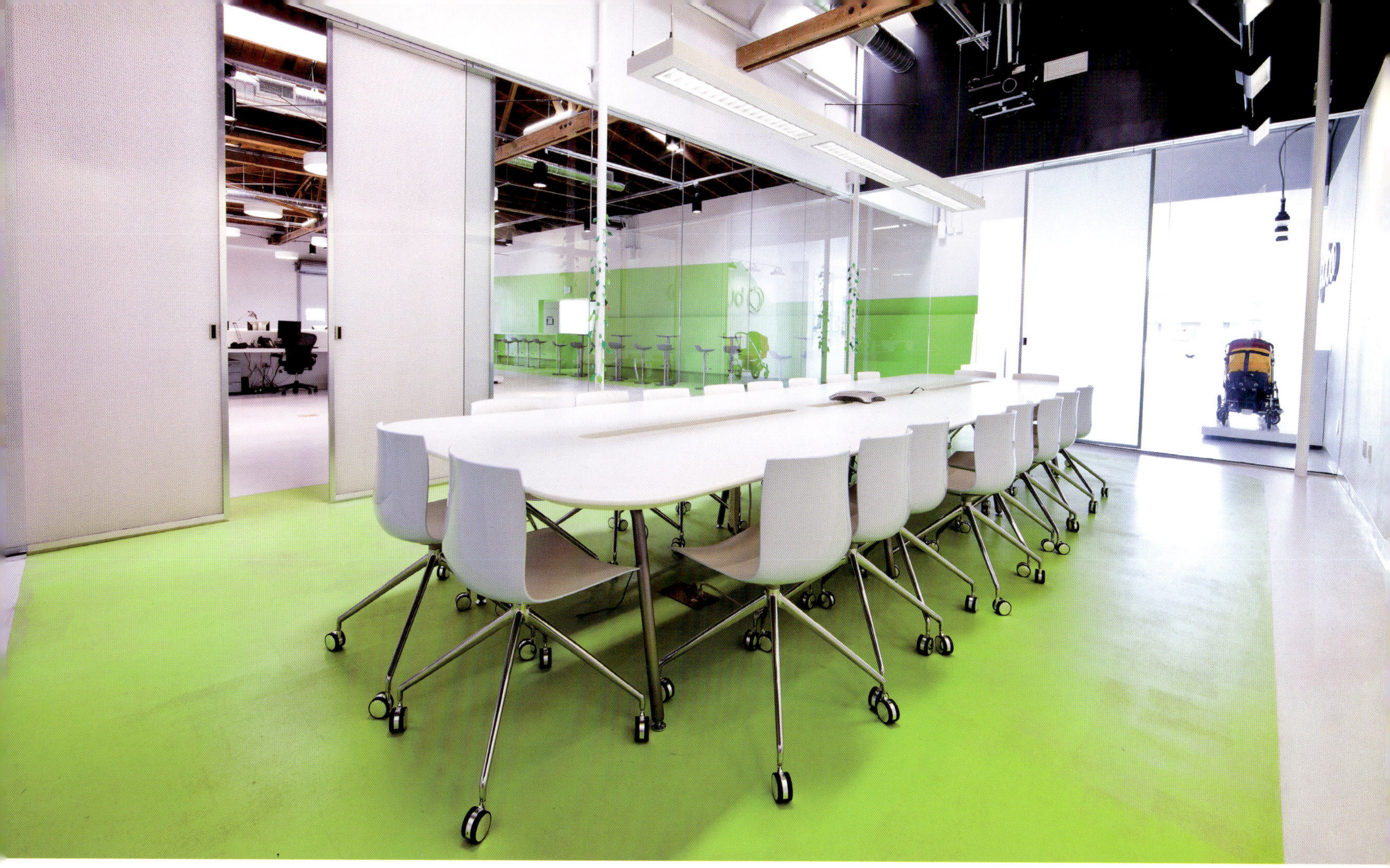

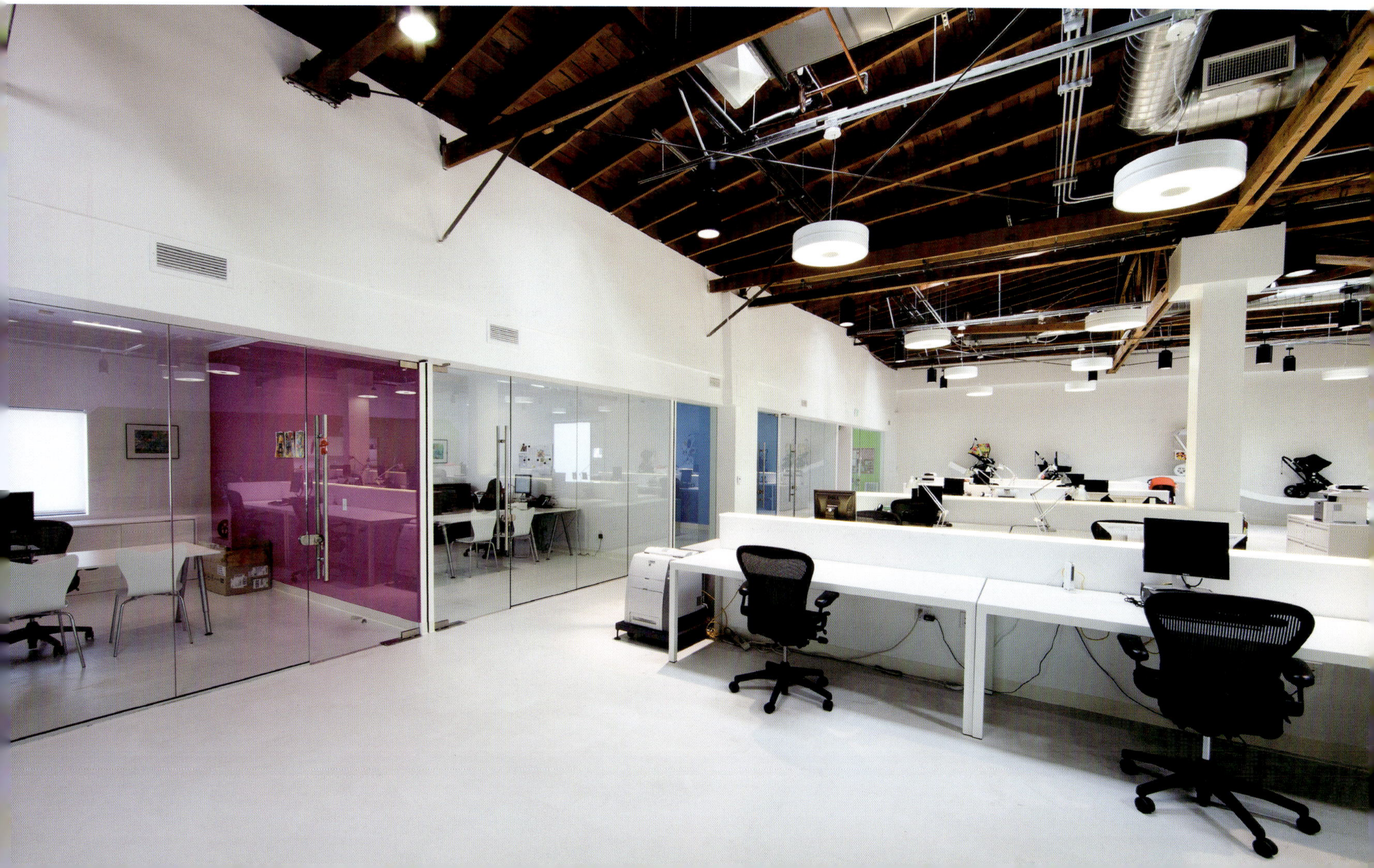

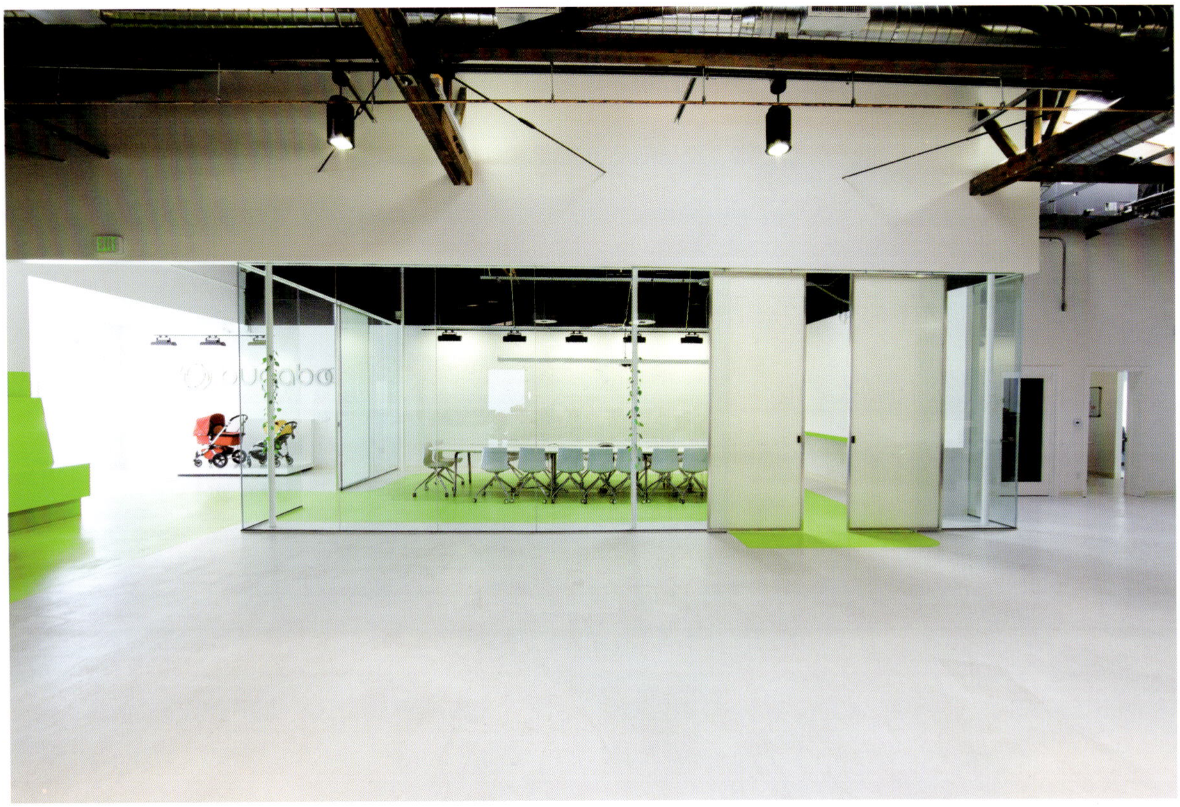

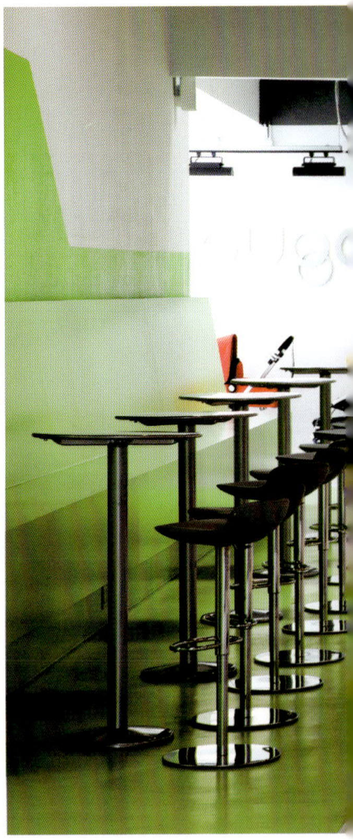

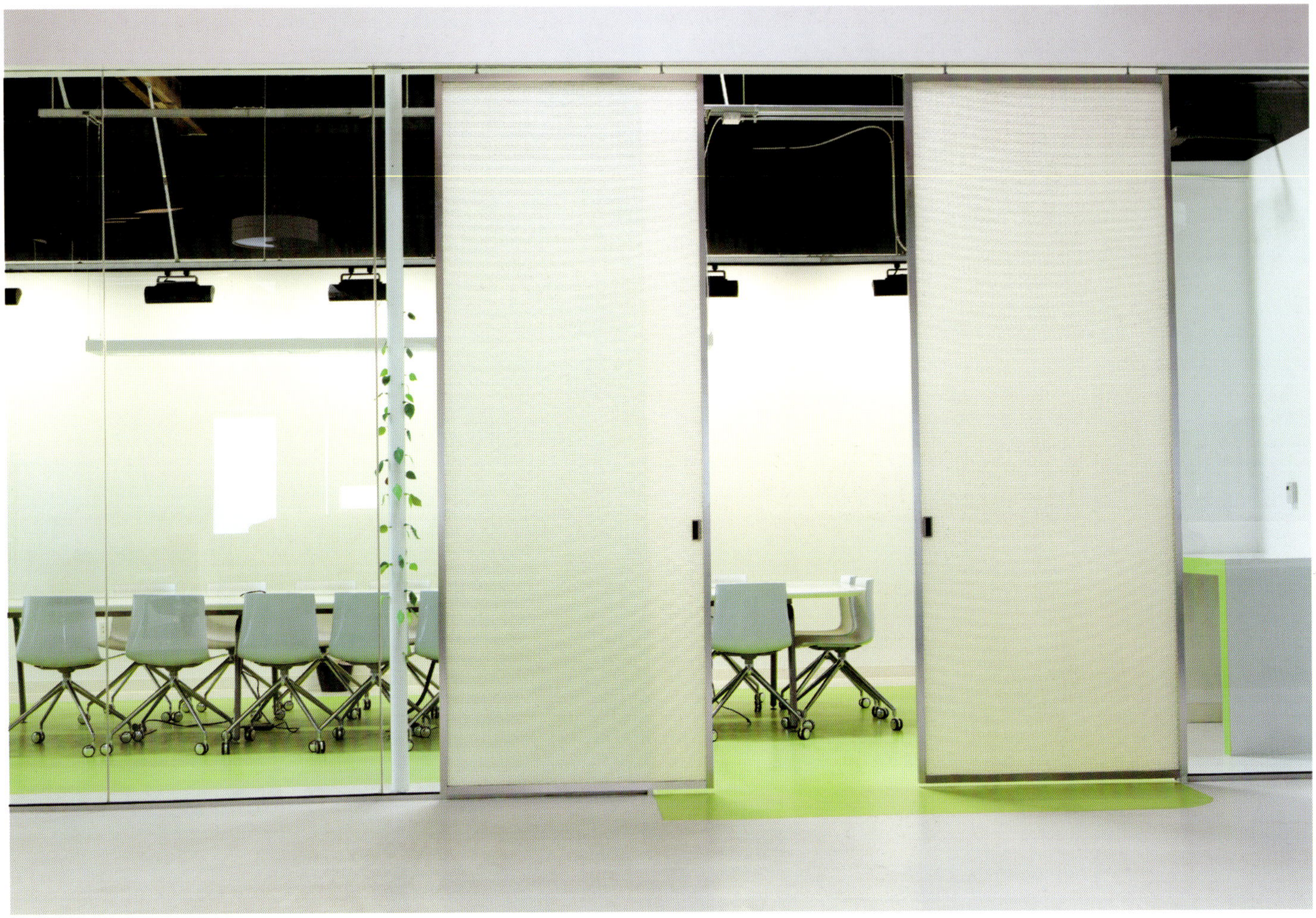

The private offices along the south edge of the main space are separated only by a transparent glass wall in order to avoid the visual separation that private offices often generate.

KDa

TBWA \ HAKUHODO HQ

Tokyo, Japan   Photographs: Kozo Takayama

Architecture:
KDa (Klein Dytham architecture),
Yukinari Hisayama, Yoshinori Nishimura,
Joe Keating, Mayumi Ito, Nazuki Konishi,
Makiko Okano, Hiroshi Ohsu
General contractor:
D Brain, Totem

TBWA is a global advertising agency that joined forces with Hakuhodo, one of Japan's largest advertising firms, to establish a Tokyo-based joint venture. The design of TBWA \ Hakuhodo's Tokyo HQ was the result of a three-way collaboration between the two agencies and the Tokyo-based firm of architecture and design KDa.

The search throughout Tokyo for a new space led to a disused bowling alley in a large, eight-storey amusement complex in downtown Tokyo, which was still in daily use. A golf driving-range and another bowling alley were operating on the upper and lower floors, but a whole floor in the middle of the building was being used as a warehouse. TBWA's corporate philosophy is "disruption", and KDa proposed that stealthily inserting the new agency into this unassuming building in a mundane neighborhood would be a potent way to disrupt the expectations of both the agency's clients and its employees.

When the existing ceiling was removed the bowling alley became a double-height space, and the 2 m (6.5 ft) beams that span the full width of the floor were revealed. As a column-free space, the bowling alley allowed complete freedom in laying out the office. The powerful rhythm of the beams suggested arranging the desks and circulation zones in a pattern that re-established the original dynamic of the bowling lanes. The wide-open space, however, inspired KDa to imagine the office as a park, so they filled it with fun "landscape" elements. The park combines both real and fake greenery – living plants and green shag-pile carpet.

Scattered across the floor are a series of shelters that serve as meeting rooms, project rooms, and director's offices. The shelters subtly divide the space occupied by the office's 340 staff into intimate neighborhoods connected by narrow lanes. The result is that the space doesn't feel like a corporate office, but like a little village in its own landscape. The double-height office is entered from an upper level – a reception area, gallery, and meeting spaces for visitors being located on this mezzanine. A wide stair descends onto the main floor into a 'village square' with its own café.

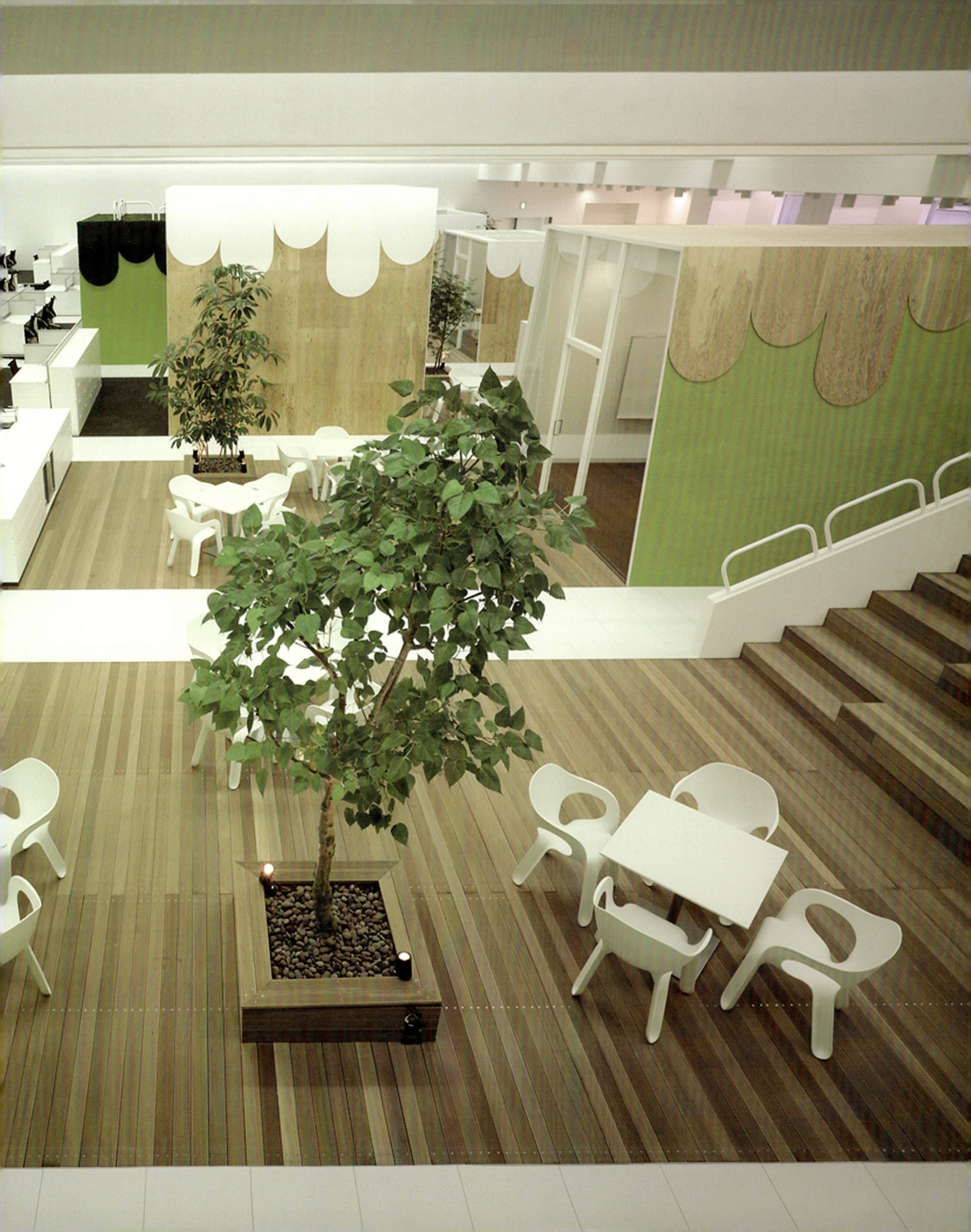

The wide-open space inspired KDa to imagine the office as a park, so they filled it with fun "landscape" elements. The park combines both real and fake greenery – living plants and green shag-pile carpet.

57

5th floor plan

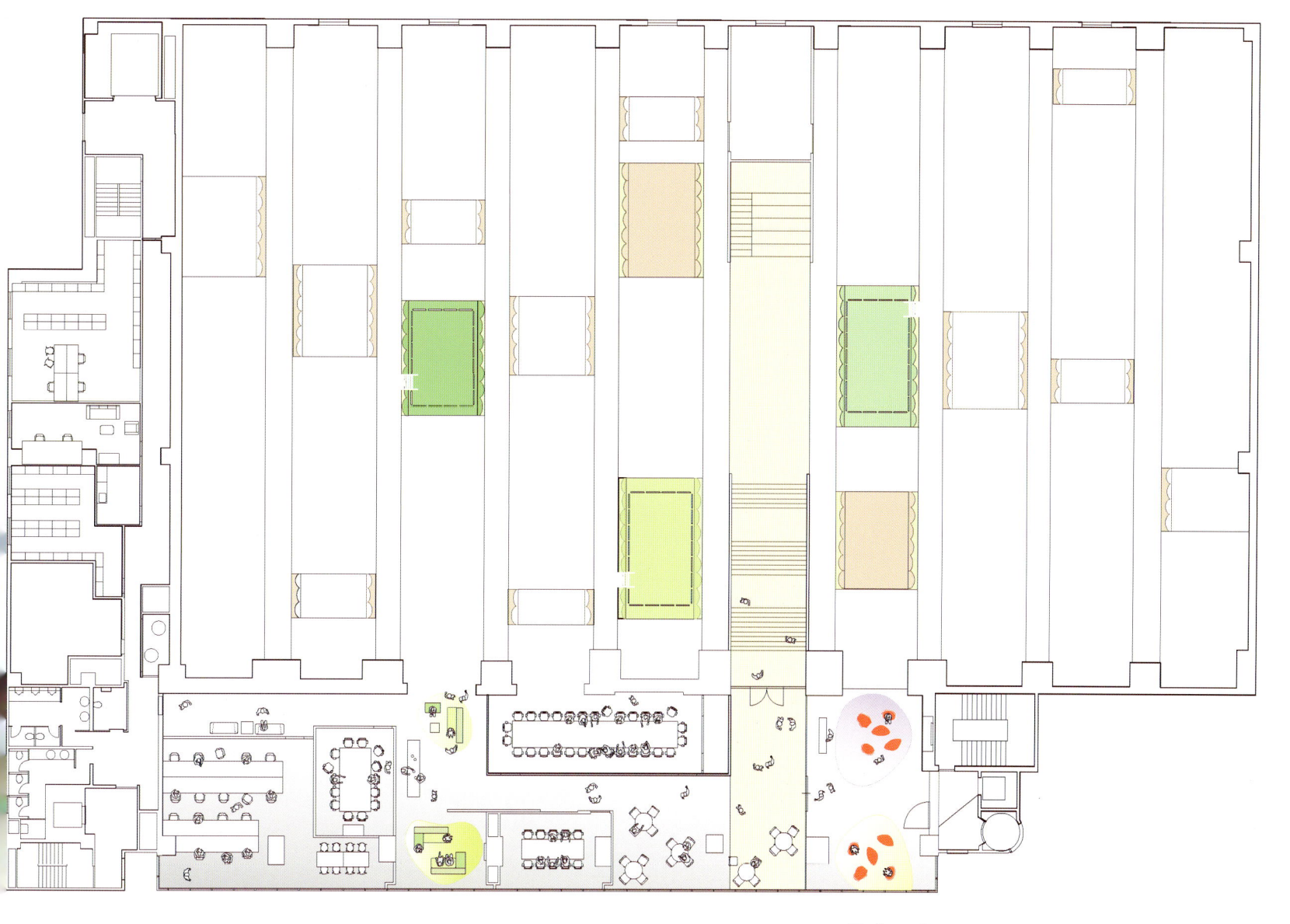

6th floor plan

A golf driving-range and another bowling alley were operating on the upper and lower floors, but a whole floor in the middle of the building was being used as a warehouse.

TBWA's corporate philosophy is "disruption", and KDa proposed that stealthily inserting the new agency into this unassuming building in a mundane neighborhood would be a potent way to disrupt the expectations of both the agency's clients and its employees.

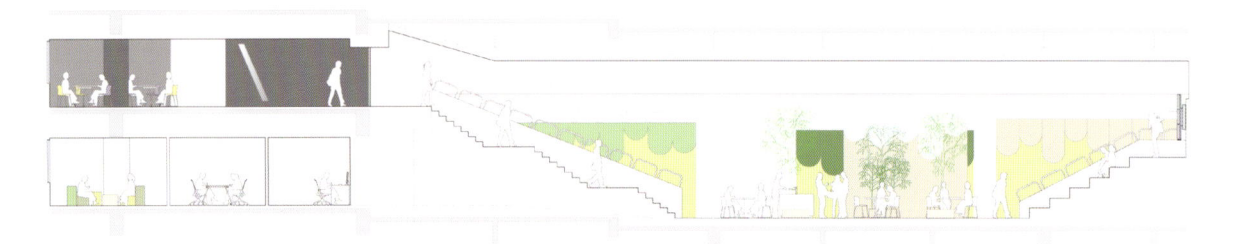

Cross section

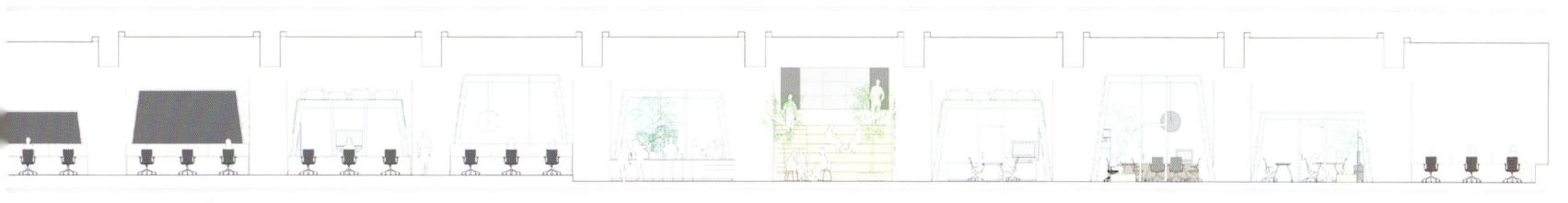

Longitudinal section

Rottet Studio

Artis Capital

San Francisco, California, USA Photographs: Eric Laignel

Artis Capital Management is a technology-focused investment advisor founded in 2001 by Stuart L. Peterson. The company's founder wanted their new office to be more of a home than a workplace, so Rottet Studio was commissioned to tailor the space to the company's culture, the San Francisco environment and its people, as well as the needs of the Artis team.

With 16,264 sq ft (1511 sqm) and only 14 employees, this project is characterized by its special features. Focused on the Artis team approach, each employee has a desk at the long trading desk in the open office as well a private office for personal calls, a home within the office. The outfit's amenities include a conference room overlooking the bay, a team room and a copy center just off the trading floor, a gymnasium, a massage room, renovated bathrooms, a pantry, a visitor centre with touch-down offices and a bathroom with a walk-in shower.

Playing on the view of the Bay, the designers wanted to merge the office space with the exterior, as if one could walk onto the water. No walls touch the perimeter of the building, so every corner has unobstructed views of the Bay and the entire city.

Along the bay side, a grand living room creates a free flowing, open space. A custom-designed carpet emulates water lapping at the shore. A dark gray cleft stone surrounds the entire floor, to reinforce the notion of rippling tides. The city side is more orthogonal as befits the urban grid, and allows the Artis team more privacy.

In the living room a mixture of custom swivel chairs and Zaha Hadid nesting stools span the entire bay side and the 54 ft (16.5 m) entertainment bar, allowing the view to enhance informal meetings. The bar has surprises such as wine storage, library and magazine racks, a monitor for video art installations, a dining table, plus workout equipment and a yoga ball for the traders to exercise while at their desks. Like the trading desks, the furniture of the six small private offices is custom-designed, with features such as a "plug and play" media component, concealed personal printers, a hidden safe, personal televisions and secret doors for storage. All six offices can double as mini art galleries.

Architecture:
Rottet Studio
Broker:
Axiant Group
Project management:
Julie Holaday Castelero
Construction:
Hathaway Dinwiddie
MEP consultant:
GLUMAC
Audio visual:
Cobalt Communication
Structural:
Rivera Consulting
Furniture dealer:
CRI

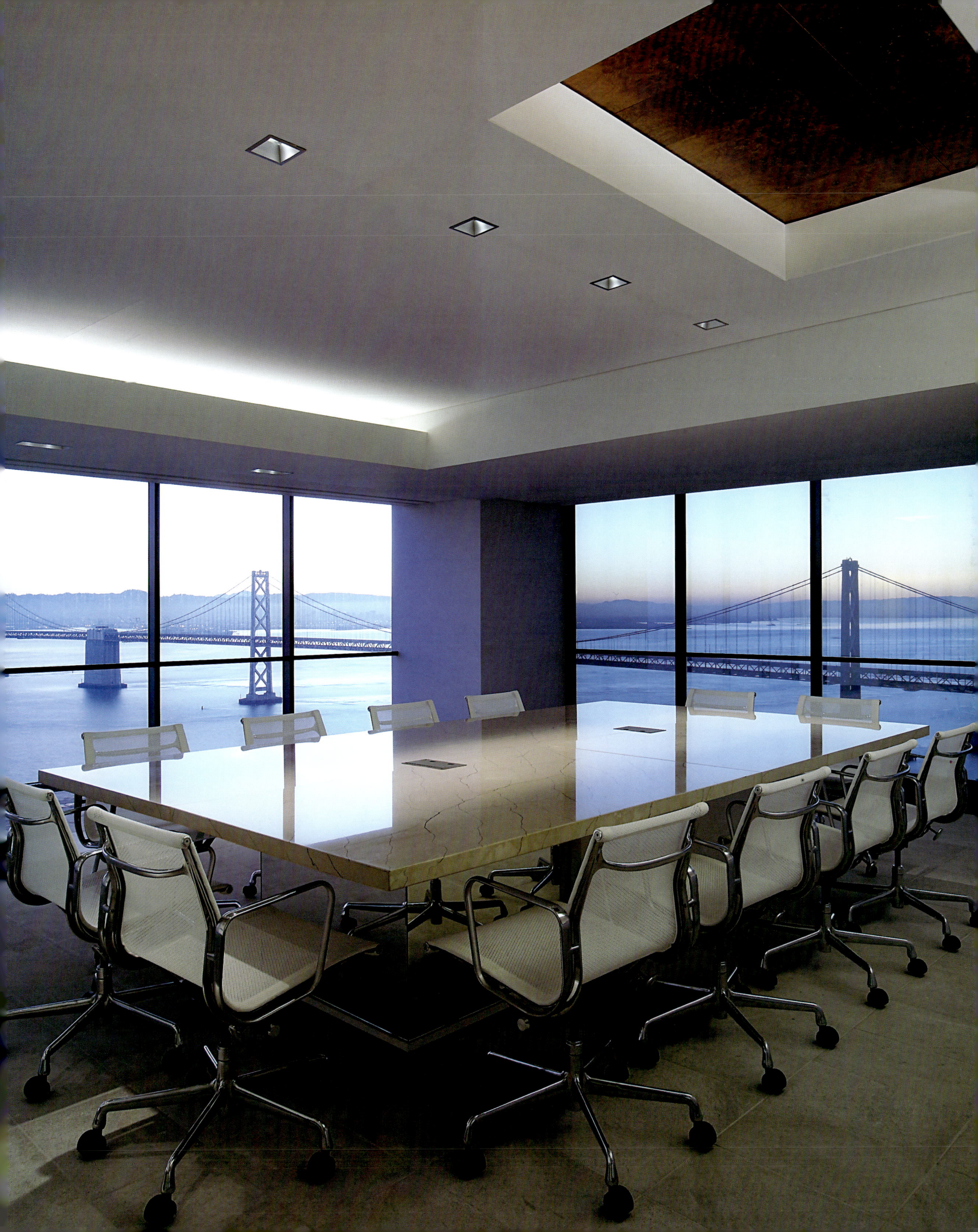

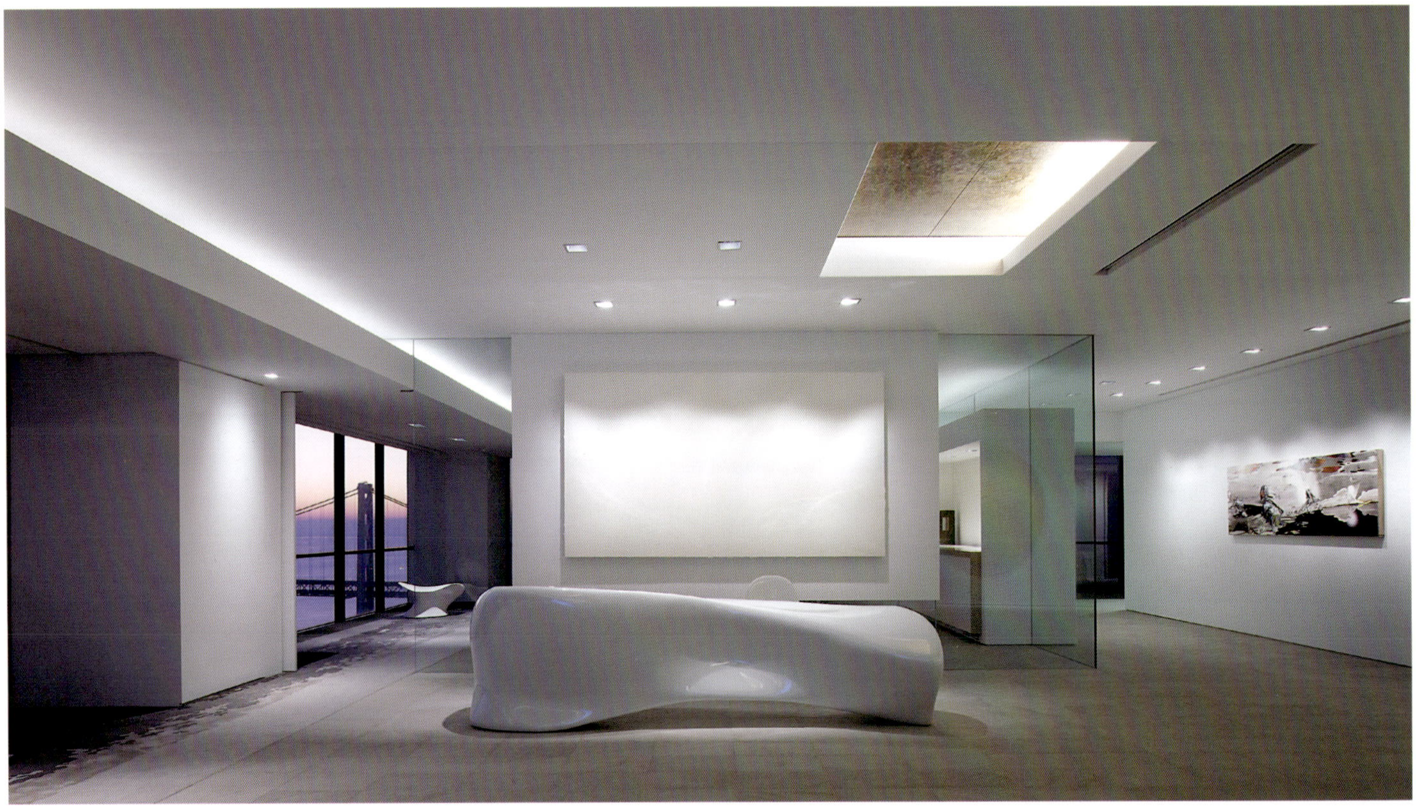

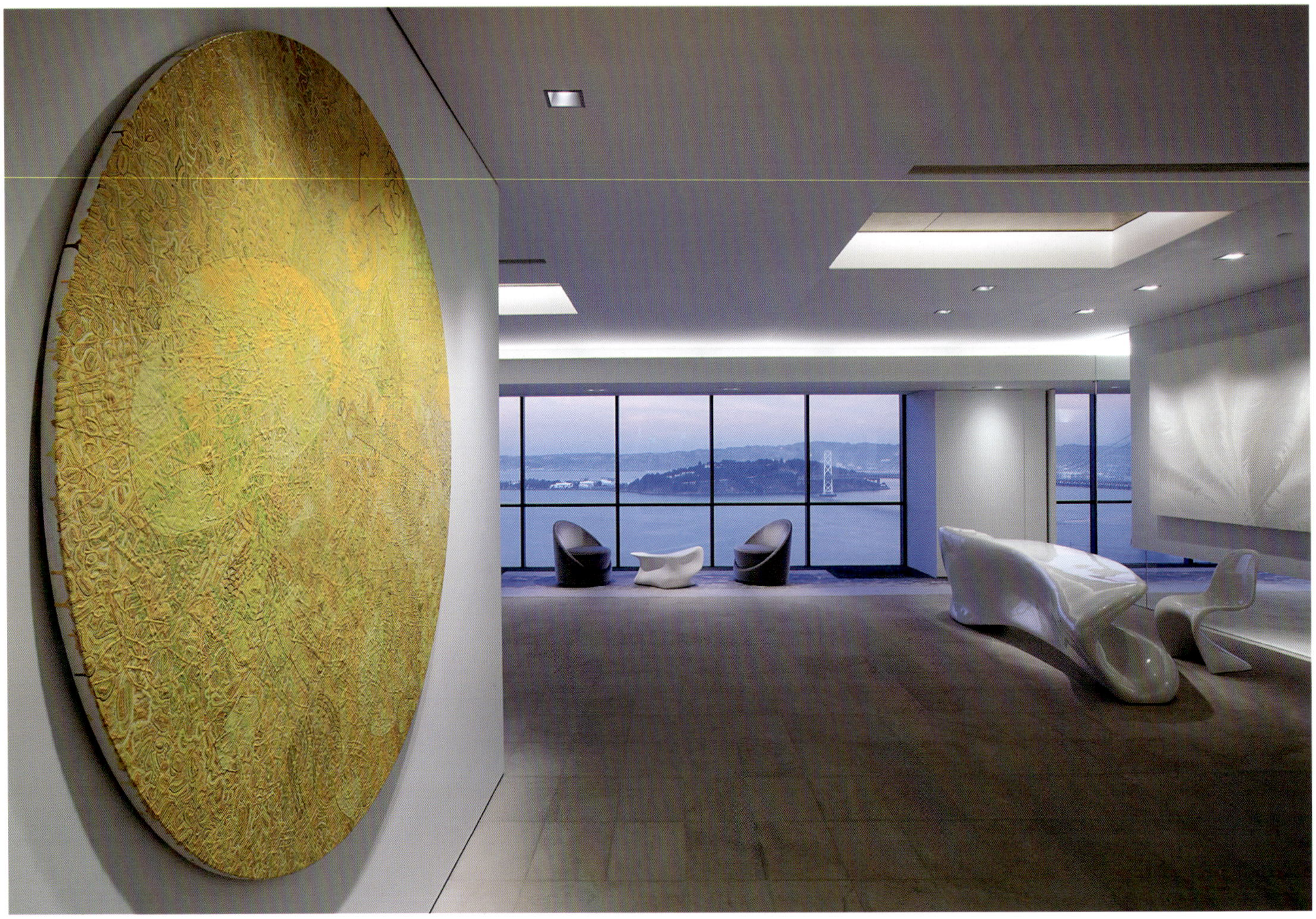

67

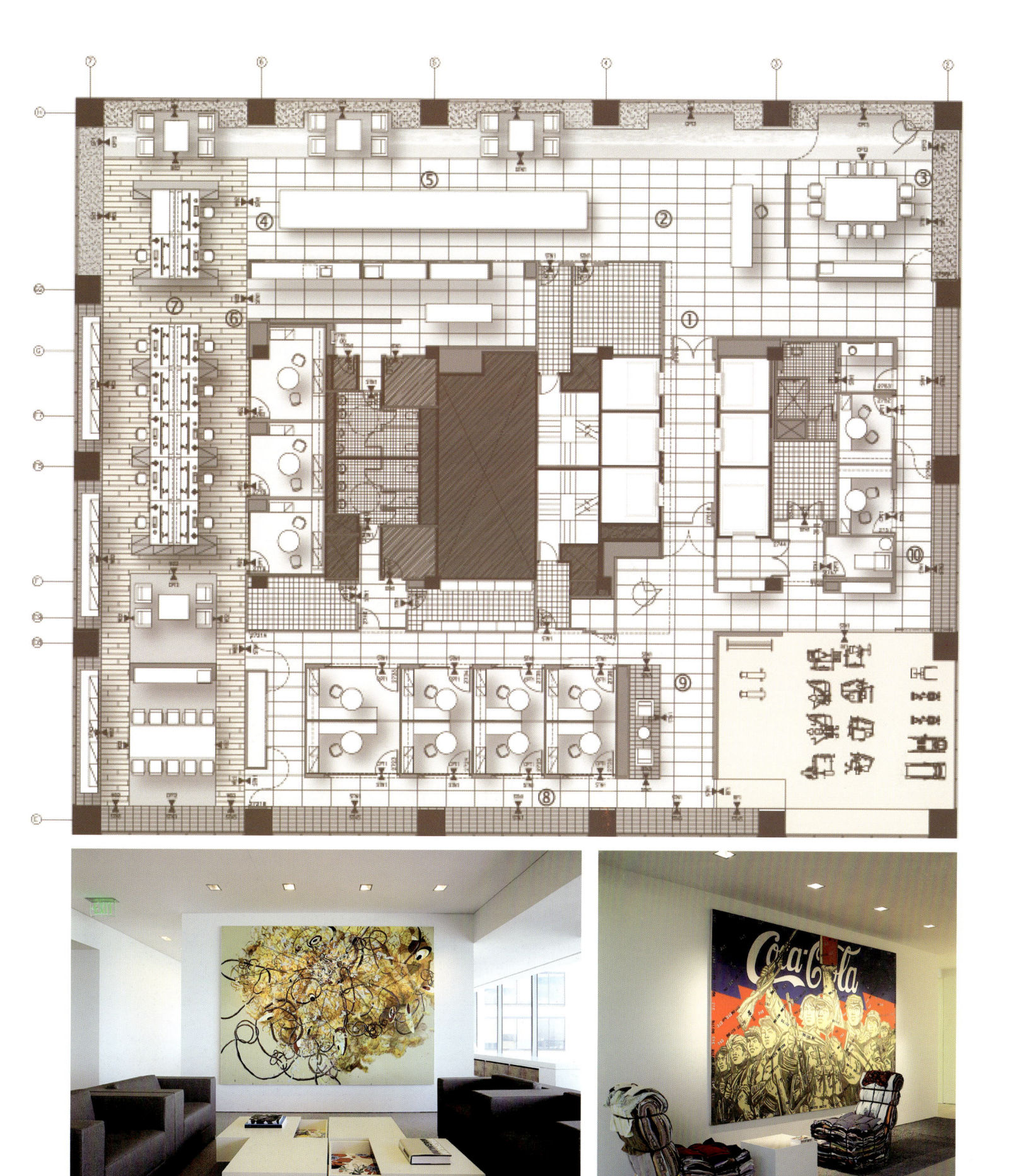

68

Looking at multiple computer monitors all day, Artis partners undergo constant visual stimulation, so the Rottet Studio designed a "visually quiet" space. The office is conceived as a "white box", but the planes peel away to reveal other materials, textures and colors, introducing an element of surprise.

69

EXIT
I CALLED DOWN TO THE D
ESK, I SAID, "IS THIS ROOM
SERVICE?" SHE SAID, "YES
"I SAID SEND UP A ROOM."

71

Studio Ramin Visch

Dupon Office

Hoofddorp, the Netherlands **Photographs: Jeroen Musch**

The former villa of the Mayor of Hoofddorp had already been used as an office space for some time by a law firm, and the series of subdivisions the lawyers had left behind were a far cry from the open office space that Dupon had in mind. What Dupon had in mind was a wide open state-of-the-art office environment that would surprise its visitors with the clear contrast between the outside and the interior of the house.

Big open workspaces were created by knocking down as many walls as possible, as those remaining were quite sufficient to allow different areas to have different characters. Light colours were chosen for the walls, floors and office furniture. As well as creating a sensation of spaciousness, this provided a neutral background to show up the few brightly colored elements that were to be added. The acoustic panels on the walls were one such item, as well as the reception furniture and a sofa in the management office.

Instead of specific colors identifying specific spaces, color has been used to identify certain objects (such as stairs or walls) that divide, connect or cut across the various spaces. This strategy enhances the sculptural and material presence of the constructive elements of the building and simultaneously allows the space to function as an undivided whole flowing through and around them. Circulation is clear. The red stairs in the hallway cannot be missed, while the main meeting room at the back of the office is visible from the entrance.

Architecture:
Studio Ramin Visch
Project team:
Ramin Visch, Femke Poppinga,
Peter van der Geer(acoustic)
Client:
Dupon Real Estate Development bv
Completion date:
2007
Area:
3,010 sqft (280 sqm)

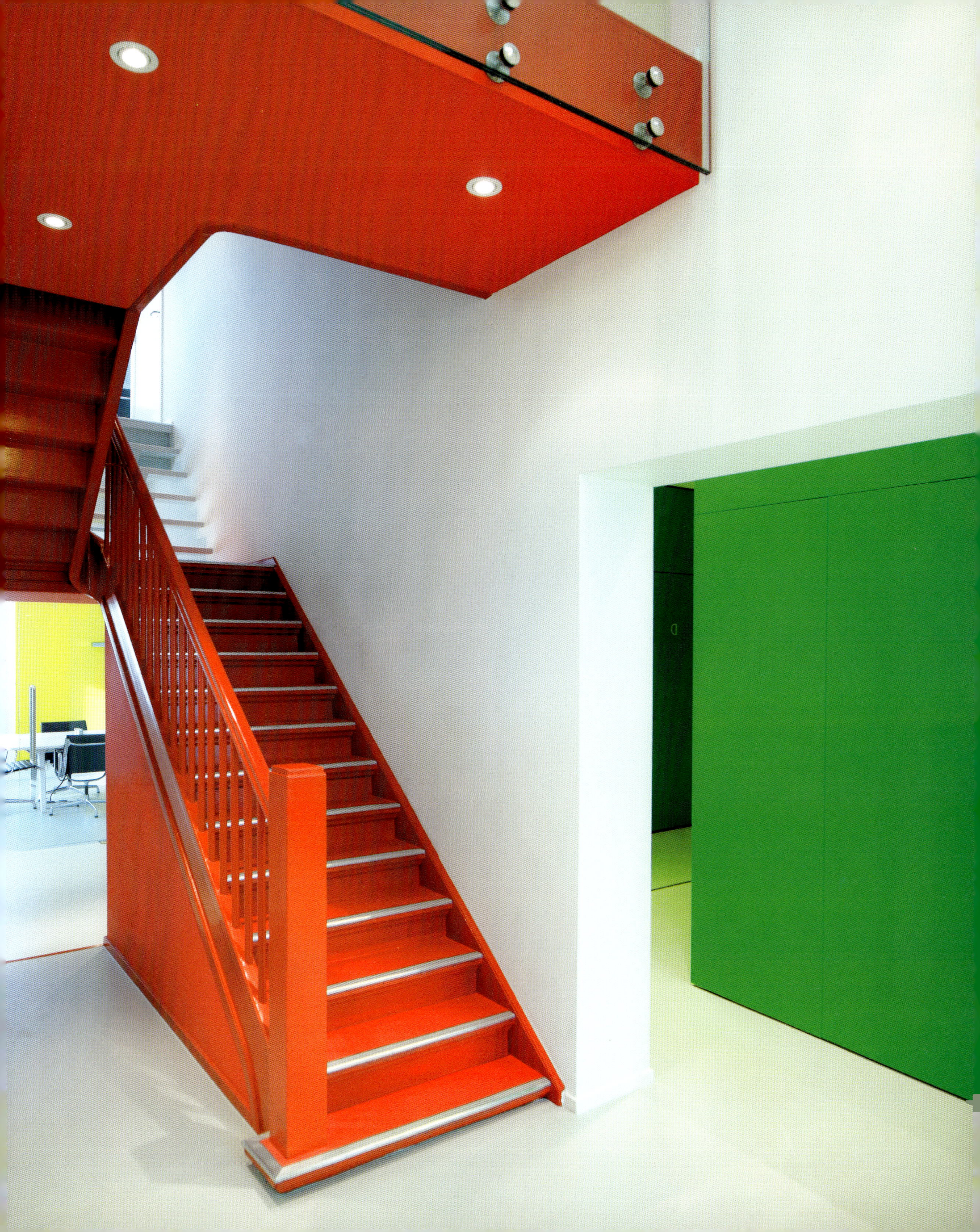

In order to prepare the villa for its open-plan office function, an almost the full height void was created at the entrance to the building, to achieve a sense of connection between the different levels and create a sense of brightness, spaciousness and transparency.

75

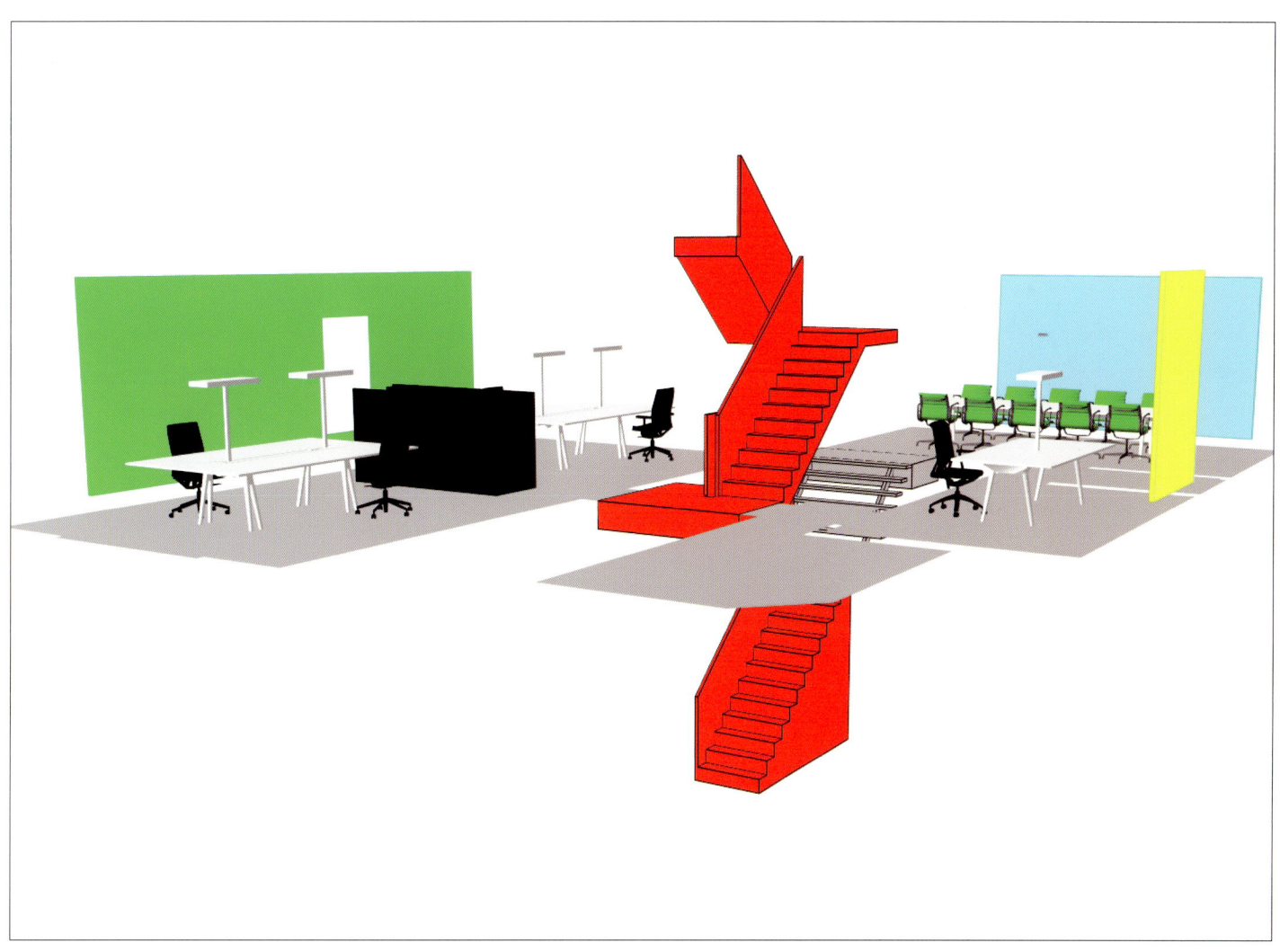

Ground floor plan

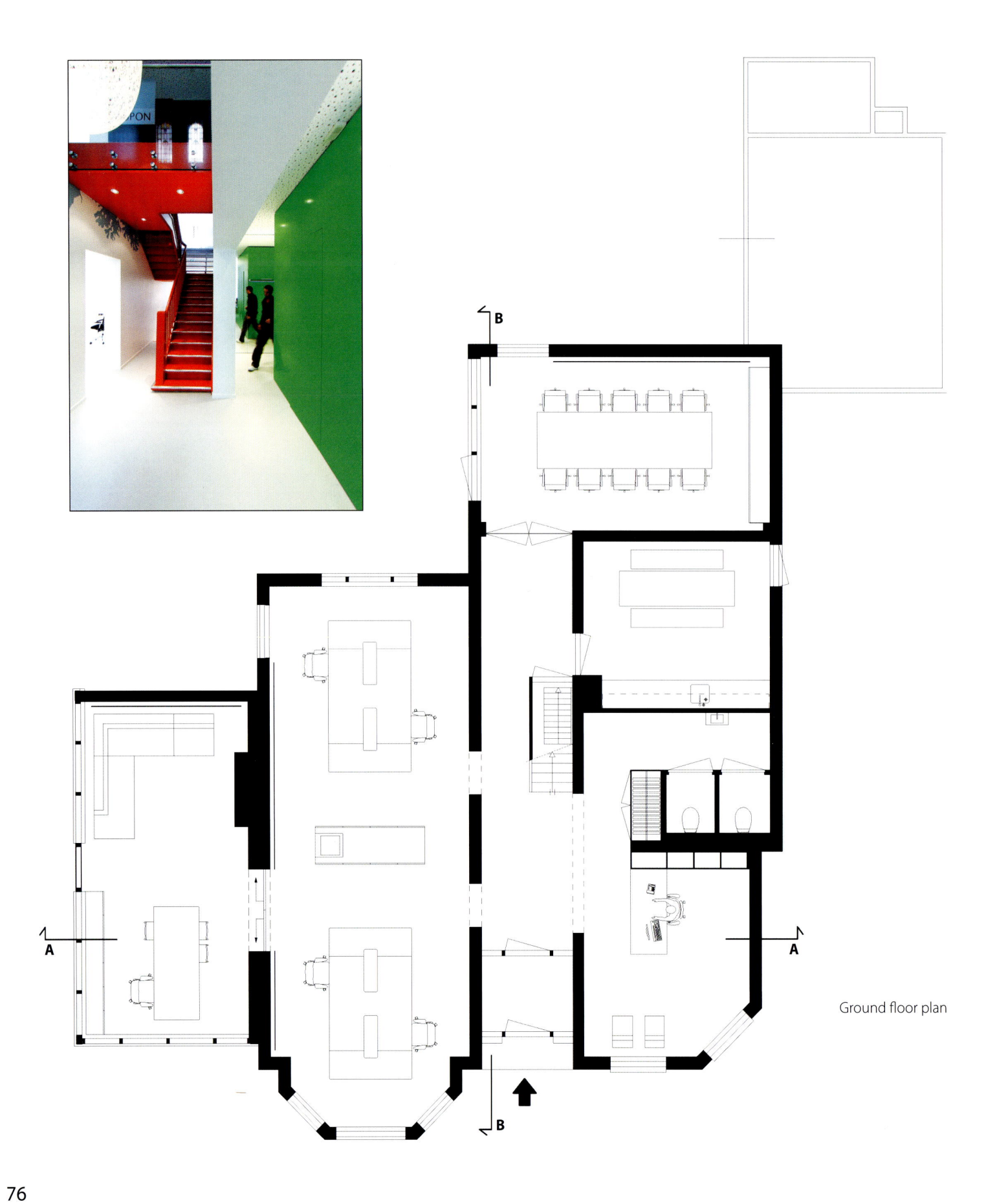

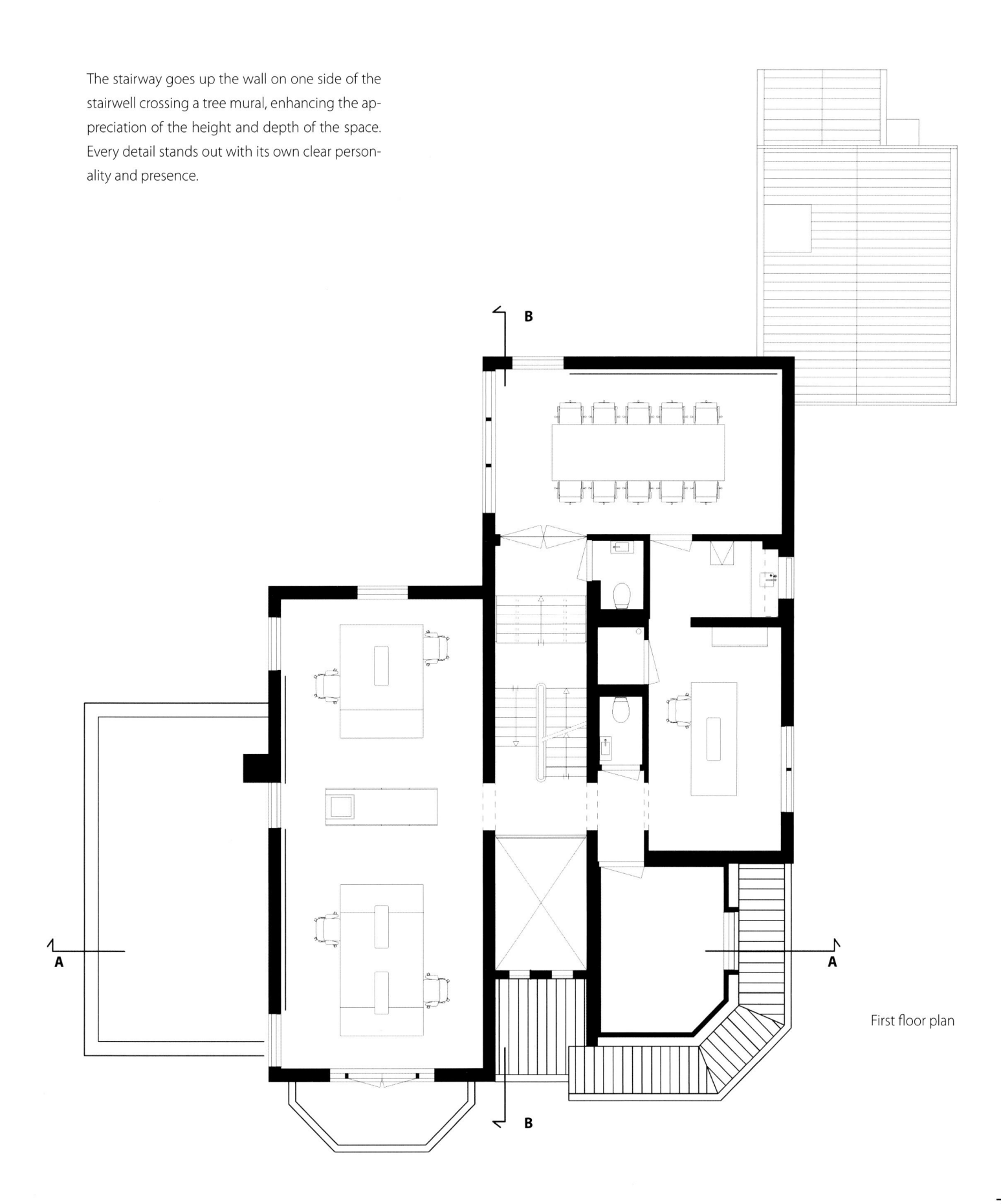

The stairway goes up the wall on one side of the stairwell crossing a tree mural, enhancing the appreciation of the height and depth of the space. Every detail stands out with its own clear personality and presence.

First floor plan

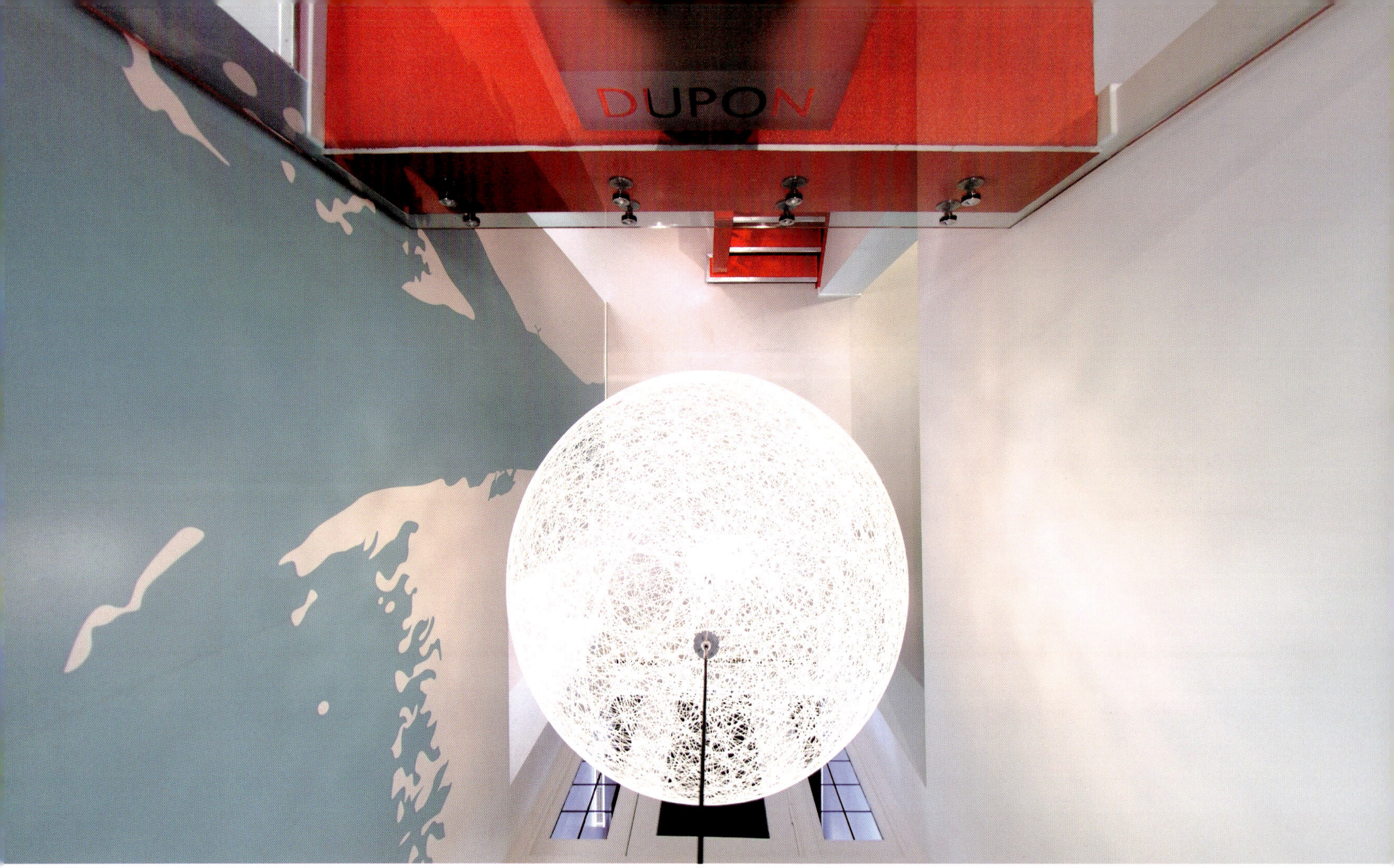
DUPON

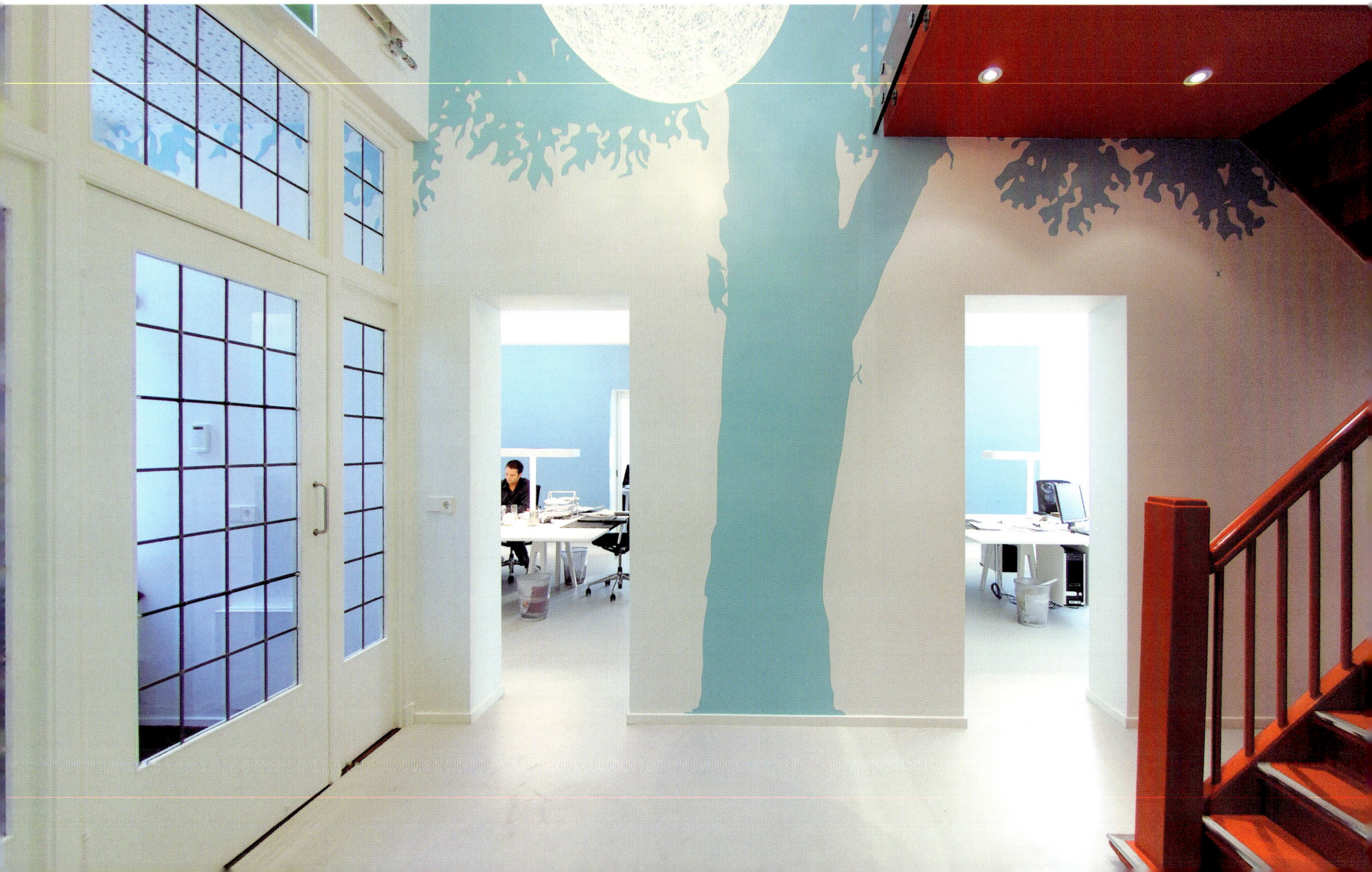

Section AA

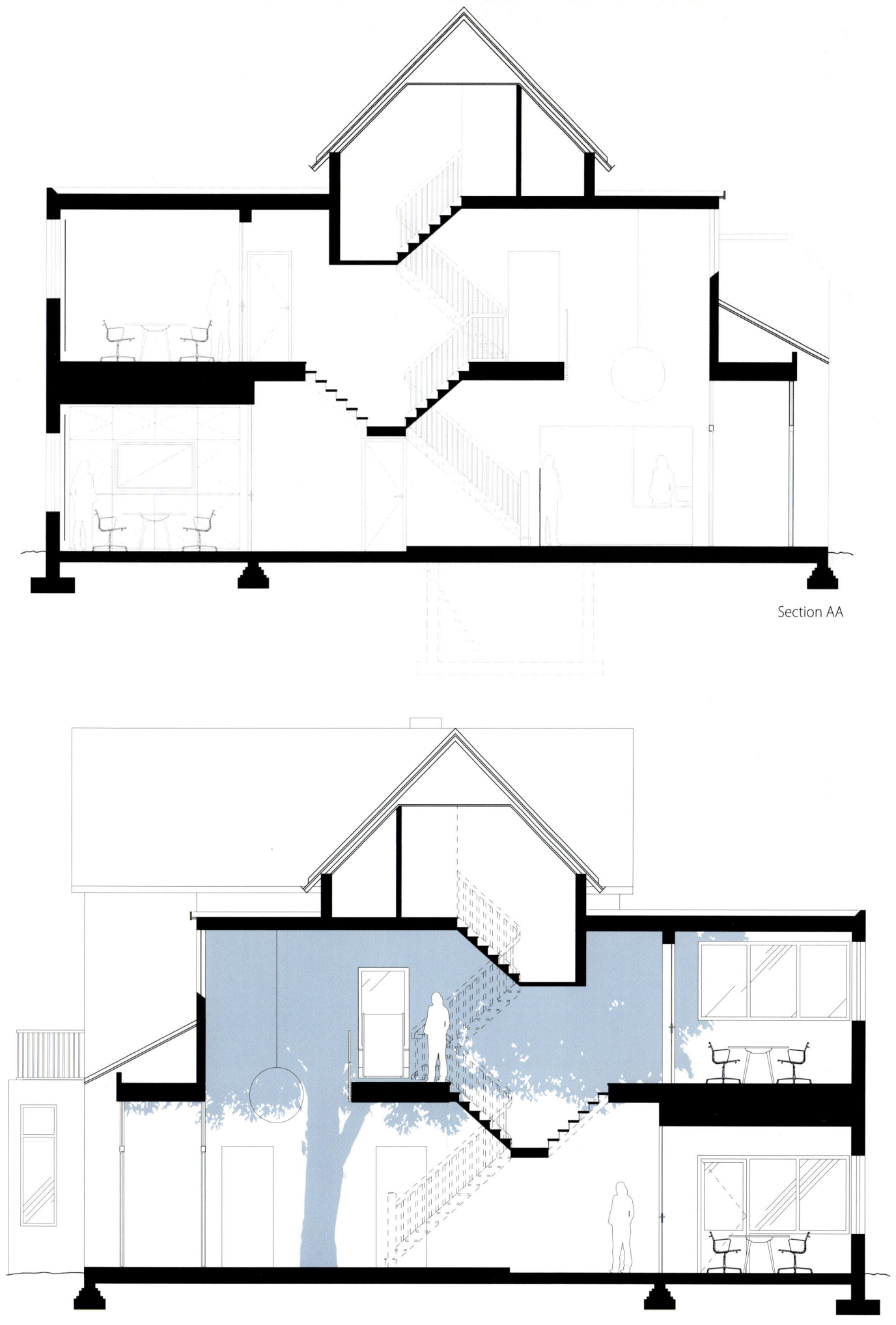

Section BB

Light colours were chosen for the walls, floors and office furniture.

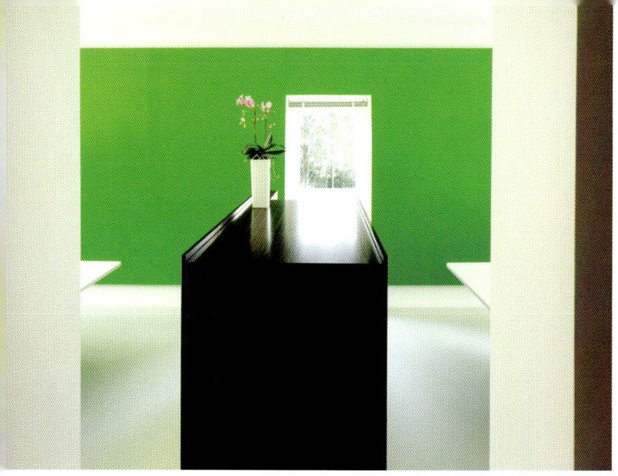
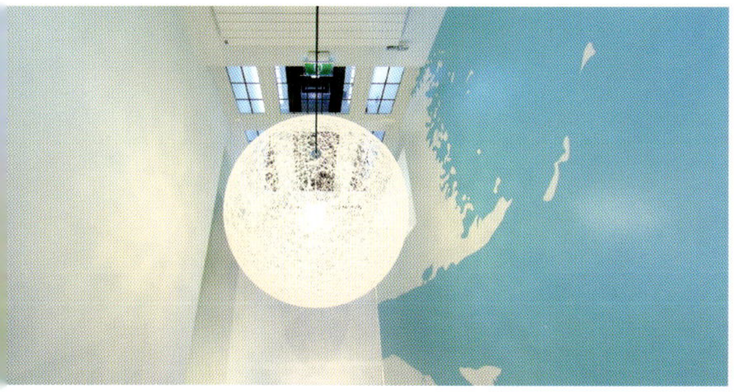
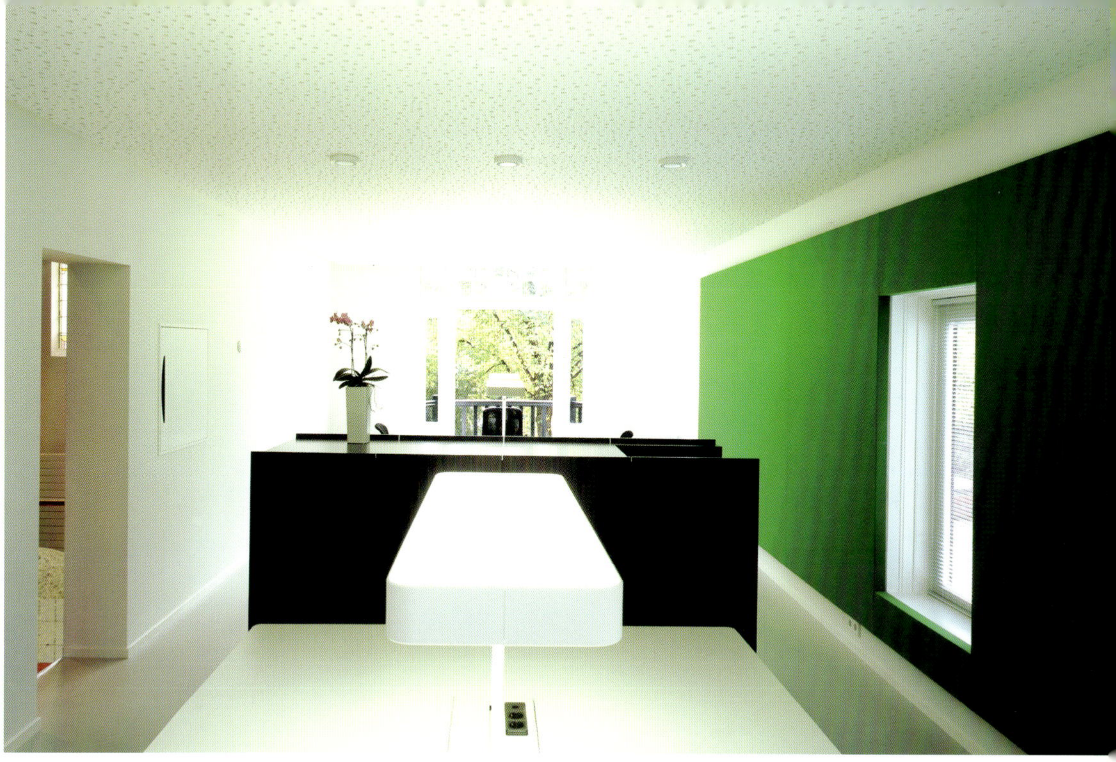
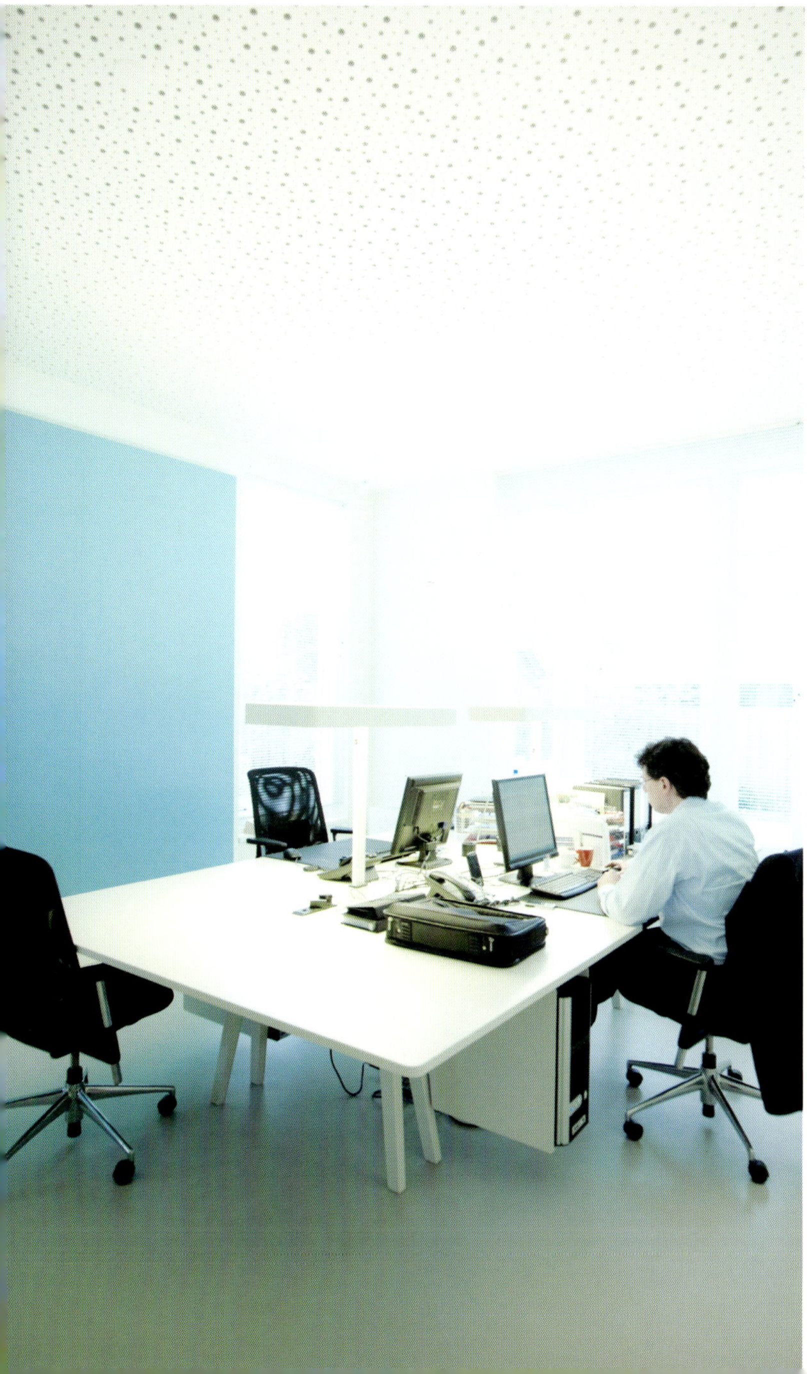
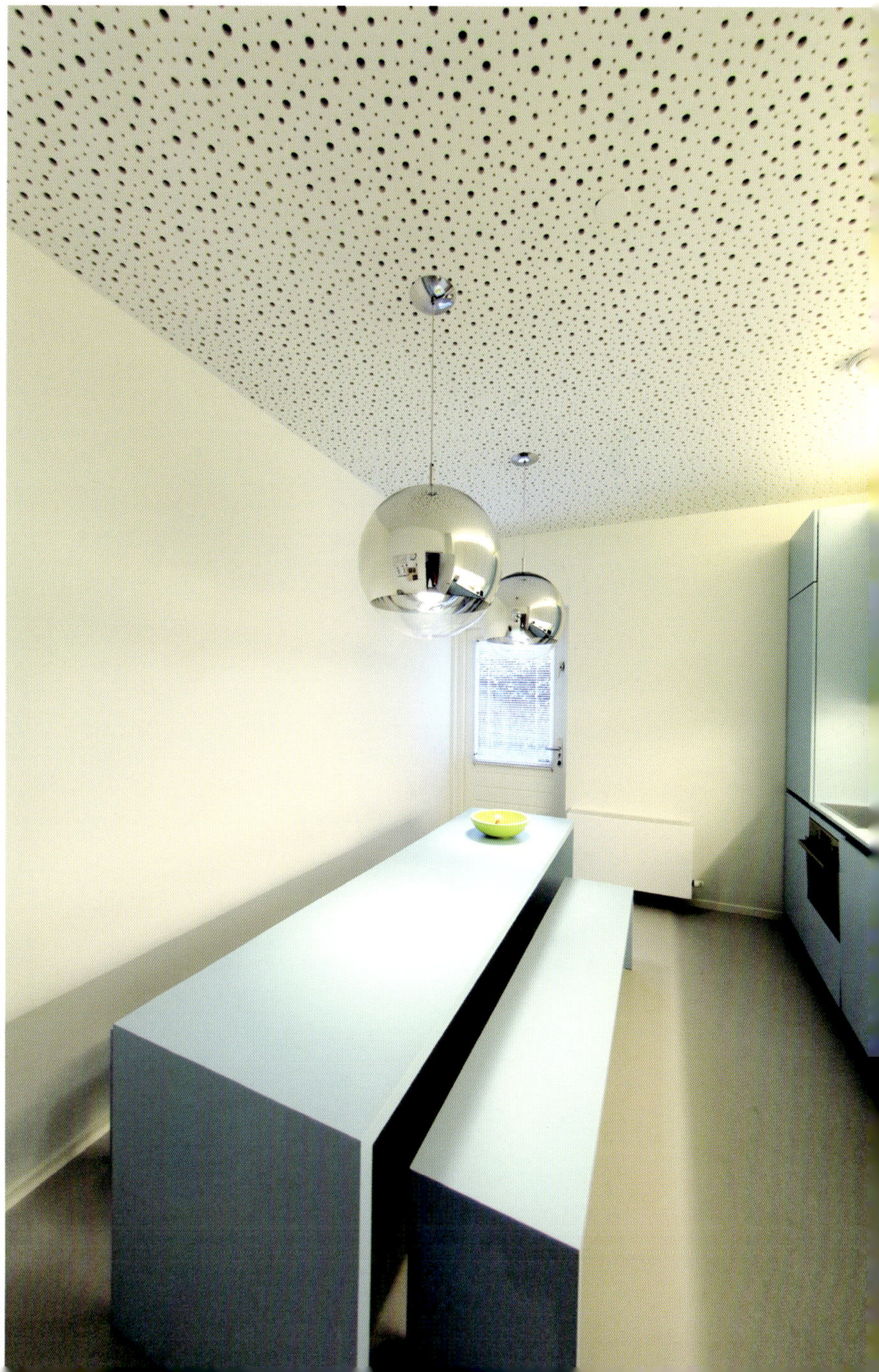

chadbourne + doss architects

HTC Office

Seattle, USA **Photographs: Ben Benshneider**

HTC, the Taiwanese cell-phone company required a new Seattle office for its user-interface team in the US, so they contacted Lisa Chadbourne and Daren Doss to create the interior they needed on one floor of a historic office building that had recently undergone a reform by SHED. The owner of HTC wanted an open-plan office, but with the addition of spaces for more private, silent, contemplative work.

Six drywall pods lined with plywood have glazed façades that look onto the main space and define the entry hall. Each pod contains a writable laminate desk and a chair, providing the company's staff with a place of retreat when extra concentration of the more individual sort is needed. Collaboration is an important part of their work-process, and wall mounted white-boards are the typical medium. A 48ft long work table with an adjacent 48ft long writable board allows for group work. A 32ft long work counter with a writable surface separates work and meeting spaces and provides space for informal gatherings and collaboration.

Several pieces of custom-made plywood furniture are also integrated into the space including a coffee table made to measure. The contractor, Fackler Construction, designed and built a customized dog bed for the office mascot. A 60ft long work table to accommodate further growth is currently in the design stage.

Architecture:
chadbourne + doss architects
Area:
5,000 sqft (464 sqm)

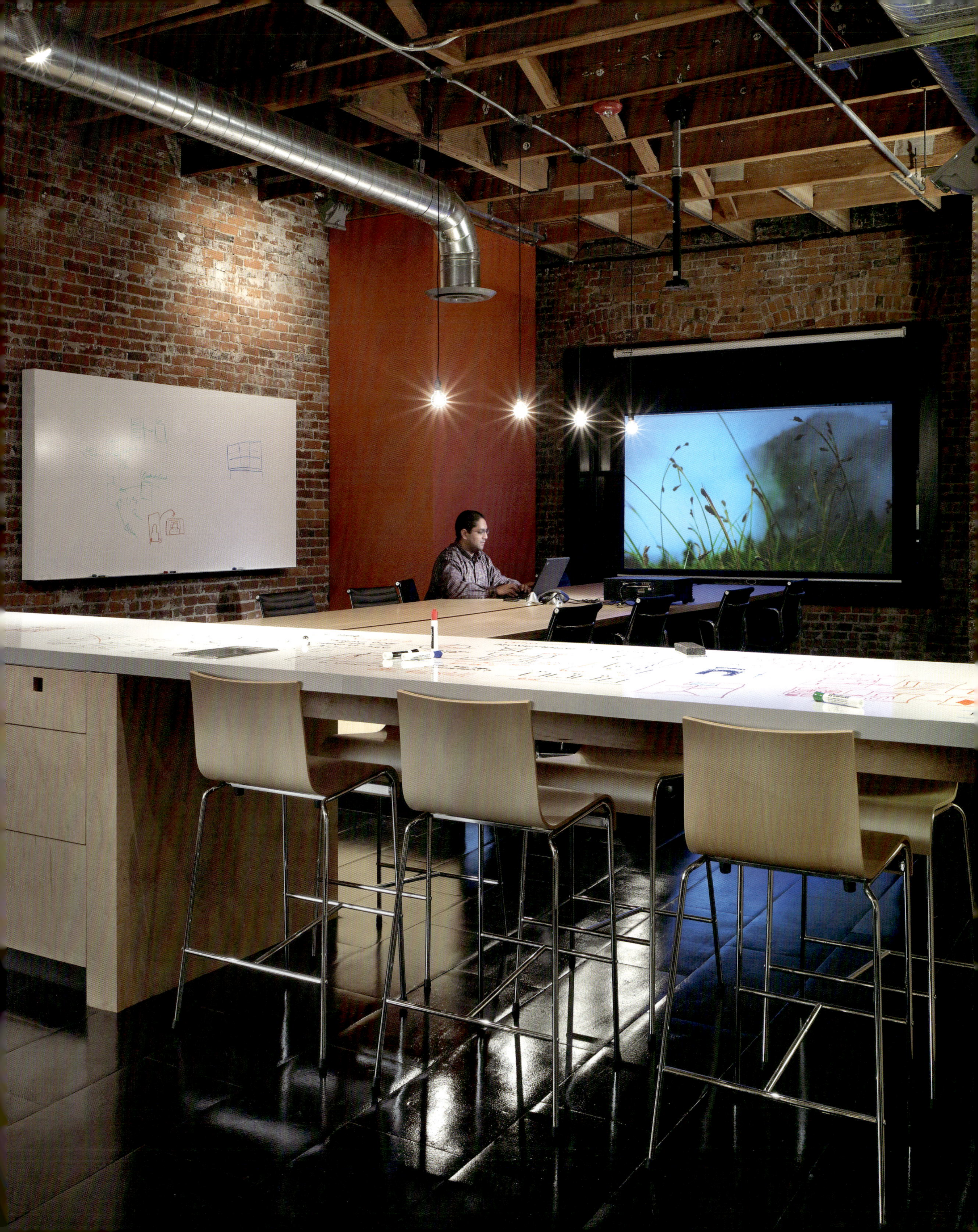

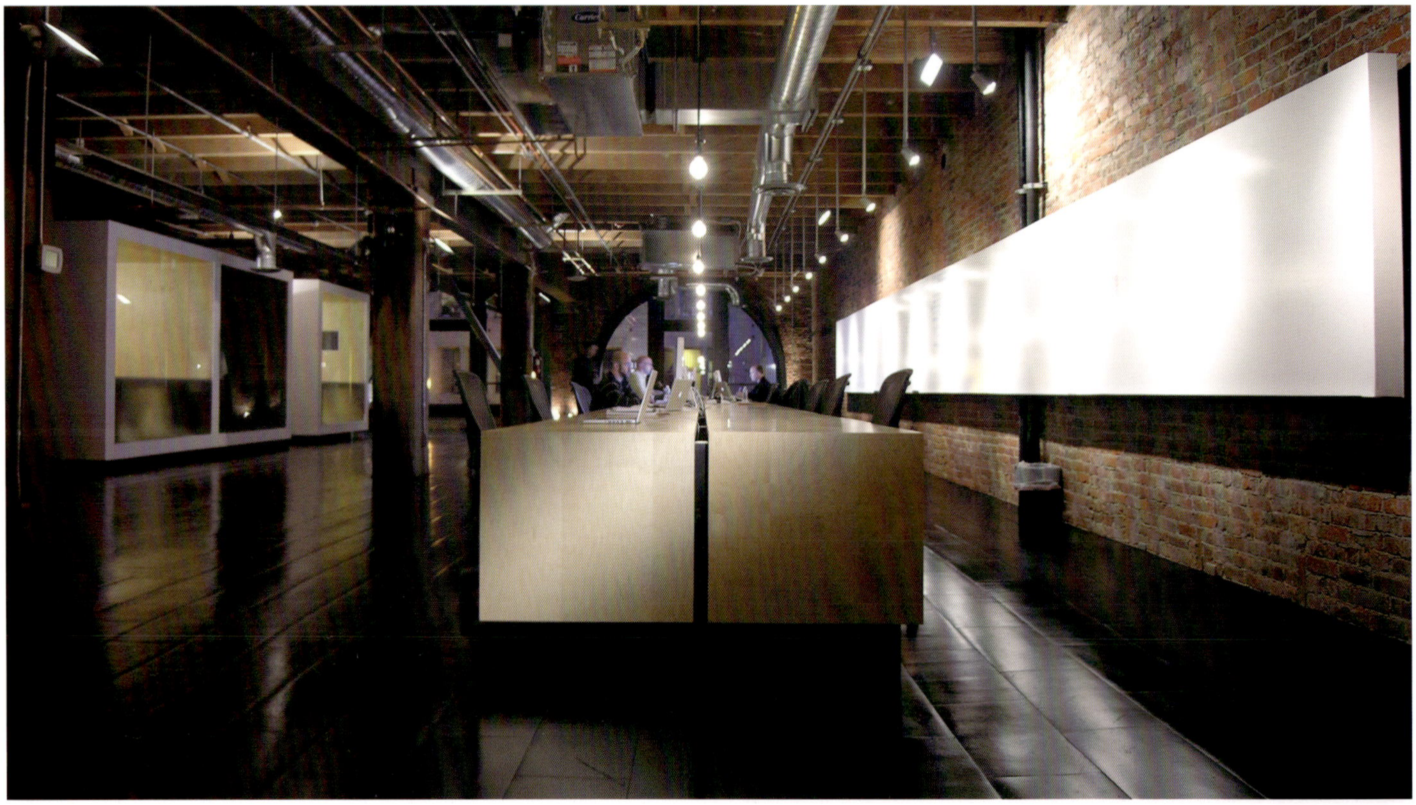

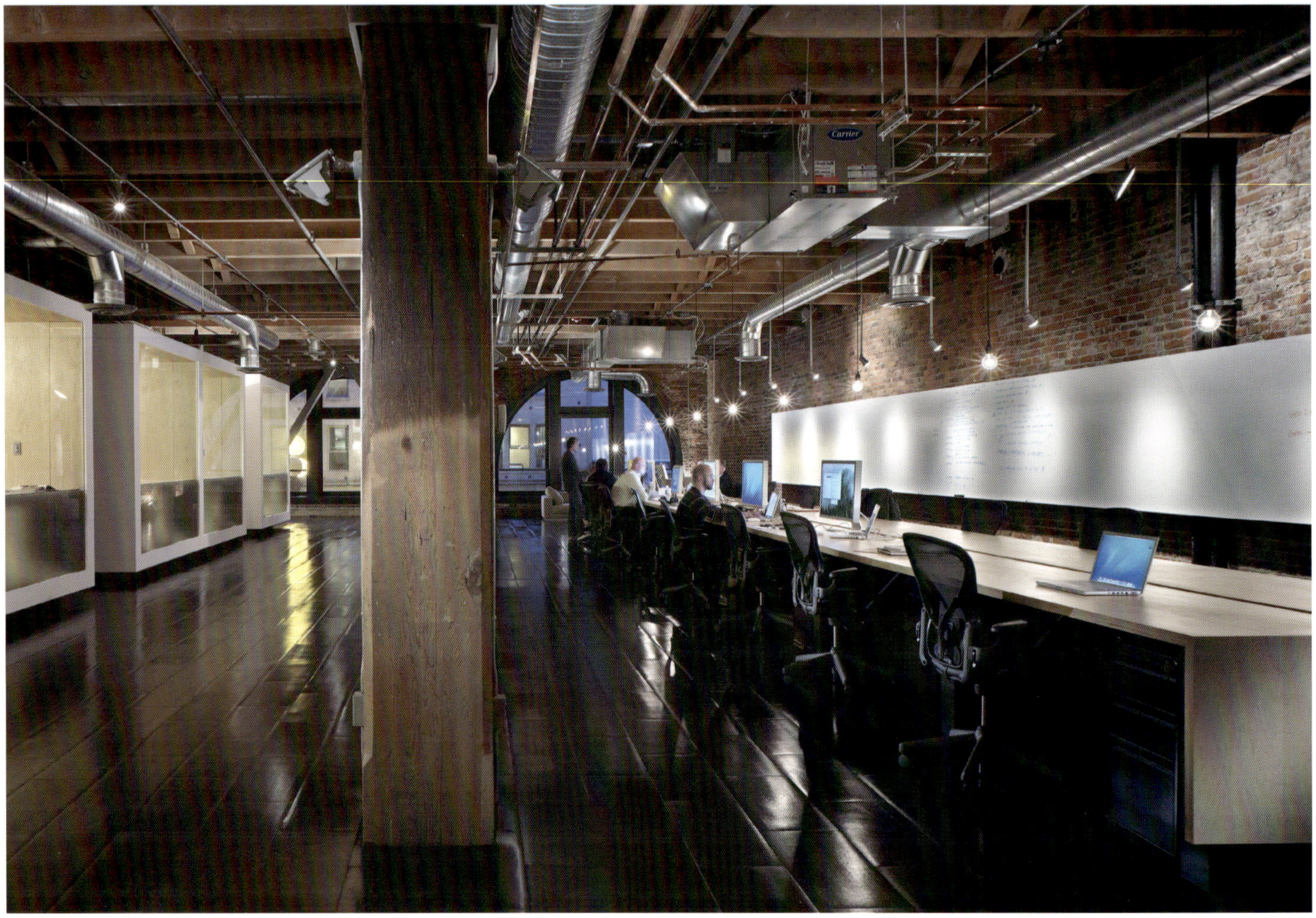

Ground floor plan

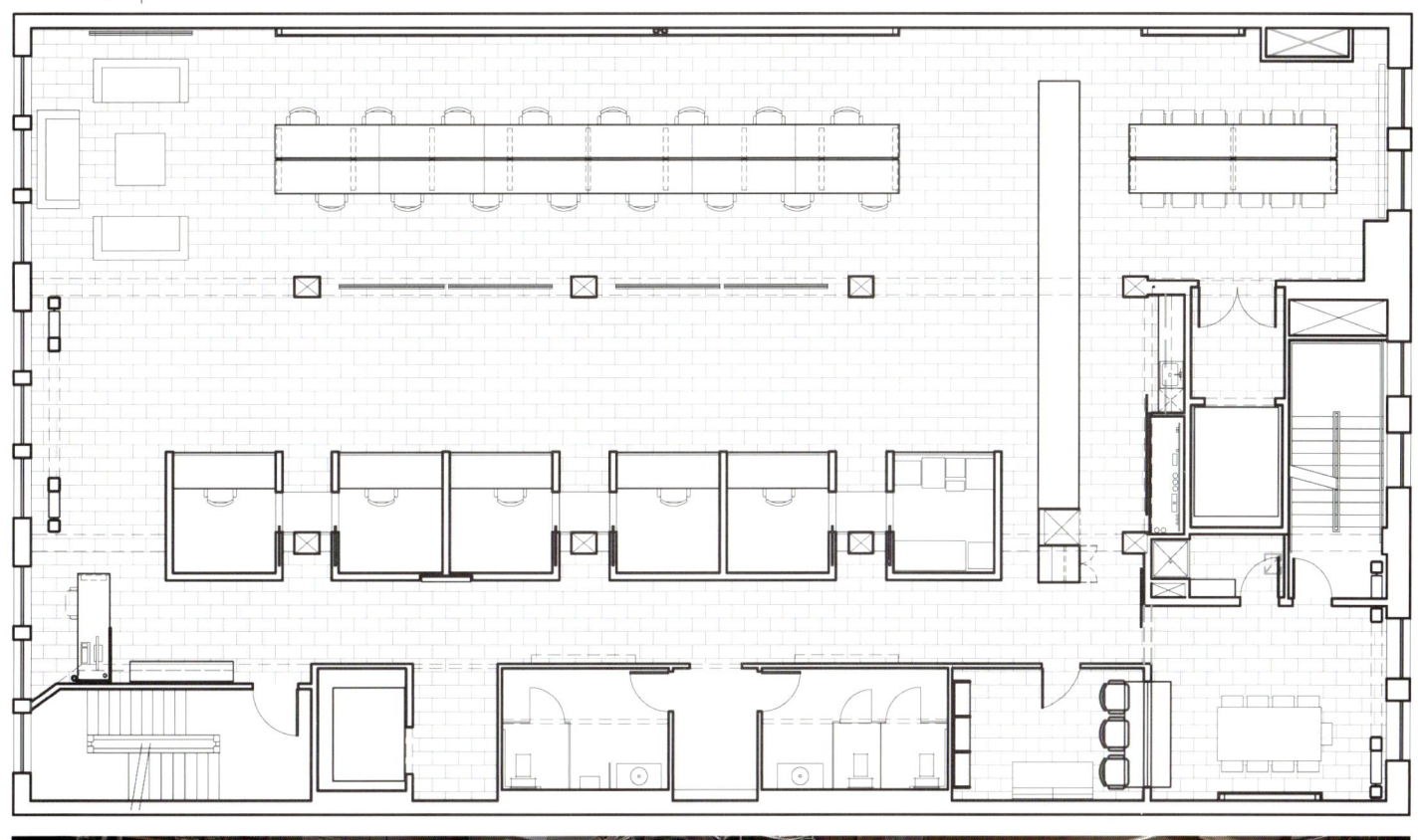

WRITABLE OFFICE DETAIL

1. Metal angle
2. Solid wood desk
3. Tempered satin etch traslucent glazing
4. Butt wall panels in/between floor at ceiling panels
5. Plywood with wax finish in interior of work pods
6. Recess at back shown dashed
7. Recess in plywood cladding for cables
8. MDF and plywood butt to glass

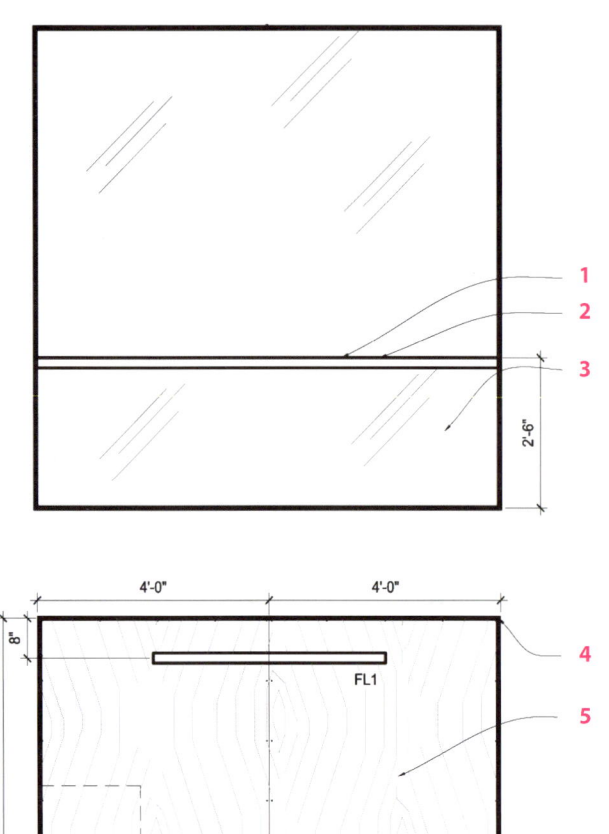

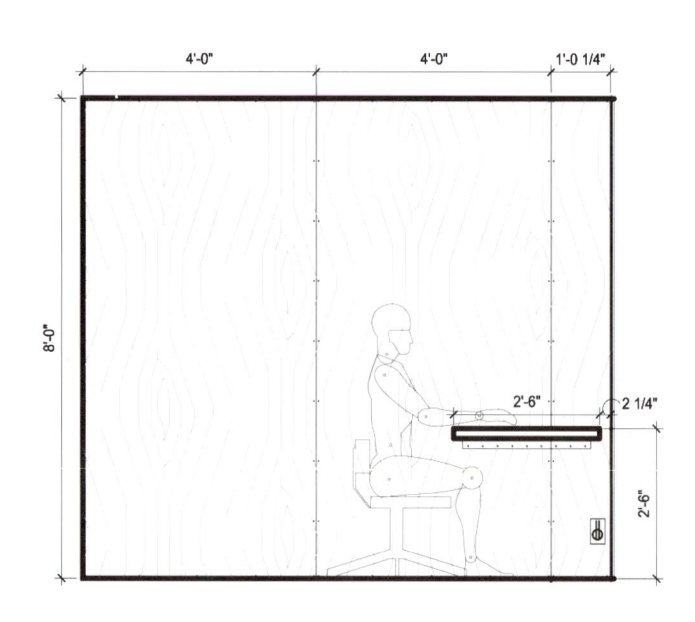

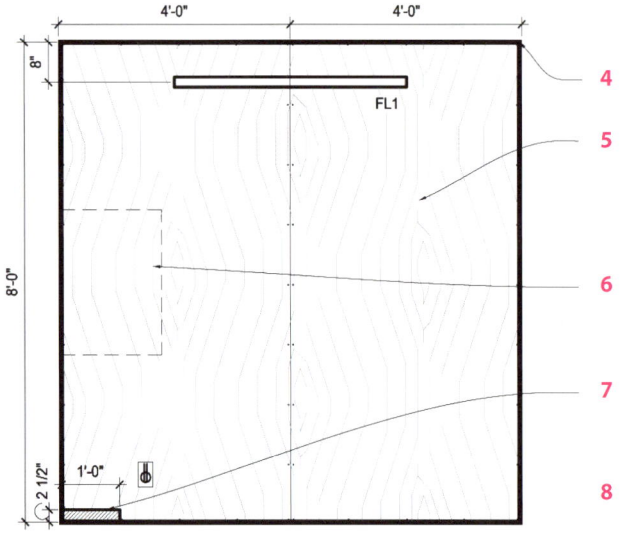

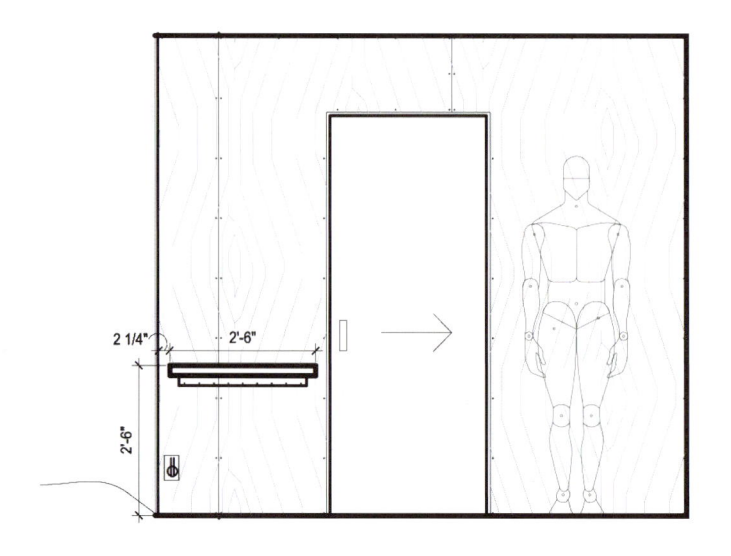

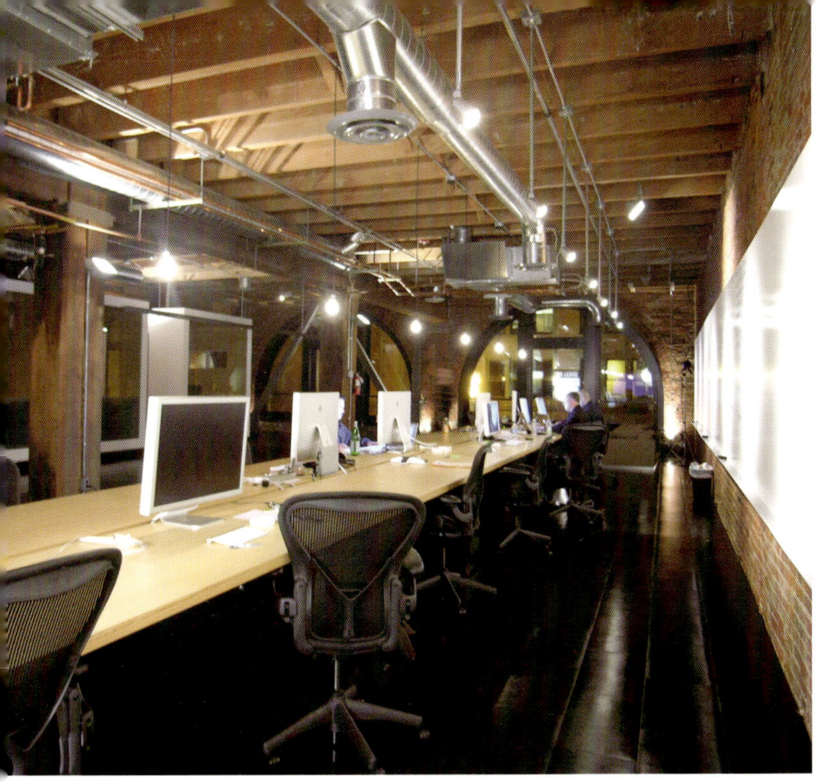
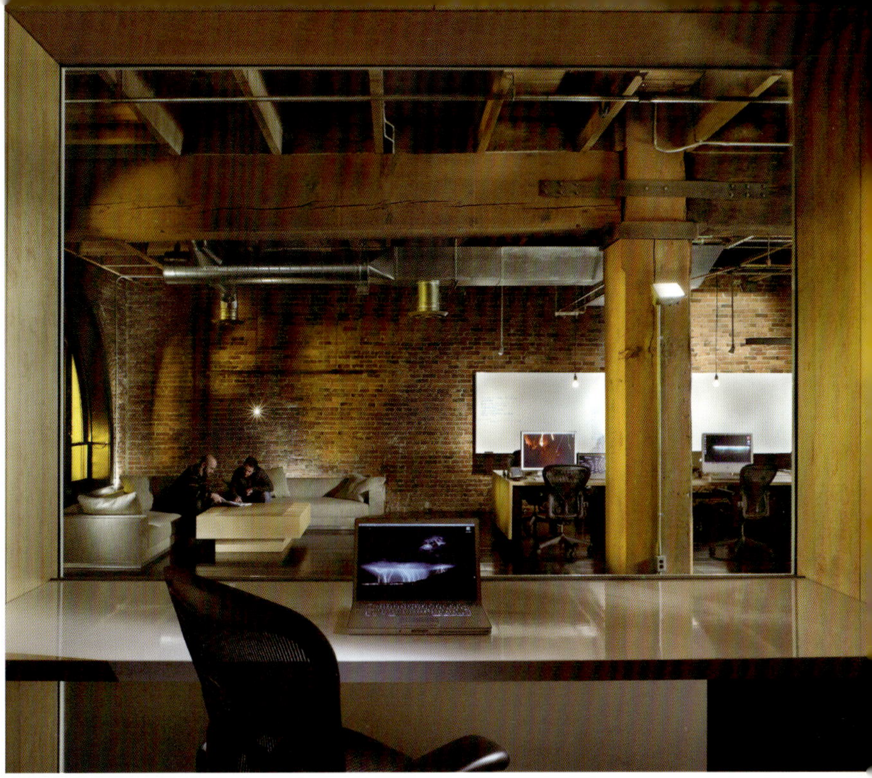
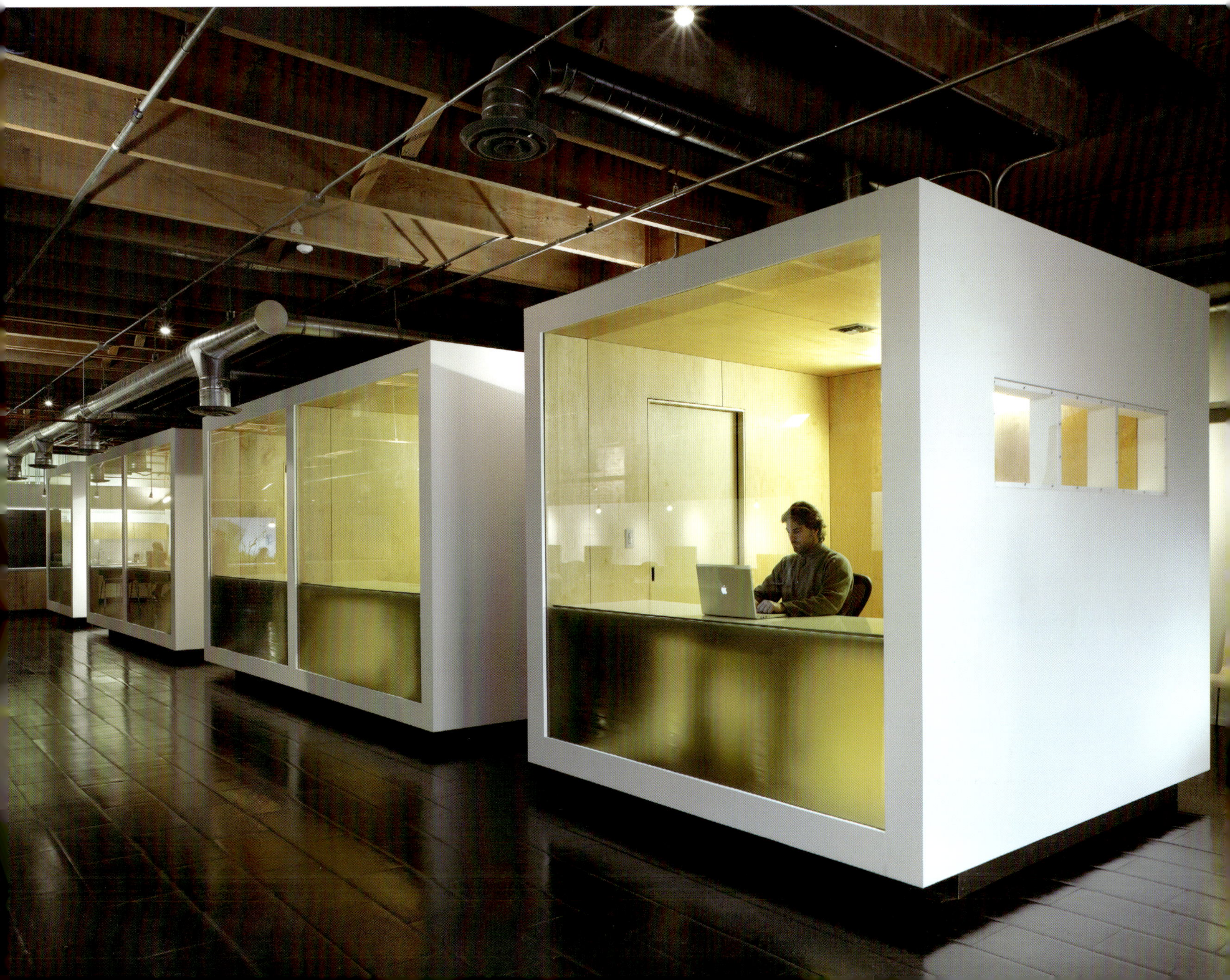

HTC, a Taiwanese cell-phone company, chose a 5,000-sqft space located on the second floor of a warehouse from the early 20th century for its new Seattle office. The client's brief demanded an open-plan workspace inspired in the term "Innovation Office".

Given the constructive quality of the building and the low budget, the architects reduced the palette of materials to plywood, glass, and plastic laminate, plus a floor of glossy black asphalt-composite floorboards.

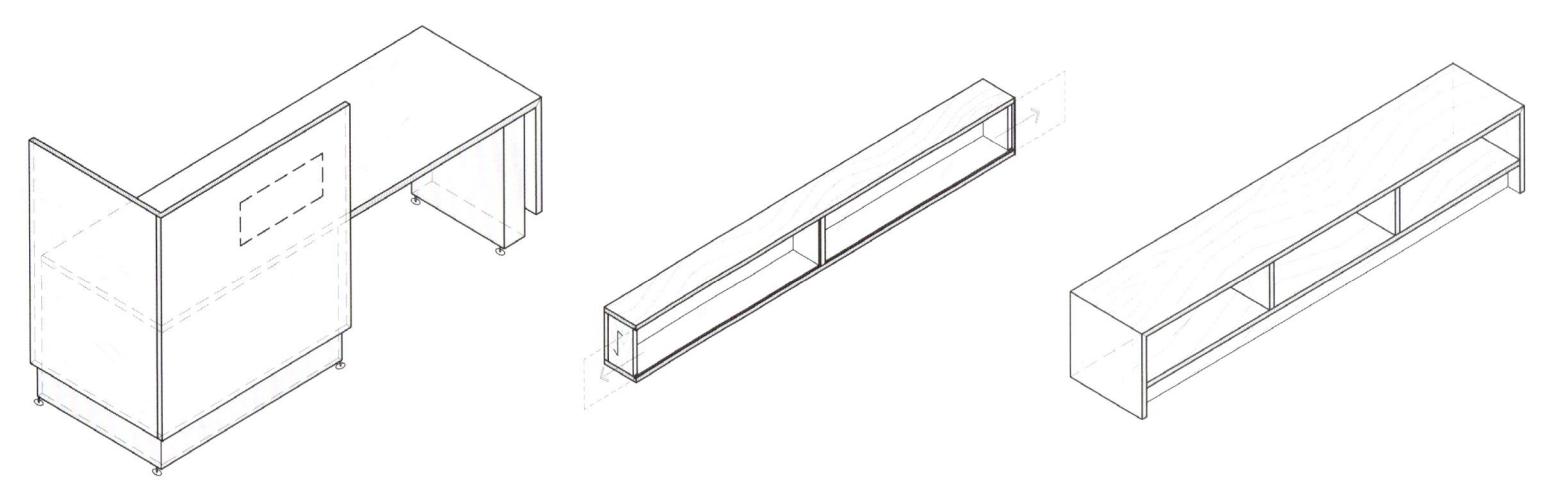

Furniture detail

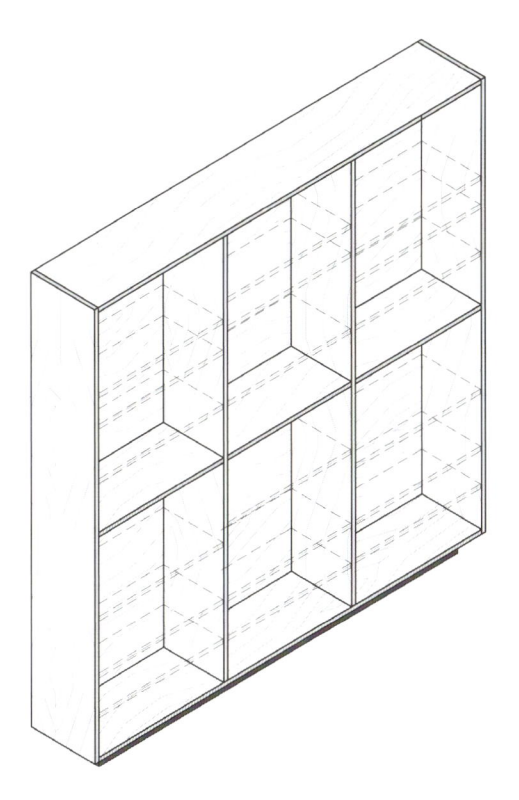

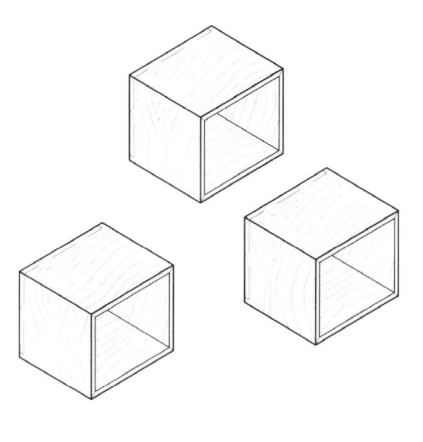

Furniture detail

arquitectura x

Ruales Izurieta Publicidad

Quito, Ecuador Photographs: Sebastian Crespo

Arquitectura x was started in 1996 by Adrian Moreno and Maria Samaniego. They have worked in architecture, urban design, interior and furniture design in Quito, Guayaquil, Cuenca, Loja and other cities in Ecuador. They have received a number of awards and nominations in urban design and architecture, such as the National Architecture Award, the 10th Architectural Biennial, Quito (Ecuador) 1996; Winners of the "National Urban Design Competition for El Barranco, Cuenca", (Ecuador) 2003; Finalists 5th BIAU (Bienal Iberoamericana de Arquitectura y Urbanismo). Montevideo, (Uruguay) 2006; First Runner-up for the Urban Cooperation Award, Santiago de Compostela, (Spain) 2007; Their work has been part of exhibitions at different national and international events in Montevideo, Cartagena, Madrid, London and Buenos Aires. They give frequent lectures and their work has been featured in numerous publications.

This small intervention for a young advertising agency is based on the requirement for a flexible and expandable space, adaptable to the multiple tasks and changing needs that will arise through the enterprise's activities and expansion. An important condition was that the budget had to be kept low, as a major proportion of the clients' overall investment was to be for the specialized tools and equipment required by the clients' work. Another defining factor was for the agency's first formal office to transmit an image of decisive, bold and refreshing decision-making.

In response to the challenge, the architects' first move was to take out all the dull finishes and claddings typical to a standard office in an office block, leaving all the ductwork and the steel and concrete structures showing; this enabled them to strip the space down to its bare constituents, to achieve a raw and flexible container in which to insert the furniture and the containers for the various activities that are likely to vary with time and may require occasional modifications. These "pieces of furniture", made of plywood and floating parquet floors have been "plugged in" to the various corresponding networks, all of which are entirely visible. The same maple finish has been used throughout (floors, walls and ceilings), achieving a strong result at minimal cost, providing a work environment that has been easy to install and offers the possibility of uncomplicated alterations in the future to adapt to a variable work context.

Architecture:
arquitectura x
Client:
Ruales Izurieta Publicidad
Project team:
arquitectura x
Adrian Moreno
María Samaniego
Construction:
Adrian Moreno
Germán Llerena
2008, with alterations in 2009 y 2010
3D:
Esteban Benavides
Maricarmen Salazar
Surface area:
882 sqft (82 sqm)

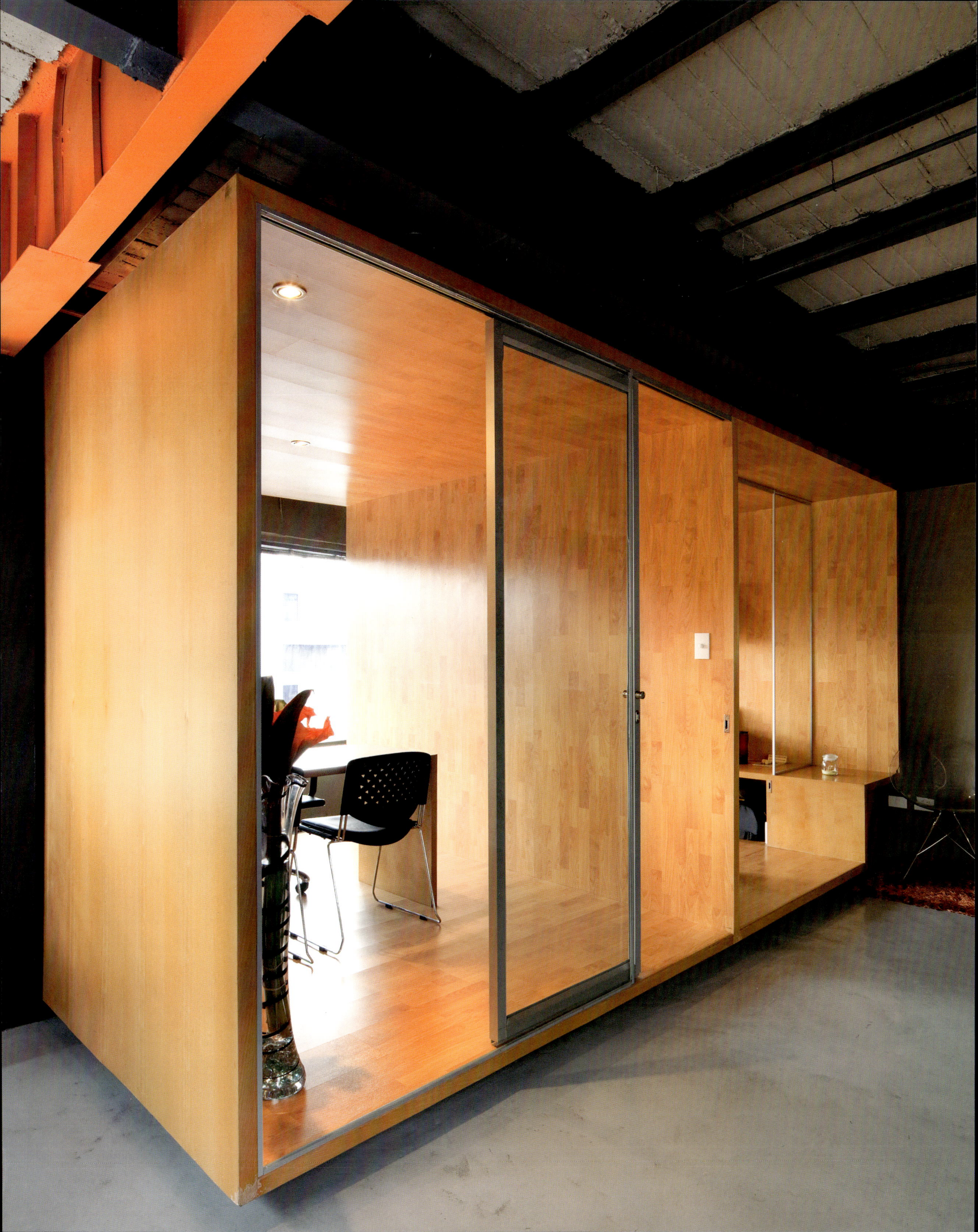

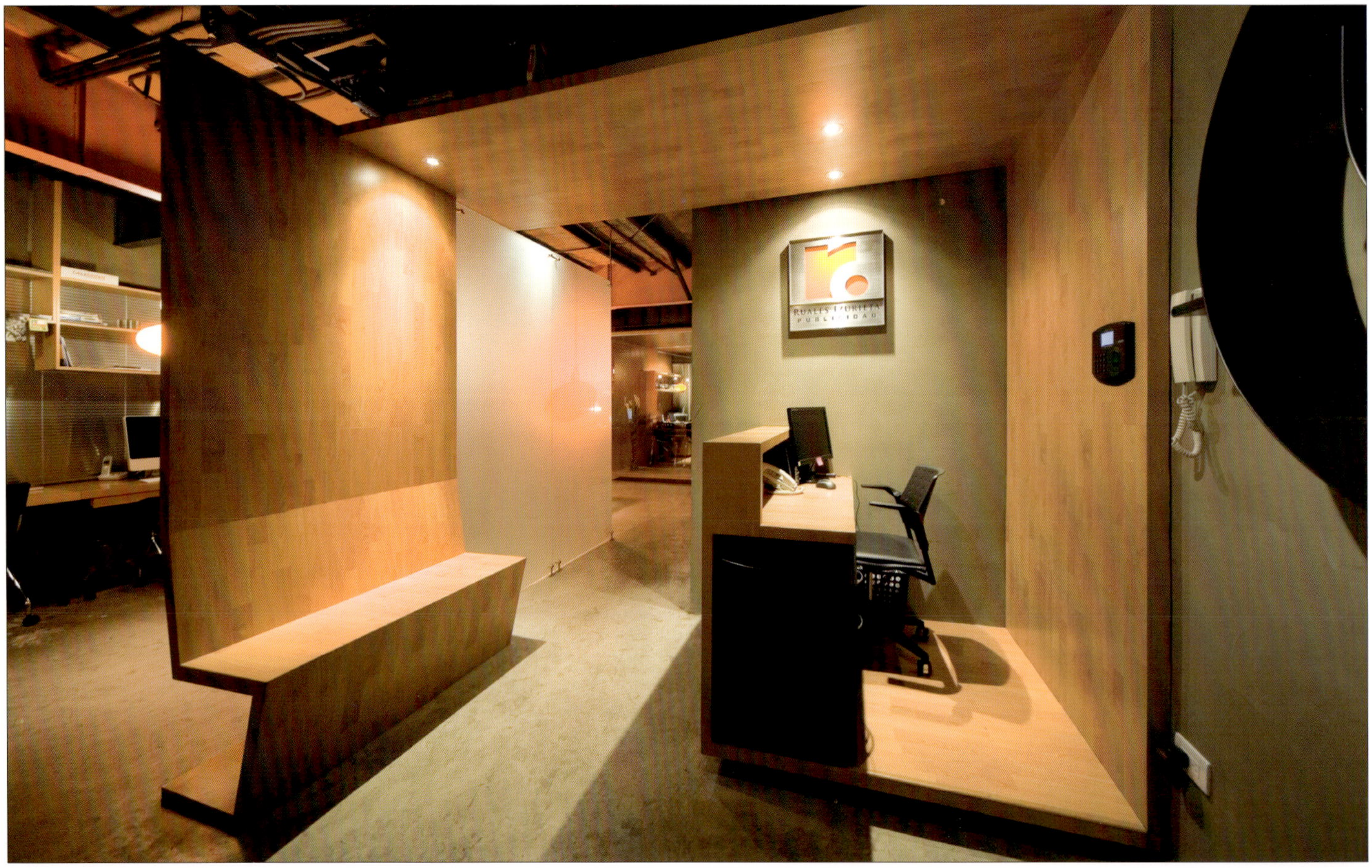
RUALES IZURIETA
PUBLICIDAD

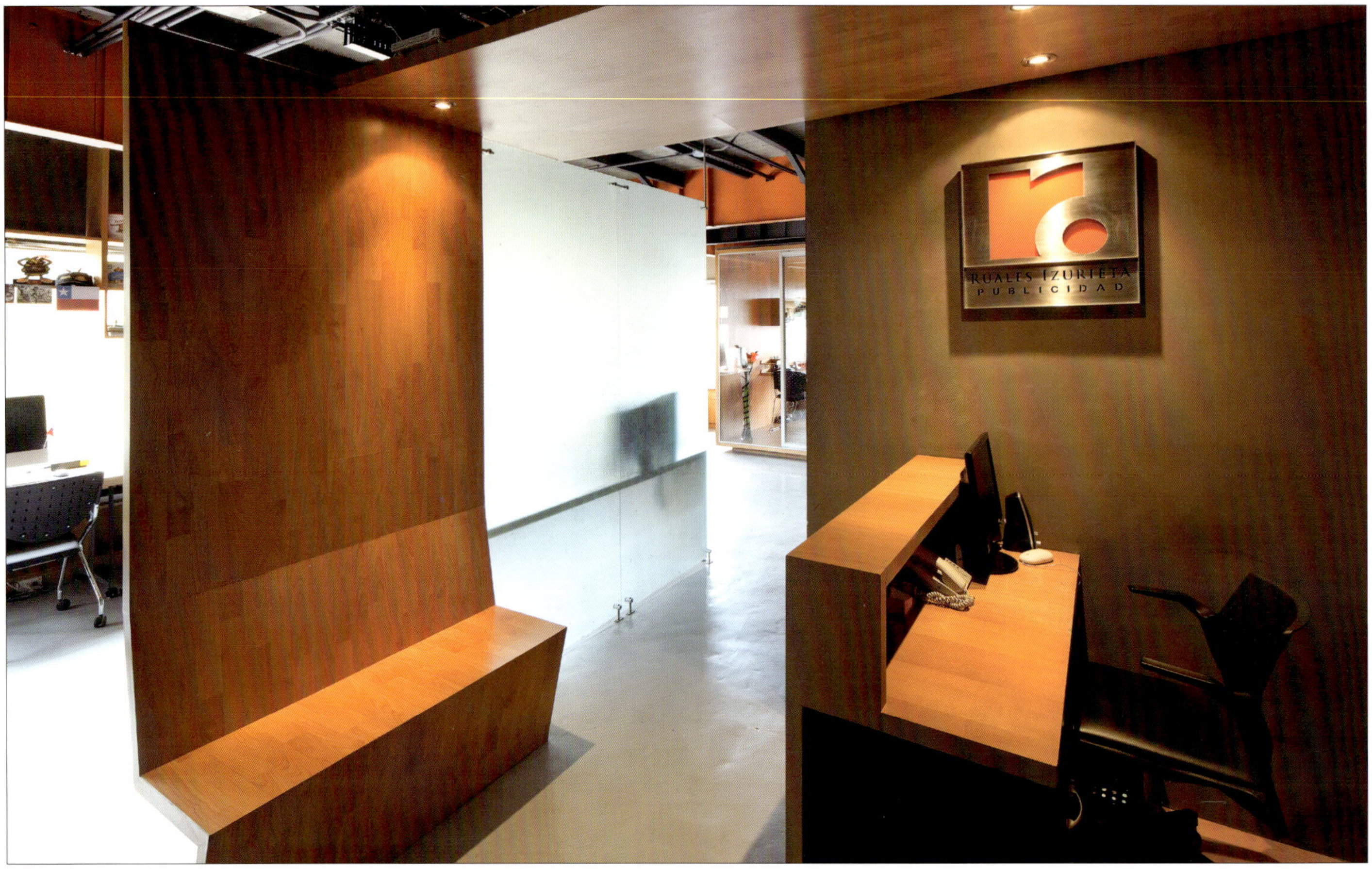
RUALES IZURIETA
PUBLICIDAD

This small intervention for a young advertising agency is based on the requirement for a flexible and expandable space, adaptable to the multiple tasks and changing needs that will arise through the enterprise's activities and expansion.

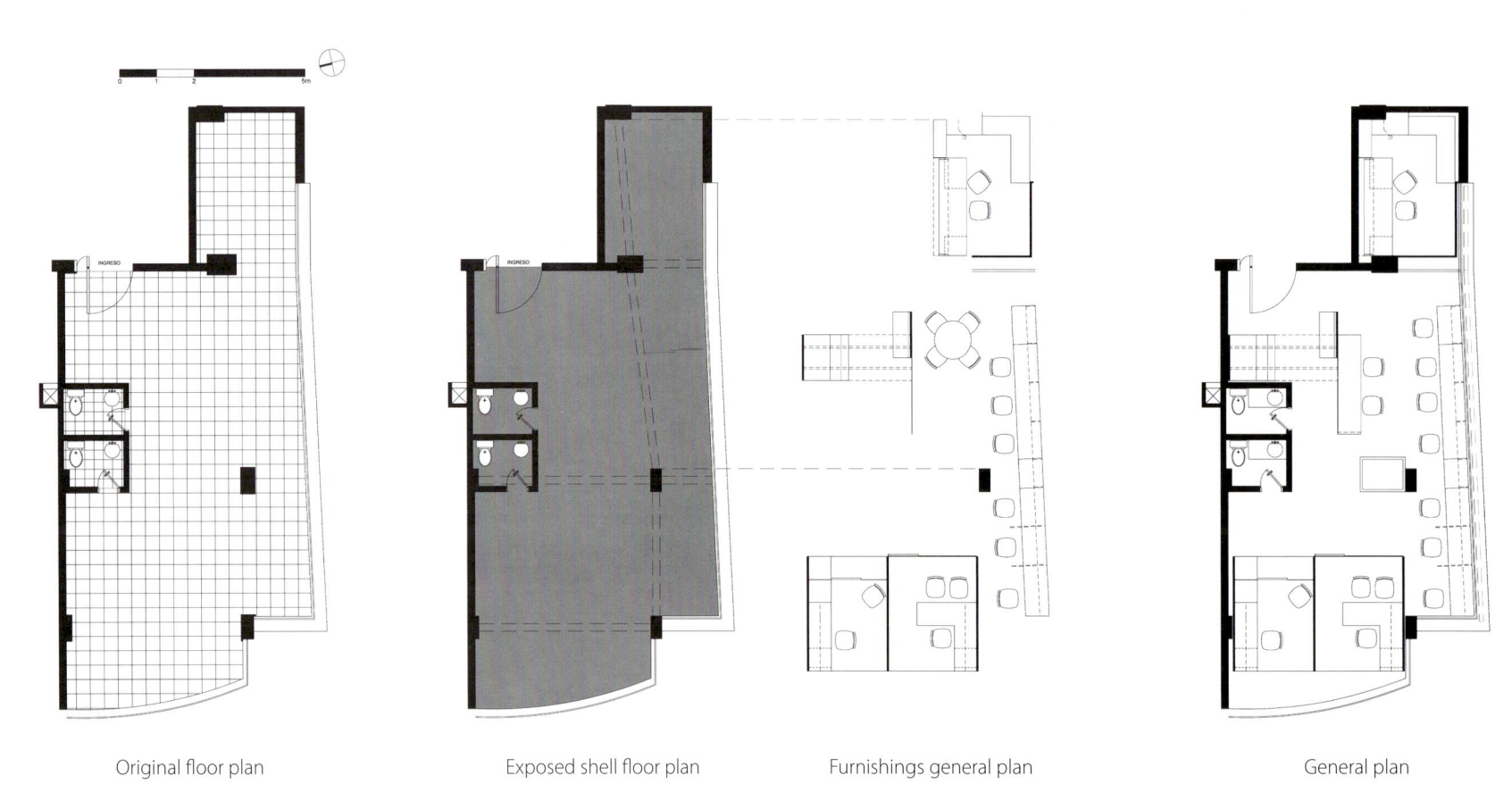

Original floor plan   Exposed shell floor plan   Furnishings general plan   General plan

Partial sections - furnishings

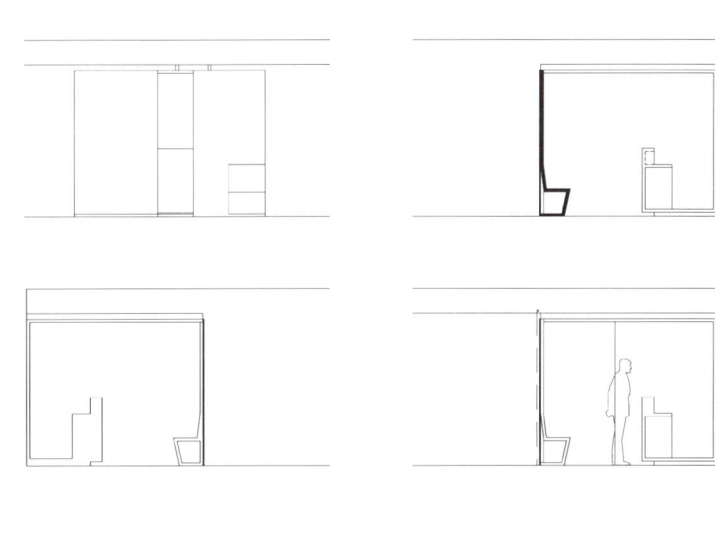

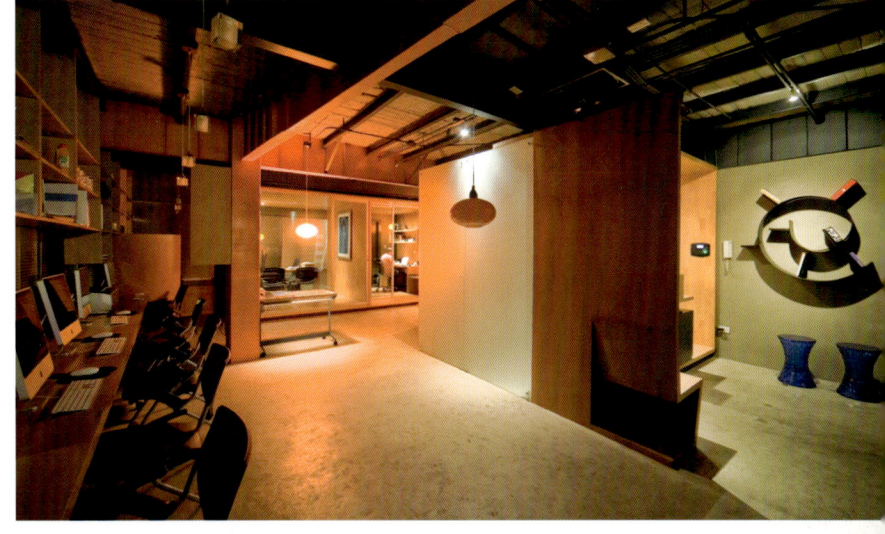

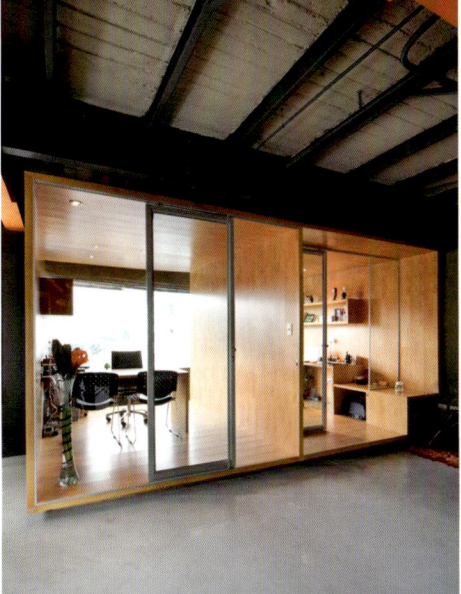

0 1 2   5m

ADDITION: cheap and flexible furnishings and services can change and grow

SHELL EXPOSED: bare structure and services

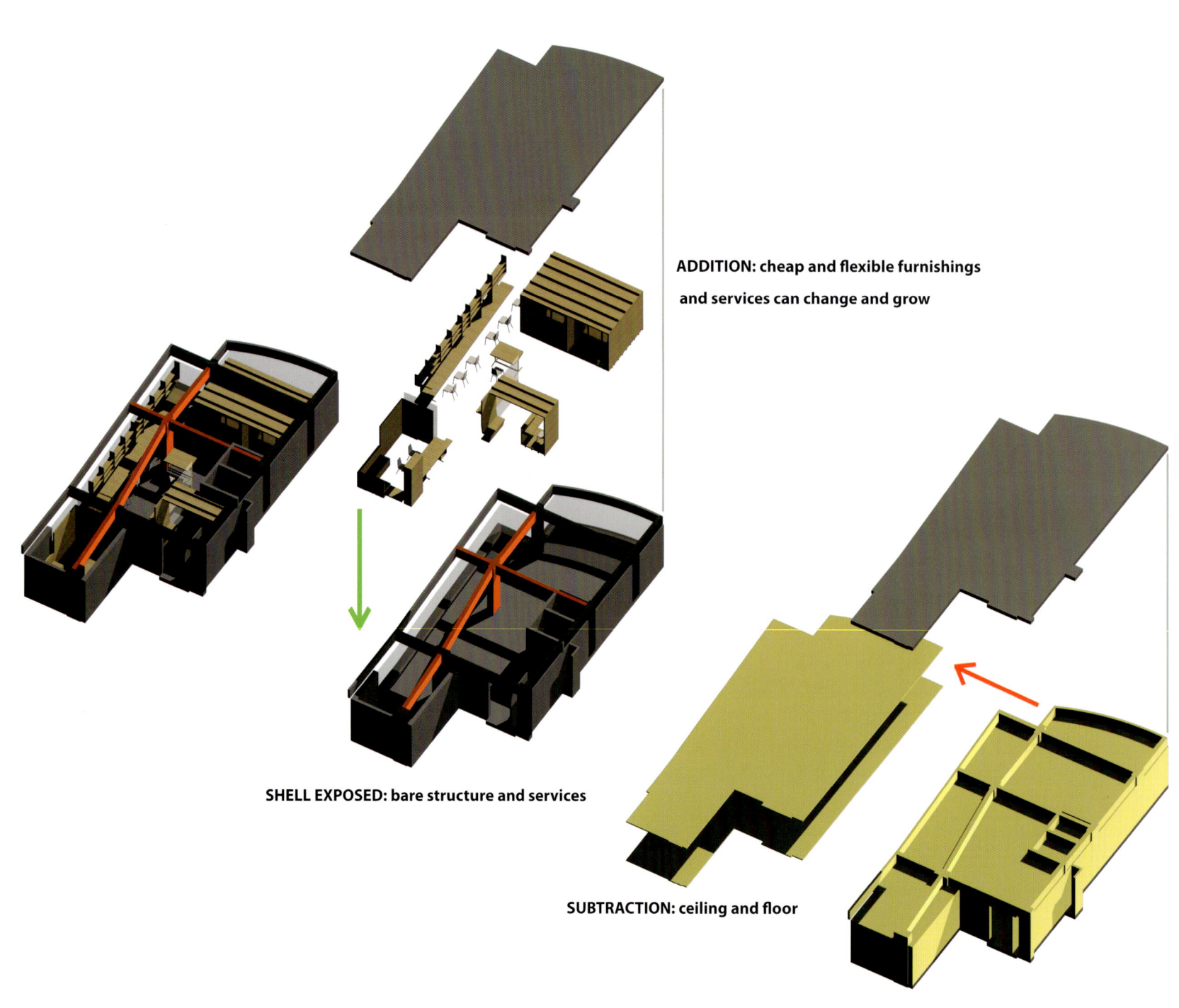

SUBTRACTION: ceiling and floor

ORIGINAL CONDITION: typical office floor

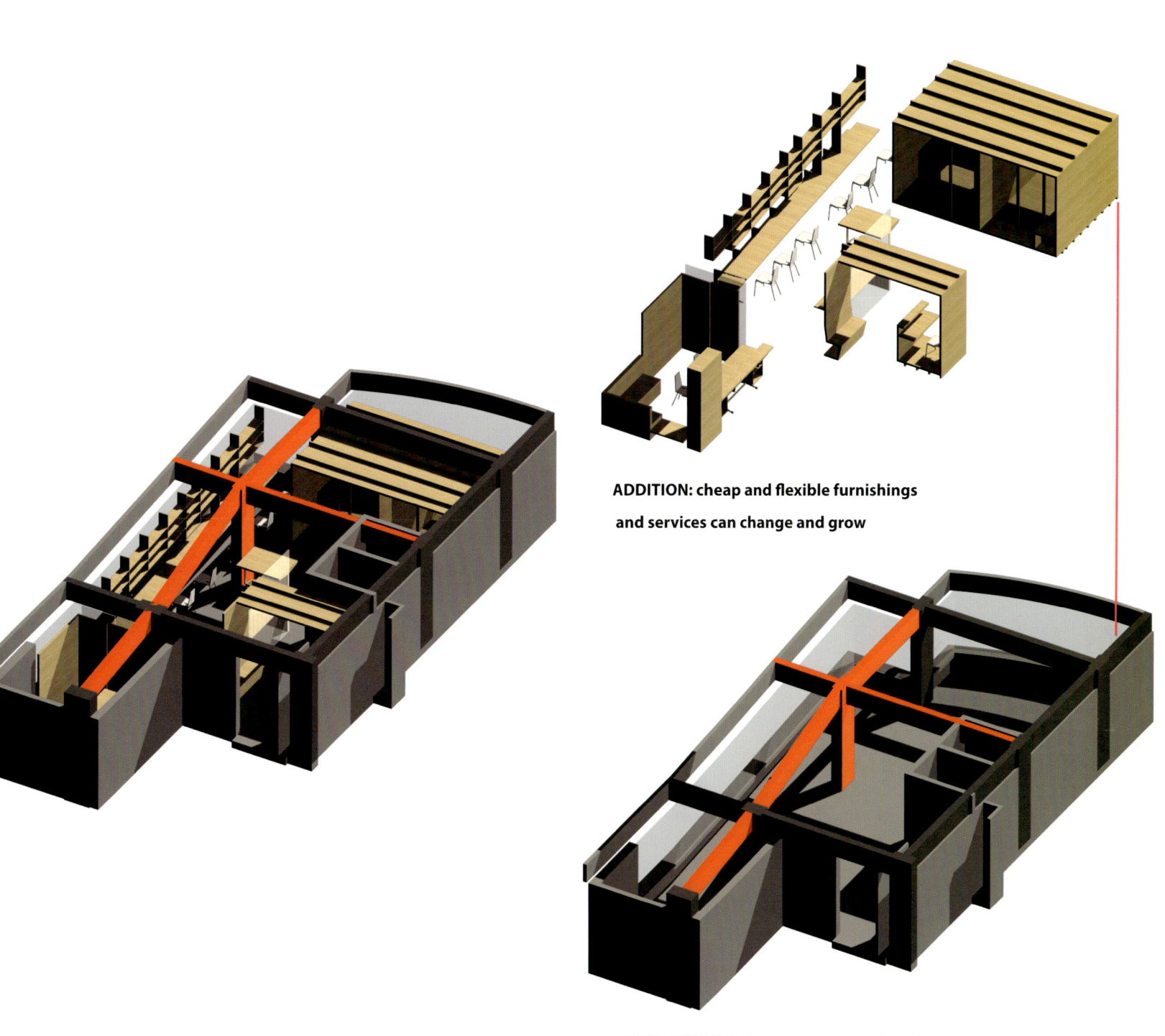

ADDITION: cheap and flexible furnishings and services can change and grow

SHELL EXPOSED: bare structure and services

HASSELL

ANZ Learning Centre

Melbourne, Victoria, Australia **Photographs: Earl Carter**

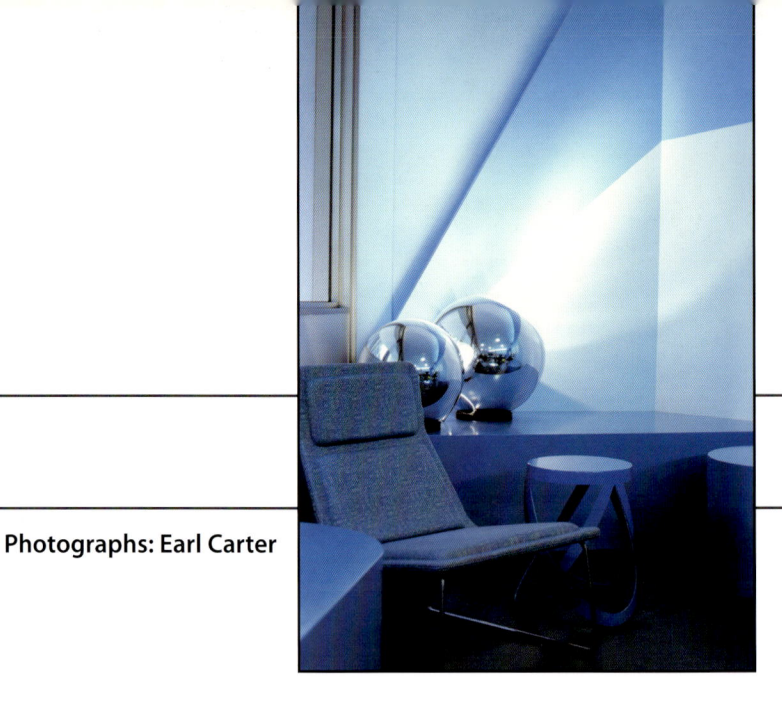

The ANZ Learning Centre is a large, multi-purpose space, designed to encourage creativity and freedom outside the constraints of a 'normal' office environment. The flexible and generous learning and meeting rooms are intended to support a range of learning activities and learning styles adapted to different psychological profiles. To reflect the client's focus on innovation, all the areas are equipped with state-of-the-art audio-visual equipment.

The experience begins with the unexpected 'Alice in Wonderland' main door and warped perspective in the lobby. The journey continues on the ground floor where the Central Forum and open courtyard provide a venue for functions and meetings. This space is large enough for the traffic entering and leaving the learning rooms during breaks, or groups of visitors gathering over coffee or drinks.

The Learning and Meeting rooms are on the first floor. Rooms are arranged around the perimeter, plus two clusters of meeting rooms located internally. Access to natural light defines the mood of these rooms, with the wall materials in one of the clusters being translucent to let in filtered light. The partitions of the perimeter learning rooms are angled in plan so that the rooms are asymmetrical. The tree-like branch patterns that appear on the walls and rubber floors are all interconnected to create unexpected pathways: an exploratory itinerary between the learning rooms, meeting rooms and nooks for informal gatherings. On the walls, colors have been applied in large trapezoidal blocks, which dissolve feelings of certainty, enhancing creativity.

Interiors:
HASSELL

HASSELL team:
Robert Backhouse
Caroline Lieu
Michael Hrysomallis
Juli Smolcic
Darren Paul
Rebecca Trenorden
Ingrid Bakker
Robert Harper
Nick Tennant

Awards:
2008 IDEA Awards - High Commendation –
Commercial Interior
2008 IDA Awards - High Commendation –
Corporate Interior

Client:
ANZ

Surface area:
32, 300 sqft (3,000 sqm)

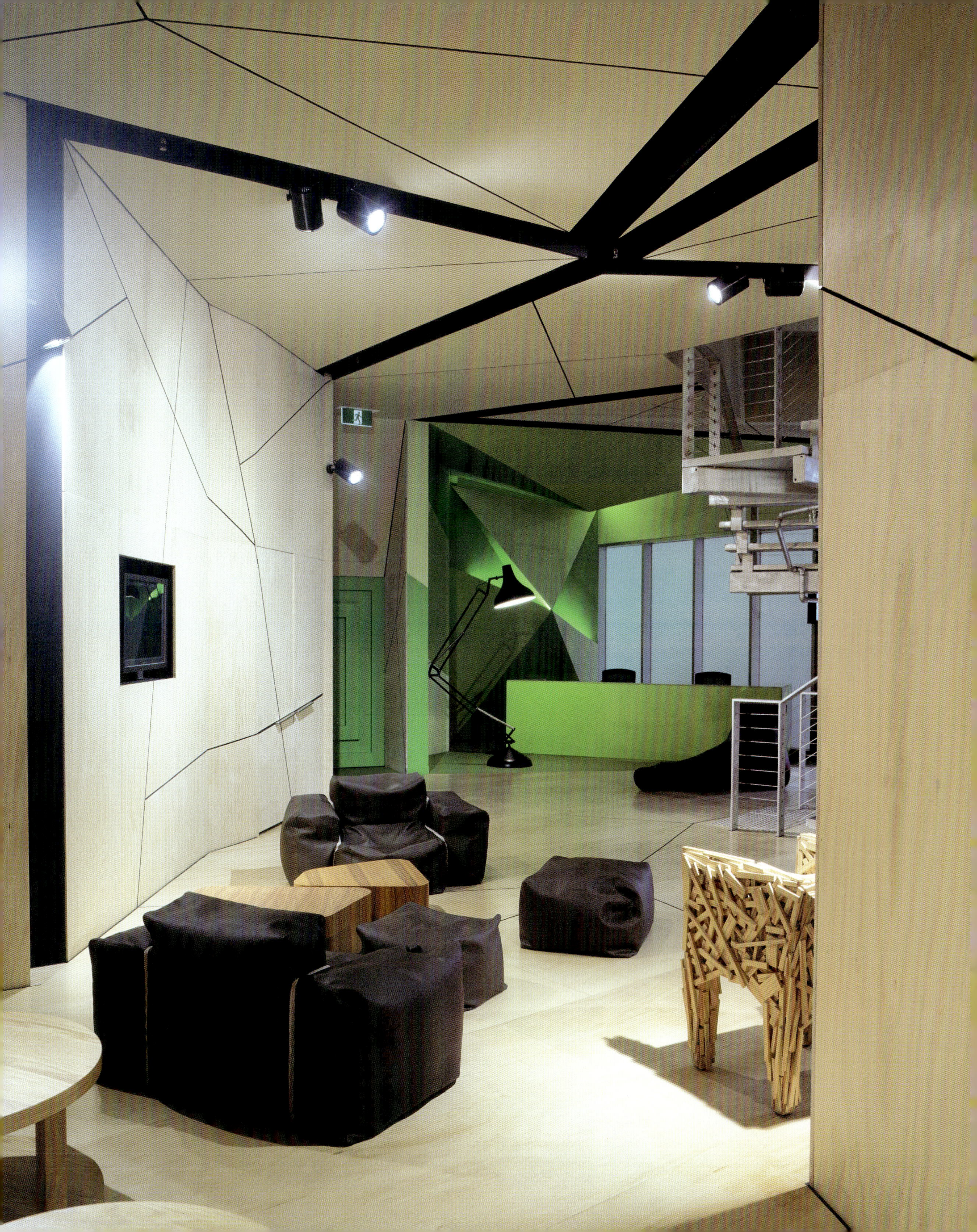

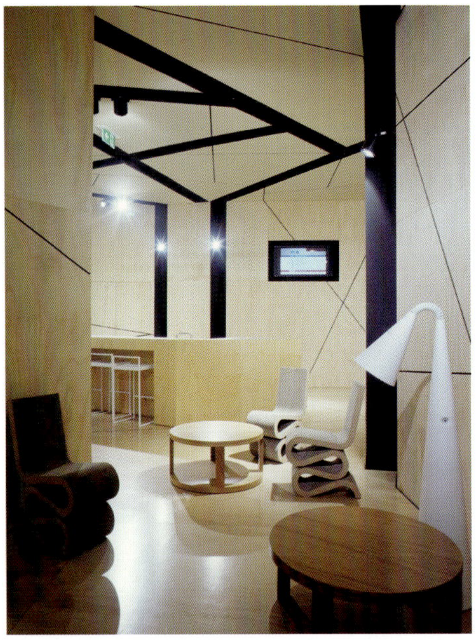

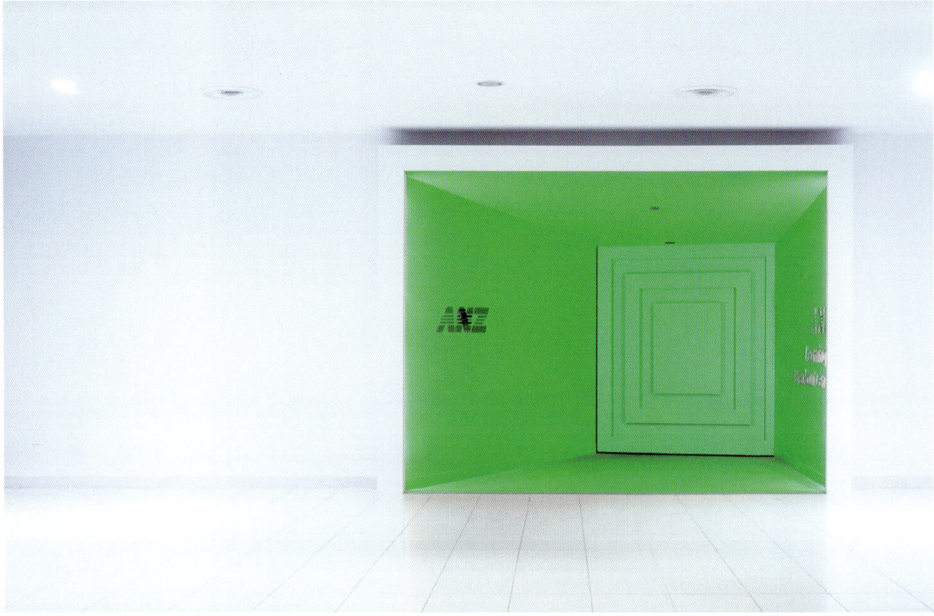

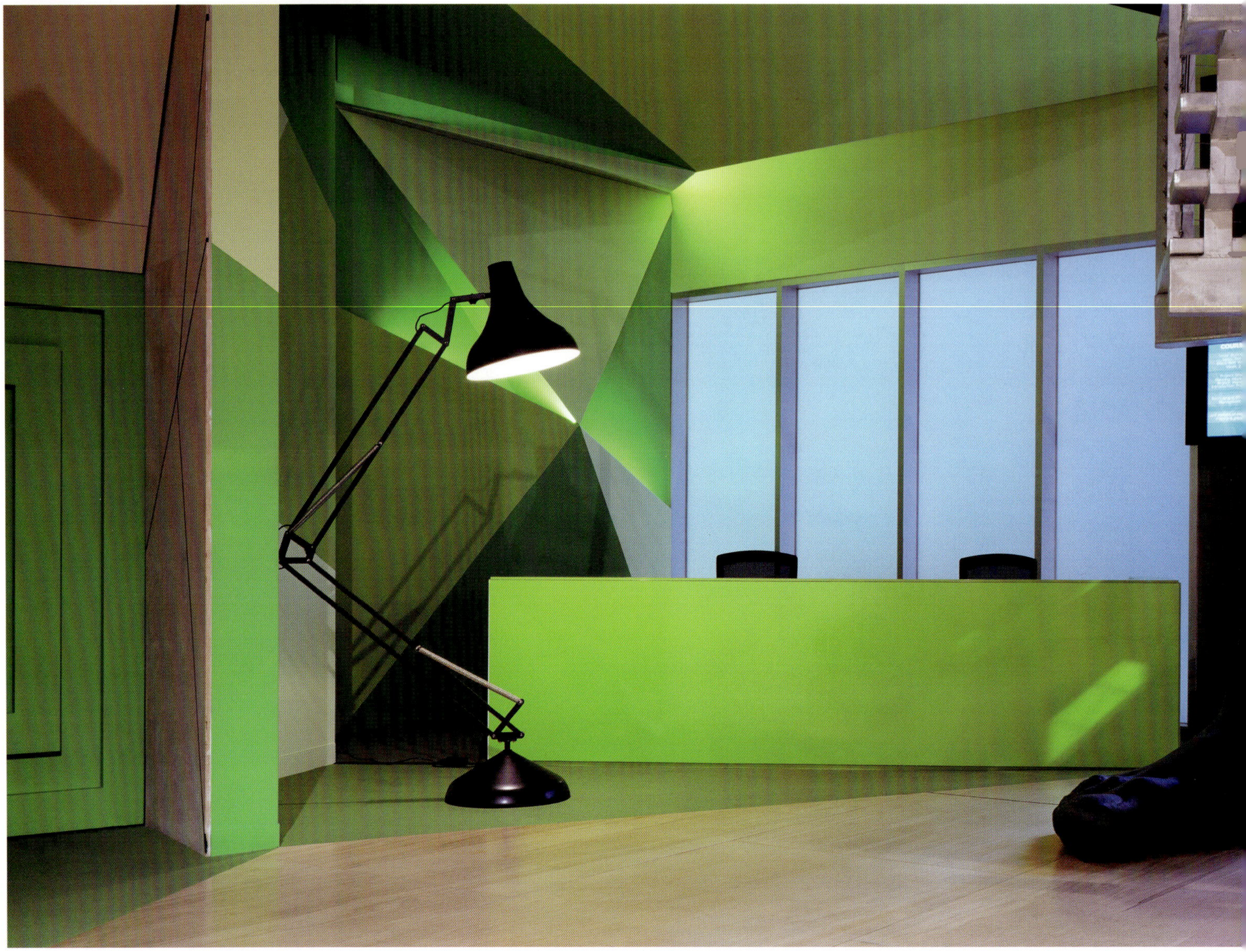

The brief asked for a design free of a formal or corporate appearance. This was achieved by the clever use of plywood, paint and patterned rubber and by exposing the services soffit to increase the volume of the space.

Ground floor plan

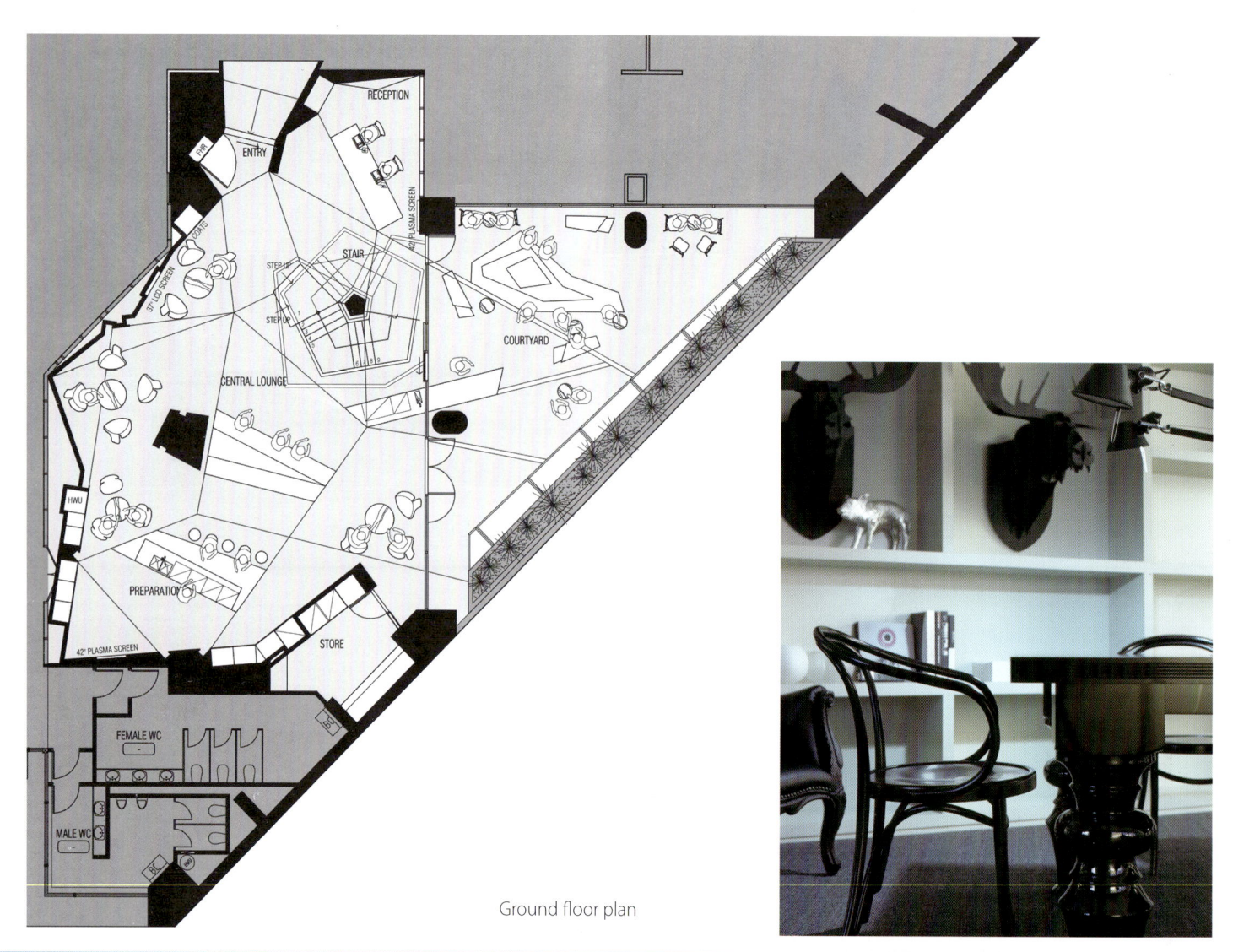

First floor plan

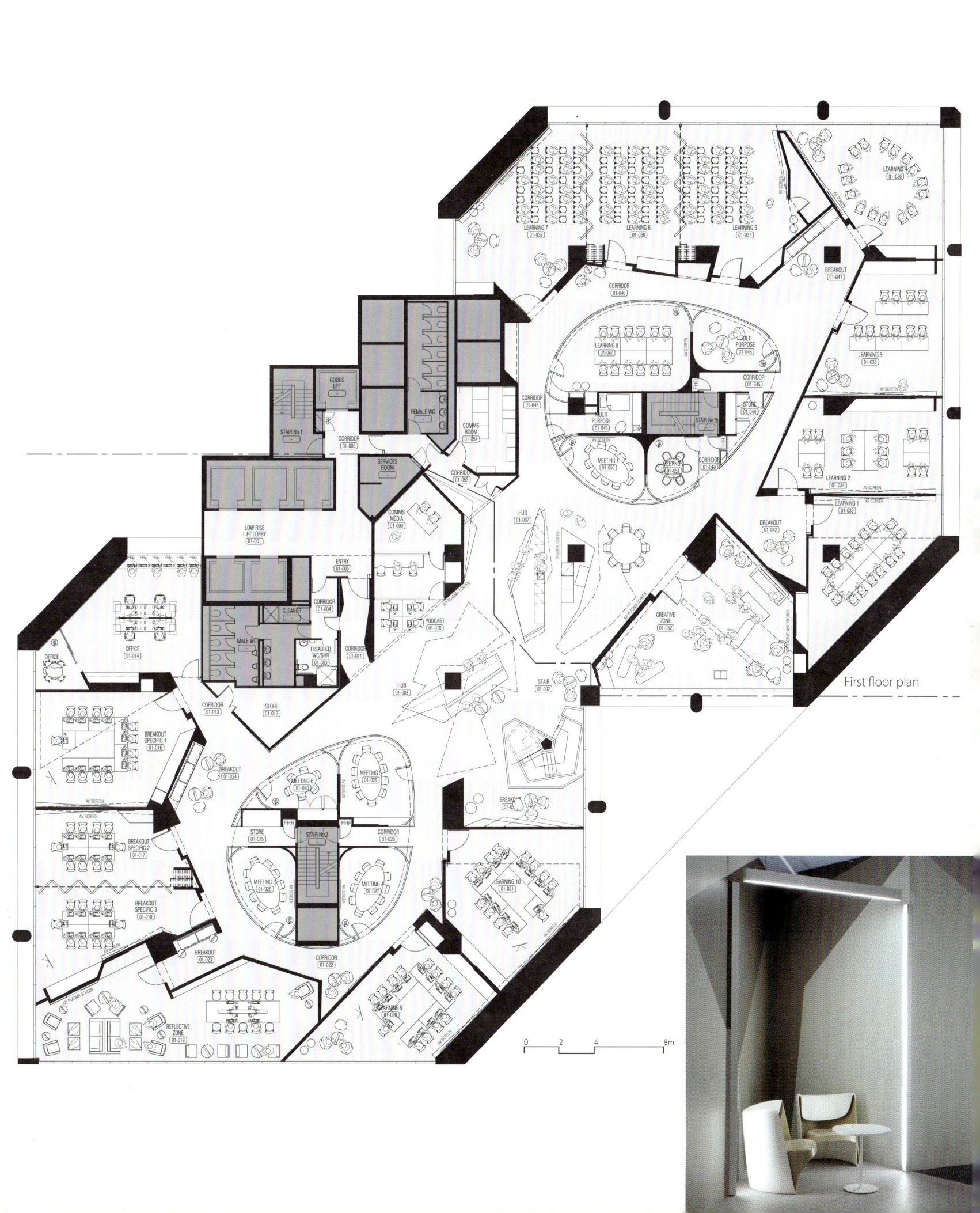

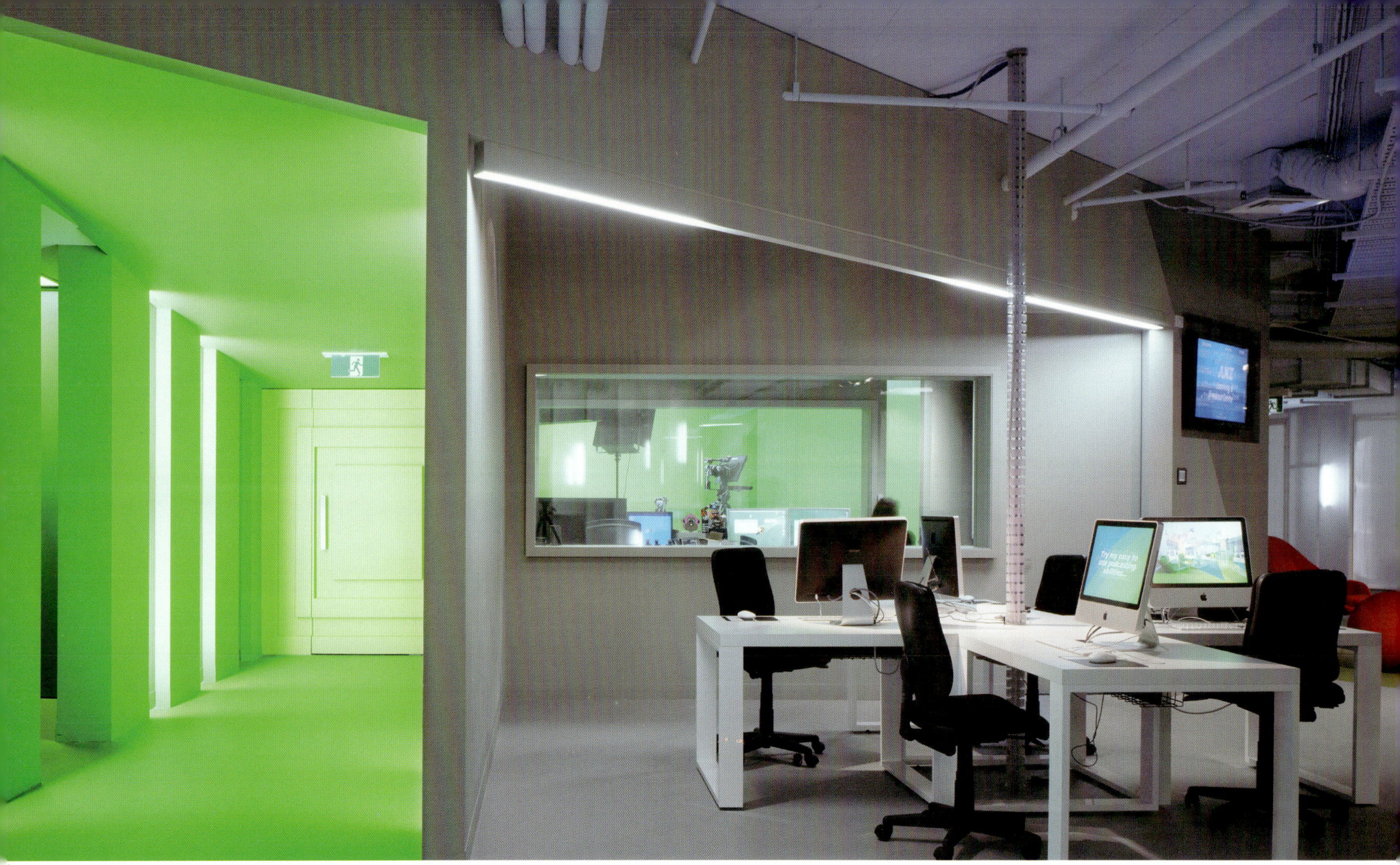

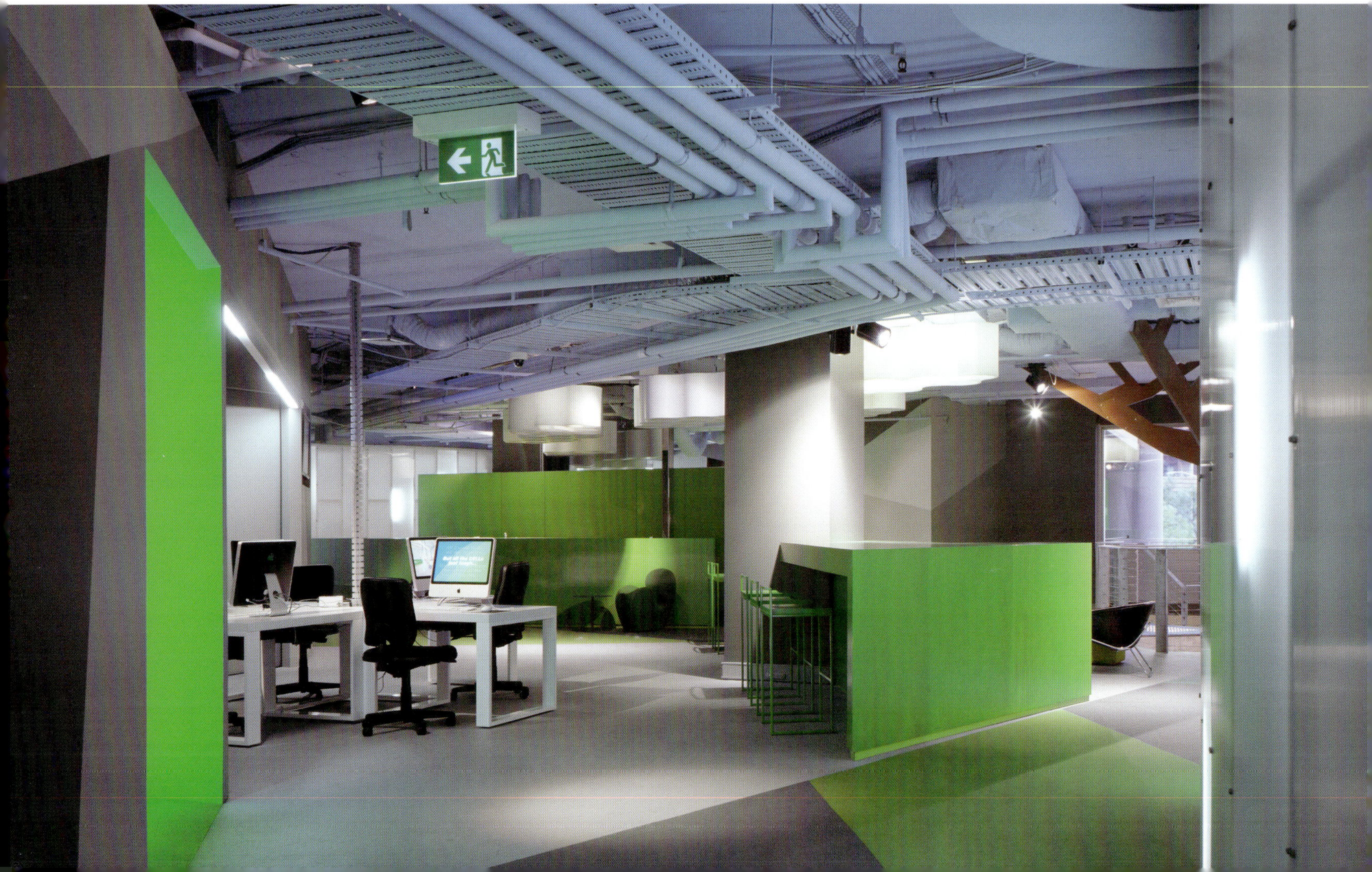

107

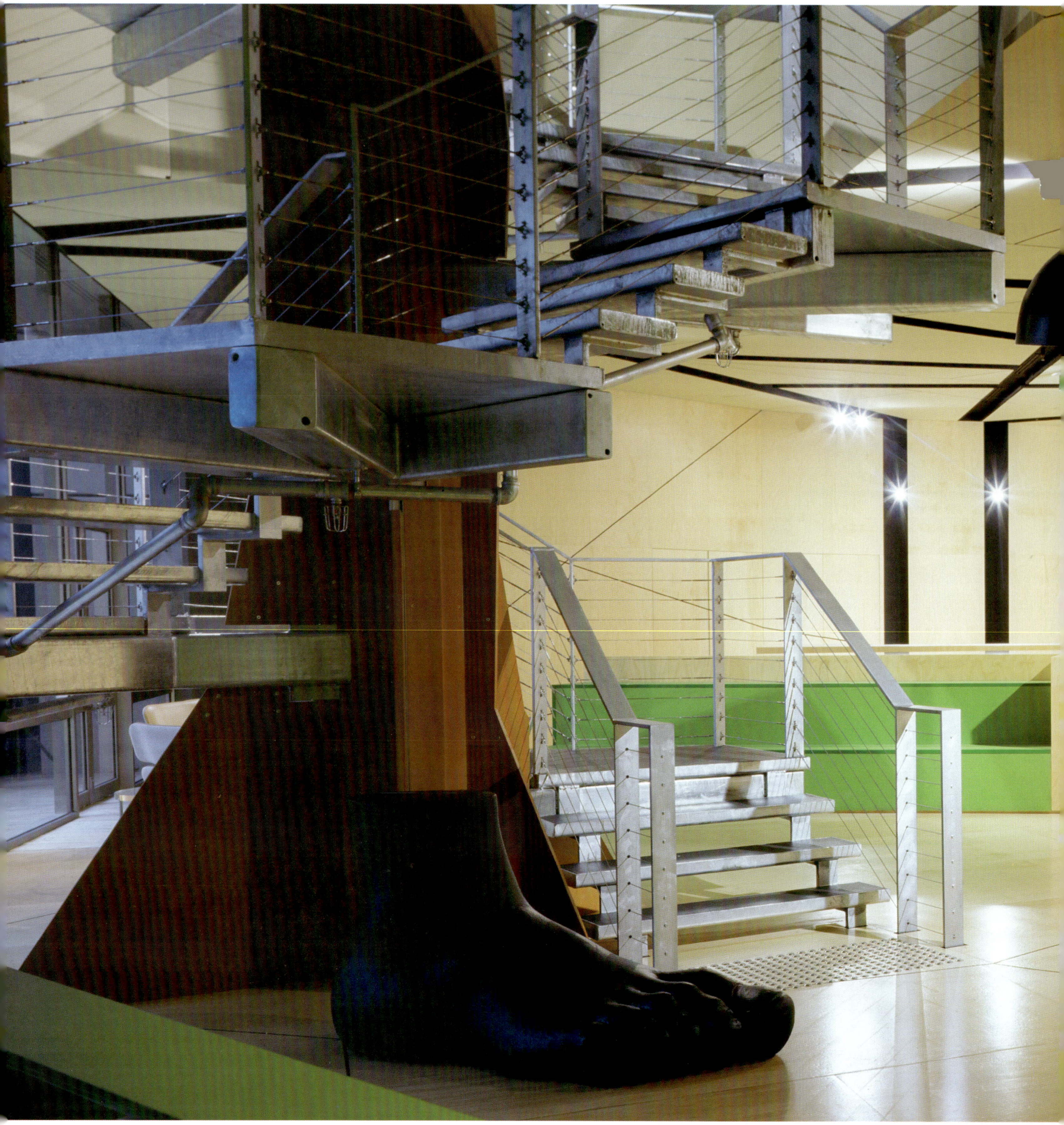

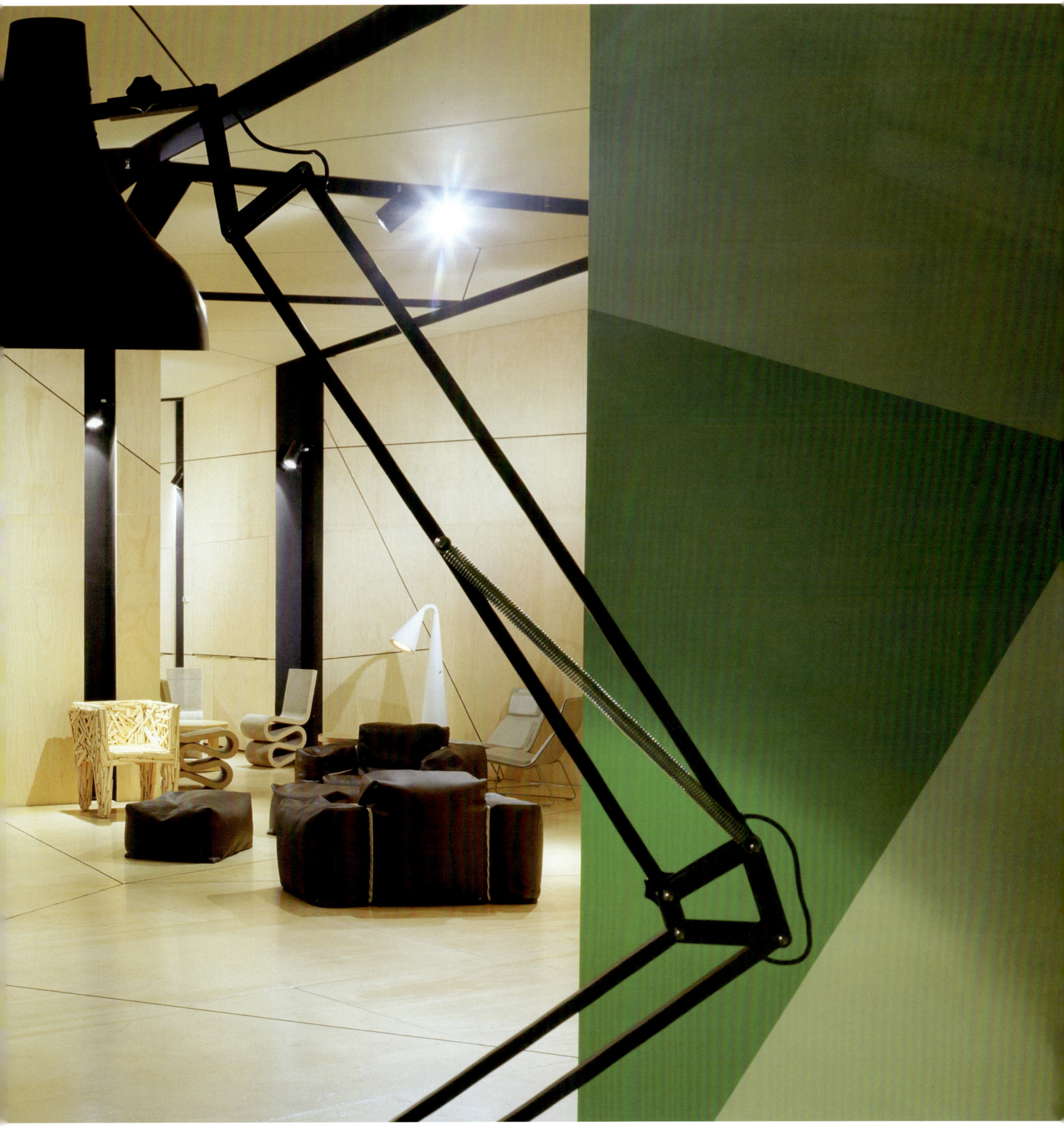

BVN Architecture

Goods Shed North

Melbourne, Australia   Photographs: Peter Clarke, Anson Smart

The refurbishment of the Goods Shed North, in Docklands, a heritage listed railway goods shed, presented a great opportunity to renew an integral part of Melbourne's history. One of the few heritage buildings left in Docklands, the Goods Shed was originally built in 1889 at the center of the Melbourne Goods Yards. It was derelict for over 30 years and became redundant in the 1980's, later being bisected by the Collins Street extension which created the North and South side.

The Good Shed North's transformation into a vibrant workplace shows what is possible when adaptive reuse of building stock is undertaken with a clear vision and a shared goal. The clients, VicUrban, Building Commission & Plumbing Industry Commission (BC/PIC) and the developer, contractor and consultant team worked in close collaboration to realize the project both from a tenant perspective and the overarching aim to set a new benchmark for adaptive re-use projects.

The end result is the creation of Victoria's most sustainable historic building (the first 5 Star Green Star heritage listed building in the state) and a dynamic versatile contemporary workplace that fosters collaboration and innovation.

Whilst the building's historical exterior has been restored, the interior has been designed to be an innovative, contemporary, office space. Key historical elements of its interior have been retained whilst incorporating state-of-the-art technology. The design enables the organizations to foster a more innovative and collaborative work ethic through increased visibility and transparency and the creation of both active and passive project spaces within the building's central zones. By locating workspaces to the east and west side wings and retaining clear lines of sight through the building's spine, multifunctional project spaces were created centrally within the base of the voids to ensure greater staff interaction and connectivity.

The Goods Shed North is a unique heritage building that naturally creates an exceptional backdrop to the workplace, including high ceilings, clerestory windows, exposed trusses, cast iron heritage columns and exposed brickwork. The design aimed to achieve an aesthetic response that built on the existing and reinterpreted elements into a new aesthetic.

Architecture:
BVN Architecture
Clients:
VicUrban + Building Commission and Plumbing Industry Commission
Interior:
Fitout
Awards:
IDA Corporate Design Award,
IDA Environmentally Sustainable Design Award

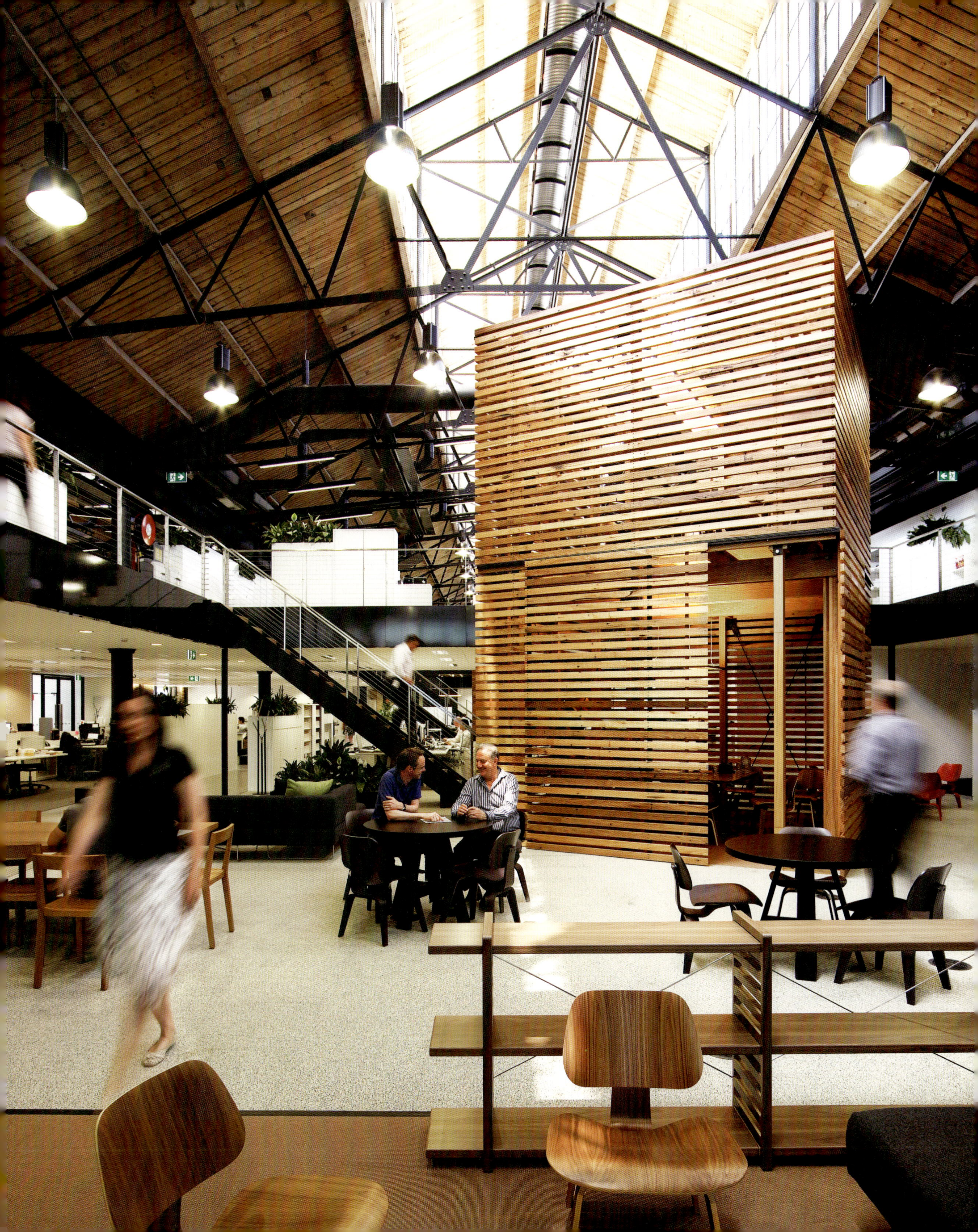

© Peter Clarke ▲▼

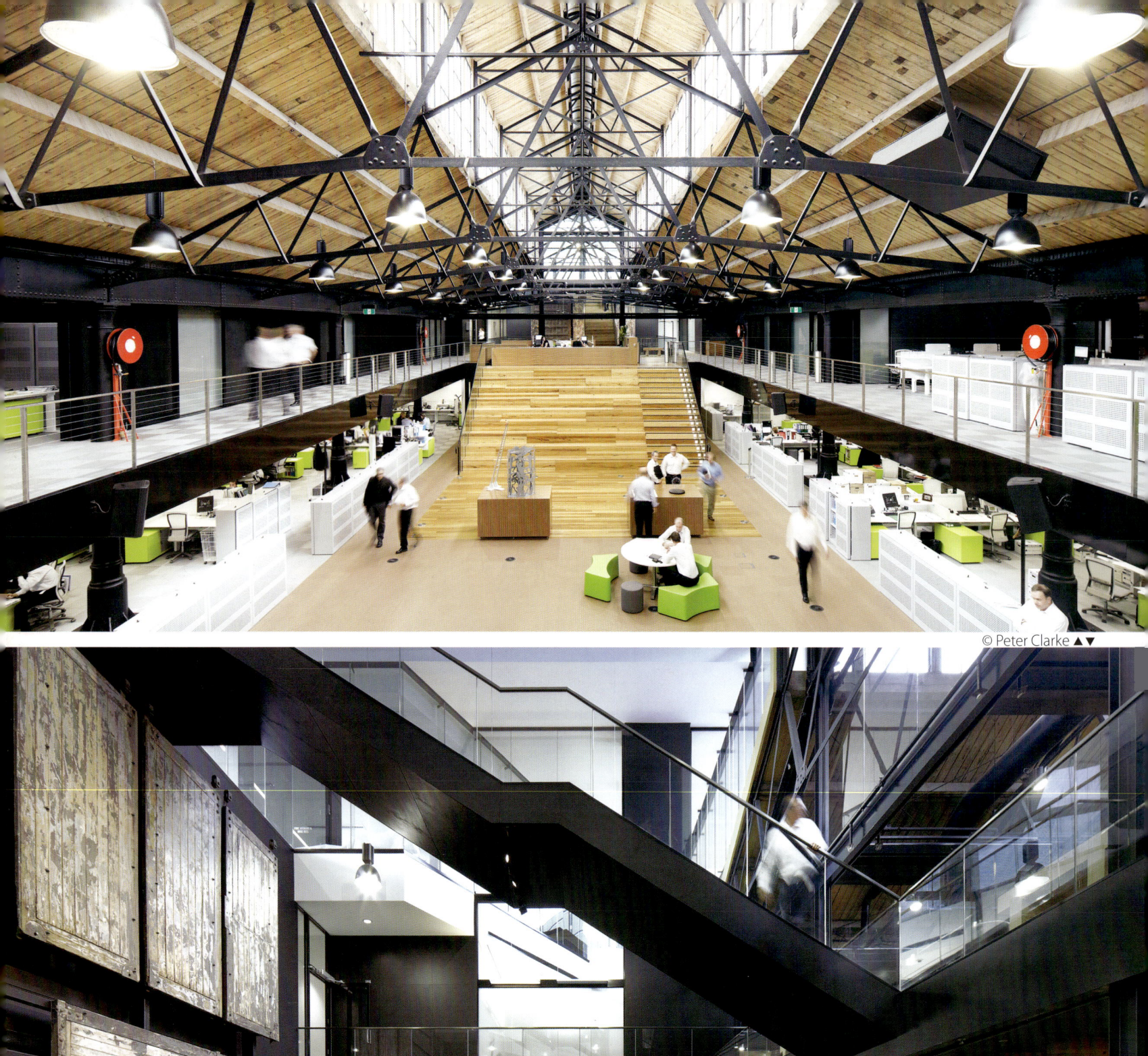

© Peter Clarke

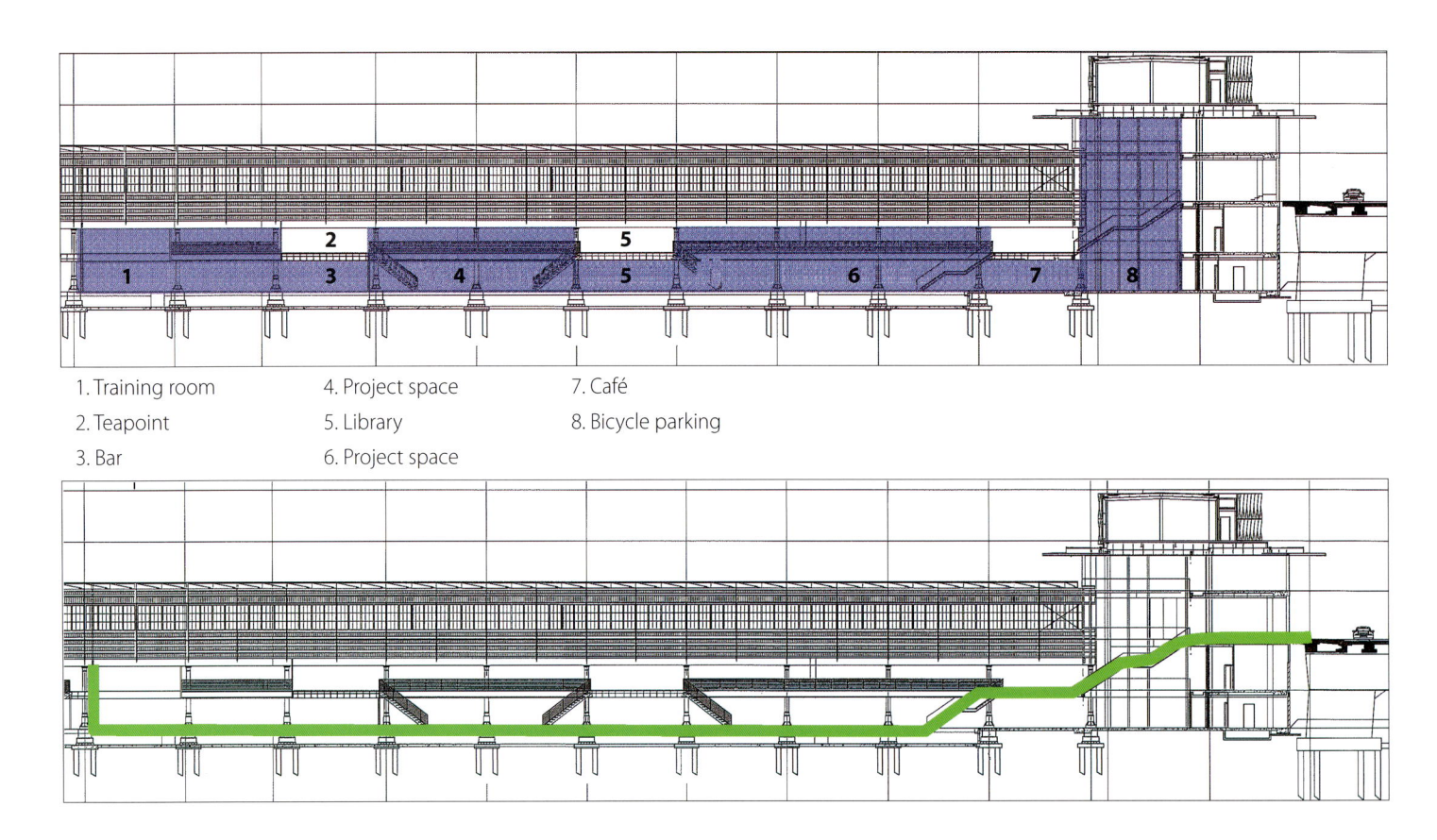

1. Training room
2. Teapoint
3. Bar
4. Project space
5. Library
6. Project space
7. Café
8. Bicycle parking

© Peter Clarke

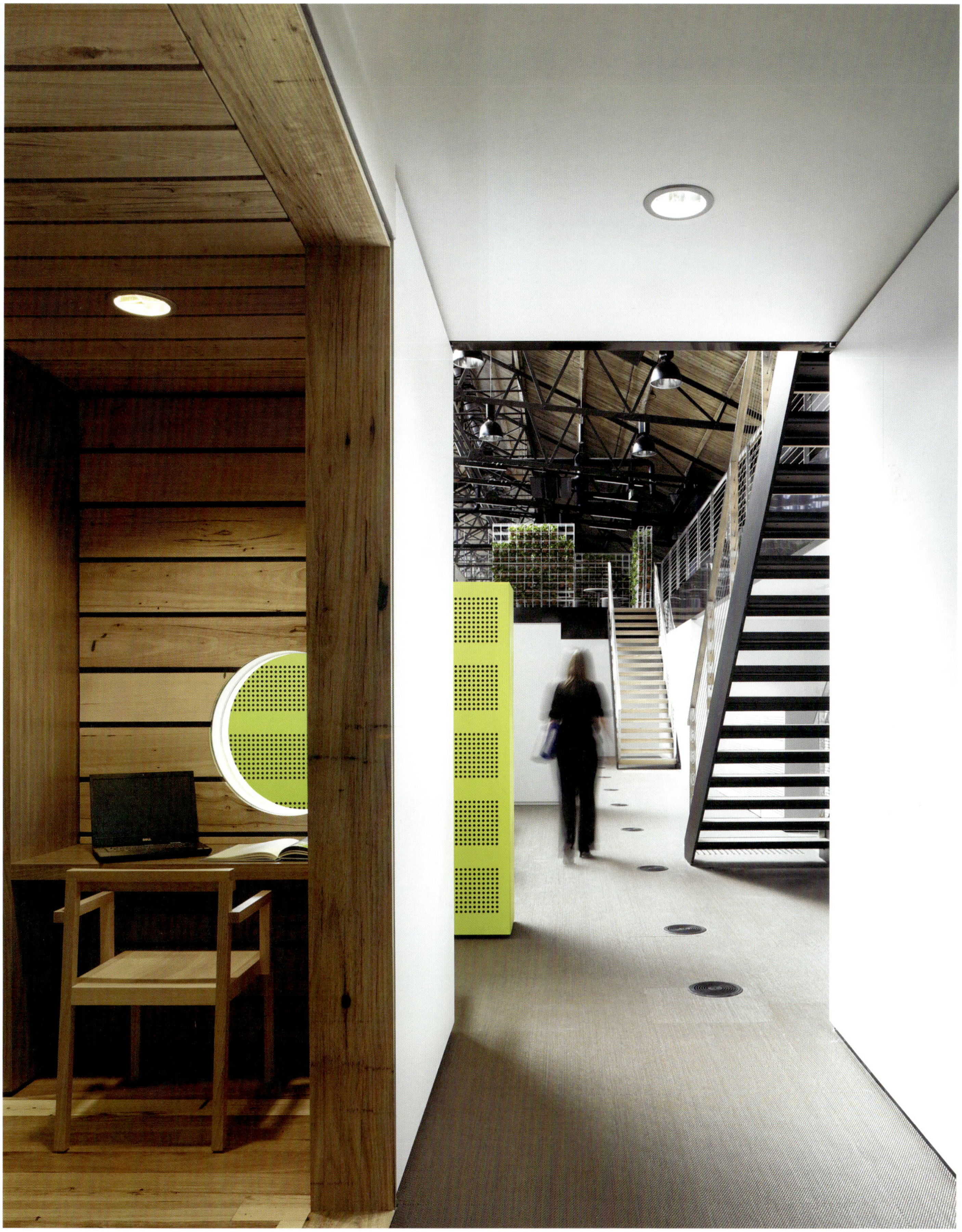

© Peter Clarke

© Anson Smart

Environmentally sustainable materials were selected with preference given to products that have eco-preferred content, low embodied energy, recycled content, minimized volatile compound content, and minimal amounts of PVC content.

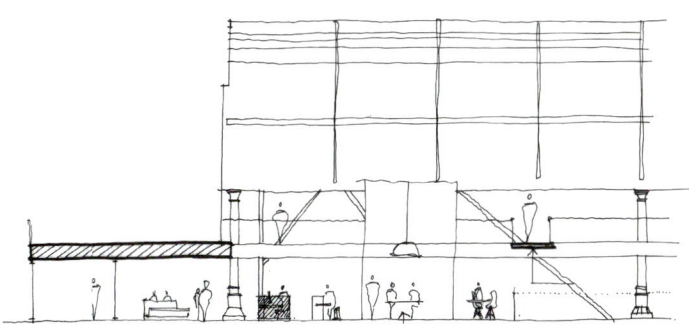

© Anson Smart ▼▲

Cross section

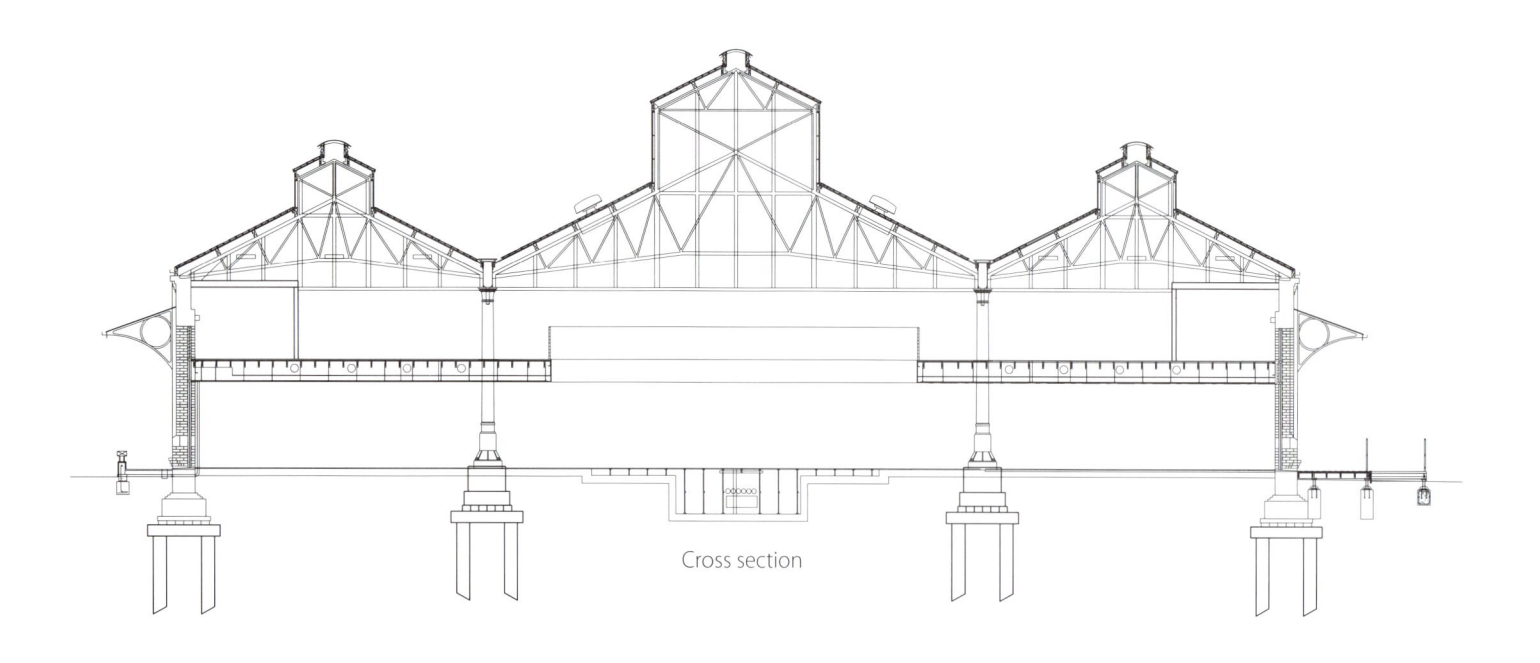

© Anson Smart

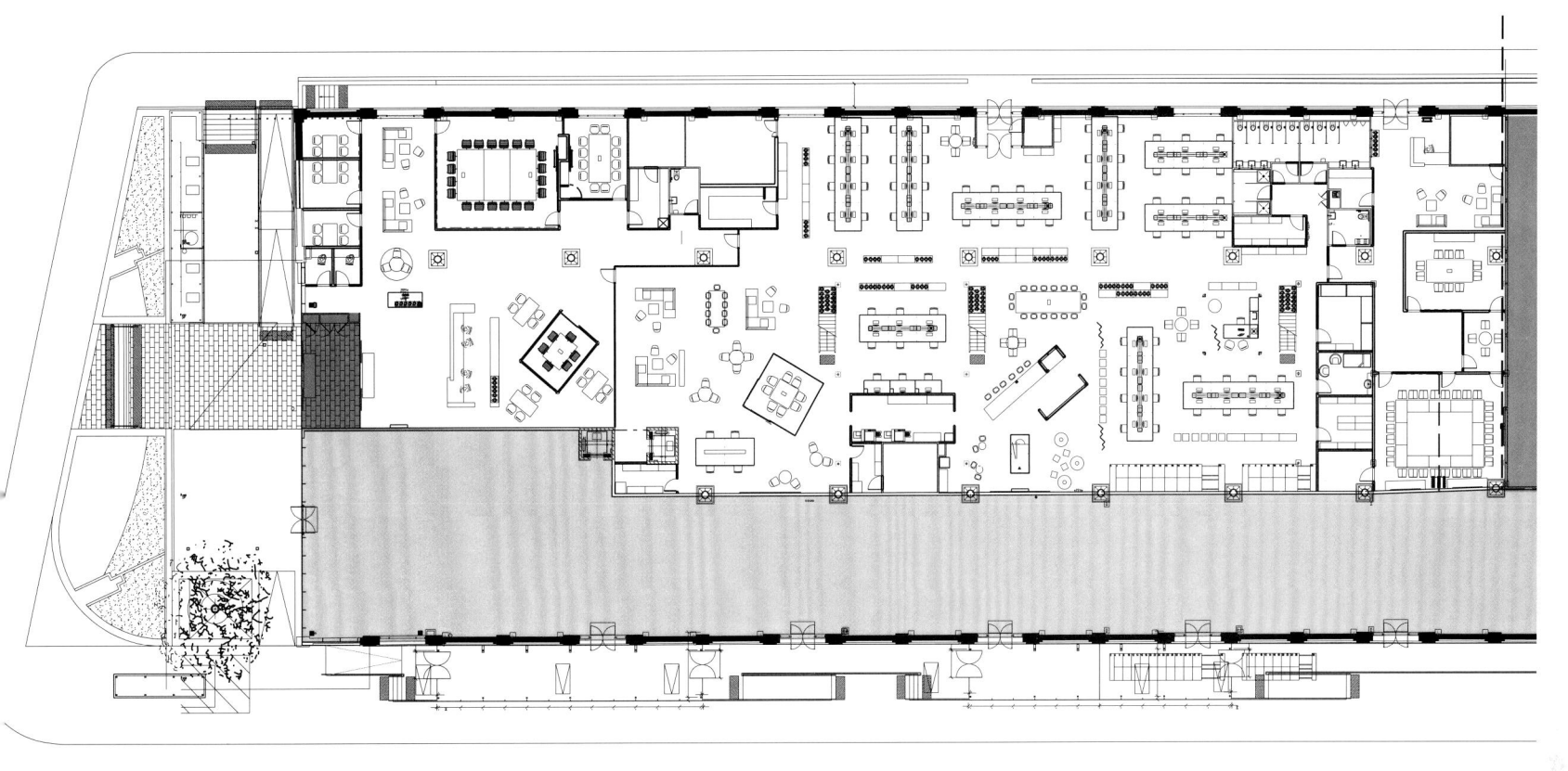

Mezzanine floor plan

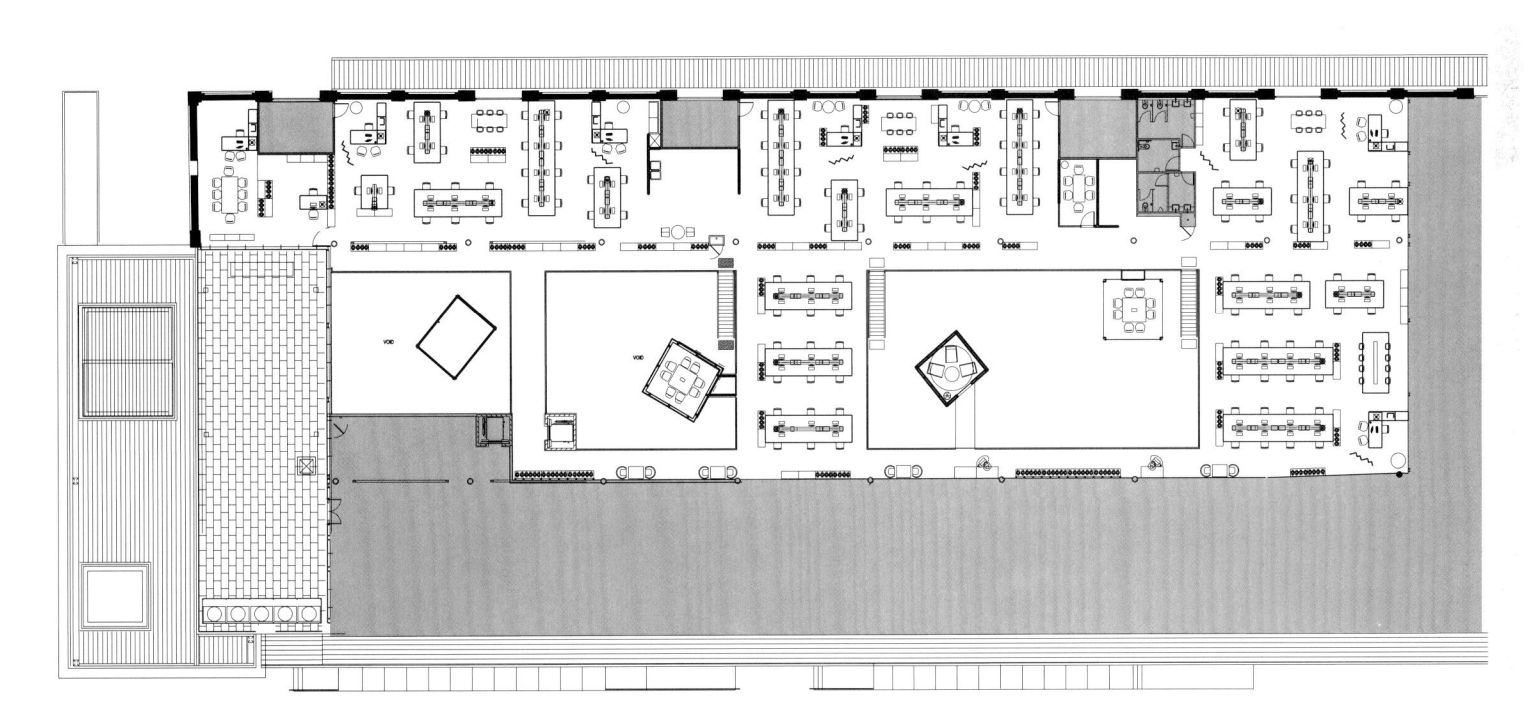

Ground floor plan

119

Jump Studios

Engine offices

London, UK Photographs: contributed by Jump Studios

Jump Studios designed an animated but suitably slick new office for London-based communications group Engine.

With 12 different companies operating under the Engine umbrella, the challenge was to create an environment that would appeal to a broad range of tastes while respecting and upholding the individual brand identities. 'We had to cater for a spectrum of cultures,' says Jump director Simon Jordan of the £3.5 million project. 'That ranged from your typical creative young ad agency through to political lobbyists who would be horrified to think that someone might come to work in a pair of trainers. We ultimately came up with a common language that each and every one of those companies could identify with.'

The move to the new building on Great Portland Street brought all 12 businesses together (across five storeys) for the first time, but while the working floors were kept reasonably generic to allow for the personalisation of space, the building as a whole is characteristically Engine.

The team worked with the concept of 'precision engineering', partly inspired by Engine company chairman Peter Scott, known to be a 'razor sharp' businessman with a passion for detail. 'We really wanted the office to look like it was machined rather than constructed,' Jordan explains. This idea is most clearly manifest in a series of perfectly formed elements that run through the building, essentially forming a backbone that links the ground floor to the fifth.

Among the many 'talking points' in the building are the seating pods on the fifth floor with their Corian shells and Barrisol light ceilings. Here employees are encouraged to interact, serviced by a café offering spectacular views across the city's rooftops and a series of conference and meeting rooms ranging in design, size and style. The idea was to offer a more refreshing alternative to the conventional table and chair.

Architecture:
Jump Studios
Design Team:
Shaun Fenandes and Markus Nonn
Floor area:
60,000 sqft (5,570 sqm)

5.3

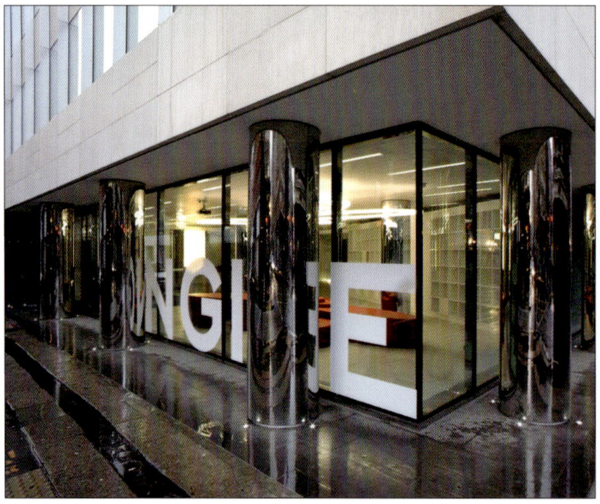

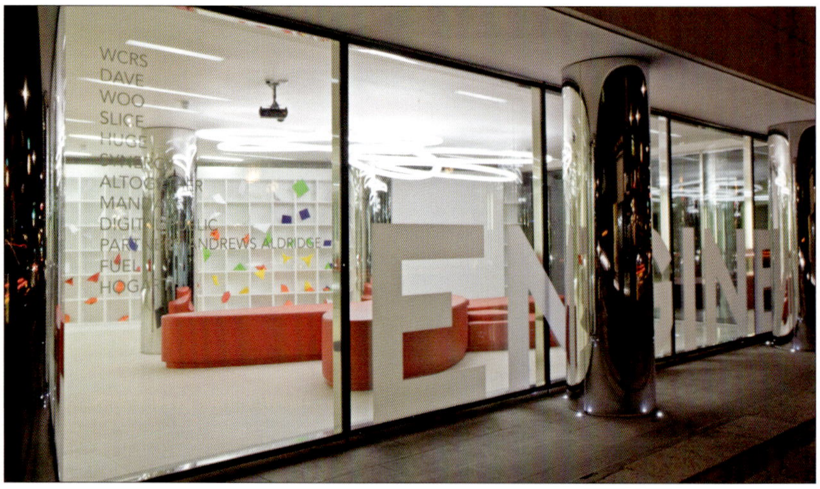
WCRS
DAVE
SLICE

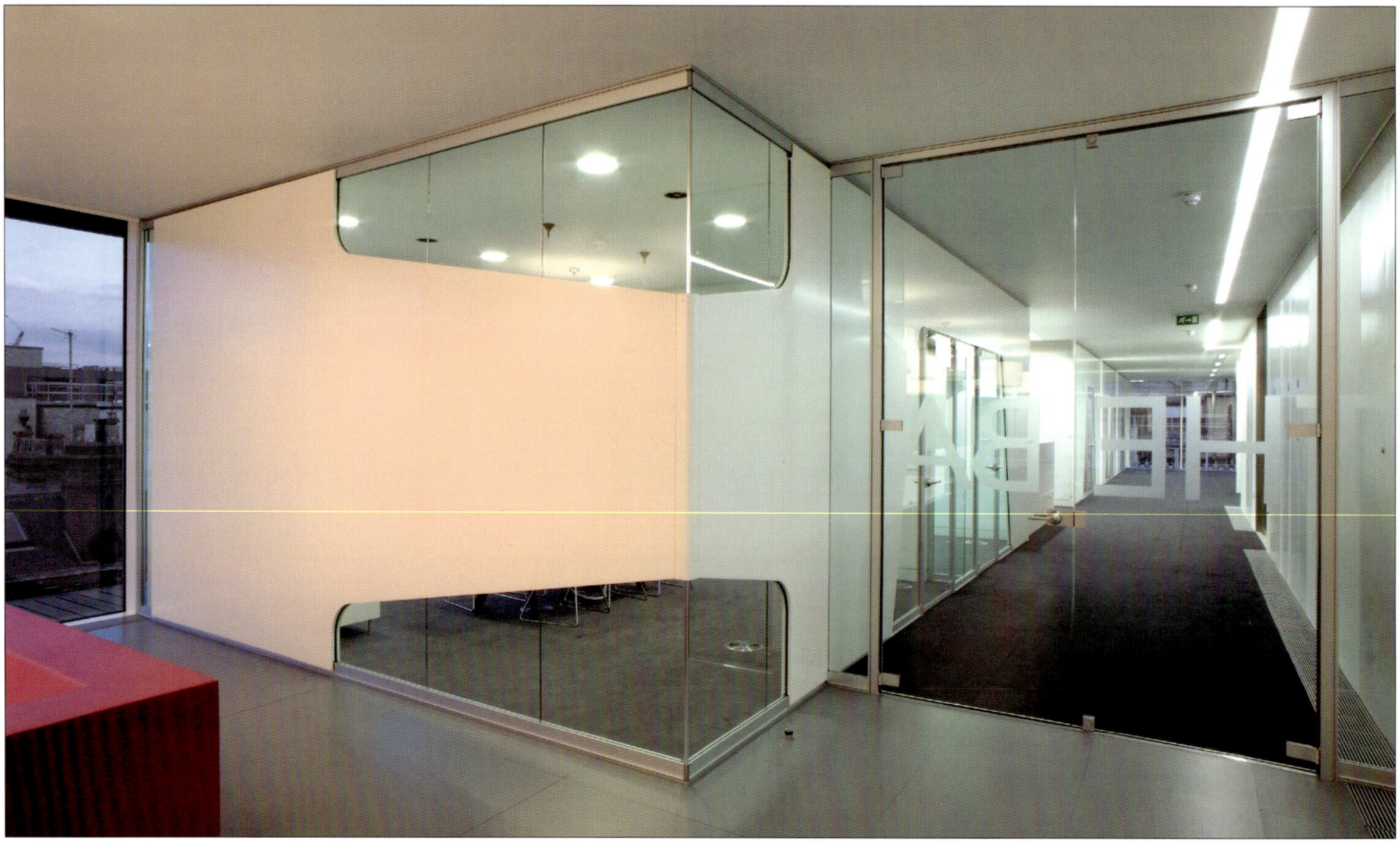

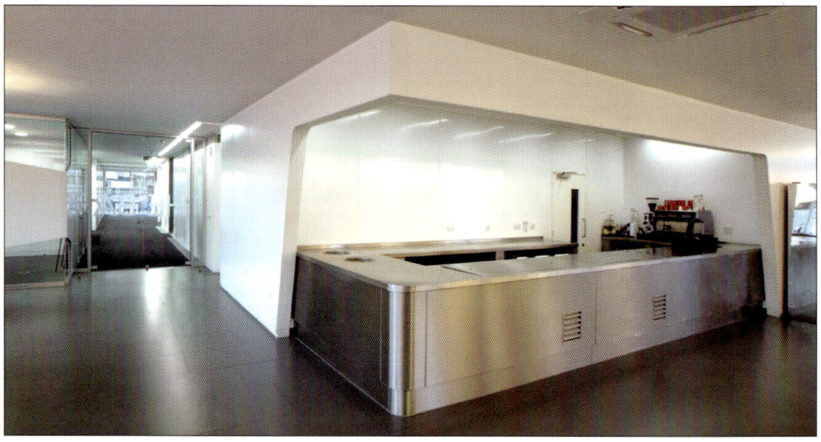

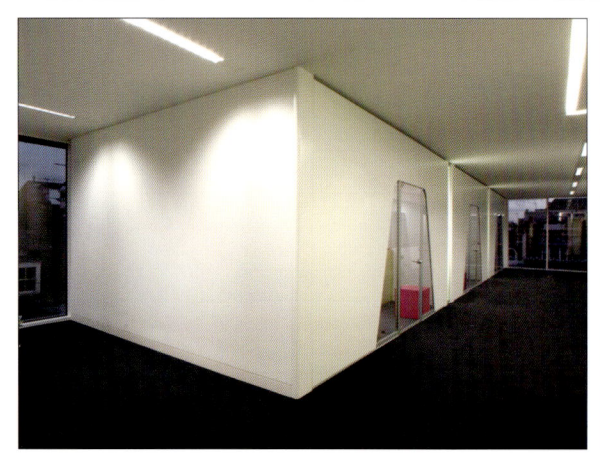

Part of Engine's appeal is that clients can opt for multilateral or unilateral engagement with the various partner companies, which meant that Jump Studios had to provide for group working as well as satisfying each of the companies' individual requirements.

123

GROUND FLOOR PLAN

1. Bar / café
2. Pods
3. Client work area
4. Open counter
5. Kitchen
6. Parlor
7. Mini auditorium
8. Board room
9. Pin-up rooms
10. Terrace

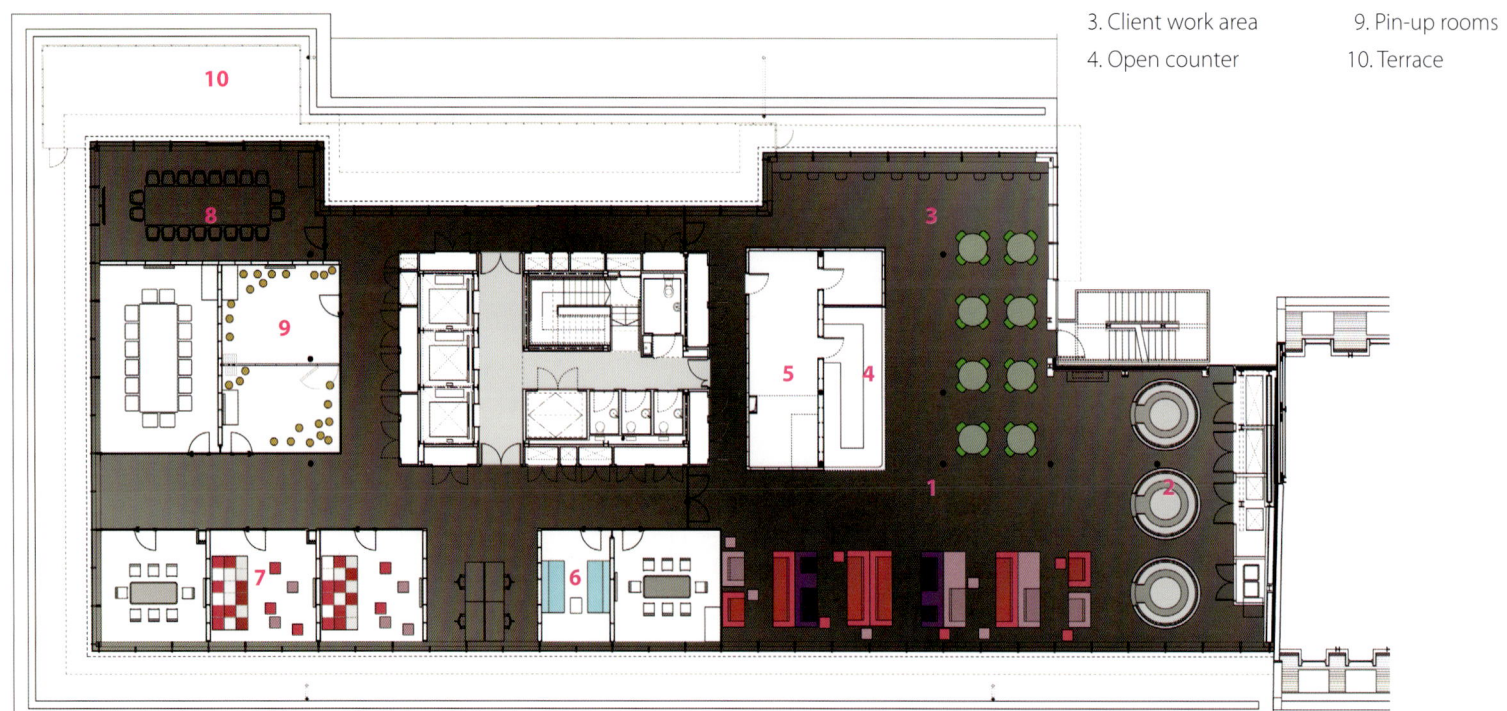

FIRST FLOOR PLAN

1. Open plan office
2. Large meeting
3. Small meeting
4. Pin-up
5. Archive
6. Cutting room / library
7. Copy point
8. Tea point
9. Cloakroom
10. Break out
11. Storage walls

125

One of the most dramatic elements in the series of 'precision-engineered' features that unify the overall design is the floating auditorium at entrance level, intended for presentations.

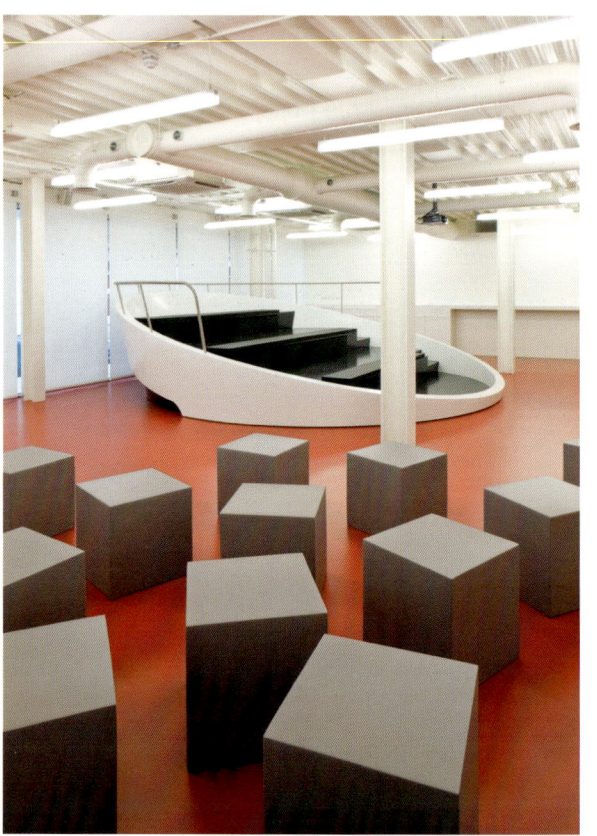

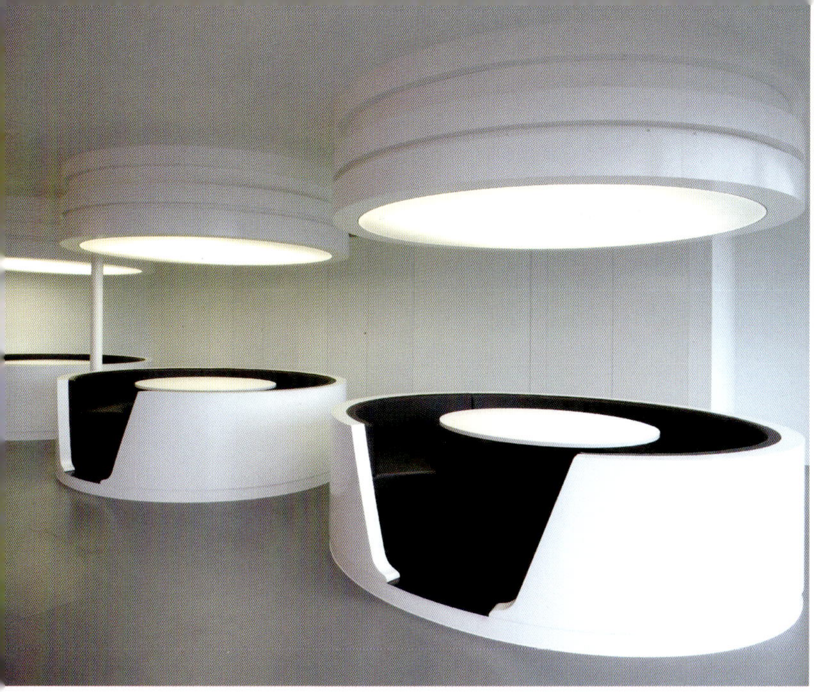
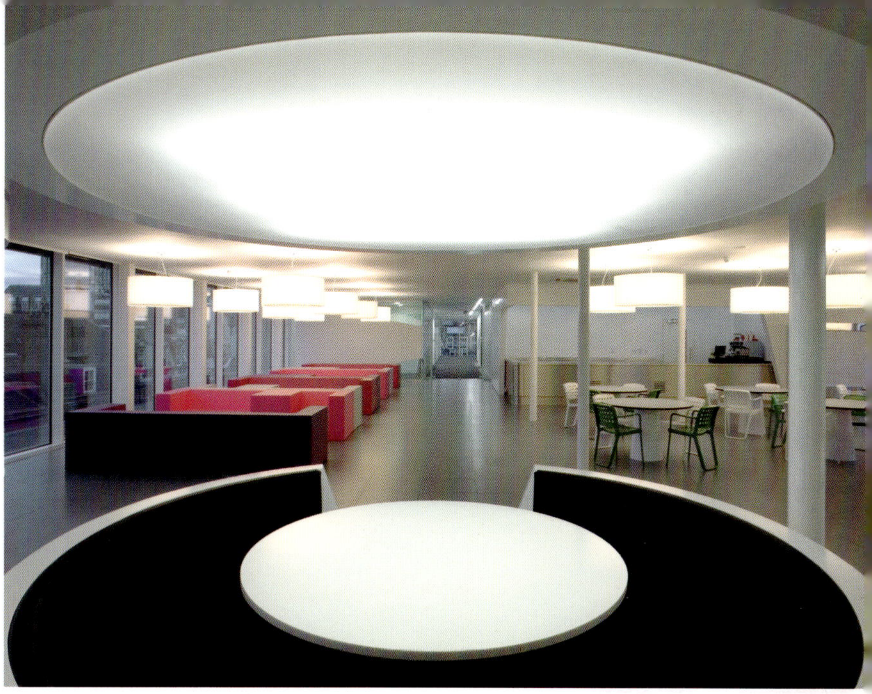
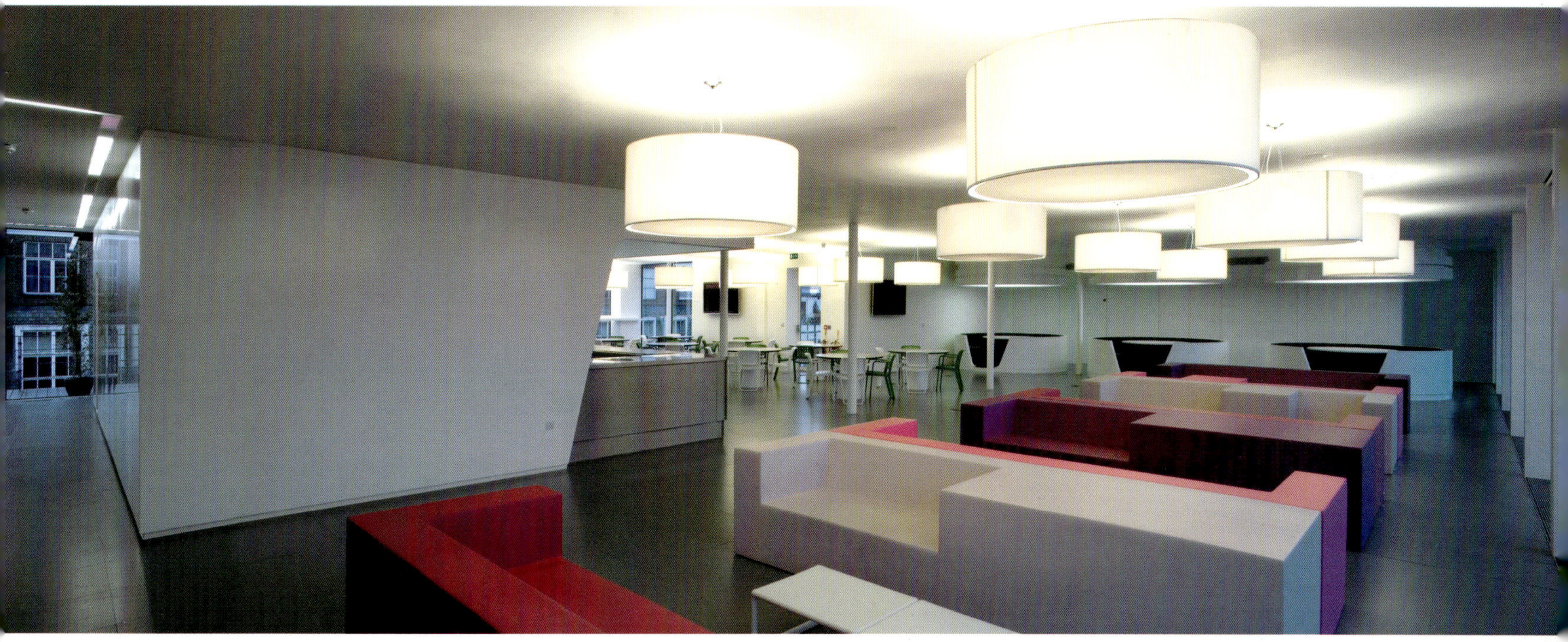
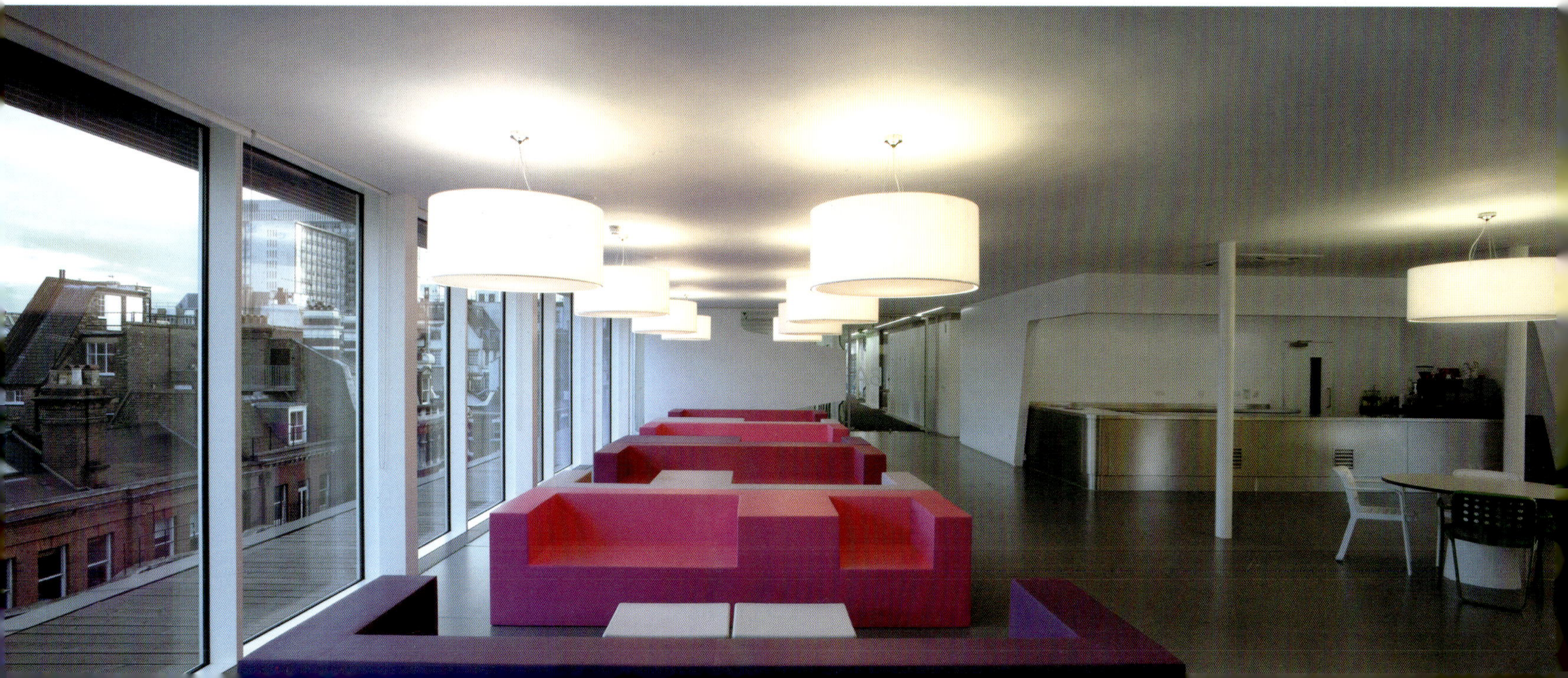

Sinato

Yuras

Tokyo, Japan Photographs: Hiroshi Ueda

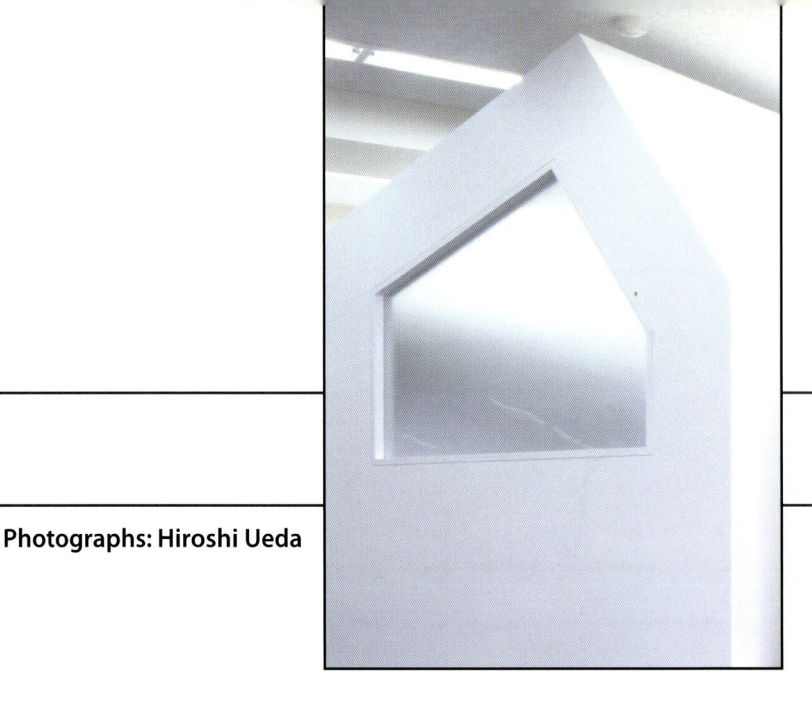

New rooms were constructed in the middle of the floor plan for this office without touching or modifying in any way the existing floor, walls or ceiling including the lights and the air conditioners. The result is a unique and interesting working environment, which offers employees here additional spaces with greater levels of privacy.

The new rooms were required to be closed, intimate spaces because of the purposes they would serve. The upper part of the partitions that separates the rooms was therefore bent so that the section form of each room might taper off as it rises. This allows those working in these spaces to feel a 'closed mass of air', which can't be sensed from rooms that have normal vertical partitions. Openings in these walls allow natural light to enter the interior and offer a connection with the surrounding office space, avoiding any sense of claustrophobia.

The bending form of these new offices, which is designed to affect the inside of the rooms, also has a direct consequence on the form as seen from the exterior. An outward appearance similar to a connection of gabled cabins or a mountain range appears by placing the aforementioned section form side by side. In addition, this symbolic mountain range mass is arranged diagonally and becomes a thick partition which divides the site into work space and common space. 'Rooms', 'Symbol', 'Partition'.

Work spaces are also formed on a second floor, which can be found nestled in the middle of the new construction, with the 'gabled roofs' forming sloping lateral walls. Furthermore at one end there is a large doorless opening, inside of which is a table with two cushioned benches on either side. This area can be used for informal meetings or as a communal lounge space for employees. Whatever the main function may be, the quality and originality of this place is provided by the curious mountain range mass which presides over the center of the space.

Architecture:
Sinato
Designer:
Chikara Ohno

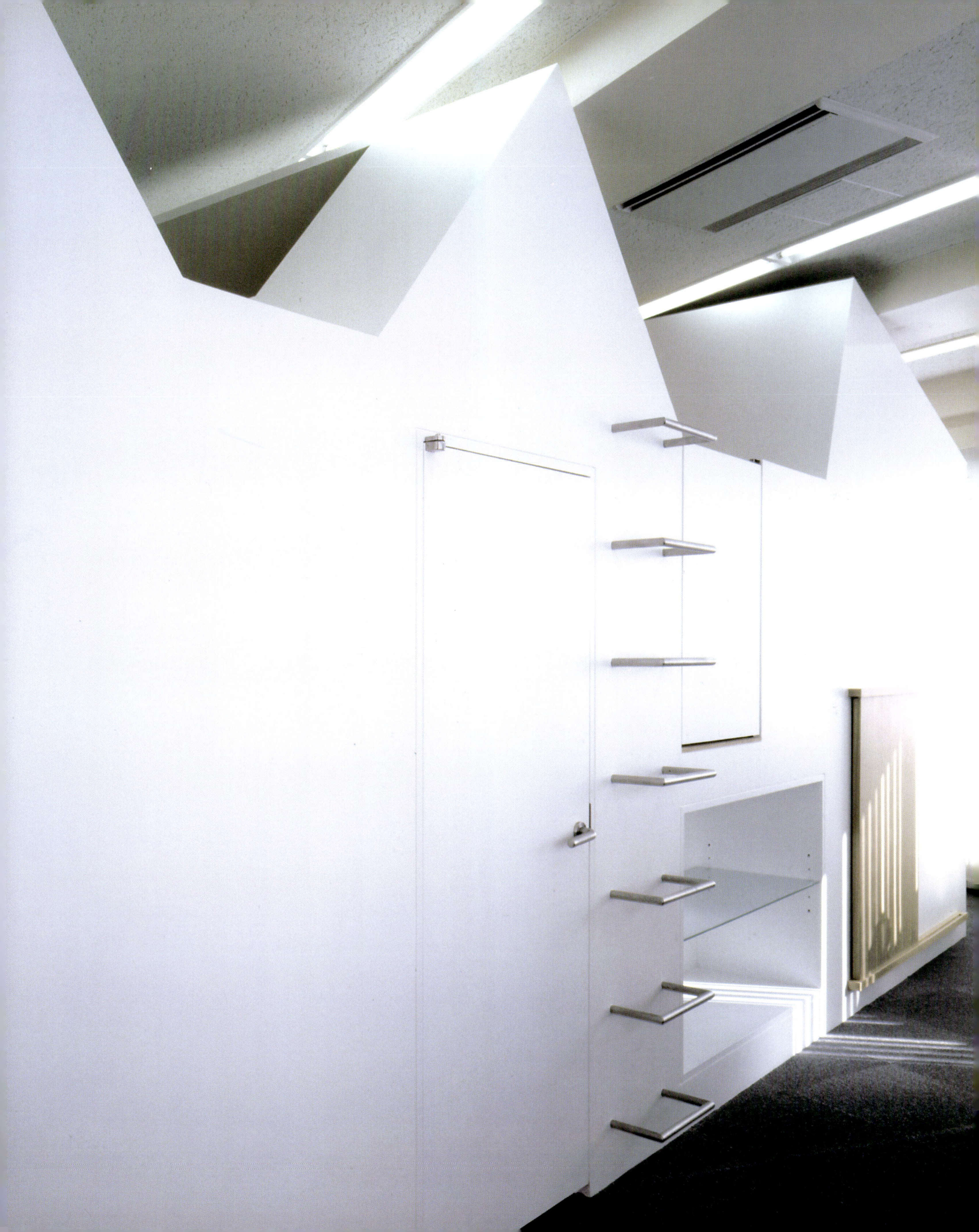

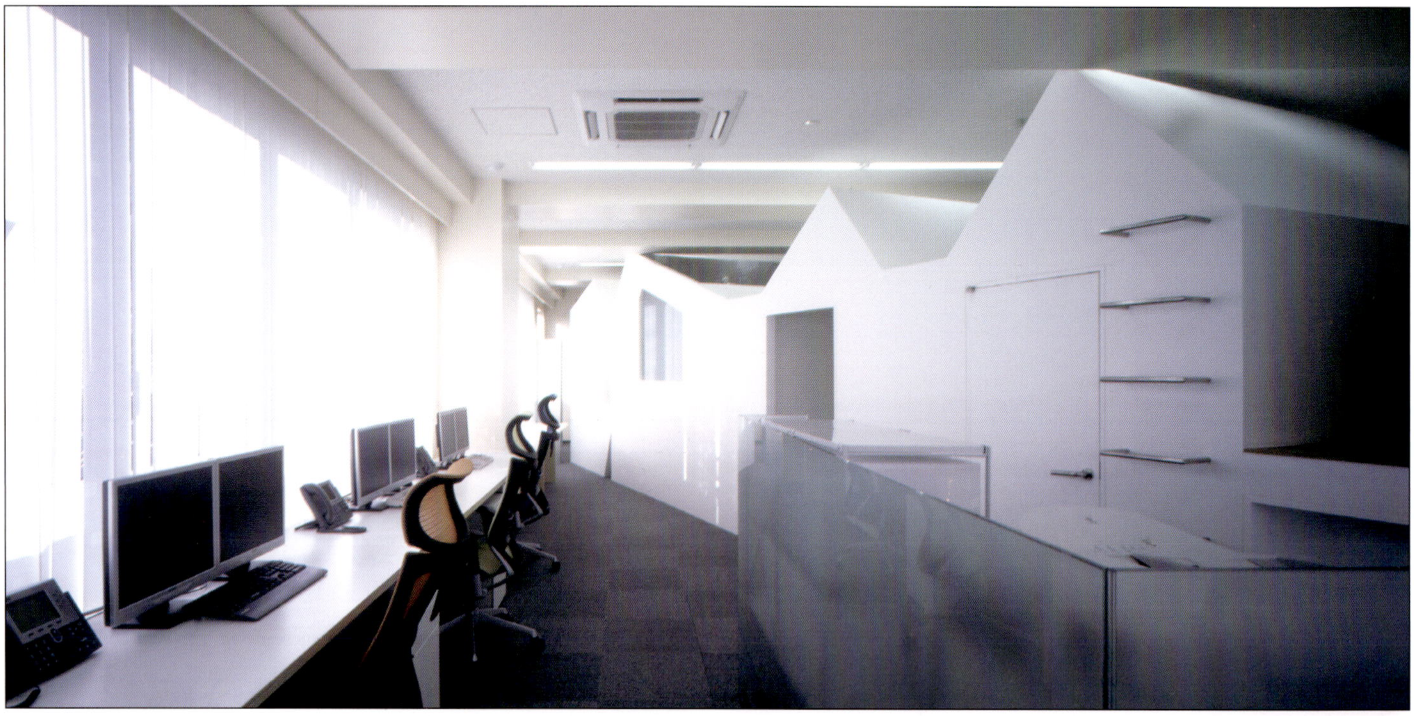

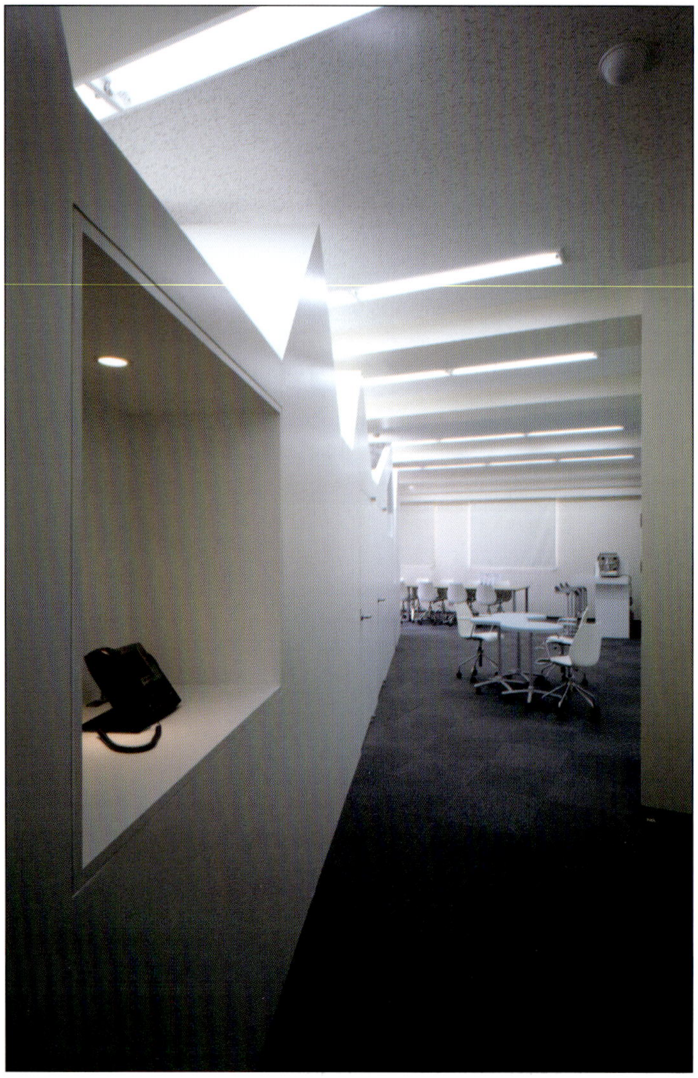

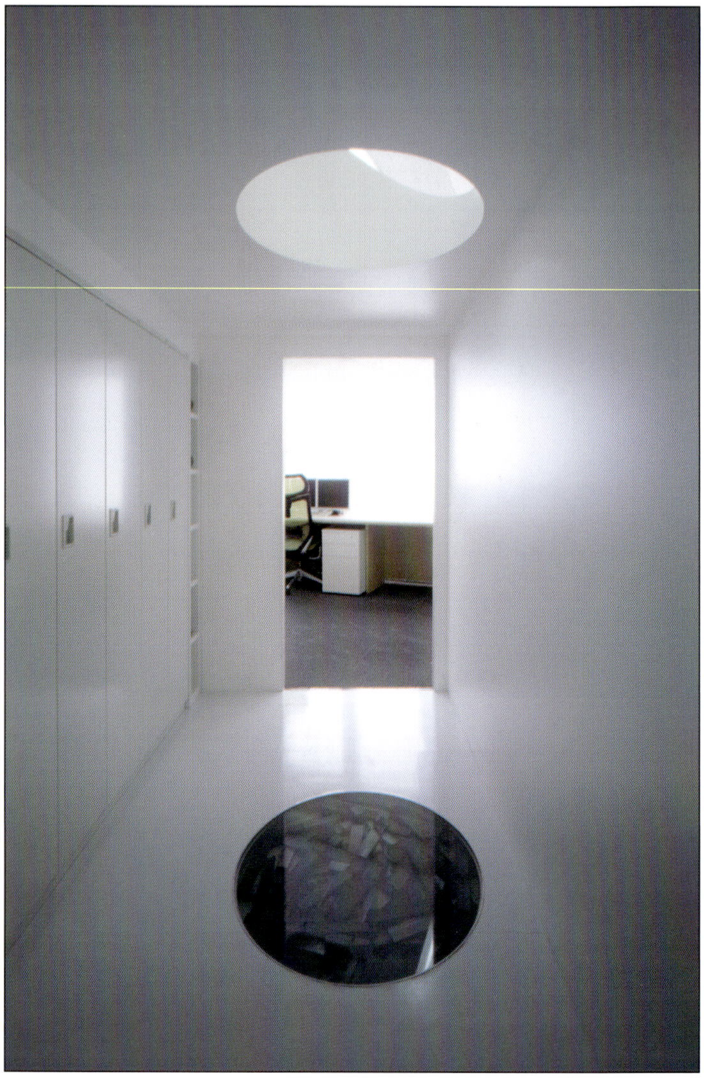

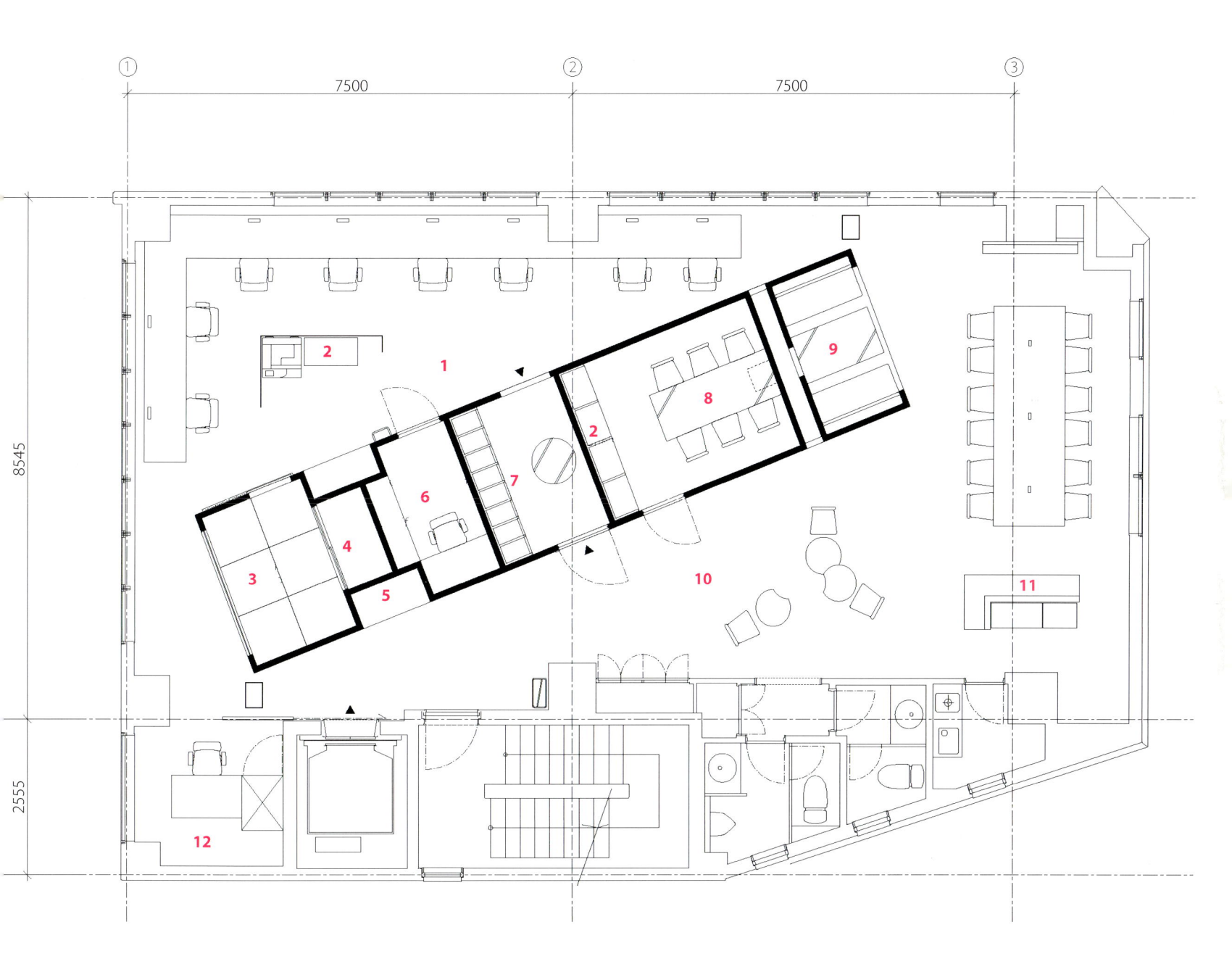

FLOOR PLAN

1. Work space
2. Shelf
3. Meditation room
4. Storage
5. Reception counter
6. Concentrated work room
7. Hall
8. Meeting space
9. Sofa
10. Common space
11. Counter
12. Server room

2900

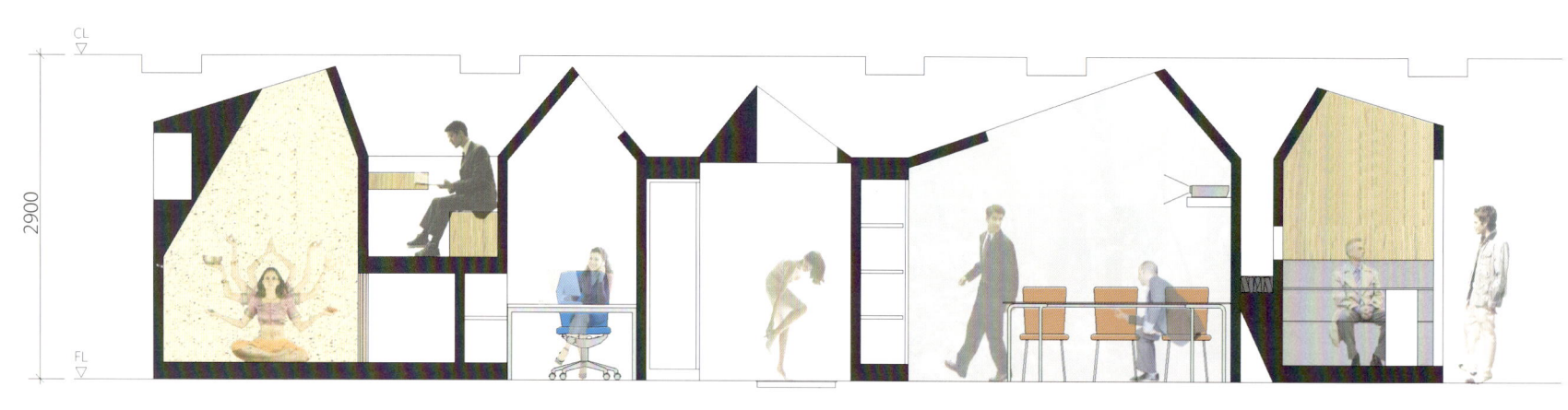

The bending form of these new offices, which is designed to affect the inside of the rooms, also has a direct consequence on the form as seen from the exterior.

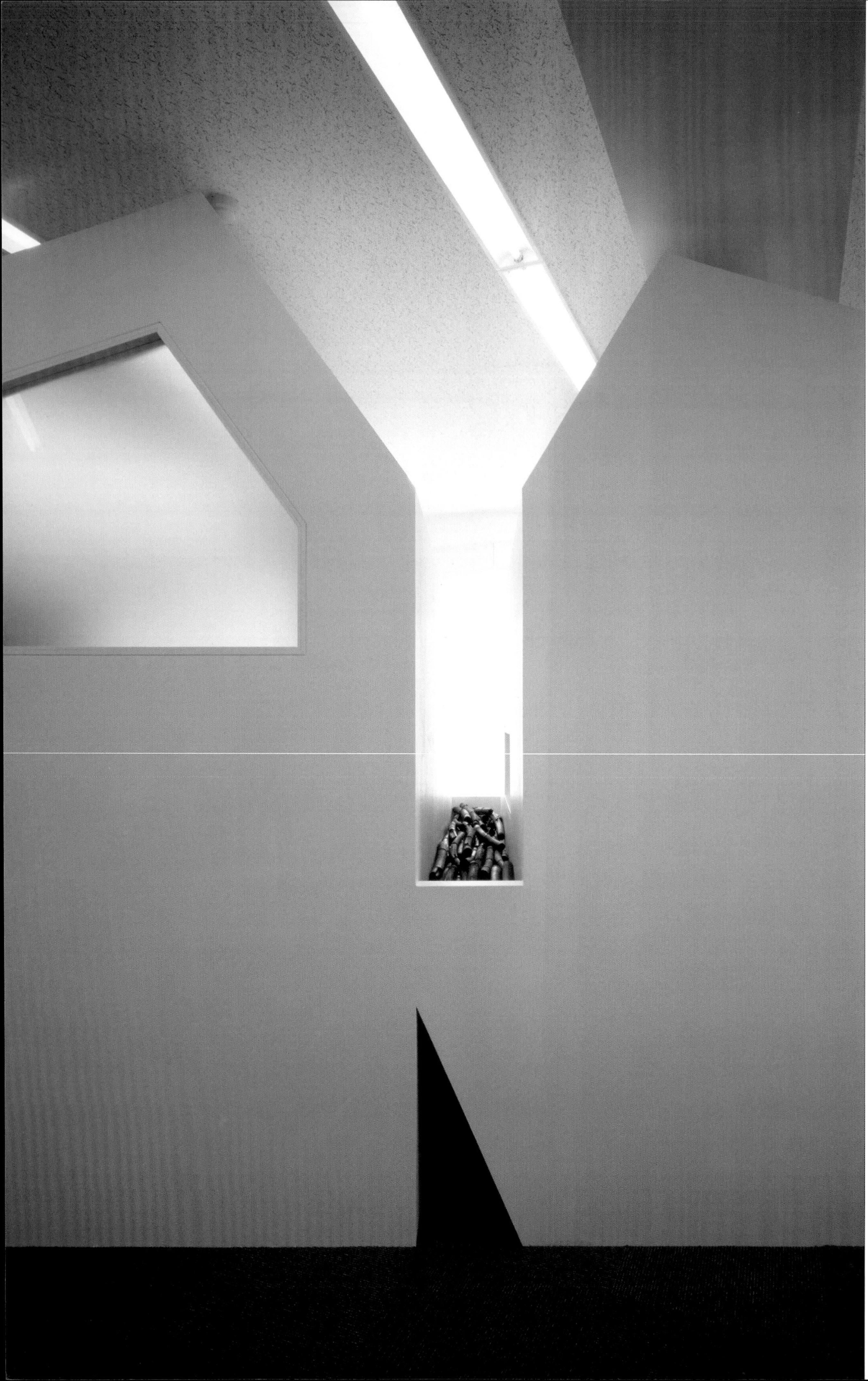

An outward appearance similar to a connection of gabled cabins or a mountain range appears by placing the aforementioned section form side by side.

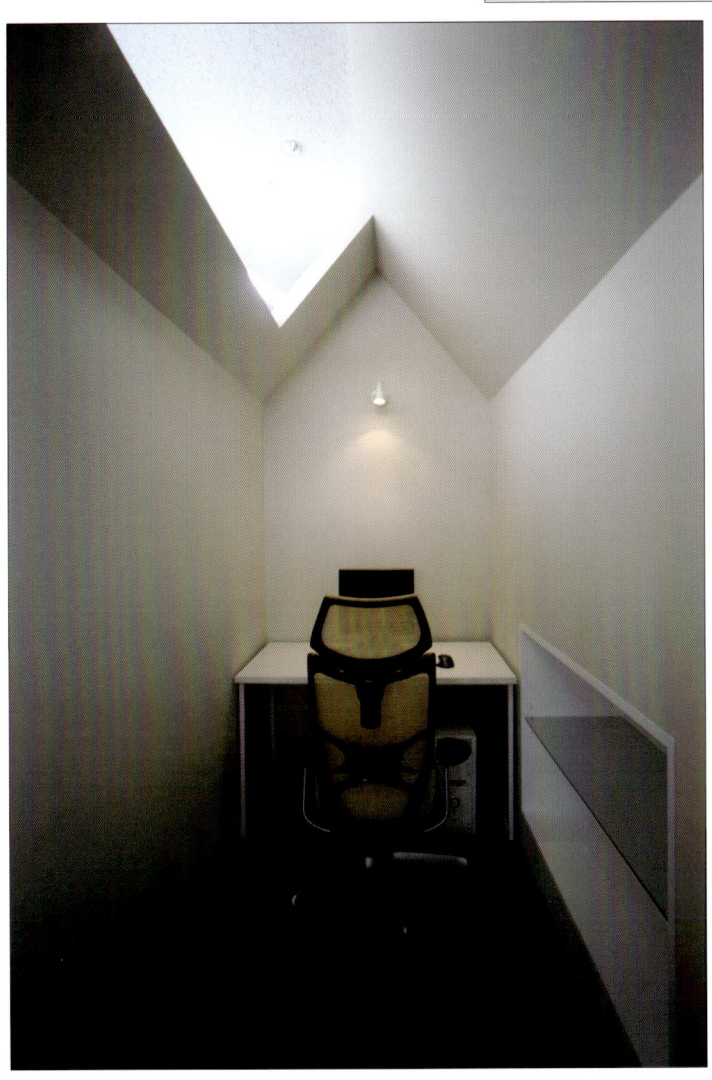

Lemaymichaud

Lemaymichaud Offices

Quebec City & Montreal, Canada **Photographs: Pierre Bélanger**

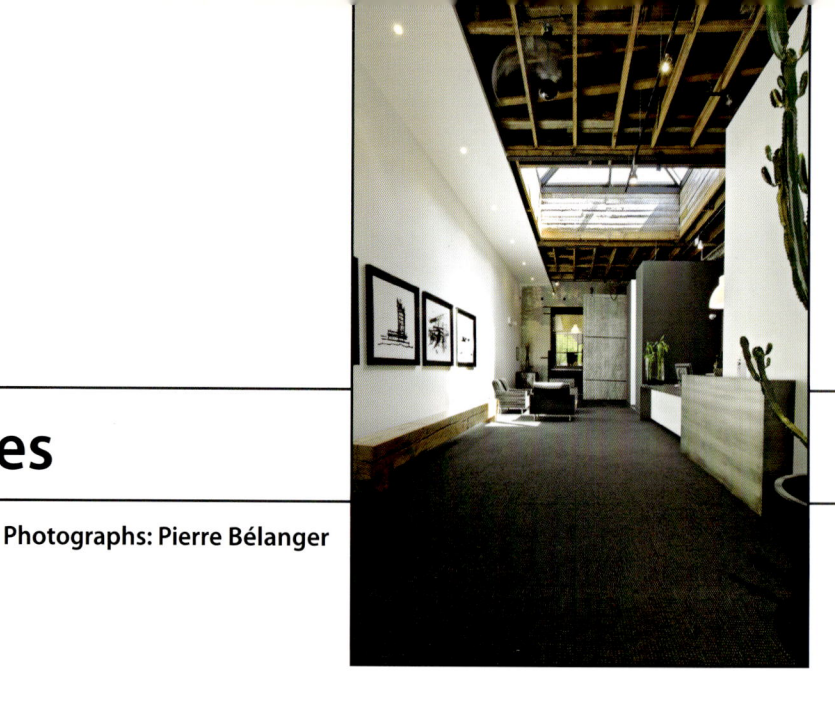

Architecture:
Lemaymichaud

One of Quebec's largest architecture and design firms, Lemaymichaud, has 63 employees in two offices situated in Quebec City and Montreal.

In 1989, Lemaymichaud acquired an abandoned building, built in 1906 for the Bank of Montreal, in the Old Port of Quebec City. Twenty years later, in 2009, with a larger team and different needs, it was time to expand and update the premises.

"It was quite a challenge," explains Alain Lemay, "because we had to expand from the inside. So we transformed a single-storey building with a nine-metre-high ceiling by constructing a mezzanine and occupying an unused attic, which has become a perfect space for relaxation, meetings, and creativity. This venture enabled us to almost double our usable area."

The Lemaymichaud team thus created two superimposed work studios, one of which was in a floating mezzanine, in order to respect the nature of the building and let the entire team take advantage of the quality of the space.

What the Montreal office has in common with the Quebec City one is that it is located in a historic building that no one wanted.

"We left the charm of 740 William [next door], with its inner courtyard and landscaping, for a windowless warehouse," recalls Viateur Michaud, who manages the Montreal office. "And yet, I thought, What a space! And for us, space is the basic necessity."

By excavating part of the building down to the foundation (1.52 m underground) and constructing a part of the floor 90 cm above ground level, they were able to create interior parking without making an underpinning. In addition, they integrated bicycle stands, a shower, and a radiant heat system; they improved the insulation and opened the interior to natural light; they had a number of pieces of furniture made from material recovered from the site, and so on.

In short, "The result is simple because the space, interesting in itself, retained its character and its volume was highlighted," concludes Michaud.

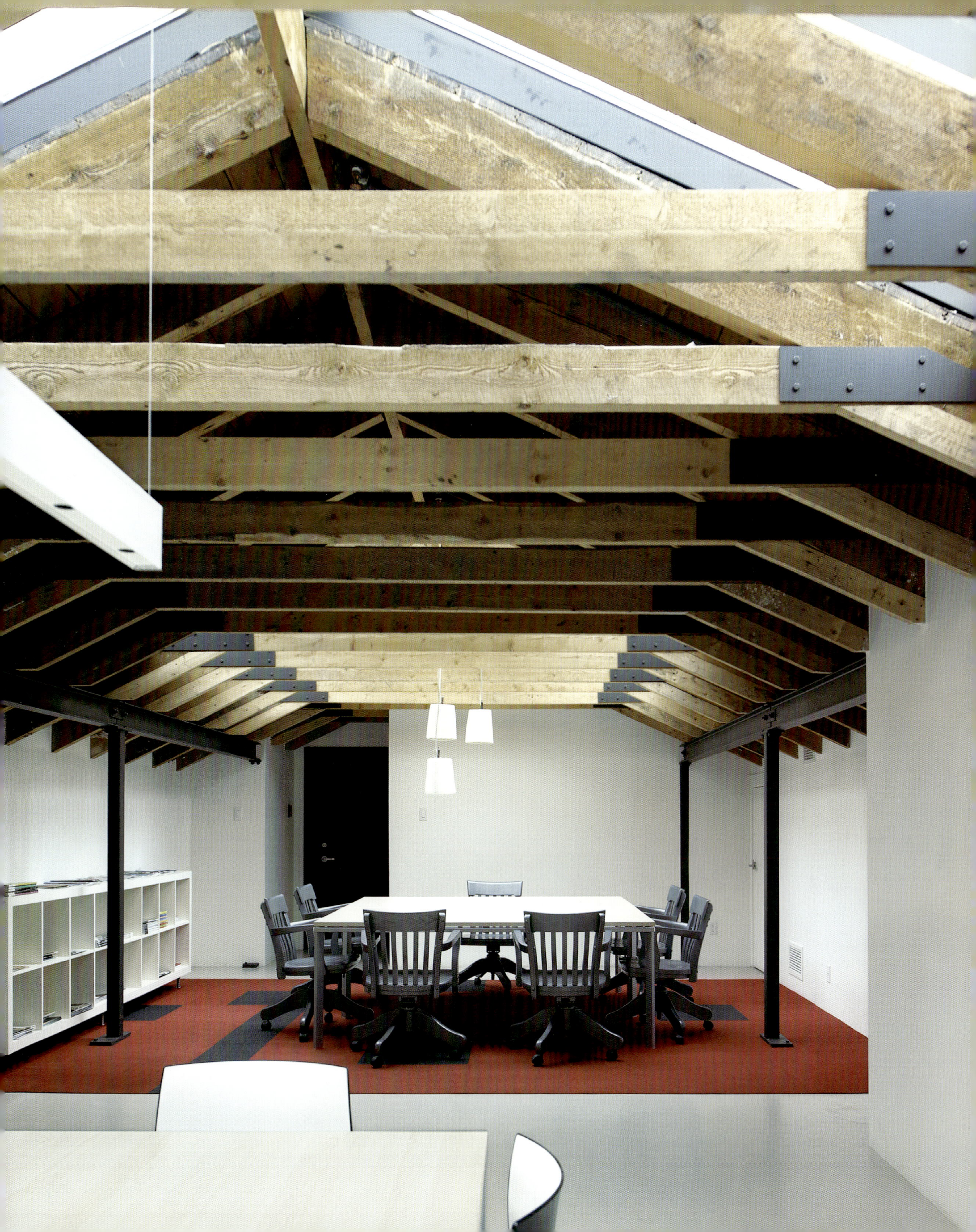

The challenge for the Quebec City office, located in an abandoned 1906 bank, was to expand within the existing building. A mezzanine was built, dividing the building's original nine-meter-high ceilings into two floor areas.

139

First floor plan

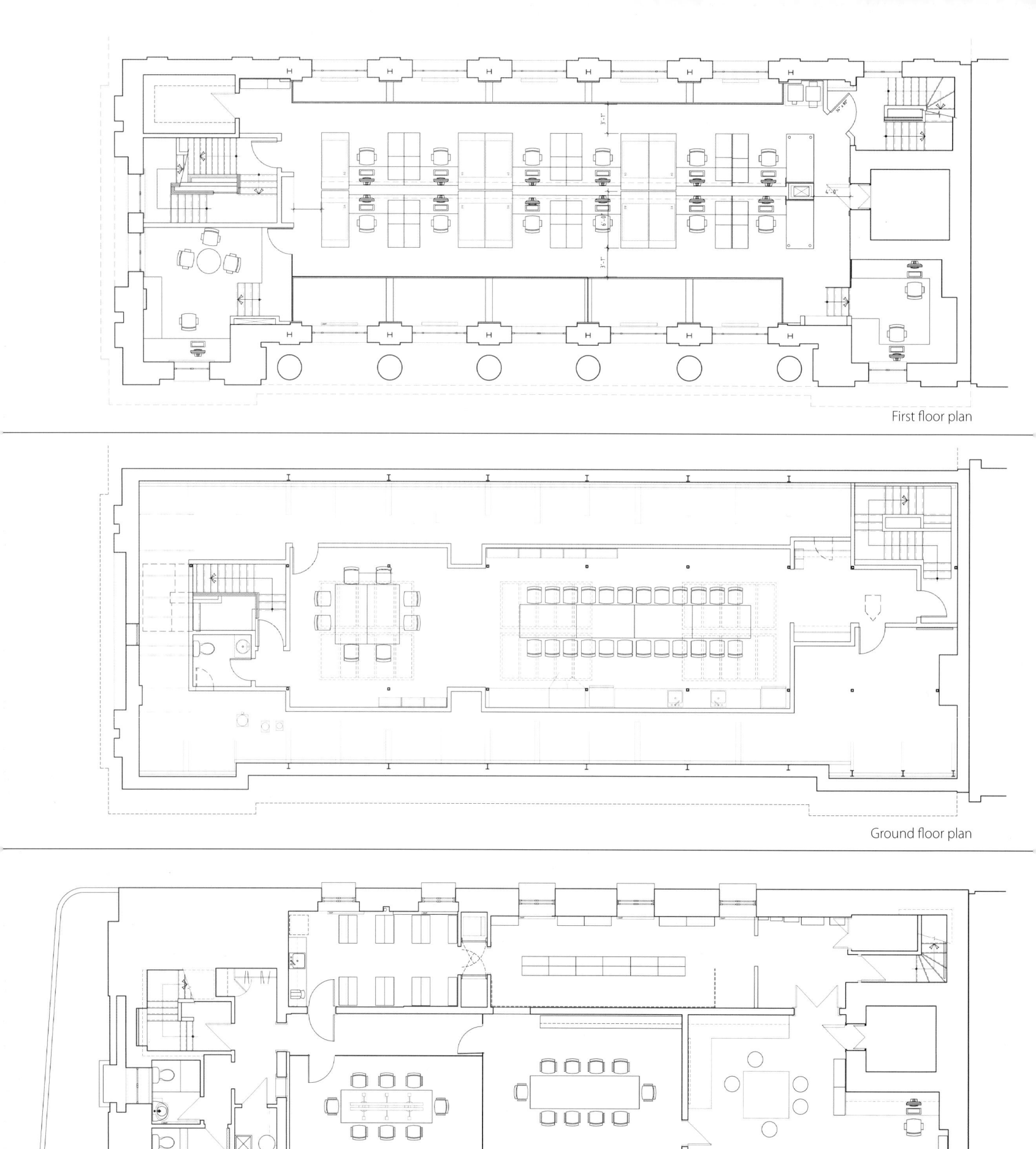

Ground floor plan

Basement floor plan

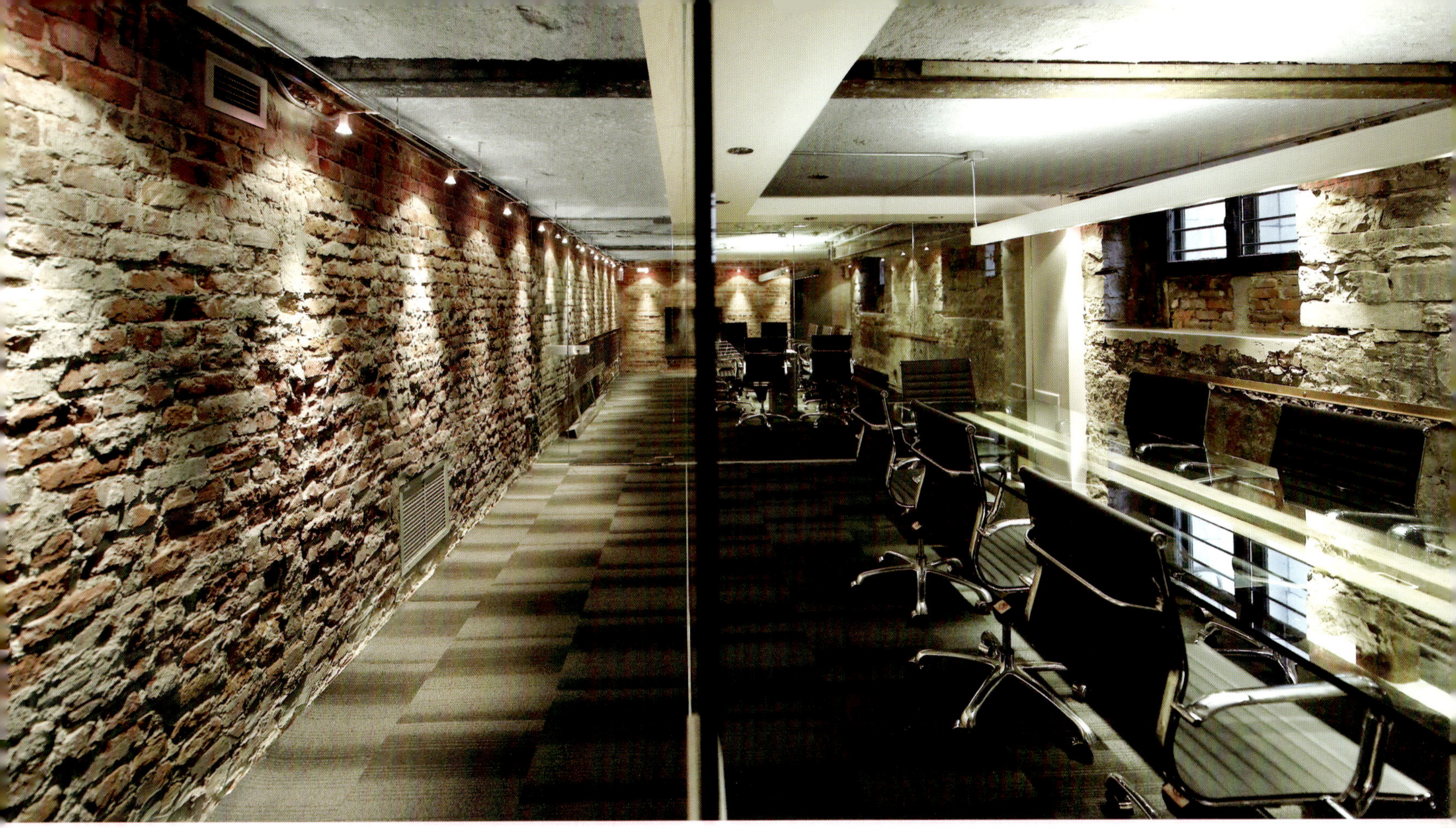
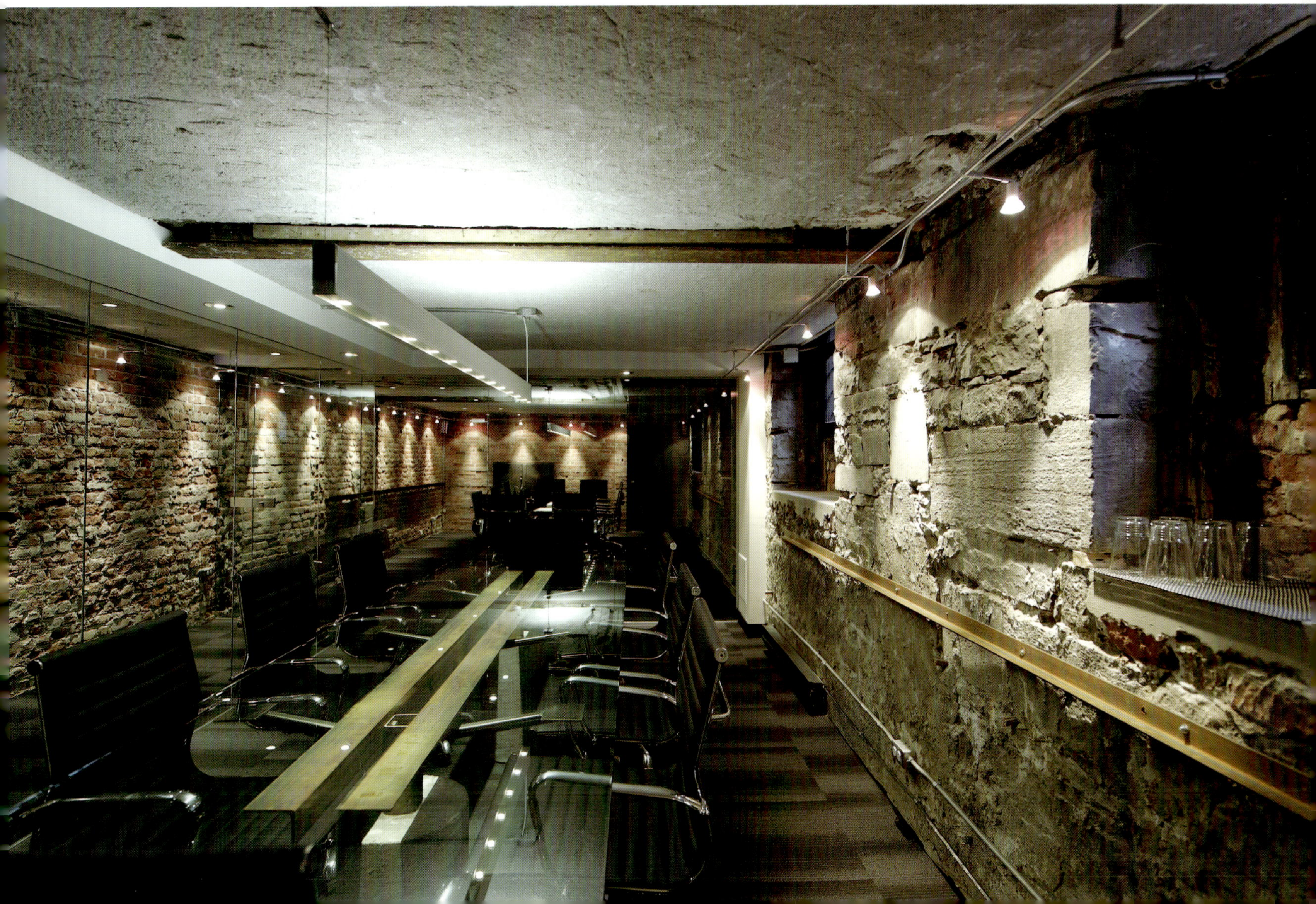

The Lemaymichaud offices resemble the company and its clients: simple and yet elegant, sophisticated but not arrogant.

143

For the Montreal office, the challenge was to integrate a touch of modernity into an old building. The Lemaymichaud architects therefore made sure to take advantage of the existing space and its constraints to transform it into a unique place.

Floor plan

146

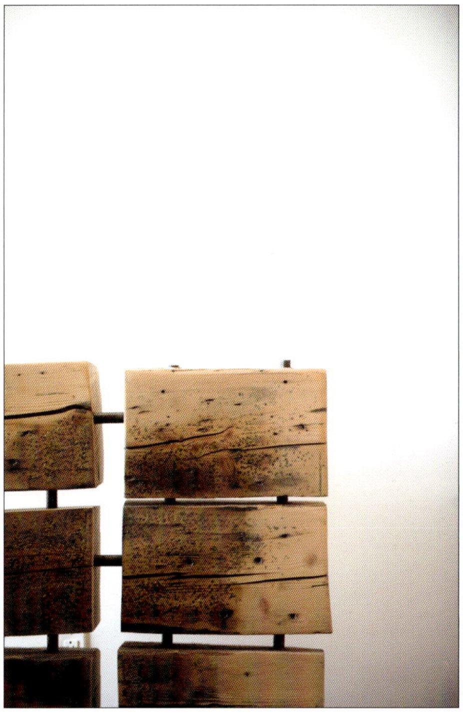
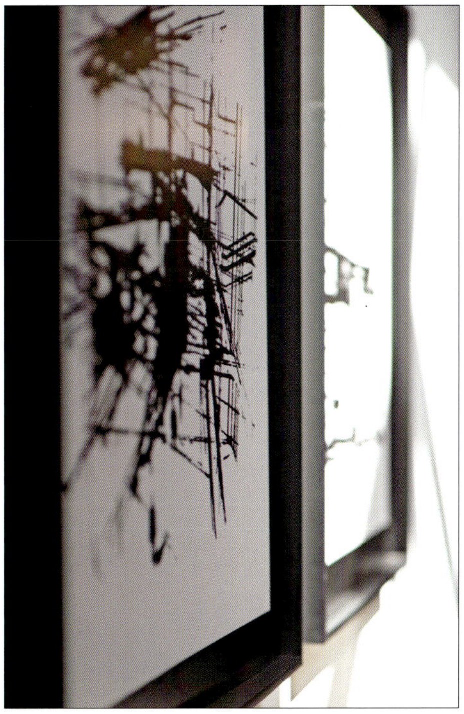
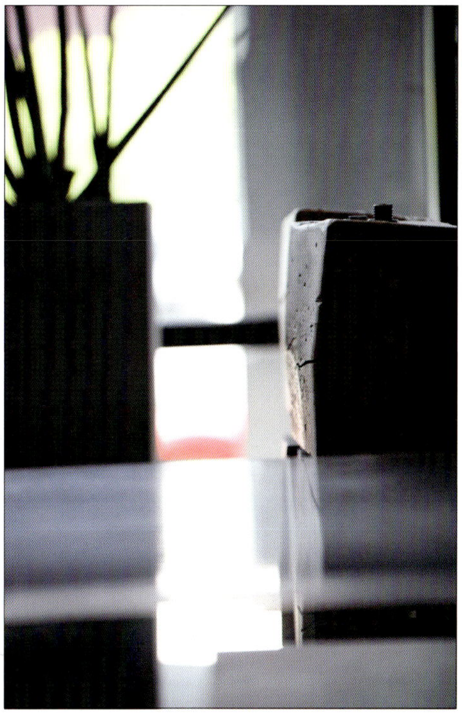
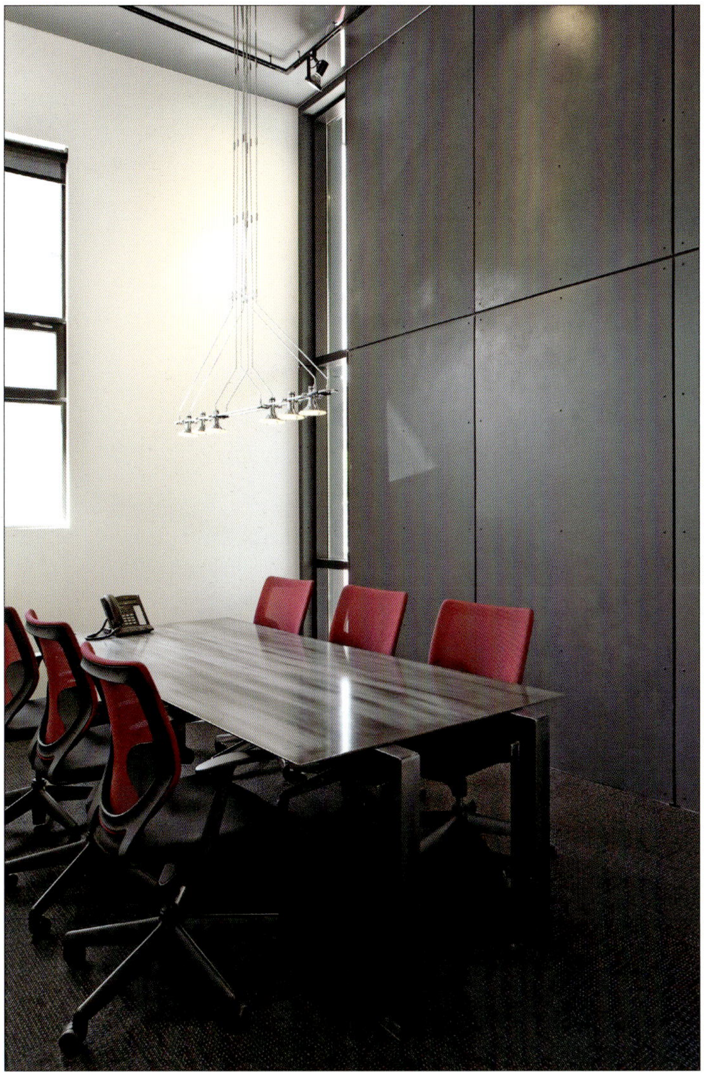
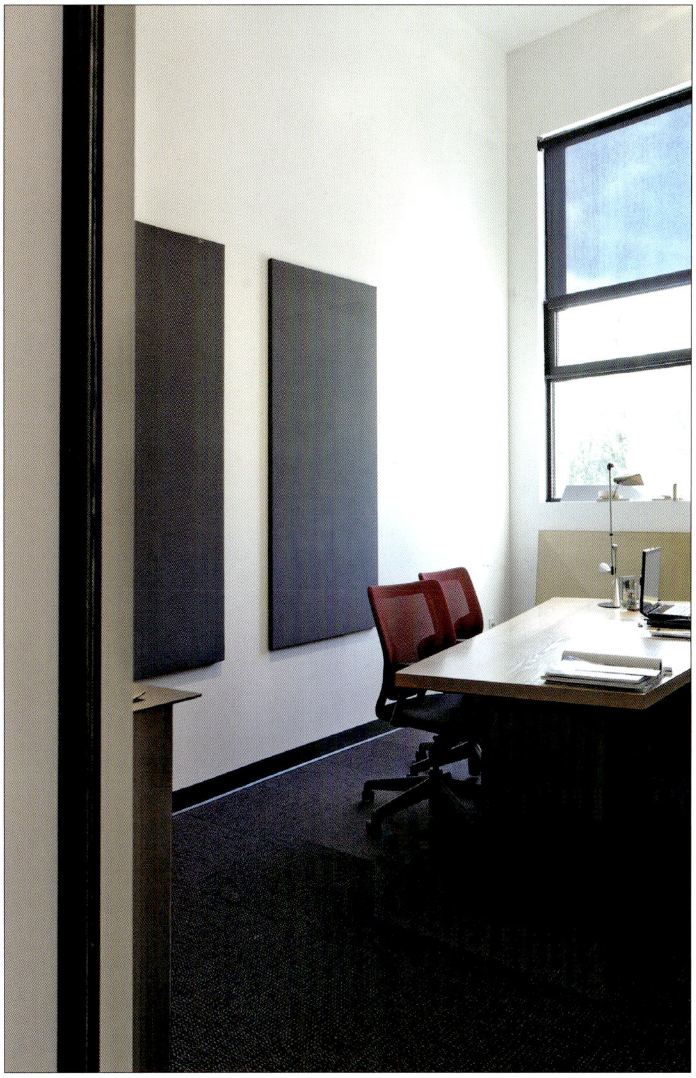

aplus arquitectes associats
Promobuilding Group

Barcelona, Spain   Photographs: Marie-Caroline Lucat

Occupying the entire 575-sqm (6200-sqft) floor of a service building and located in one of Barcelona's most representative areas, the Promobuilding Group has moved its three work centers and its workforce of over 30 employees bringing them together in a single space. The main idea behind the project was to be able to create an environment that would reflect the philosophy of this young property developer by way of a modern, open-plan and transparent space, which would also be functional. The existing floorplan was characterized by the small distance between the pillars, the services nucleus that interrupted the continuity of the space, and a façade excess which was deeper than it needed to be.

The 'major players' in this project are the three organically shaped glass volumes. They contain the more closed spaces such as the meeting rooms, the technicians' rooms and small storage spaces, which in turn conceal the ventilation shafts found on this floor, as well as providing different access points to the functional areas. Around these bodies is a continuous open space that allows a constant variety of visual perspectives thanks to the use of different types of glass. This facilitates one of the requirements made by the client: to create a perimeter route that would show all the operative departments of the property developer and allow quick communication. The glass bodies are curved, thus creating a tension between them, providing the aesthetics for the circulation space and adapting to each of the different conditions of this triangular floor plan.

The skin of the three amorphous bodies, identified by their Bordeaux color, which also interprets the company's corporate color, makes the most of all the possibilities of a material like glass. They are curved, transparent, translucent, or opaque depending on what is required. Tinted and curved glass blurs the limits of the spaces, its transparency creating a visual relation between the meeting rooms and work areas, and connecting the exterior with the interior of this deep floor plan. It then becomes opaque however for the more private, non-visiting areas. This project is a physical representation of what it means to intervene in and remodel a space while also transmitting the values of a group, in this case a property developer.

The opacity and reflections on the glass combine in a play of light and color, creating the impression of an abstract and almost virtual space.

Architecture:
aplus arquitectes associats,
Elsa Bertran Brancós, Ignasi Pérez Arnal,
Stéphane Villafane, Gregor Mertens

Project director:
Gregor Mertens

Interior design and construction management:
Rosa Gomez

Associates:
Claudia Stolte

Glass fabrication:
CRICURSA, Cristales Curvados S.A.

Glass assembly:
MECRIMAR

Constructed surface area:
6,200 sqft (575 sqm)

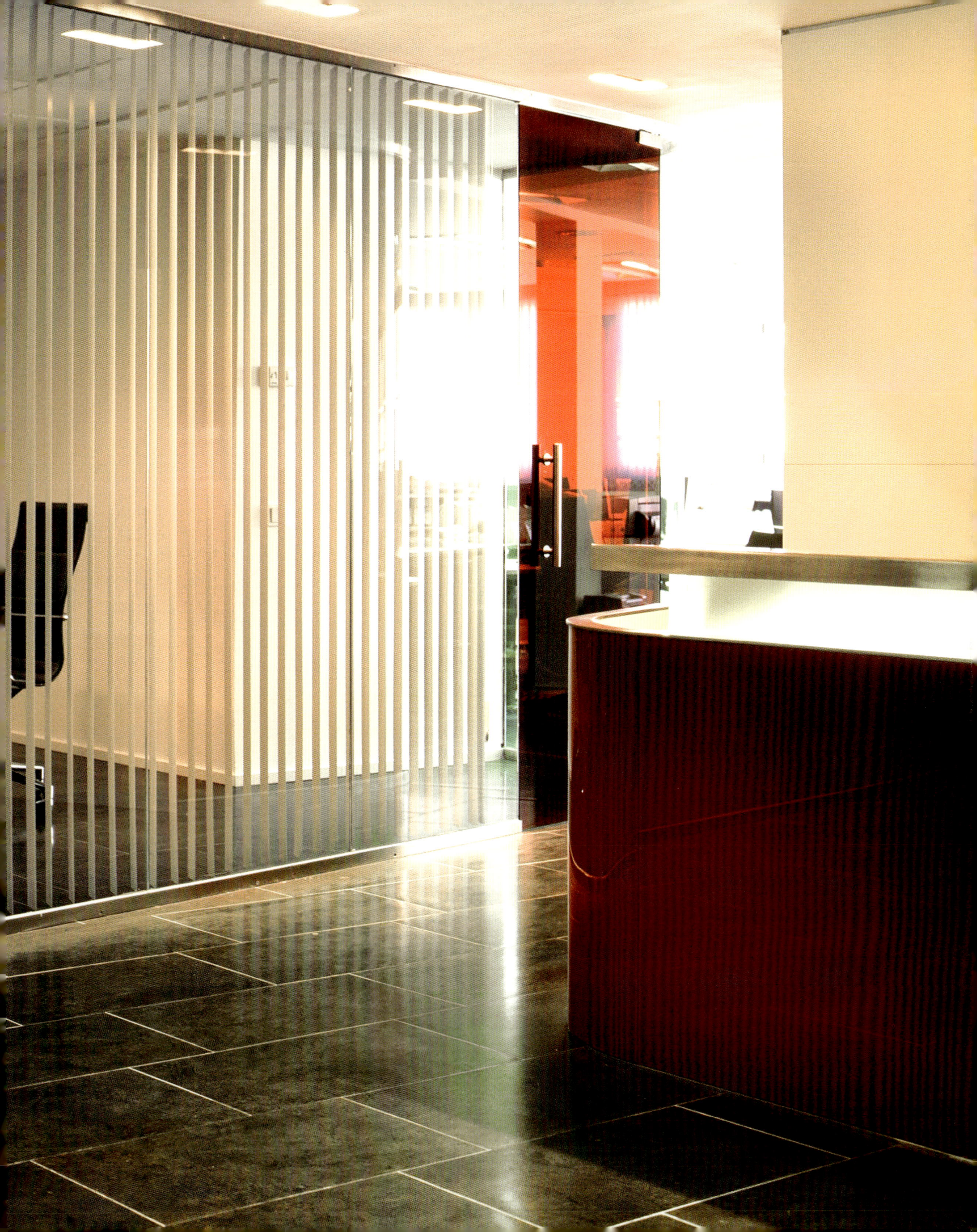

150

The 'major players' in this project are the three organically shaped glass volumes. They contain the more closed spaces such as the meeting rooms, the technicians' rooms and small storage spaces, which in turn conceal the ventilation shafts found on this floor, as well as providing different access points to the functional areas.

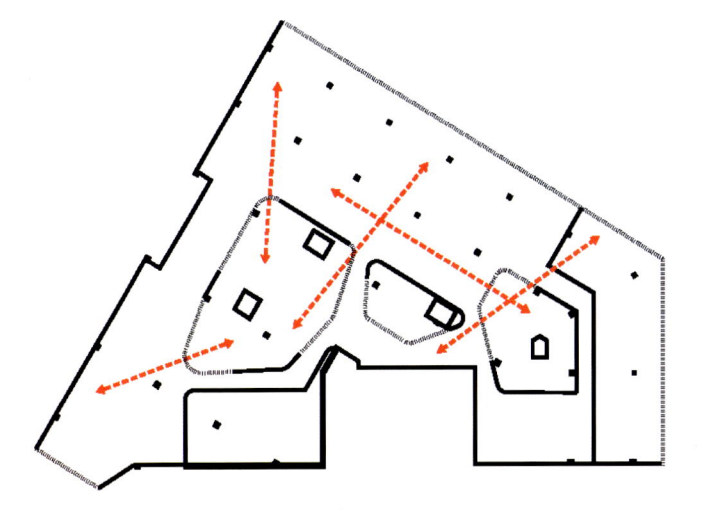

visual communication

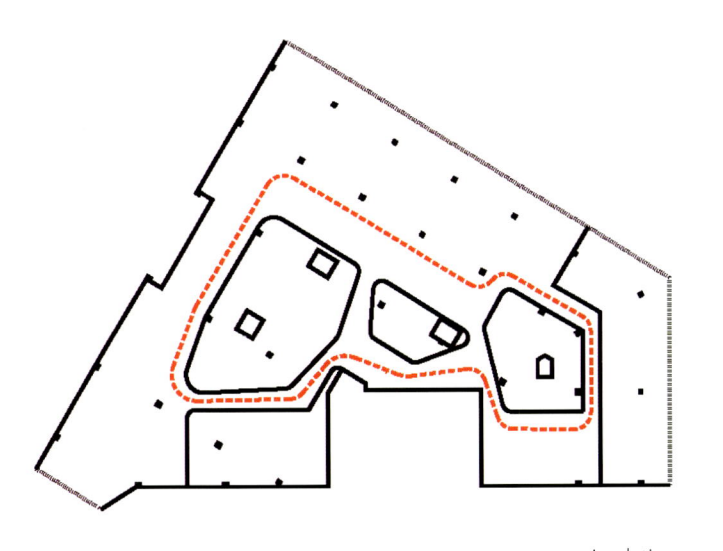

circulation

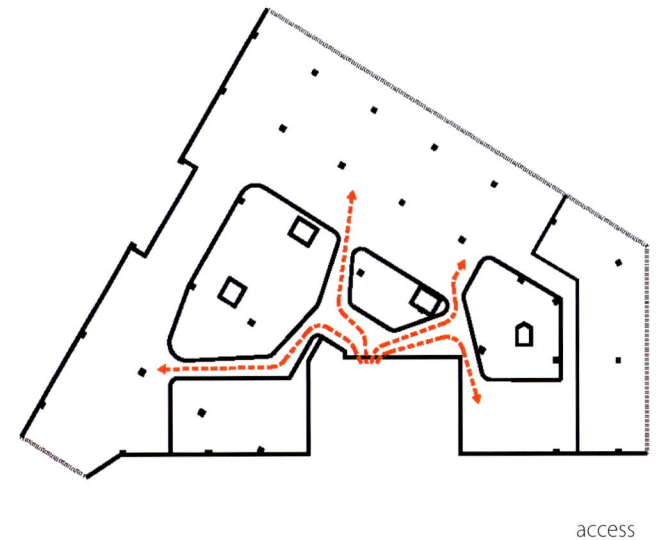

access

zoning

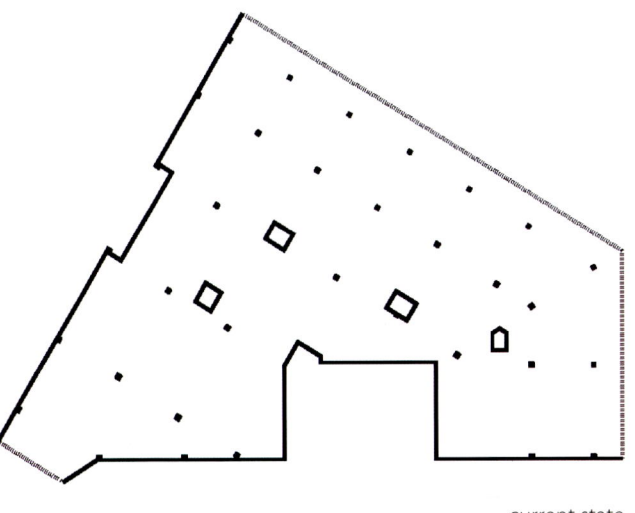

current state

152

Floor plan

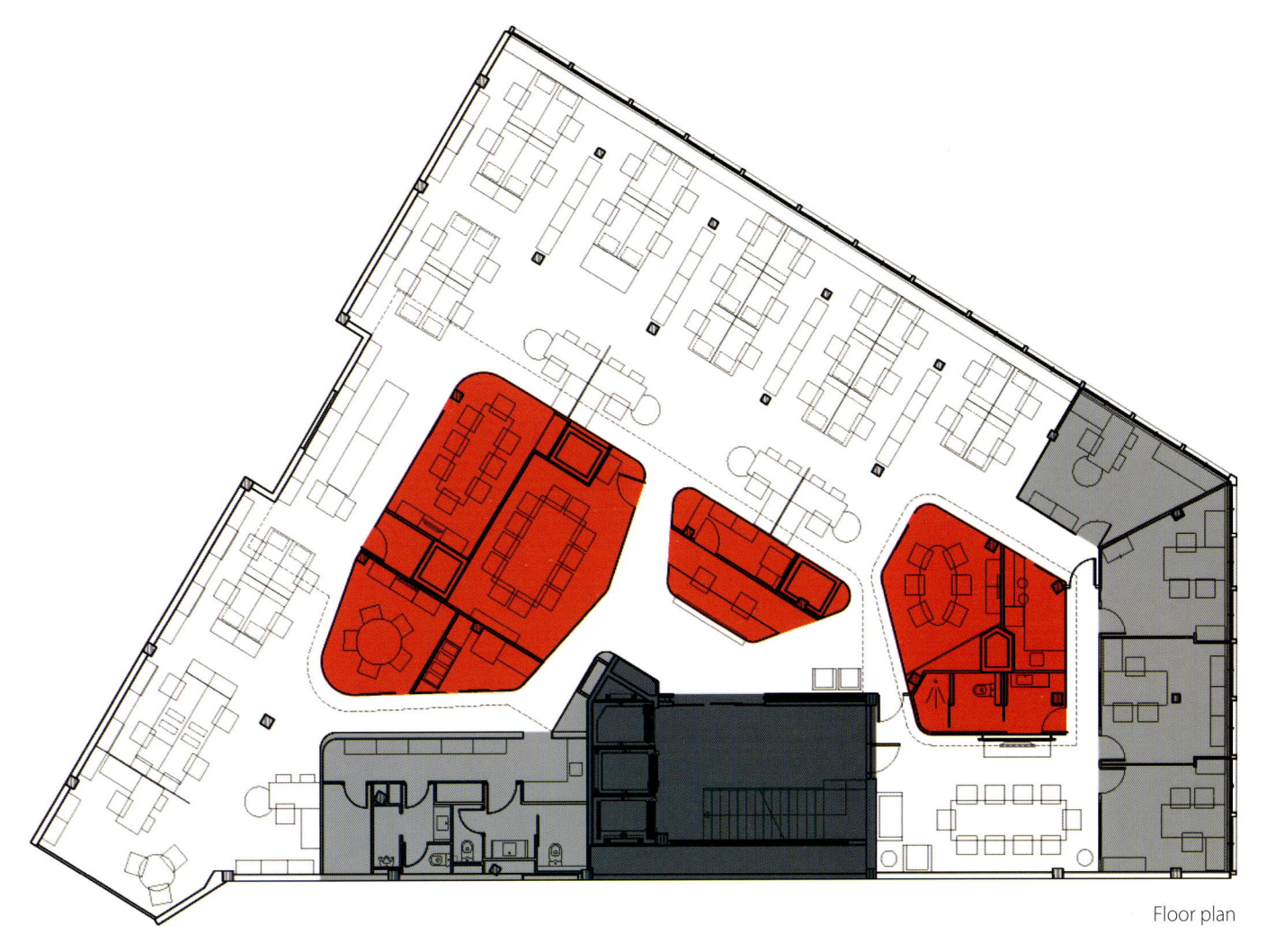

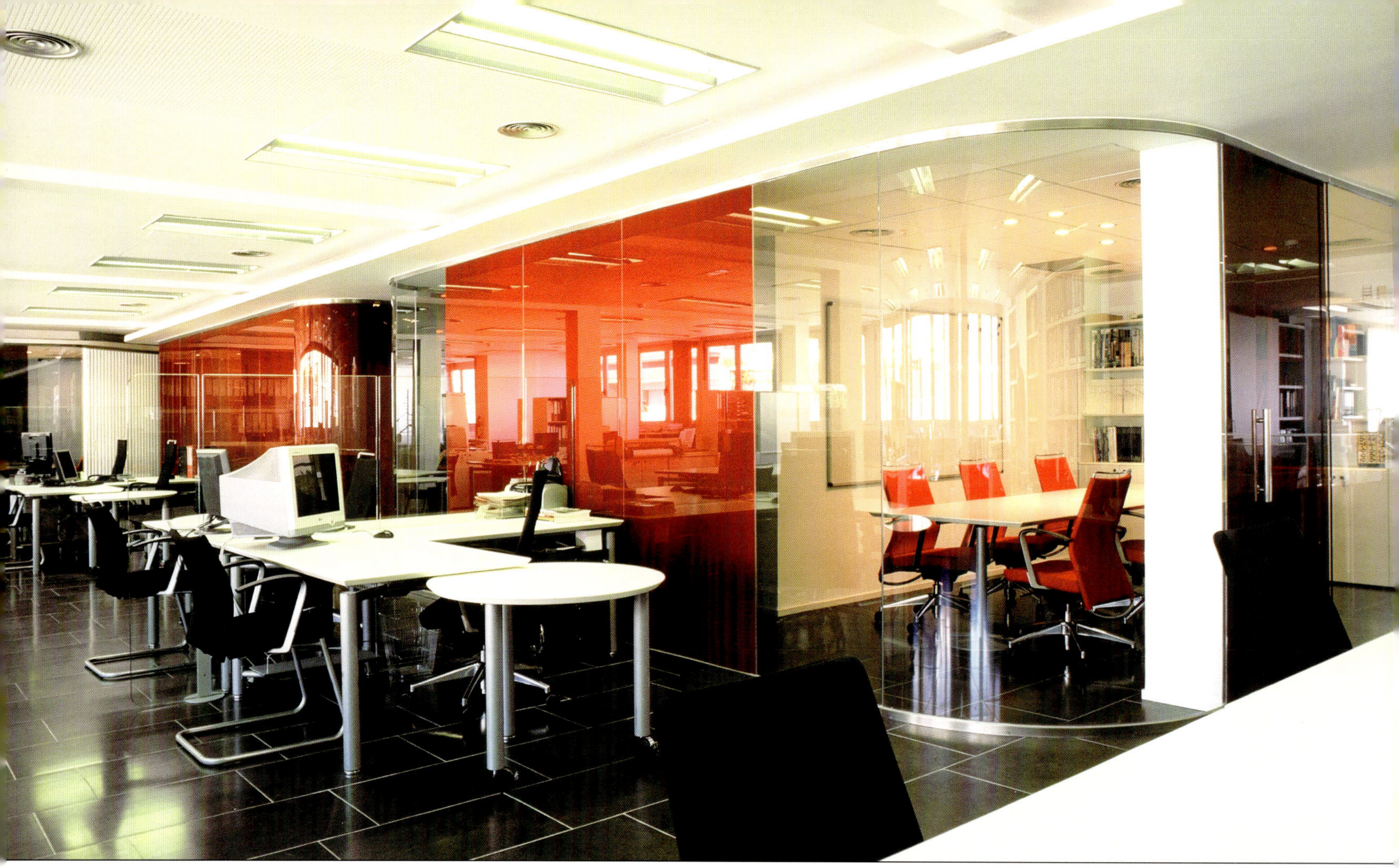

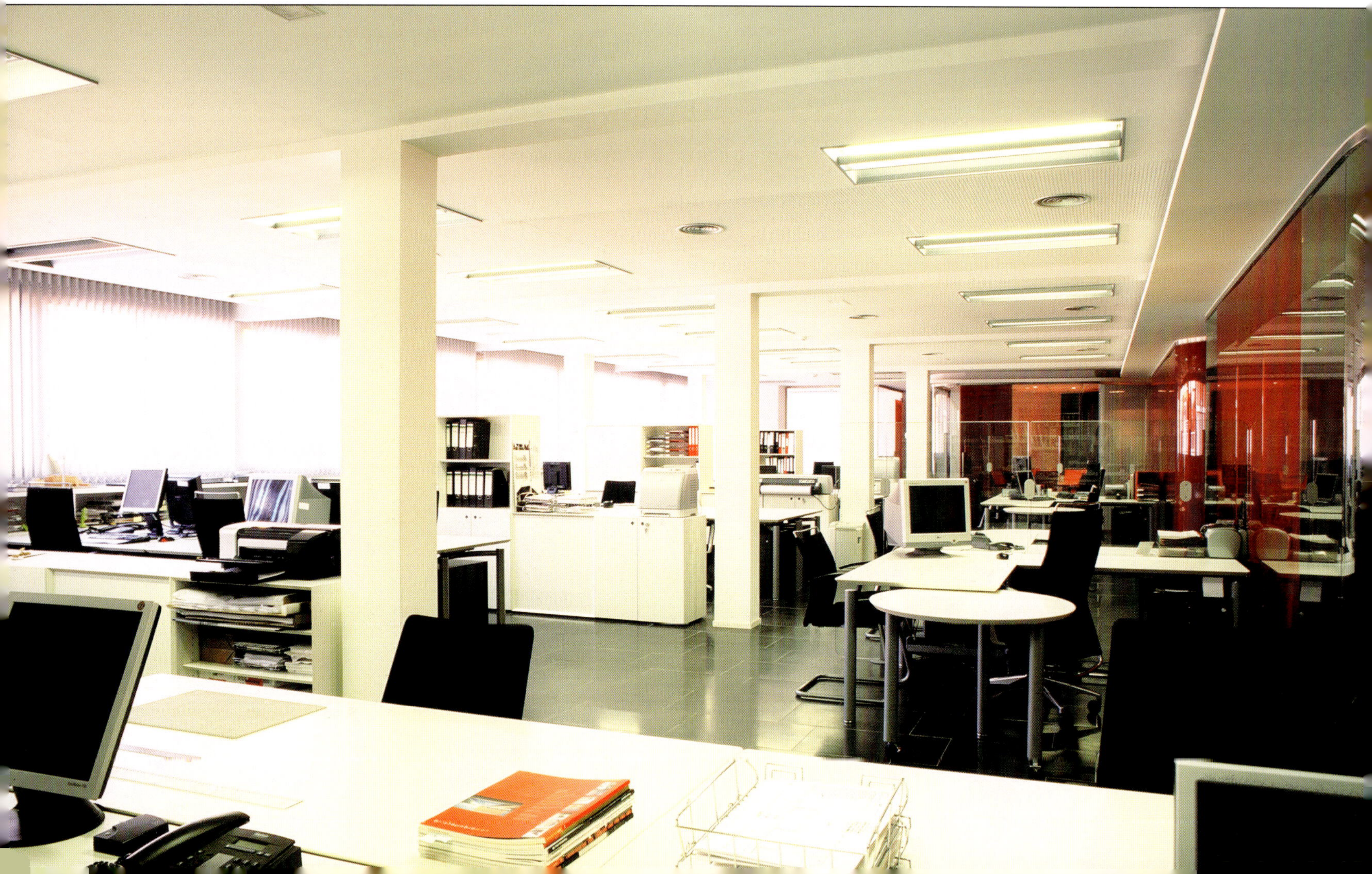

The skin of the three amorphous bodies, identified by their Bordeaux color, which also interprets the company's corporate color, makes the most of all the possibilities of a material like glass.

The opaqueness and the reflections from the glass combine in a virtuous play of light and color, creating the impression of an abstract and almost virtual space.

157

Maurice Mentjens

PostPanic Office Space

Amsterdam, the Netherlands Photographs: Arjen Schmitz

When PostPanic moved to a new building in the Westerdoksdijk in Amsterdam in 2008, Maurice Mentjens was commissioned to design an interior that would be both workable and inspiring. Functionality was a priority.

PostPanic combines a design/animation studio and a production company, producing commercial projects for the international advertising, retail, broadcast and music industries as well as its own internal projects. Clients include Nike, MTV and Coca-Cola. The image of creative free spirits hides a company of highly motivated professionals focused on image and perception. This directly influenced the new studio's layout.

The starting point was an empty ground floor space over five meters high, with large concrete columns and big windows in the slanted façade overlooking the river.

To stay true to their original vision and ensure quality throughout, PostPanic produces, directs, designs and animates in-house. This requires that various departments have their clearly defined areas, yet maintain as much openness and transparency as possible. The workforce fluctuates from 14 to 40. Dimensions of the subsequent areas are defined by the distance between the columns. The production room, meeting room and staff room measure the span between two columns; the studio on the mezzanine is twice this size. The mezzanine creates the required floor space without compromising the studio's open feel.

The concrete columns, smooth concrete floors, absent thresholds, fluorescent ceiling lights and unconcealed ductwork emphasize the raw, industrial look. Designer Maurice Mentjens has fitted up PostPanic's Amsterdam studio as a professional playground that emphasizes the company's creative attitude. In accordance with the brief, every department has a distinctive atmosphere, yet the space reads as a whole. The different areas are segregated, not isolated. The informal feel of the design emphasizes PostPanic's philosophy: a dynamic, inviting environment giving PostPanic room to play.

Architecture:
Maurice Mentjens Design
Project manager:
Elan Bouwkundig advies
General contractor:
Elan Bouwkundig advies, Castricum
Electric installations:
KS elektro, Heemskerk
Climate control:
Installatiebedrijf Kamlag, Castricum
Lighting:
Rexel
Floor:
betonlook: RW vloeren, Oudewater
carpet: Ege Flooring, Trickstyle Castricum
Painting:
Schilder- En Onderhoudsbedrijf Carlo Res, Castricum
Interior:
Adrichem interieurbouw, Heemskerk
Total floor area:
6,080 sqft (565 sqm)

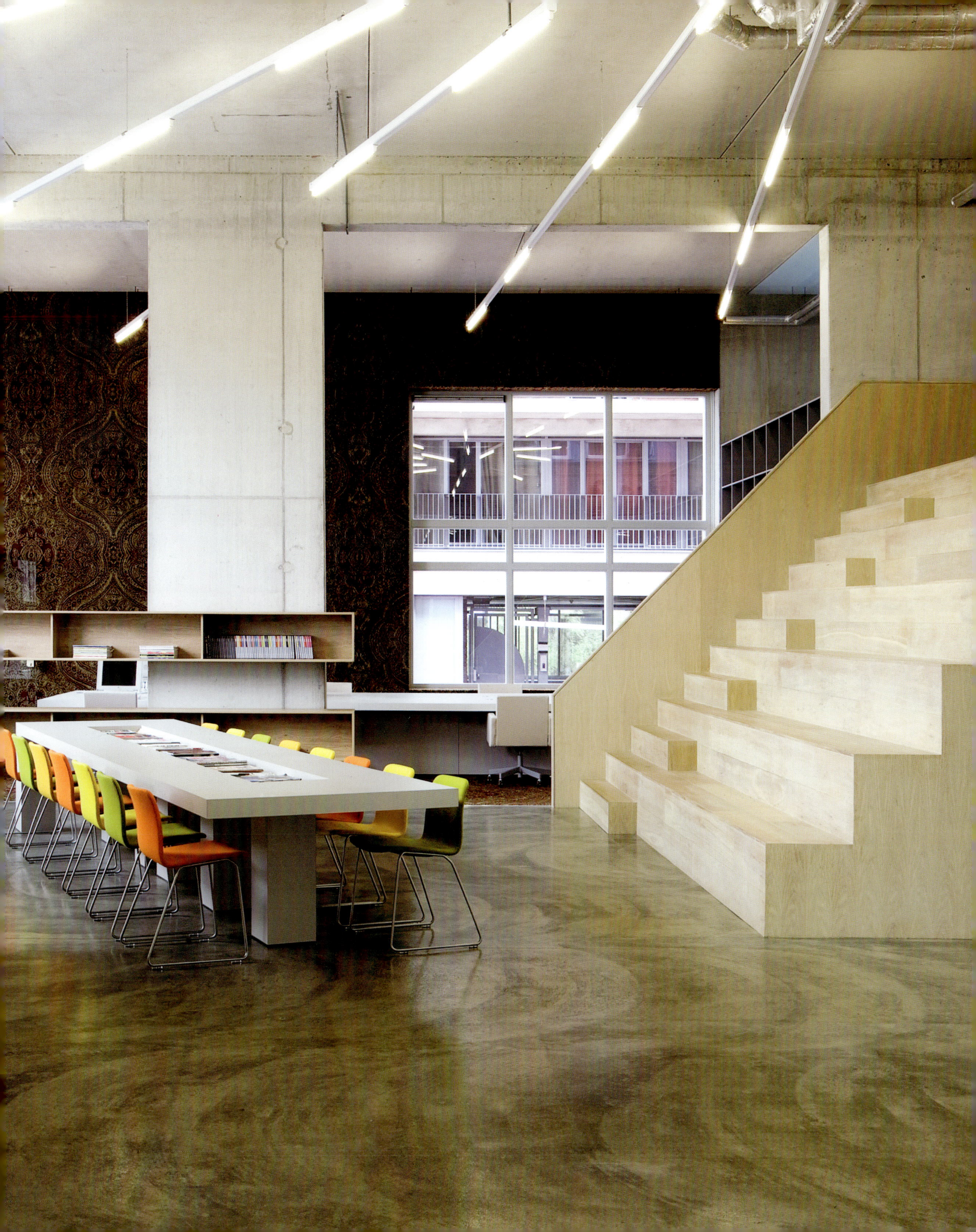

The hall, 5-meters high (15 feet), is used as a hallway/living room; to hold exhibitions, seminars and film screenings. Wedged between two columns a monumental oak grandstand, a quarter of the studio's width, doubles as stairs to the mezzanine.

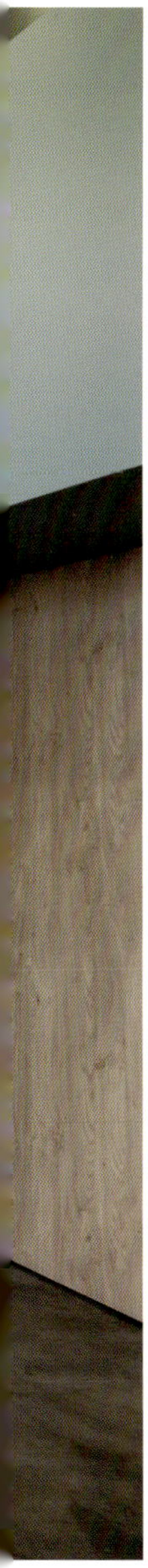

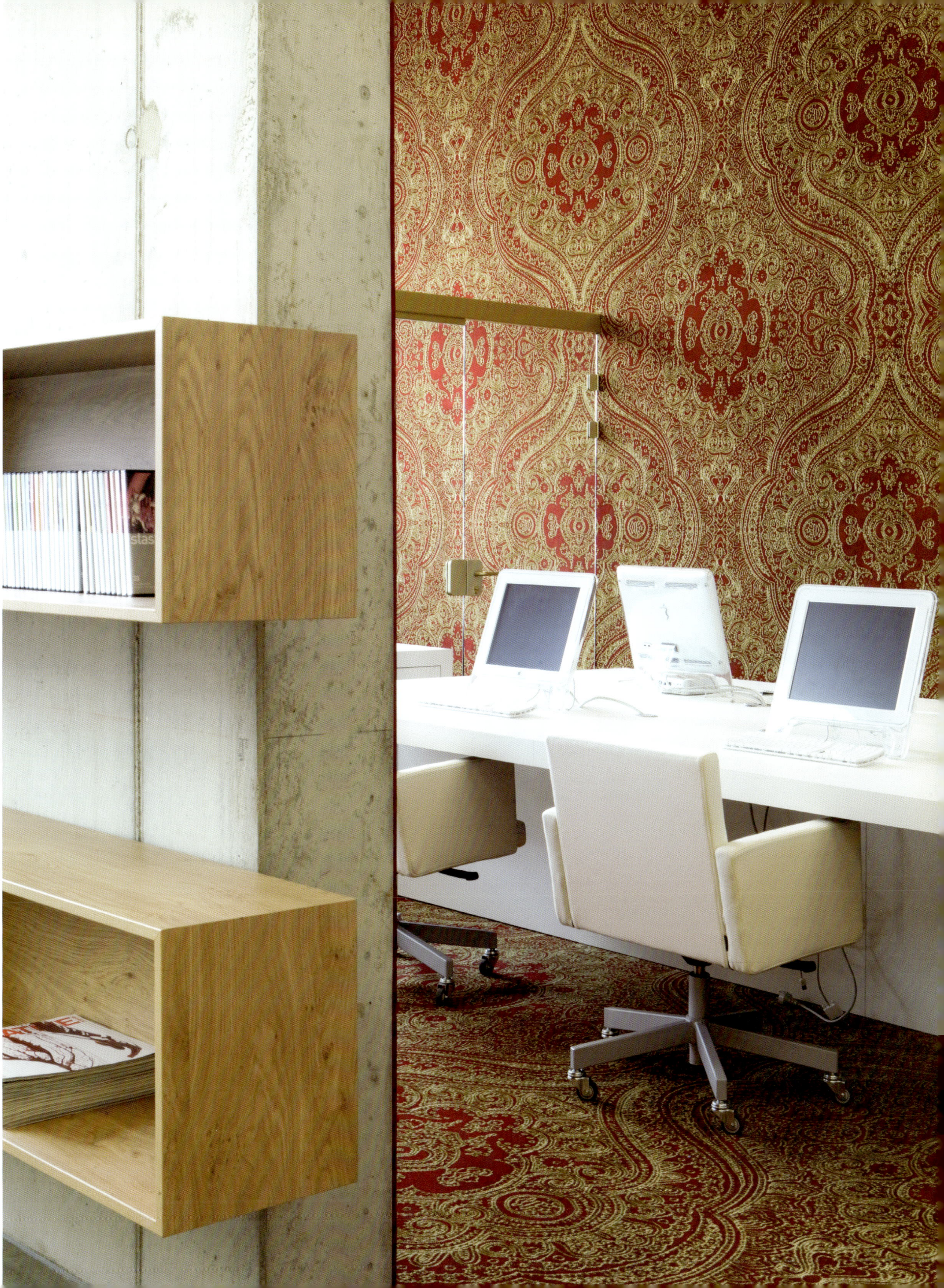

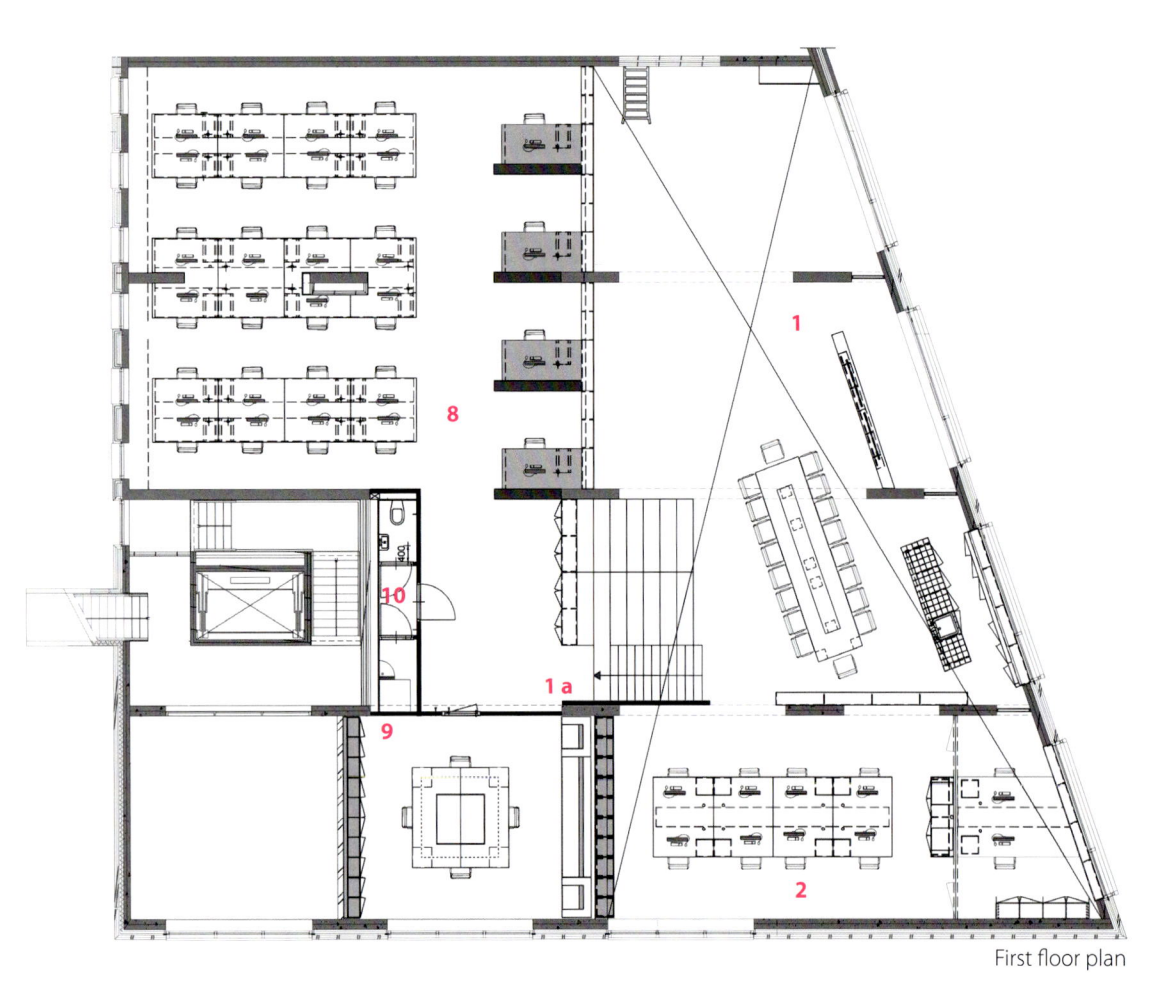

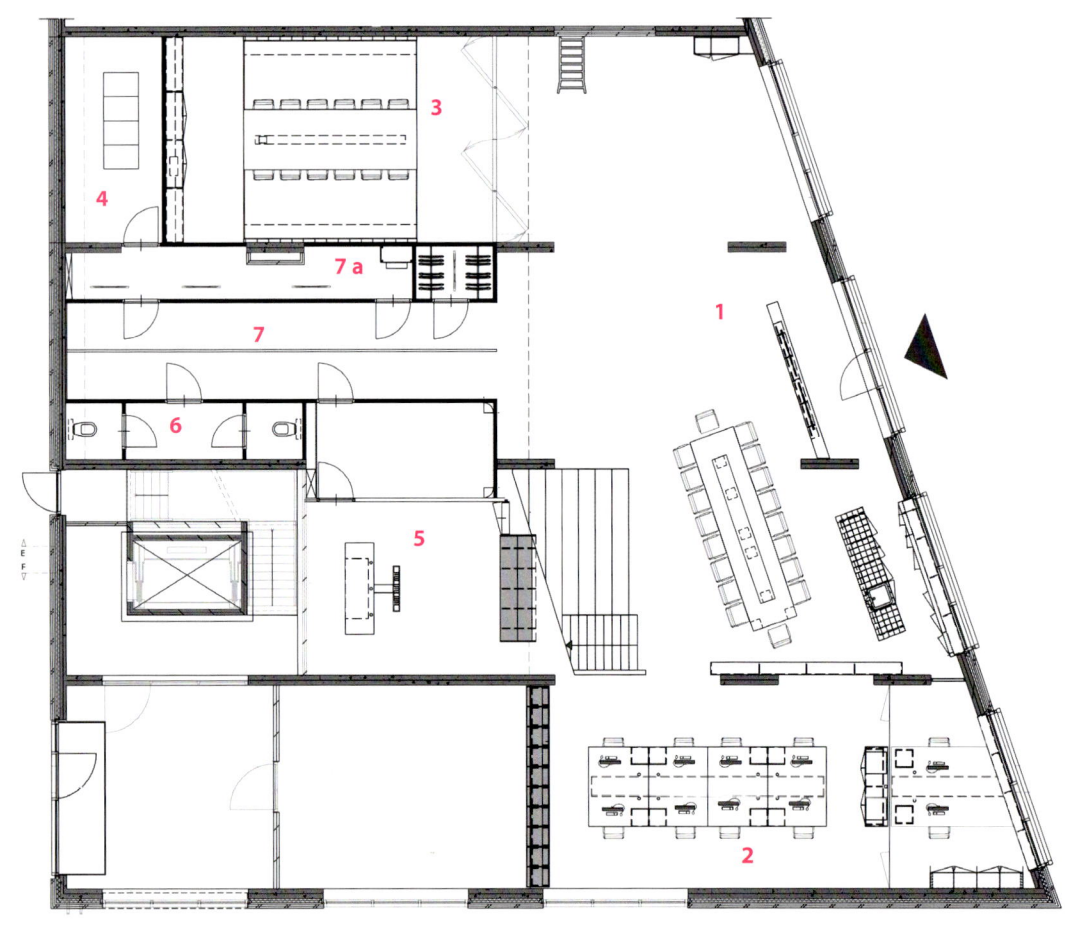

1. Entrance
1a. Stairs/tribune
2. Production area
3. Meeting room
4. Server room
5. Editing room
6. Toilet
7. Corridor
7a. Storage room
8. Studio 2D/3D
9. Office Mischa/Jules
10. Toilets/shower room

First floor plan

Ground floor plan

Parallel to the façade but diagonally placed, the 16-seater (5m x 1.20m) table meant for reading and dining has a hollow middle to store books and magazines. Bar, grandstand, table and screen provide the office's 'recreation zone'. Occasionally the employees can sit on the grandstand, beer in hand, enjoying a film or a match.

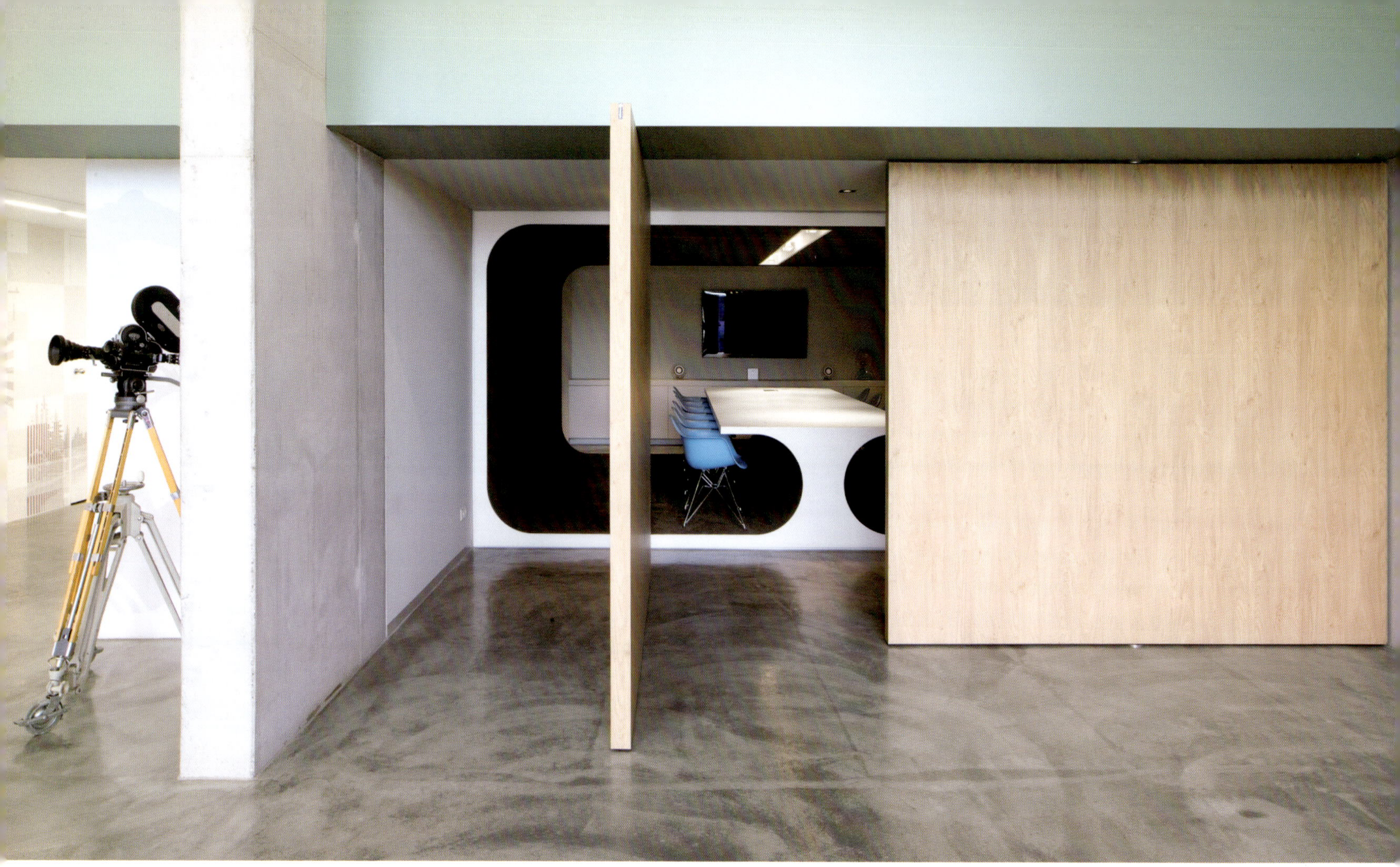

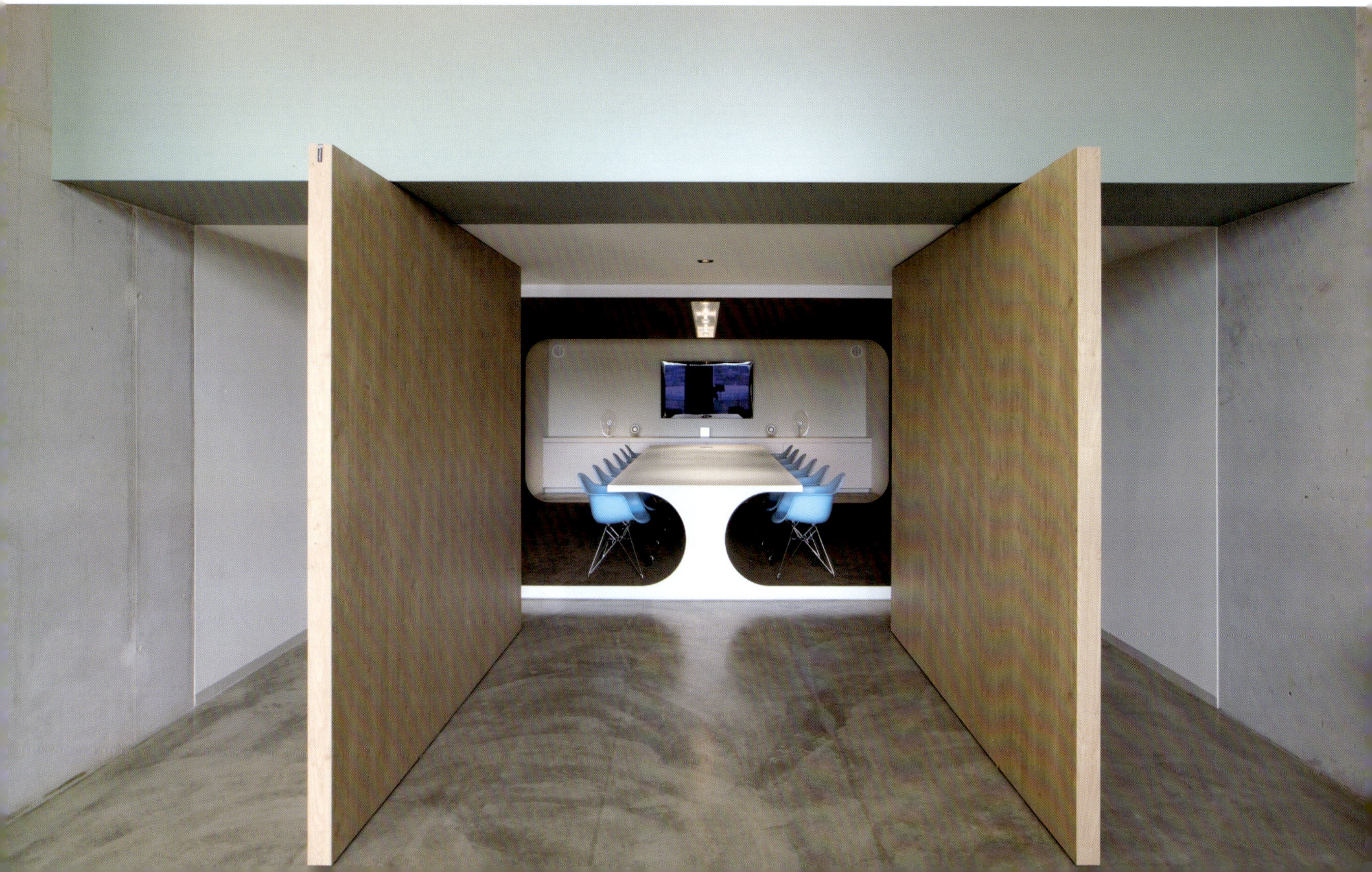

Large pivoting wooden doors separate the meeting room from the hall. Carpeted as a single object, the fluid lines of the floor, walls and table create a futuristic grotto.

165

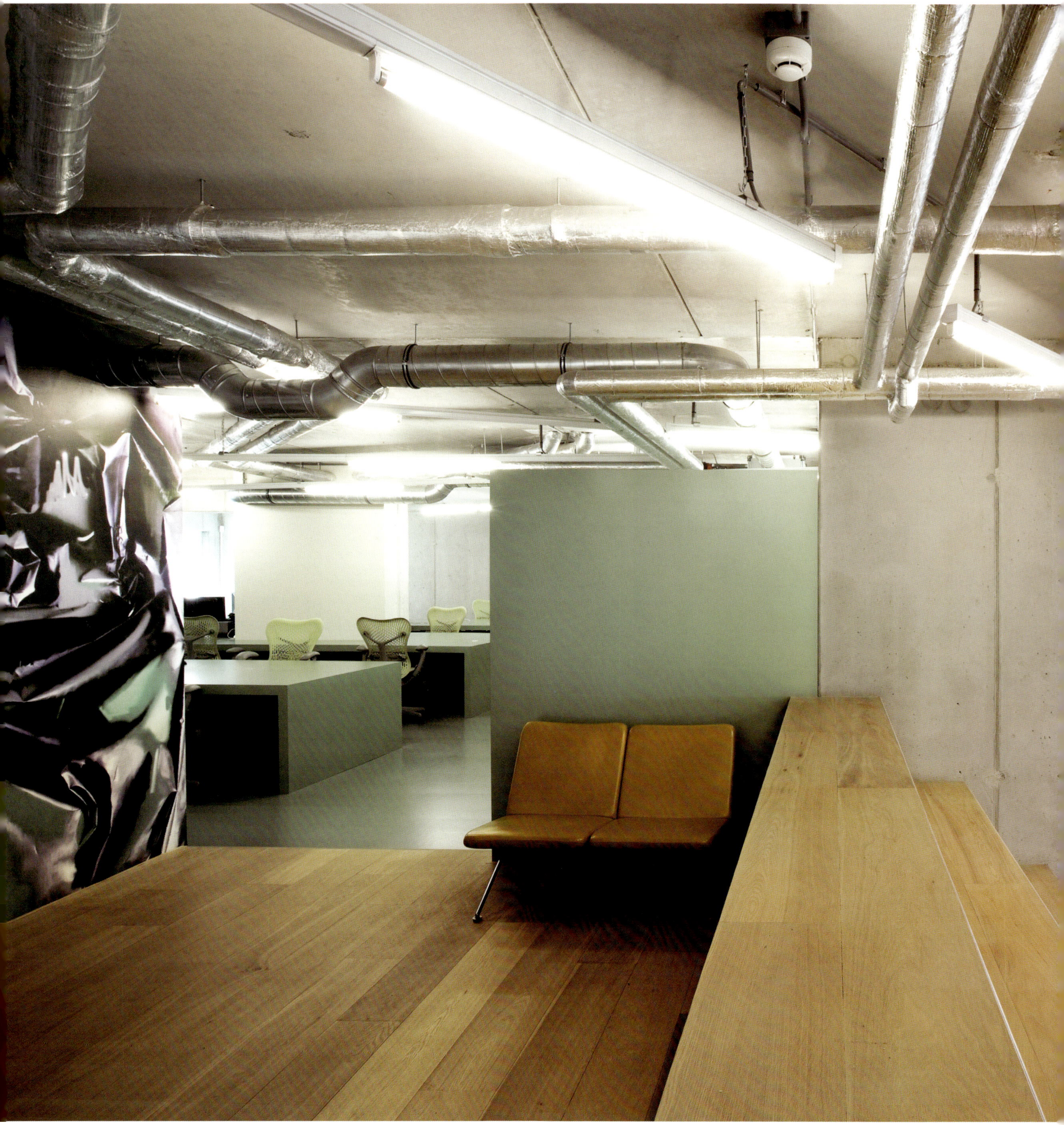

The First floor houses the staff room and the design studio on opposite sides of the landing. Landing and grandstand, both in oak, form one integrated object. The steps continue above the landing level, forming a cupboard to house the beamer. The balustrade over the entire width visually connects the different areas.

The studio on the mezzanine houses three large tables, with eight workplaces each. Floors, walls, and balustrade are all the same quiet shade of green. The balustrade contains cupboards. Storing employees' computers in trolleys under the tables makes it easy to vary the work-teams.

i29 l interior architects

Herengracht Office

Amsterdam, the Netherlands   Photographs: i29 l interior architects

The board of directors of an investment group in capital stock wanted to have what they described as a 'power office'. i29 l interior architects and Eckhardt&Leeuwenstein, the two design teams which collaborated on this project, decided to achieve this by placing every board member in the spotlight in a playful way.

The design of all three boardrooms and the lounge are firmly submitted to an overall design concept. Large round lampshades, spray-painted gold on the inside, seem to cast oval areas of light and shade throughout the entire space. This playful pattern of golden ovals contrasts with the angular cabinets and desks, which are executed in black stained ash wood. On the floor the oval forms continue by using light and dark gray carpet. Also, these ovals define the separate working areas.

In the lounge area, the white marble flooring combines with the light/shadow patterns that continue in the silver fabrics which cover the bar and benches. This area can be used for presentations or social working, with an integrated flat screen in the bar and data connections in all the pieces of furniture. The existing space is set in a 17th century historic building, facing one of the most famous canals of Amsterdam, the 'de gouden bocht'. All existing ornaments and details are painted in white.

The keynotes for this company are money and power. The design concept expresses this by setting all the members of the board literally under the spotlights. The golden and silver ovals slice through the spaces like golden coins. Which is what it is all about in the world of investment and stock trading.

Architecture:
i29 l interior architects / eckhardt&leeuwenstein architects
Constructor:
Van Zoelen bv
Cabinet maker:
Jehago bv
Commission:
Interior design boardrooms, head office of an investment group
Materials:
Stained ash wood, spray-painted MDF gold/silver, perforated steel, white marble, and plastering.
Area:
2,580 sqft (240 sqm)

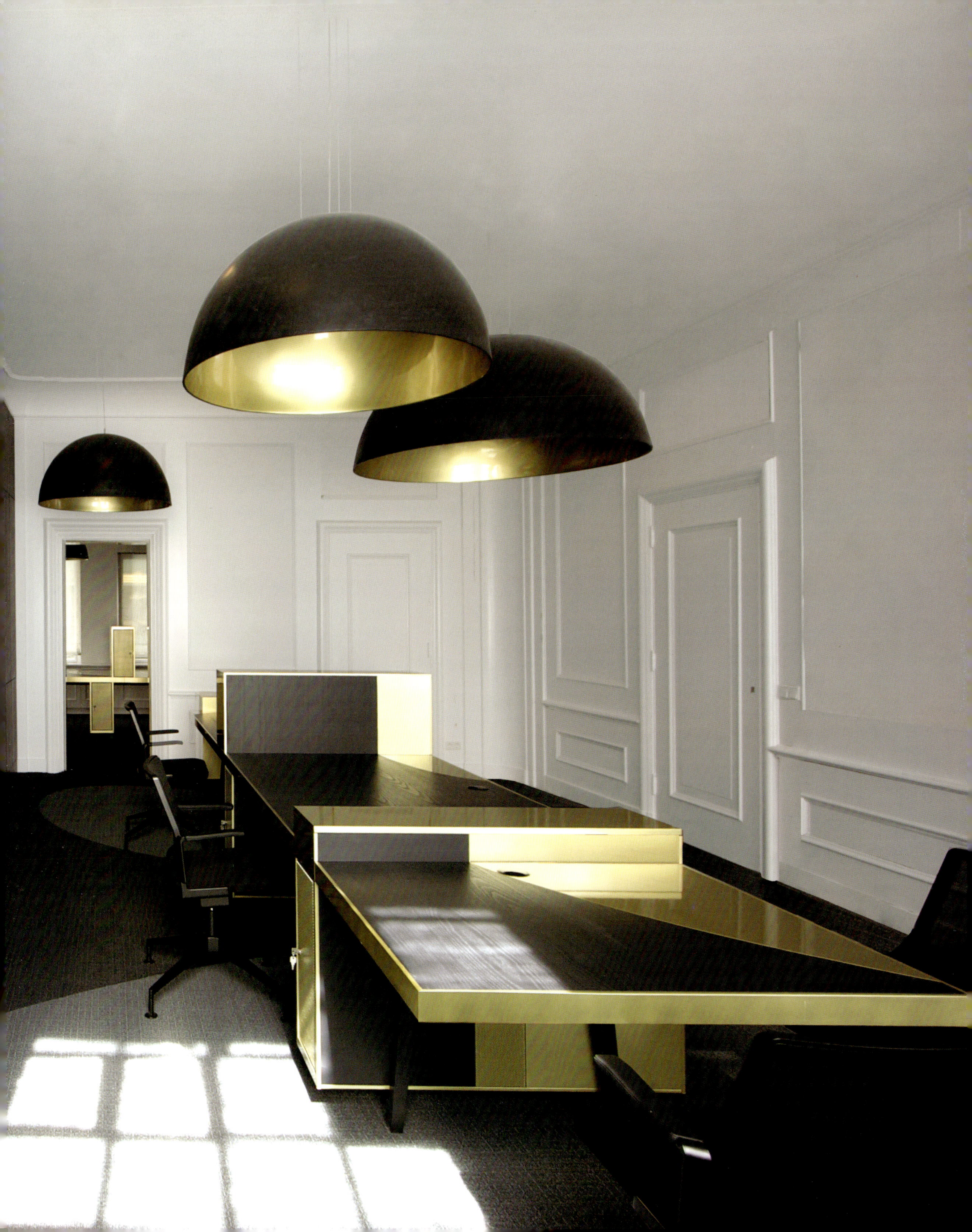

The leitmotiv for the entire composition of this investment group's head office is the theme of the spotlight; this suggests fun and suggests gold, but at another level it also suggests seeing what may be invisible for others; it suggests the knowledge and power the enterprise intends to represent.

By playfully representing the difference between light and shadow in a variety of materials, from the carpeting to the upholstery or the wall-cladding, an element of fun, creativity and relaxation is allowed to permeate the otherwise heavy atmosphere that is customary in a financial context.

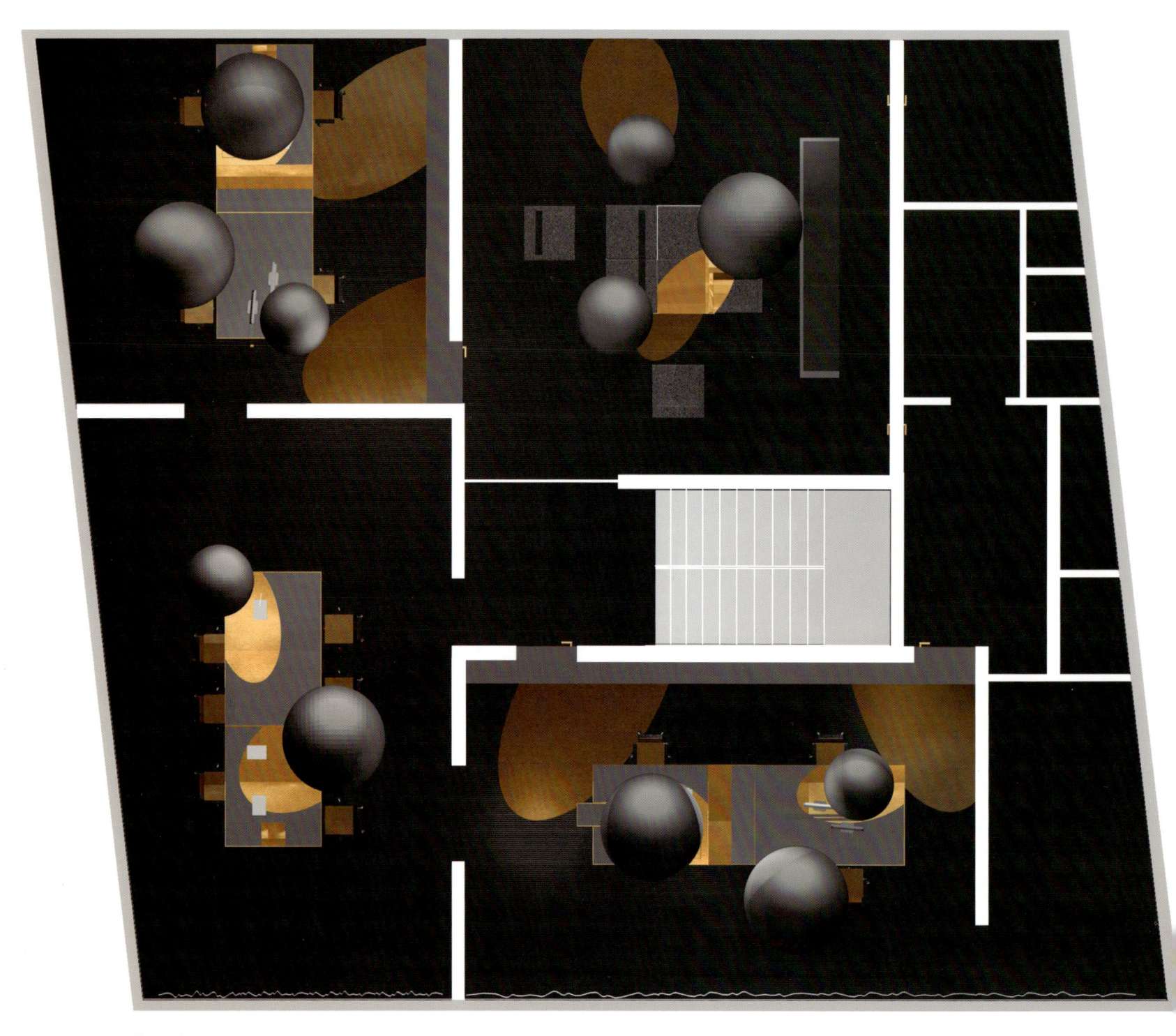

Floor plan

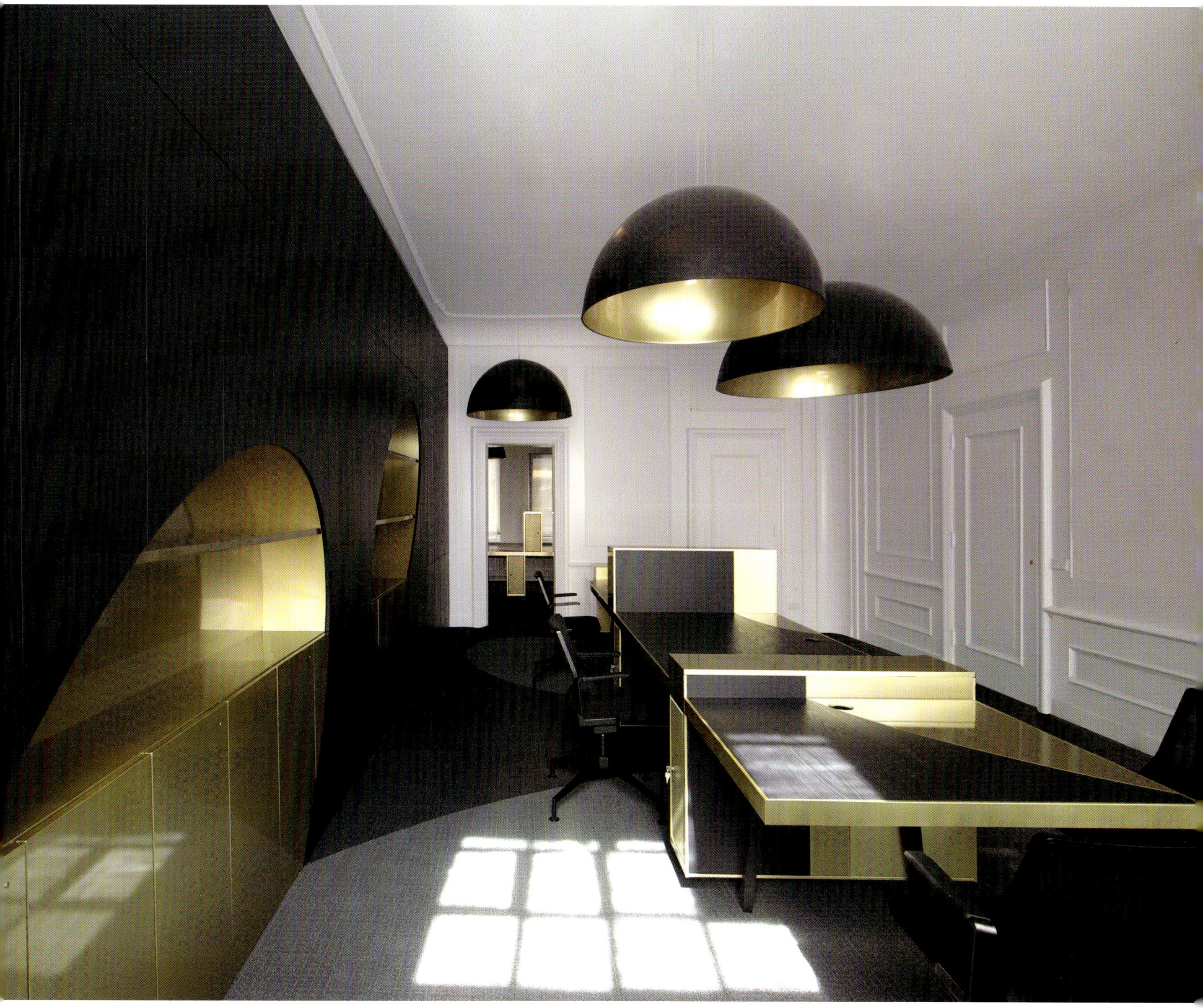

4300

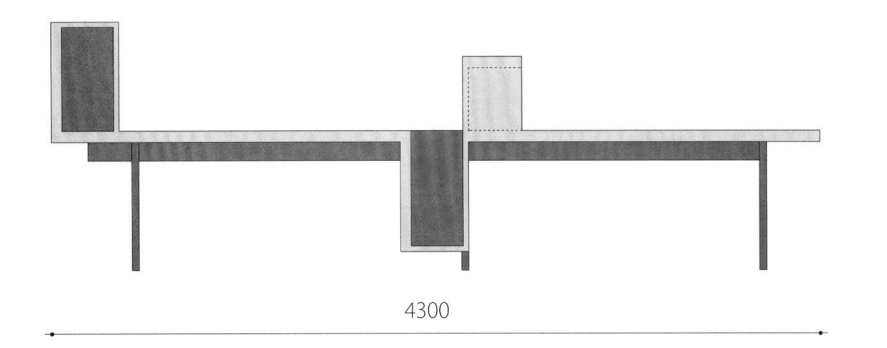

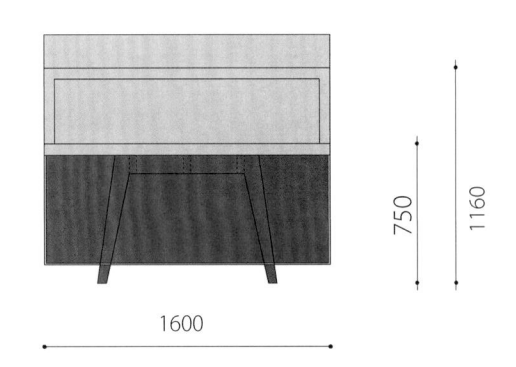

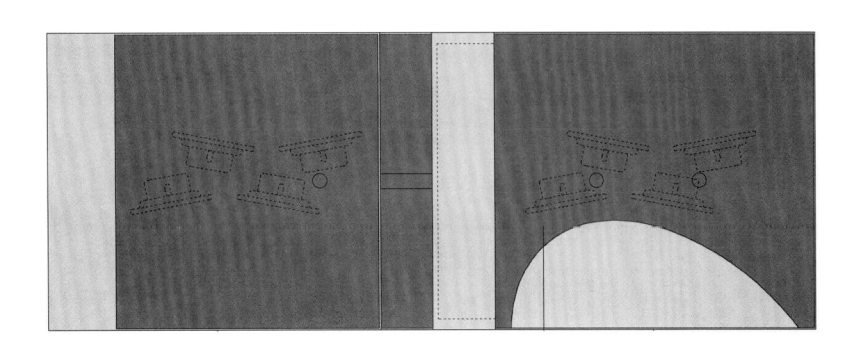

1600

750
1160

Office desk A

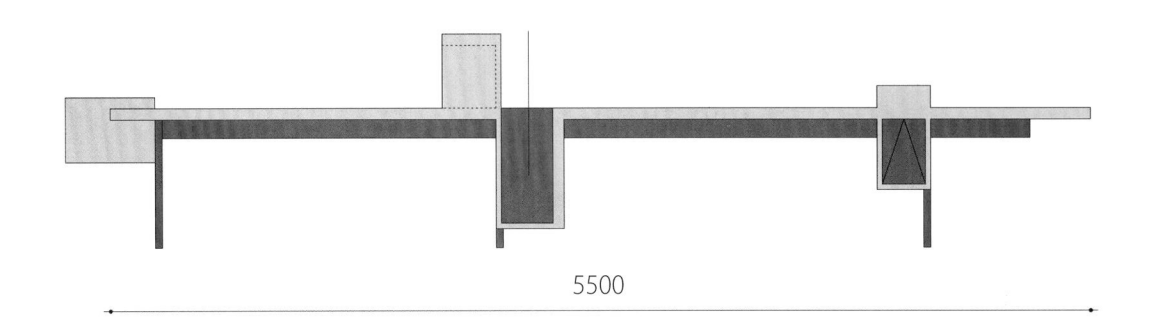

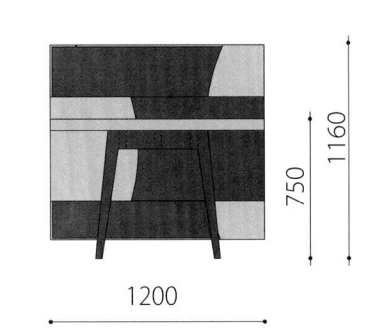

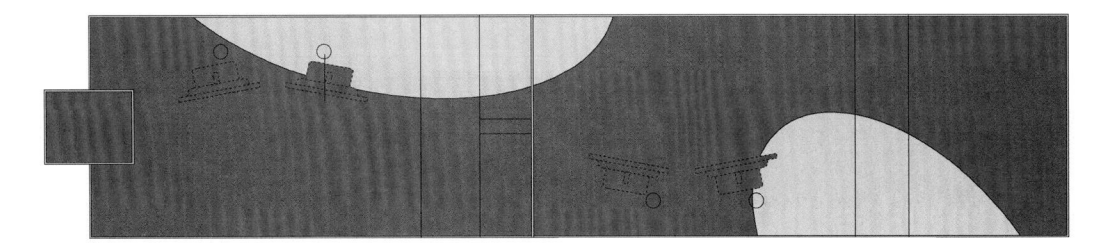

5500

1200

750
1160

Office desk B

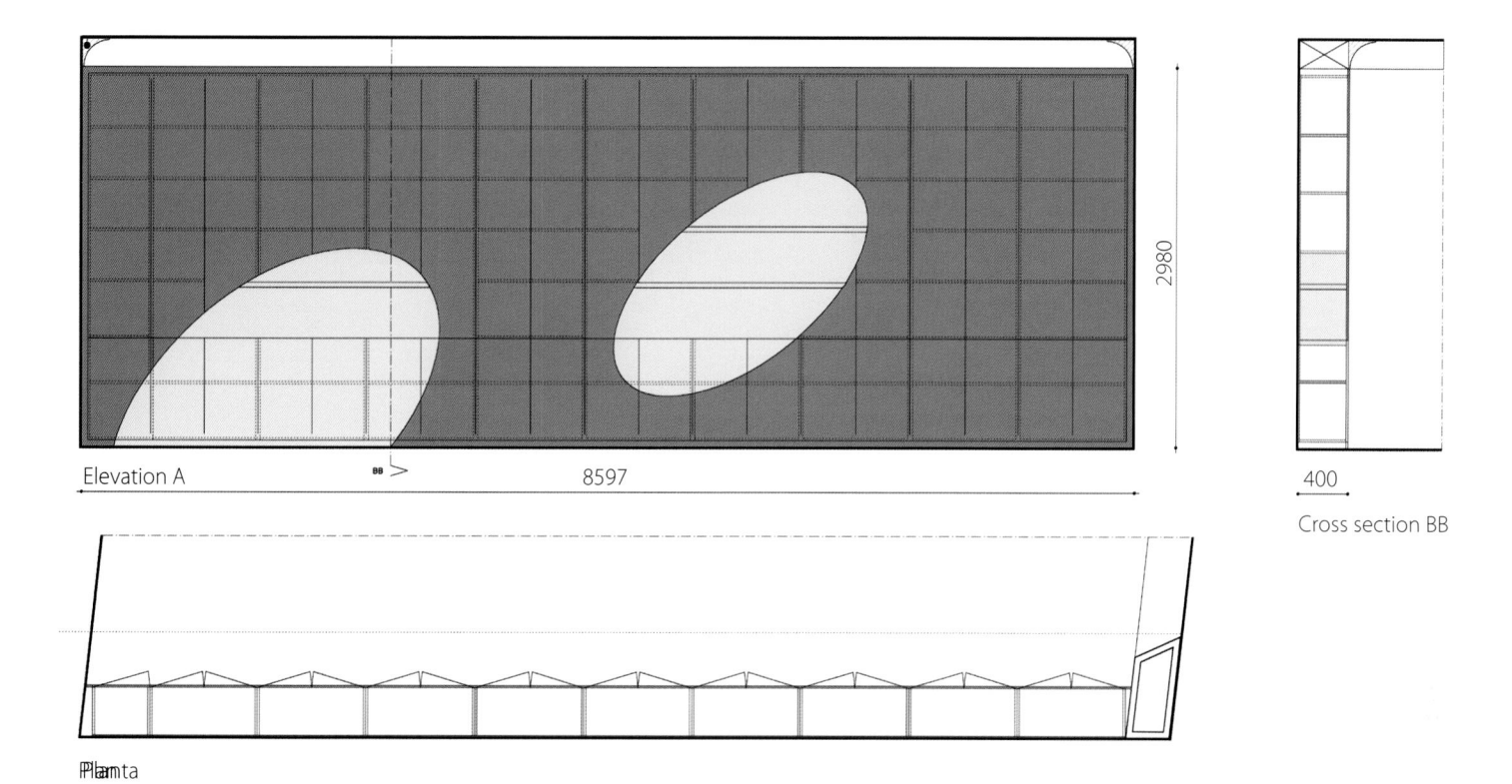

Elevation A — 8597 — 2980

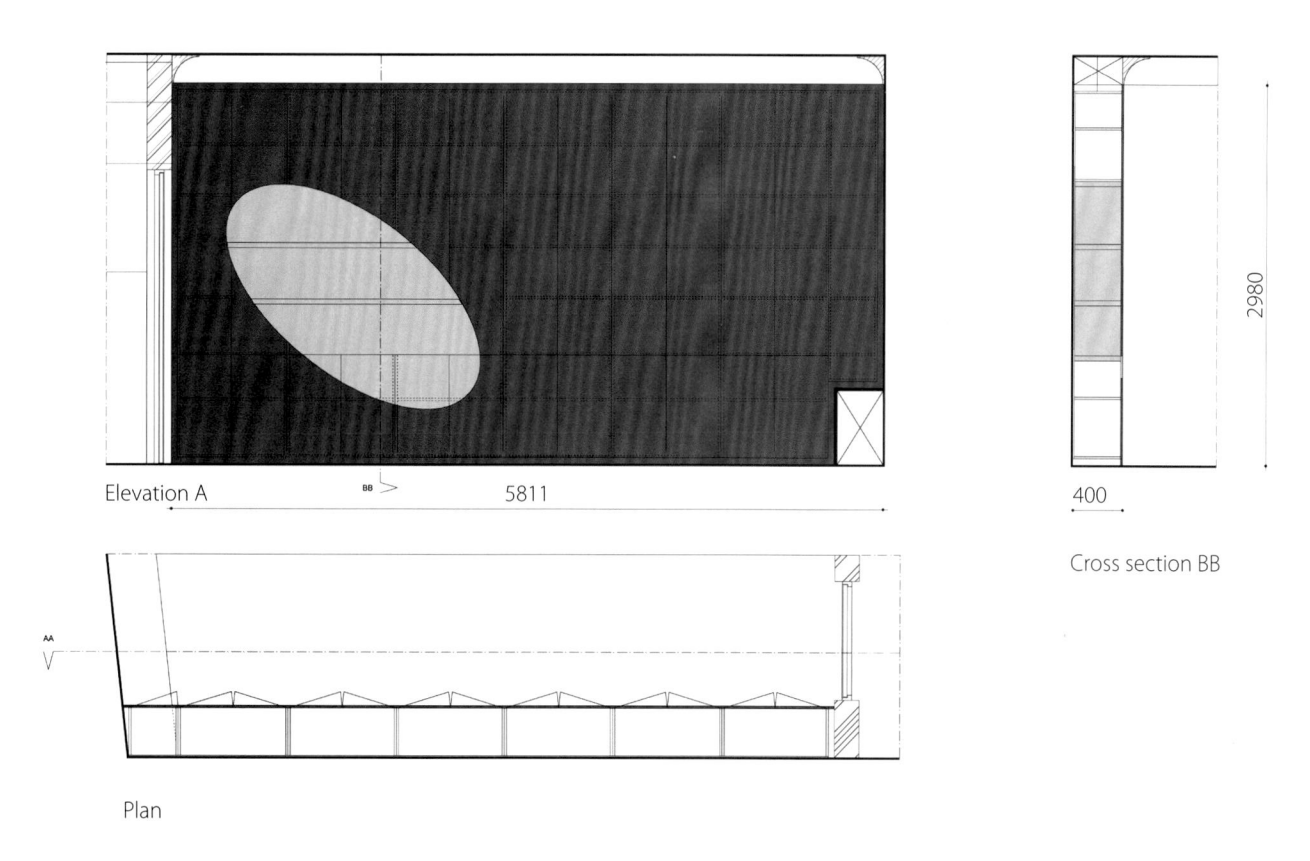

Cross section BB — 400

Plan

Elevation A — 5811 — 2980

Cross section BB — 400

Plan

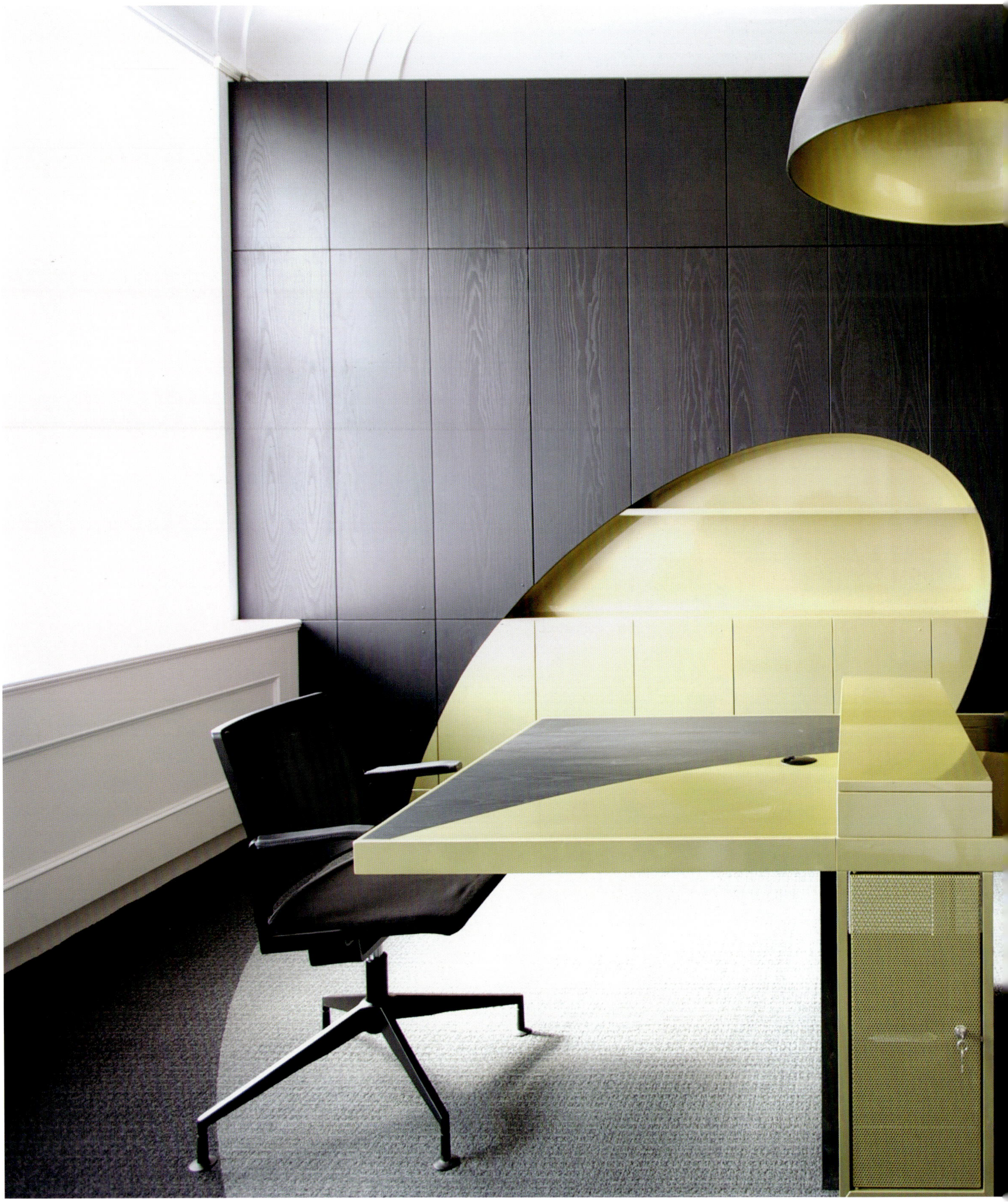

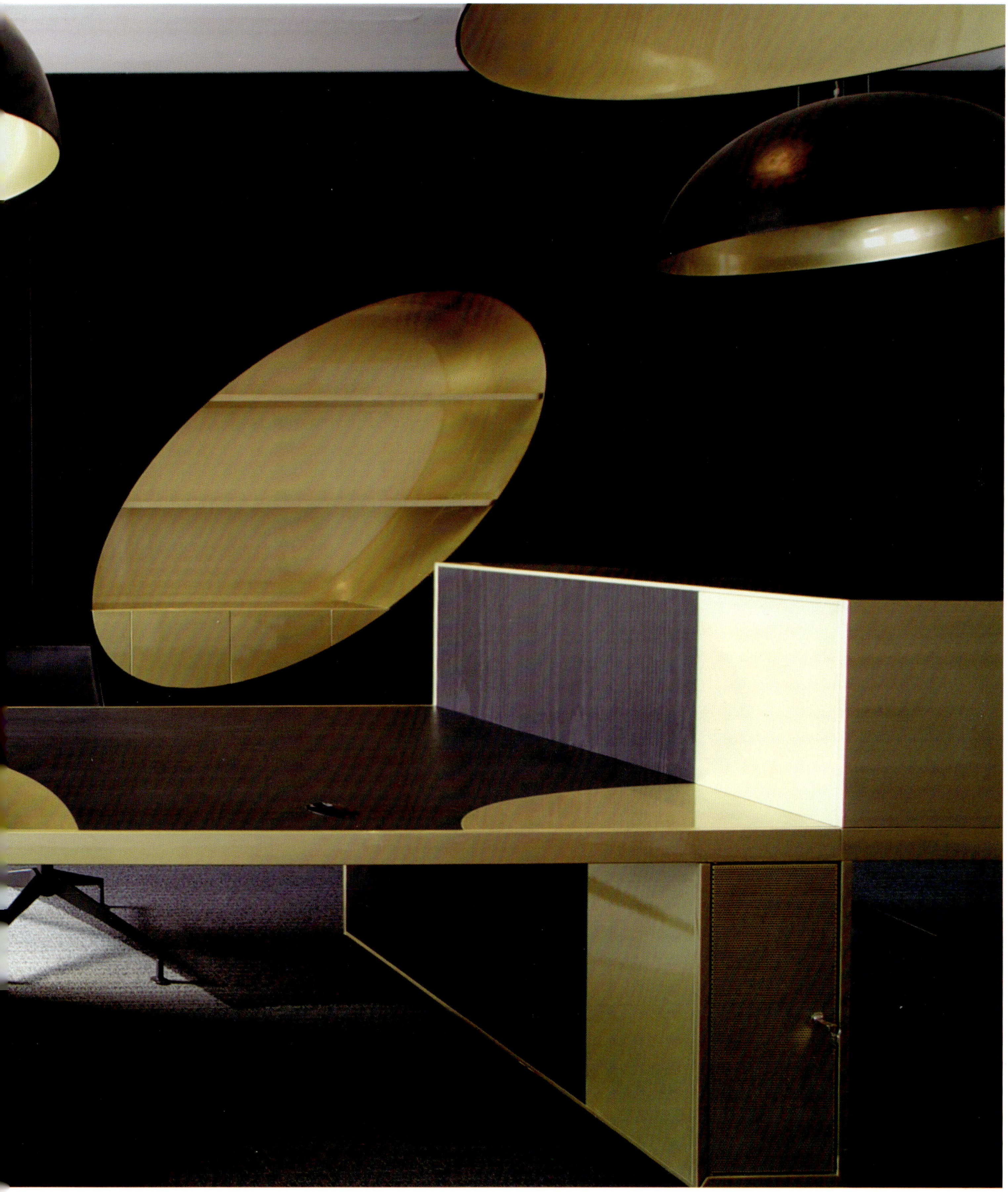

eins:eins architekten

Syzygy agency

Hamburg, Germany **Photographs: Studio Uwe Gärtner**

The Hamburg-based architecture firm, eins:eins architekten, developed and completed the interior design for the well-established European marketing agency Syzygy in downtown Hamburg, Germany. Syzygy moved its central offices into a monumental building located on a prominent corner in the immediate vicinity of Hamburg's town hall.

The clients envisaged a working environment in which all employees would be seated together at a single desk. eins:eins architekten took this idea to another level and developed an item of furniture that allows all employees to effectively sit "in" a single desk.

The single desk-units can be arranged in various configurations but always result in a whole. This allows a great variety of arrangements, which would be impossible to achieve with conventional desks. The major benefits of this innovative office furnishing is that it can establish a highly communicative constellation of workstations, and, in addition, presents an opportunity to furnish oddly shaped spaces, which may otherwise be hard to utilize.

The design of the work space is based on both clear and pure lines. The white surface of the desktop contrasts sharply with the furniture's dark brown body and thus underlines its soft contours. The assembled desk measures a generous 3.2 x 17 m (10.5 x 56 ft). Office chairs in an array of bold colors represent a stimulating addition to the otherwise brown and white decor.

The amorphous textile ceiling is sound-absorbent and features an integrated lighting system. It emphasizes the impression of being seated in one snug enveloping piece of furniture.

Architecture:
eins:eins architekten
Christoph Roselius & Julian Hillenkamp

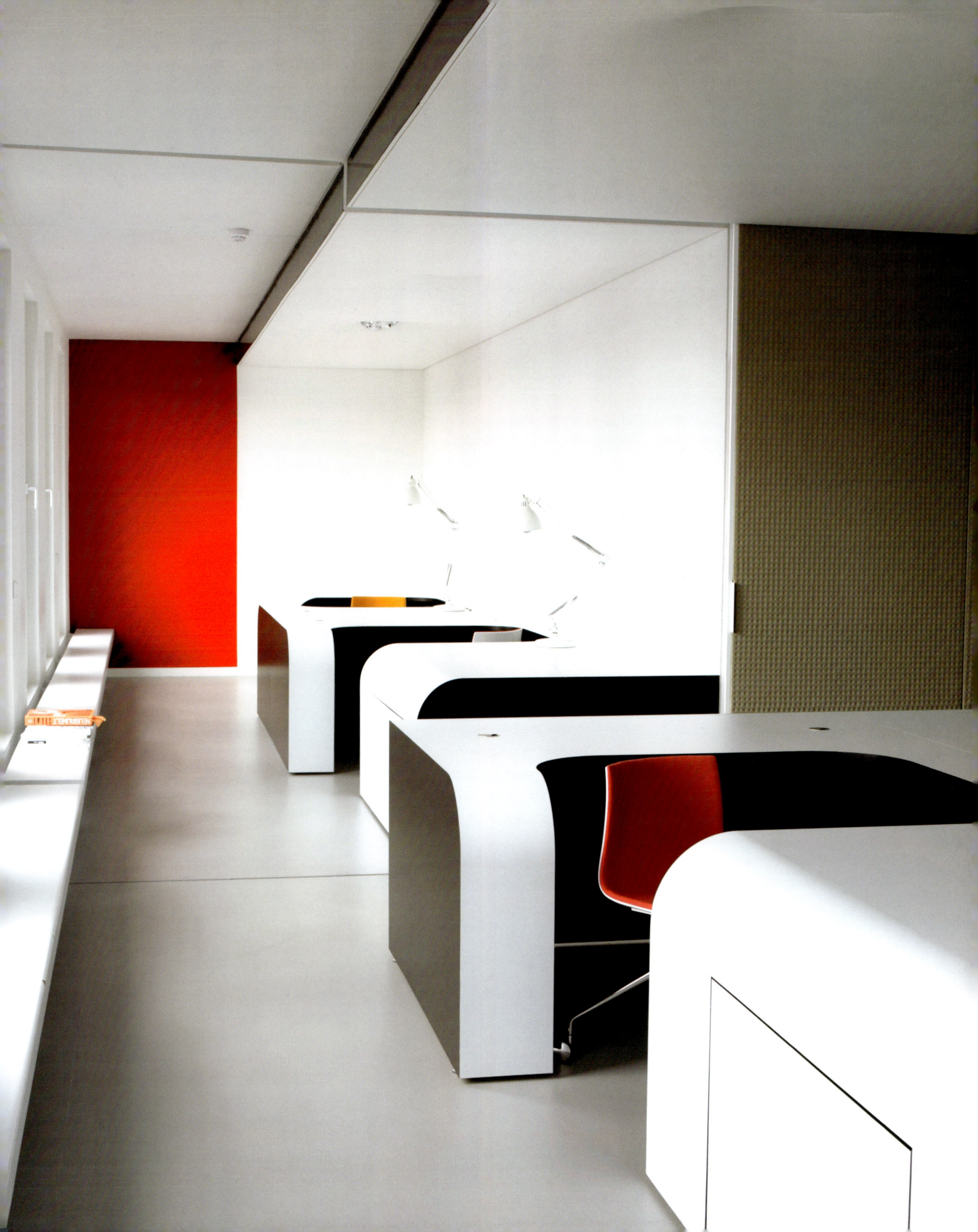

The individual workstations fit together to create a single piece of furniture that molds itself to the form of the office.

Clean lines afford a sense of order and generate a calm working environment, which is conducive to both concentration and the exchange of ideas.

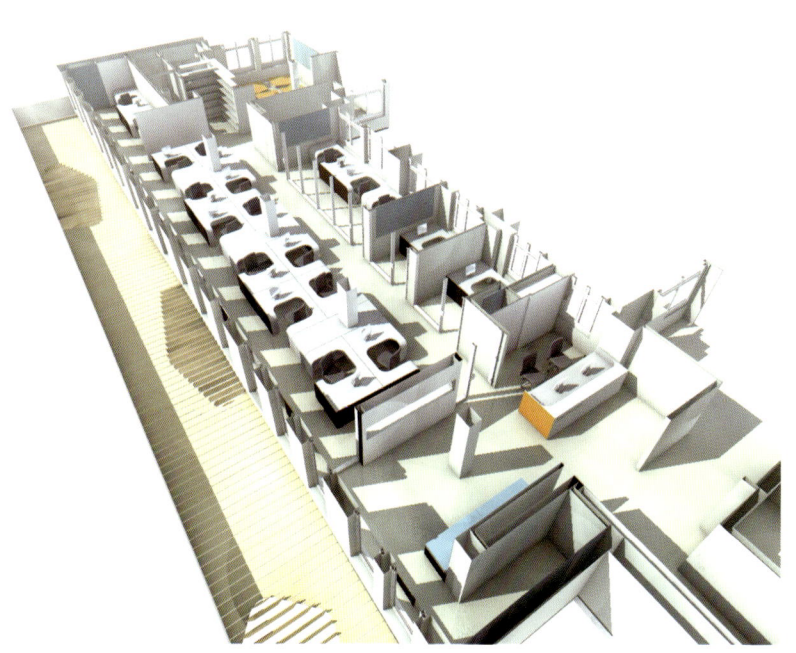

182

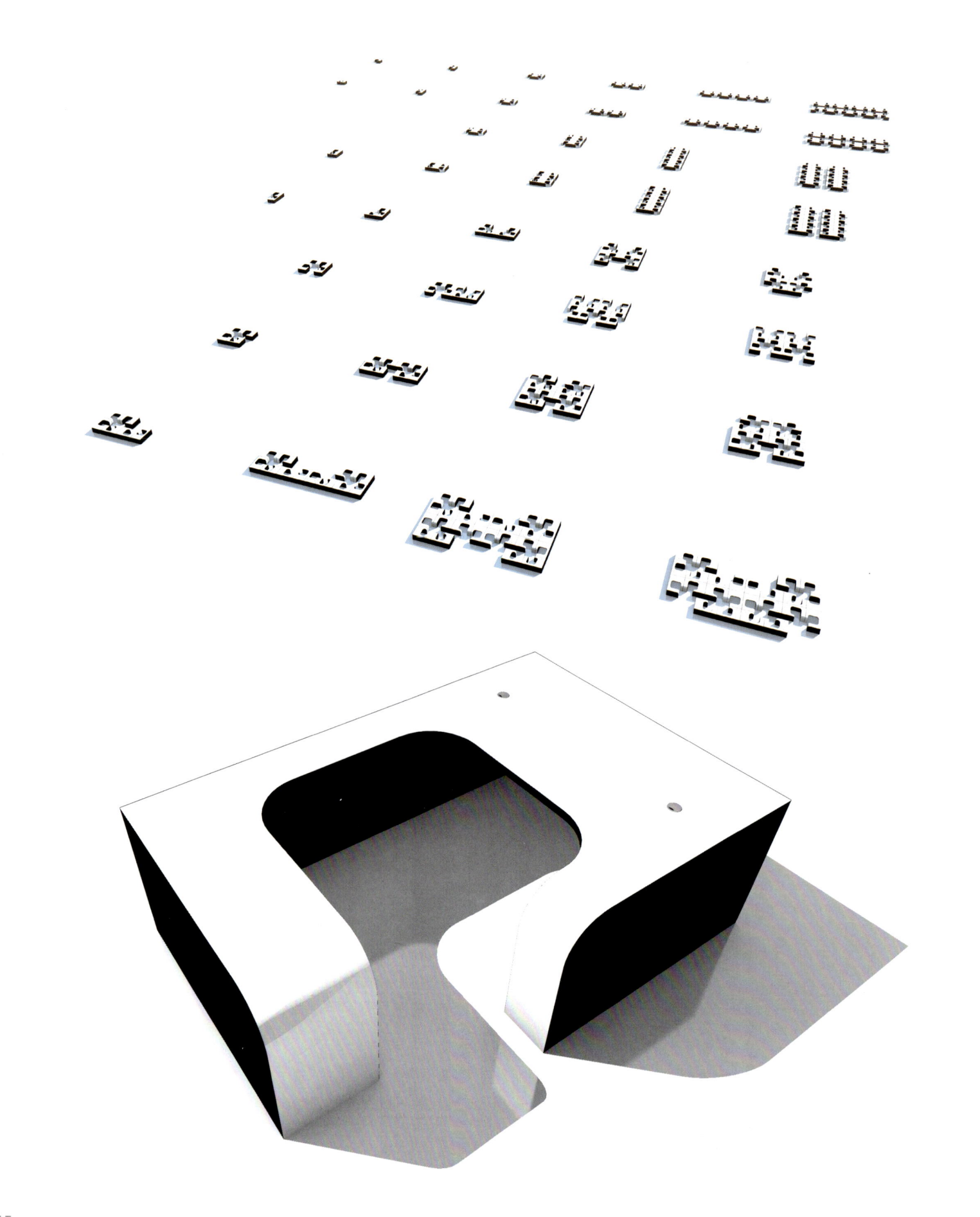

183

DEGW

Ericsson Telecommunications

Rome, Italy   Photographs: contributed by DEGW

The client's brief defined the Ericsson Experience Center (EEC) as a flexible space designed to experience new facilities and solutions that anticipate the future of telecommunications. The center will show-case the conjunction of innovation with Ericsson's established tradition.

To resolve the project a curved sign was inserted to organize and integrate the various functions it is required to contain. The ease with which this can be reconfigured will guarantee more comfortable uses of the space for the various activities likely to take place there.

The determining position of the sanitary area and the length of the available space suggested its division into two zones:
- Reception area/ open lounge
- Demo and exhibition area.

Located on opposite sides of the sanitary facilities, both zones are conceived as multiple use areas. When there are no visitors, the reception area can also be used by the Ericsson personnel for their breaks. The Demo area is divided into 4 zones, each dedicated to a particular theme, though it can also be used as an auditorium or TV studio. One side of the space is characterized by the "Memory wall", where glazed niches display historic Ericsson products.

The project achieves a strong integration of technology with design. The Swedish brand's warm and human corporate imageis represented with the use of natural materials and light colors. The challenge was to humanize the space by implementing Hi-tech solutions.

The key to this project is that all the technology required for a centre like EEC has been located inside the gap between the original walls and the new envelope. The ceiling, the walls and the floating floor provide a seamless curtain that contains the technological infrastructure and reinstates the recognizable "Swedish look". The space is enlivened by soft tones, birch wood finishes and the fluid uninterrupted spatial arrangement, making it emotionally reassuring. The branding and the communicative aspects of the project were studied in cooperation with Ericsson's marketing experts.

Architecture:
DEGW
Project architect:
Giuseppe Pepe
Site supervisor and P.M.:
Sabina Arcieri
Interior designer:
Laura Duenas
Technical project:
Qprogetti

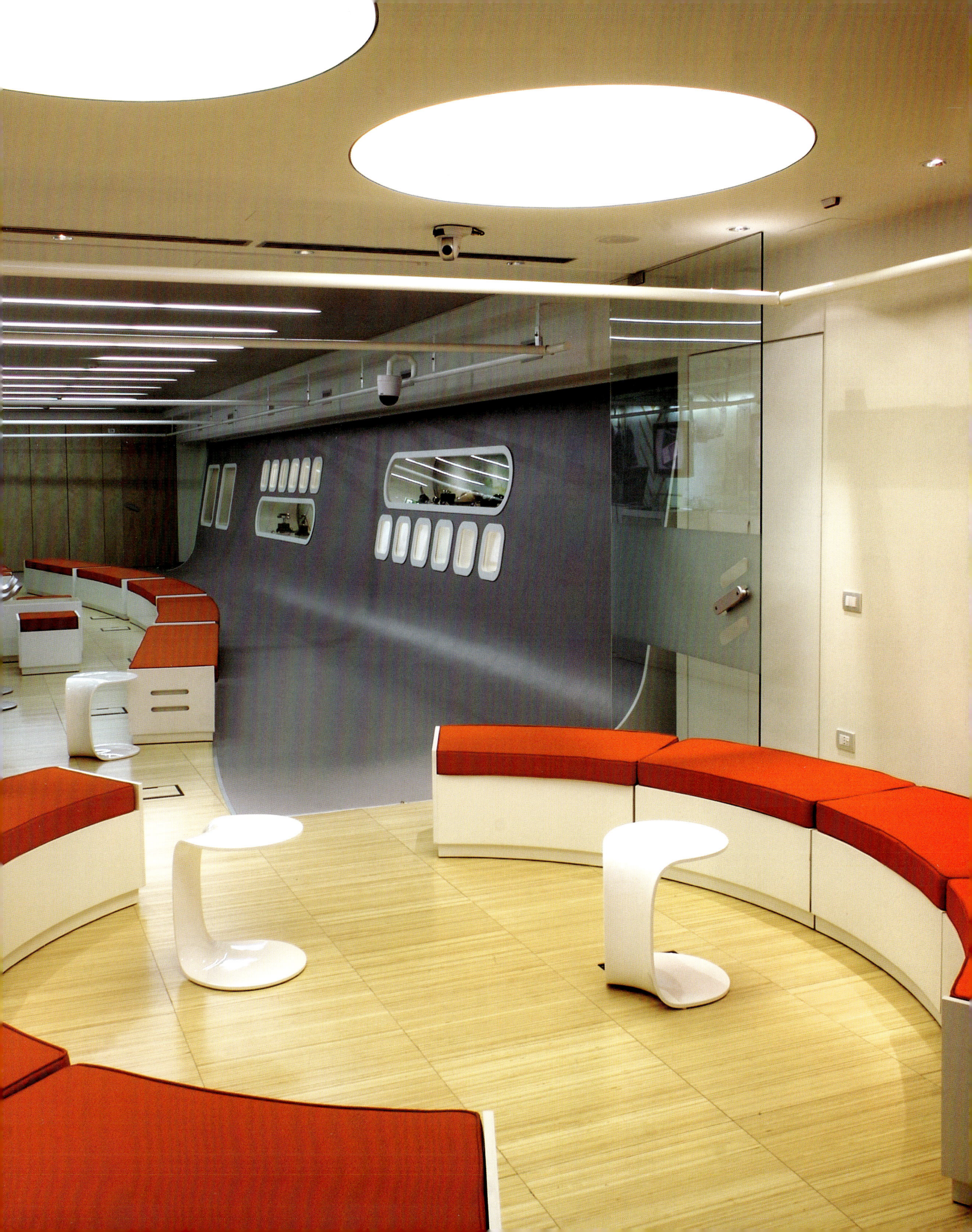

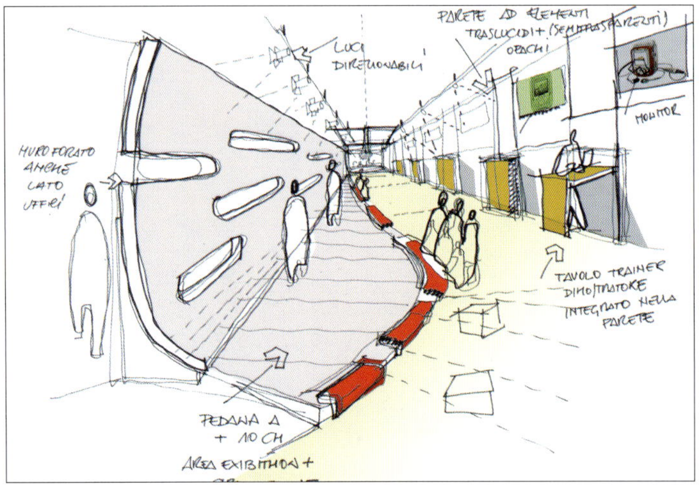
PARETE AD ELEMENTI TRASLUCIDI + (SEMITRASPARENTI) OPACHI
LUCI DIREZIONABILI
MURO FORATO ANCHE LATO UFFICI
MONITOR
TAVOLO TRAINER DEMO/MOTORE INTEGRATO NELLA PARETE
PEDANA Δ + 10 CM
AREA EXIBITHON +

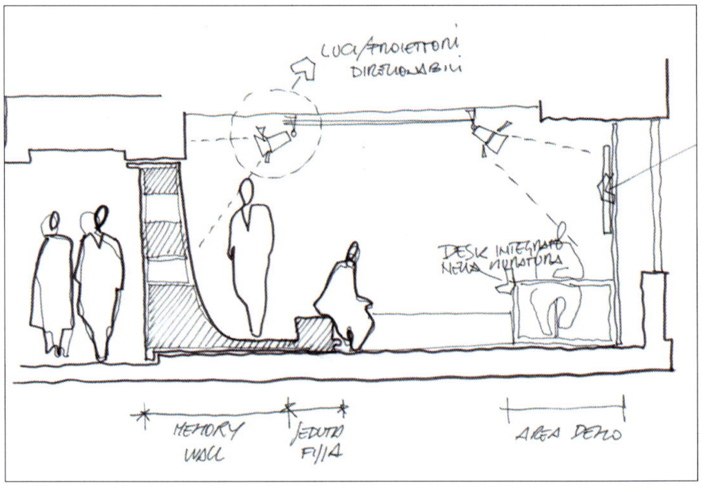
LUCI/PROIETTORI DIREZIONABILI
DESK INTEGRATO NELLA MURATURA
MEMORY WALL
SEDUTE FILA
AREA DEMO

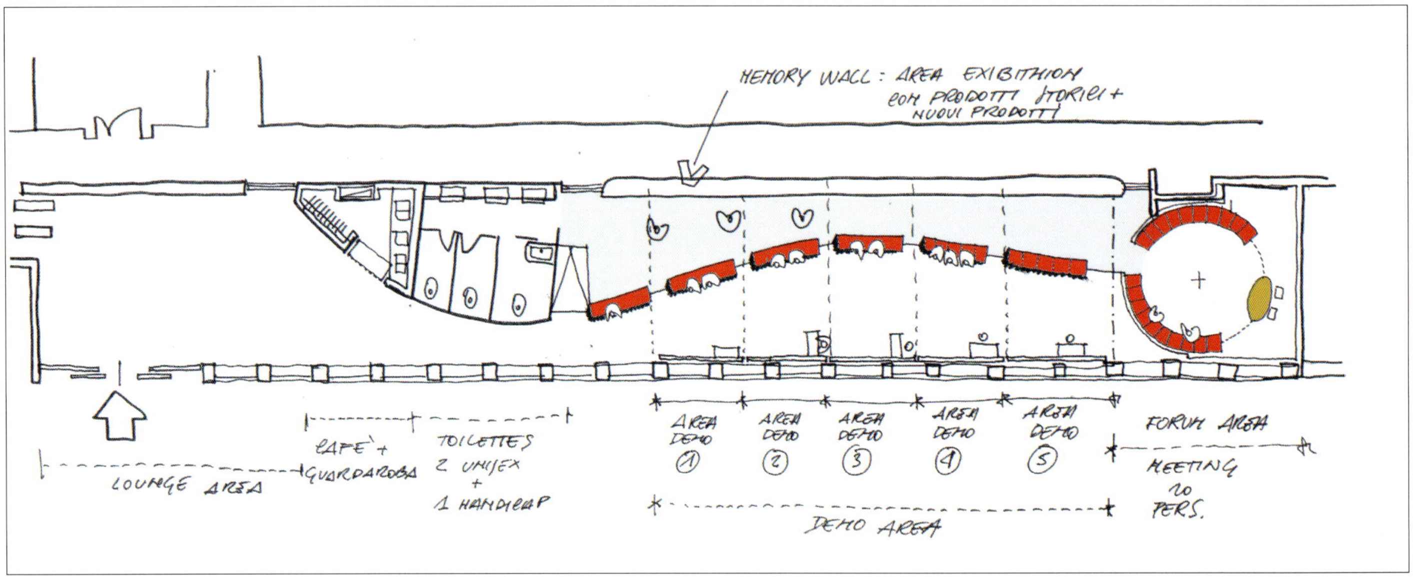
MEMORY WALL: AREA EXIBITHION CON PRODOTTI STORICI + NUOVI PRODOTTI
LOUNGE AREA
CAFE' + GUARDAROBA
TOILETTES 2 UNISEX + 1 HANDICAP
AREA DEMO 1
AREA DEMO 2
AREA DEMO 3
AREA DEMO 4
AREA DEMO 5
FORUM AREA
MEETING 20 PERS.
DEMO AREA

ERICSSON

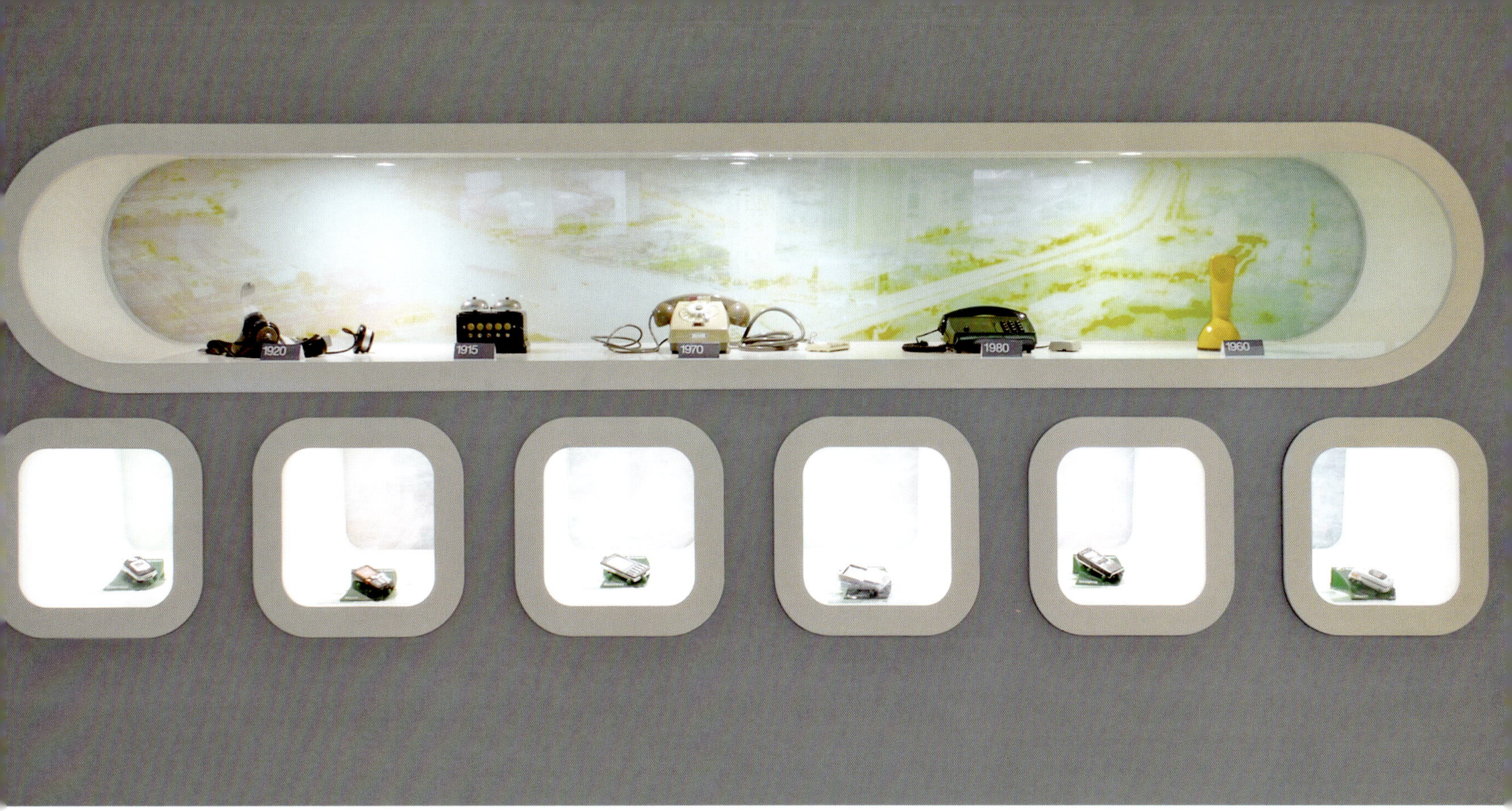
1920
1915
1970
1980
1960

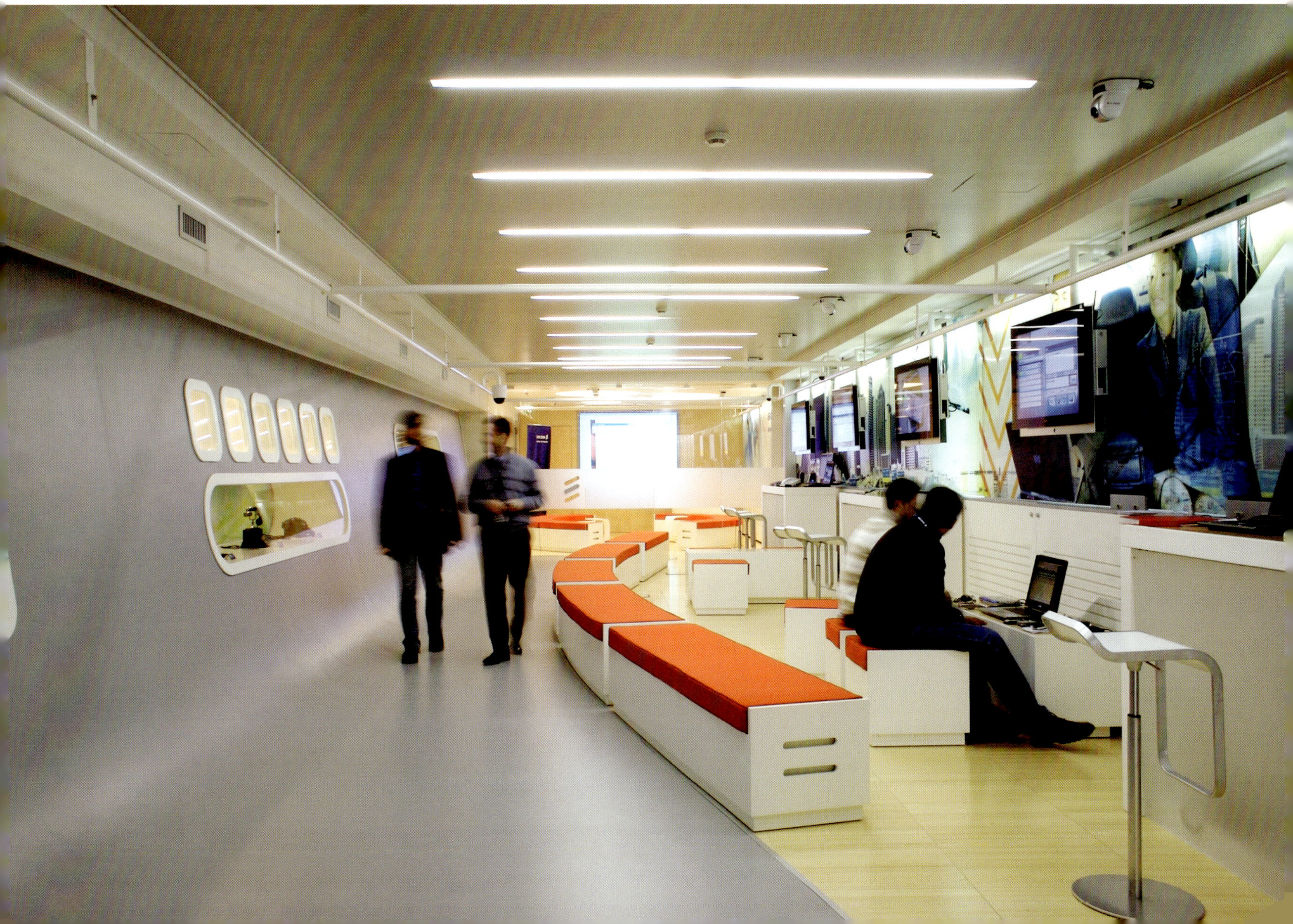

General floor plan

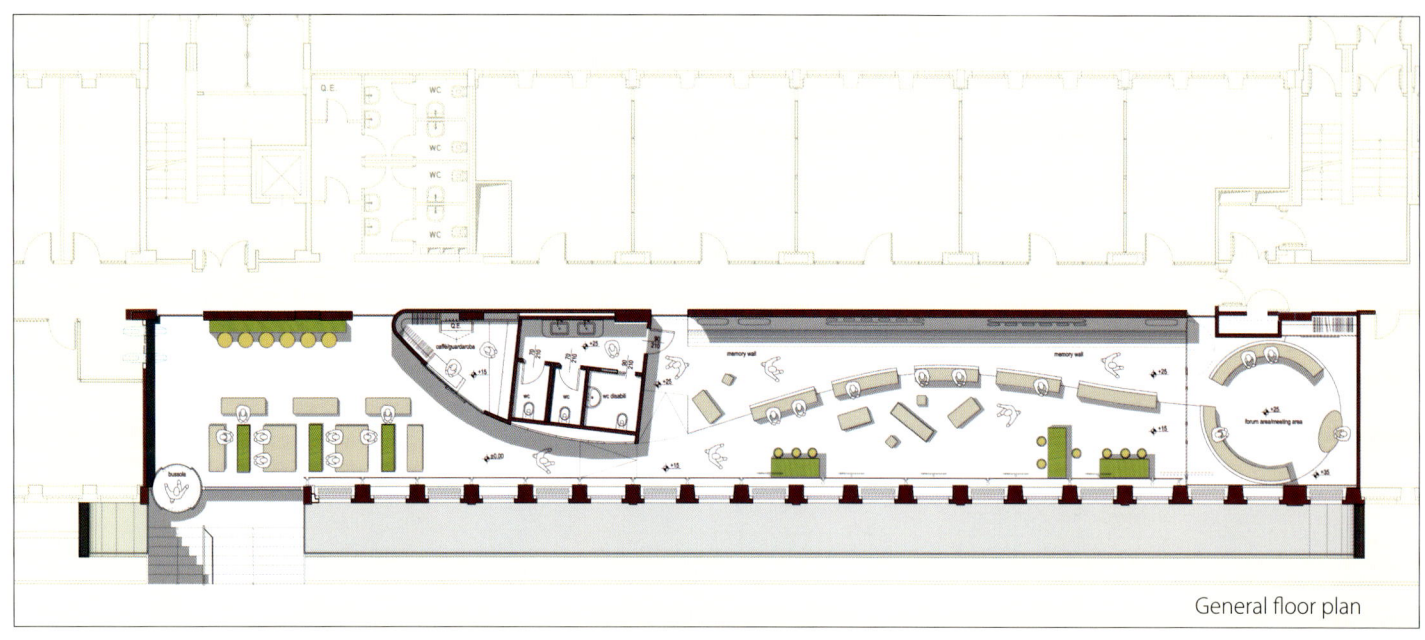

Ericsson Experience Center

To reconfigure the spaces every item was especially designed and built to measure, to allow for easy reconversions without having to call in a specialist, embodying the "do it yourself" attitude embodied by the Swedish furniture industry.

189

| AA section |
| BB section | DD section |
| CC section |

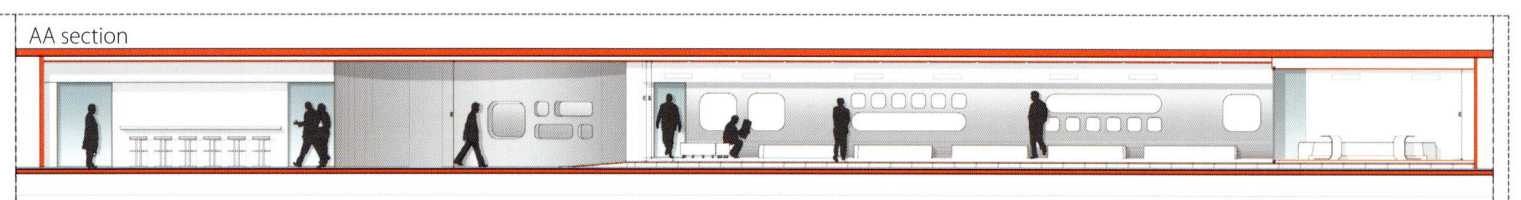

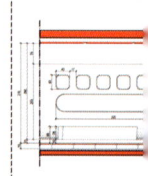

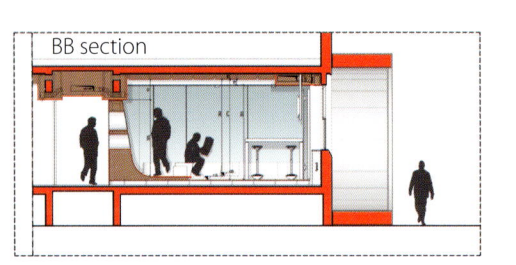

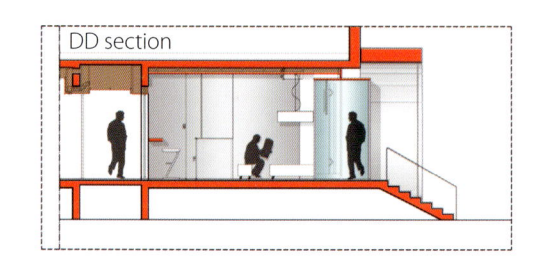

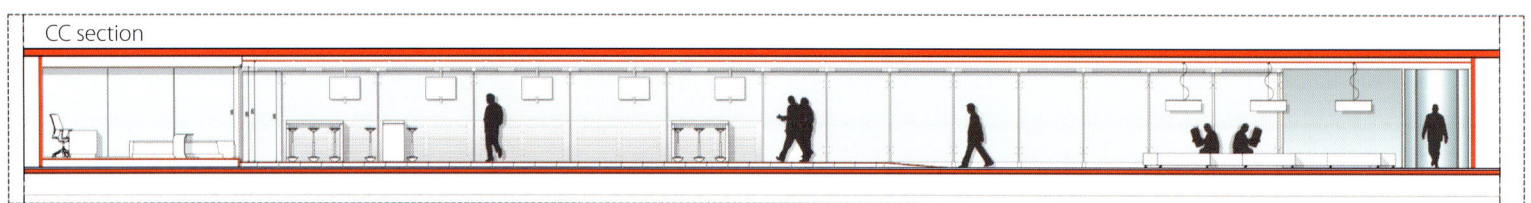

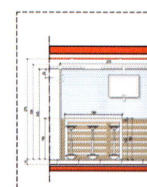

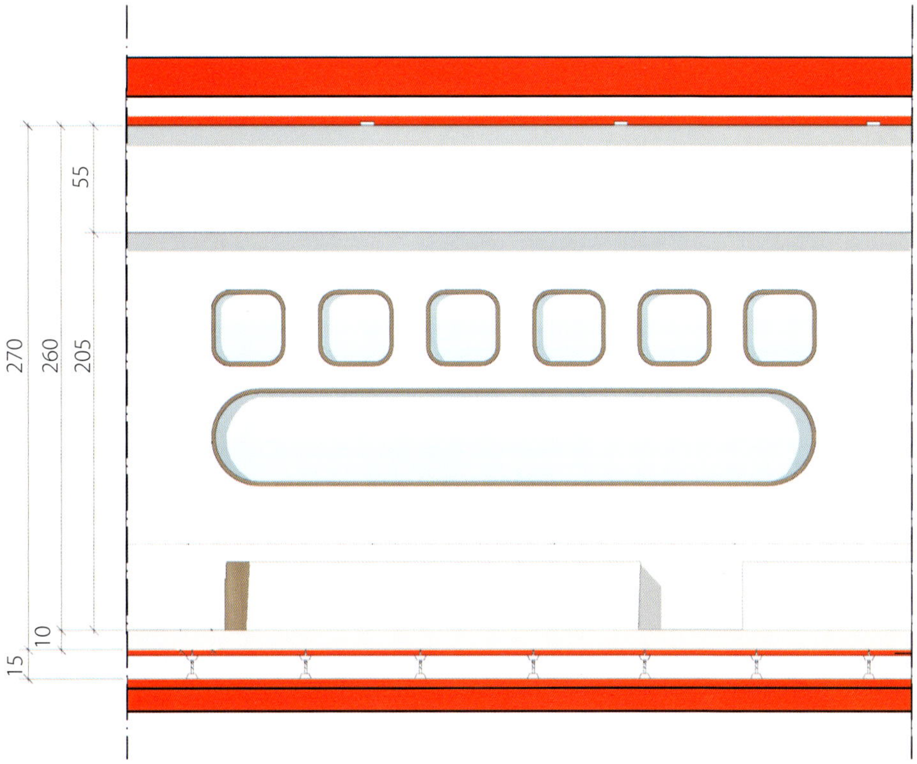
55
270
260
205
10
15

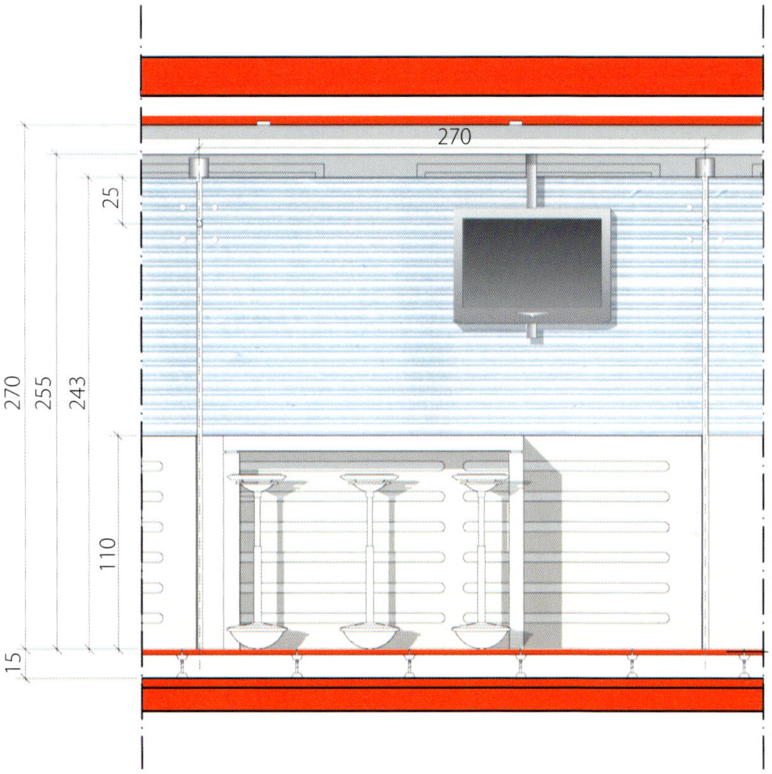
270
25
270
255
243
110
15

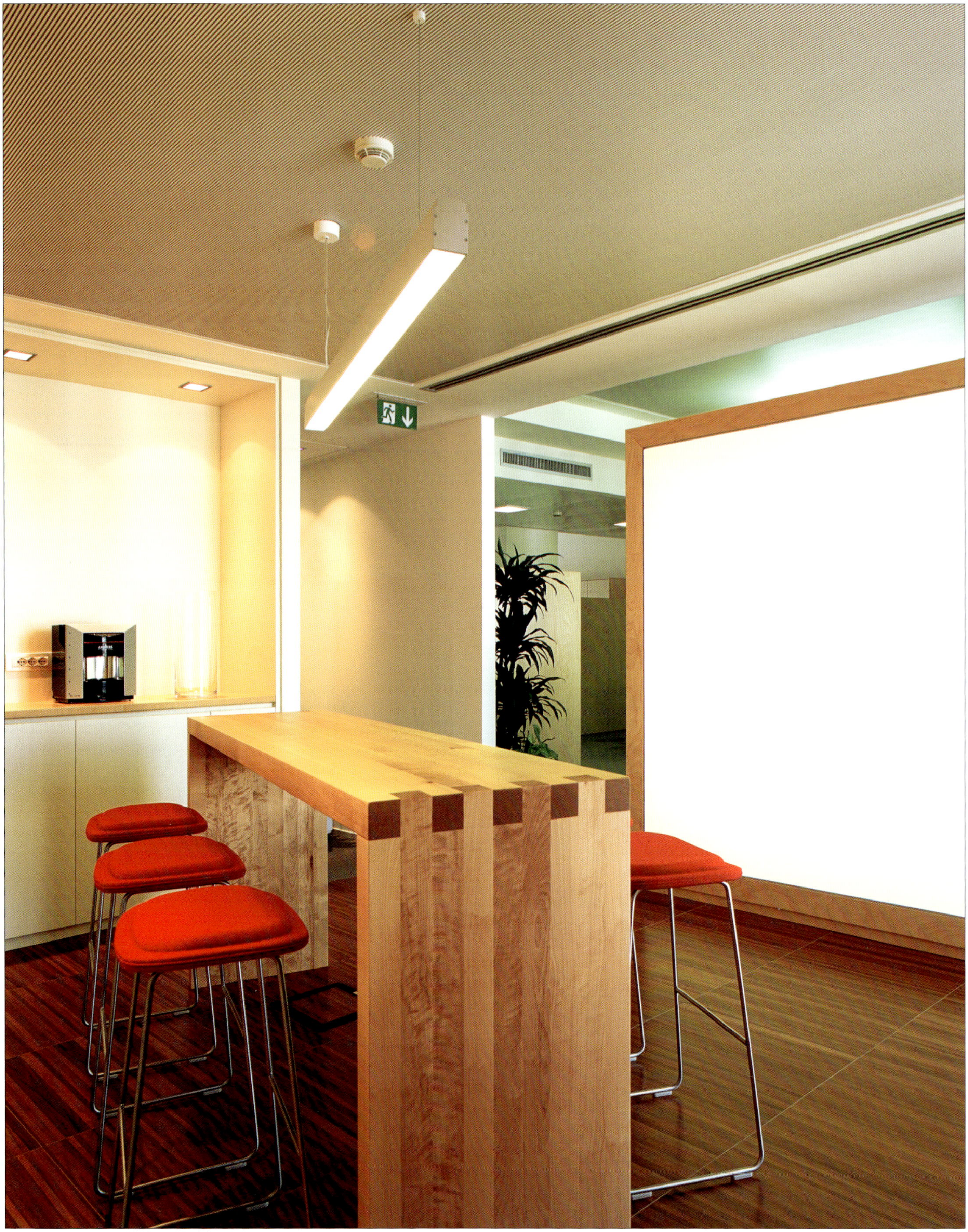

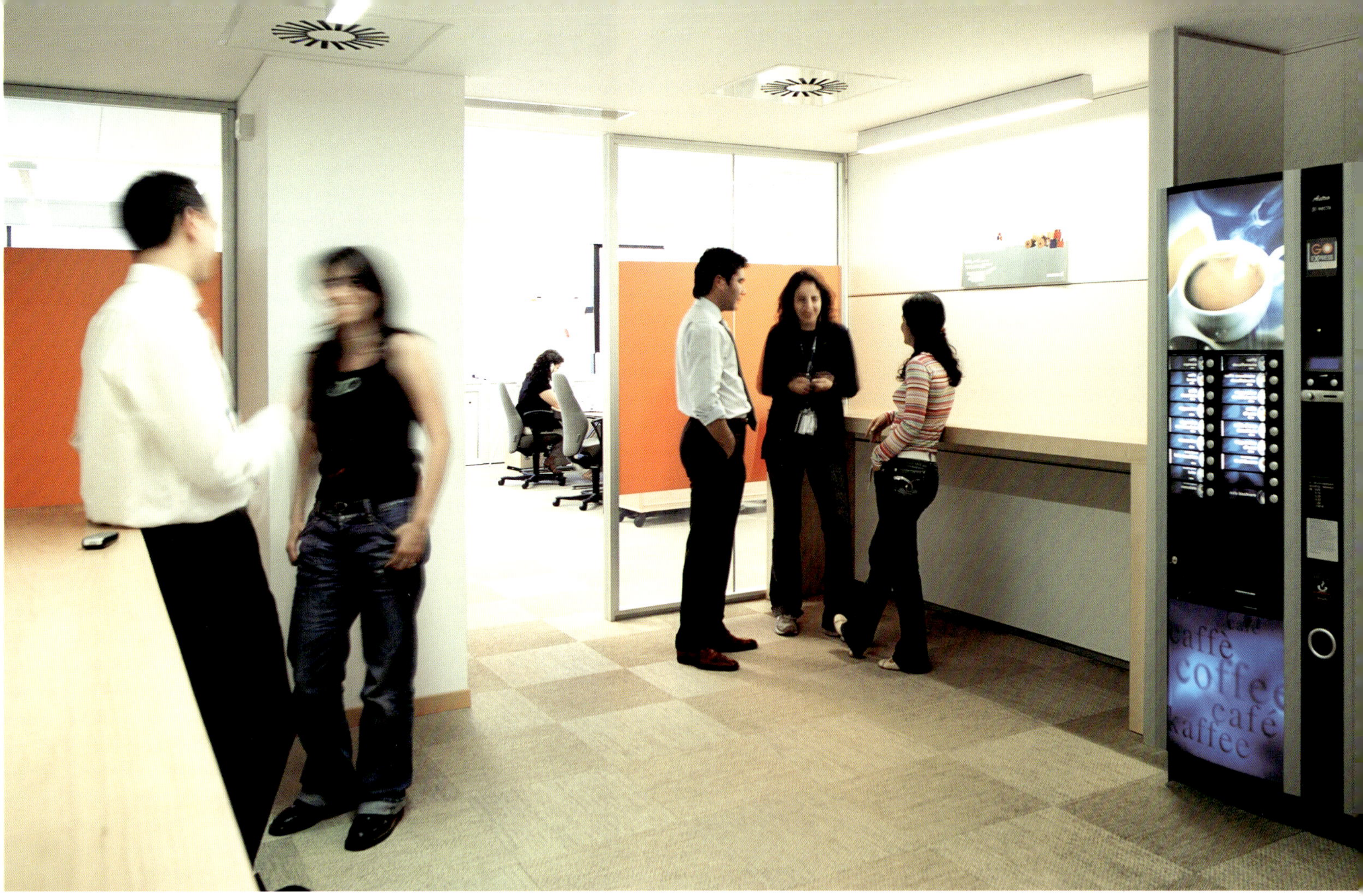
caffè
coffee
café
kaffee

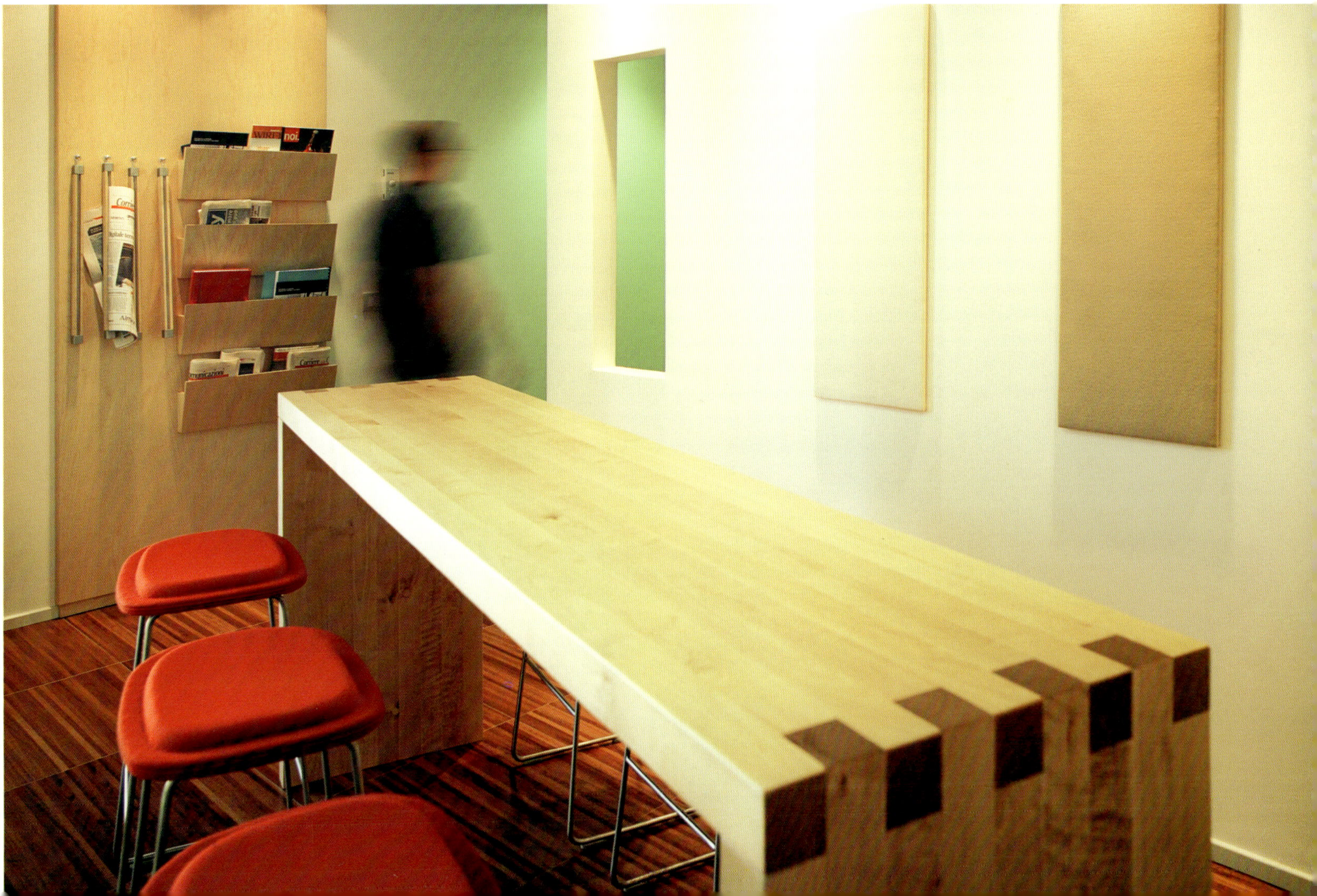

HASSELL

dtac House

Bangkok, Thailand Photographs: Pirak Anurakyawachon

HASSELL designed the new workplace for dtac, one of Thailand's leading telecommunication providers, to accommodate 3,500 staff members occupying 62,000 sqm over 20 floors.

The design successfully reflects dtac's corporate philosophy of 'play and learn', challenging conventional notions of arrival, meeting, concentration and relaxation spaces. This was the principal aim of the new workplace - to communicate this philosophy to both staff and visitors. The client requested an environment to develop and encourage this approach, already evident in the creativity and enthusiasm of the dtac staff.

In addition to the goals defined in the brief, the client demanded efficiency in the overall timeline and budget. HASSELL relied heavily on both to keep within the short one-year time-frame from the moment the design competition was won to occupation of the finished premises. A phased construction program was implemented to maximize contractor productivity and competitiveness. In total, there were four different contractors over a three phase construction program, driven by the client's business group needs. Moreover, in keeping with dtac's marketing philosophy of accessibility to everyone, the project was carried out on a modest budget that benefited all concerned. Intensive project team and base-building consultation and integration was required to achieve this structurally.

The team-based environments created by HASSELL encourage dtac staff to be mobile and creative in their selection of a work space, enabling them to choose between their regular work point, a meeting lounge, or the open terrace overlooking Bangkok's skyline. Open workspaces are supplemented with indoor plants, and the incorporation of a floor dedicated to relaxation and fitness, further enhancing staff amenities and promoting a healthy work environment.

The majority of materials and loose items of furniture were sourced locally. This was informed by the client's aesthetic design direction and their preference for supporting Thai products and designers. Rich and varied use of local timbers for the floors, screens and ceiling battens provides direction and framework across this activity-based workplace. Locally made cotton and silk fabrics were also used throughout. It was understood from the start that imported materials and loose furniture would not only hinder progress but also affect the budget. Instead, custom joinery was applied in many areas, resulting in an integrated and concept-driven result.

Interior design:
HASSELL
Gross floor area:
667,000 sqft (62,000 sqm)

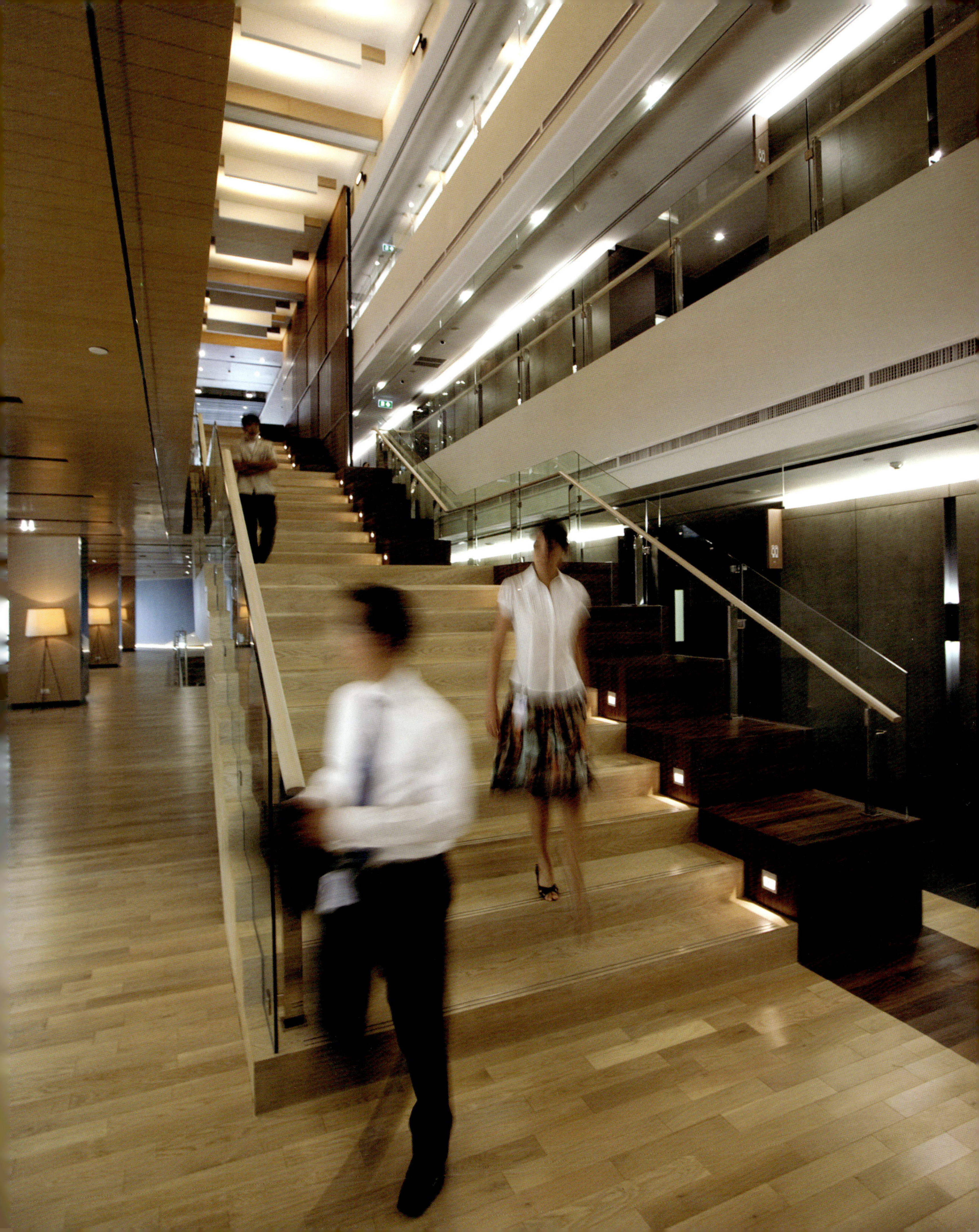

31st floor plan

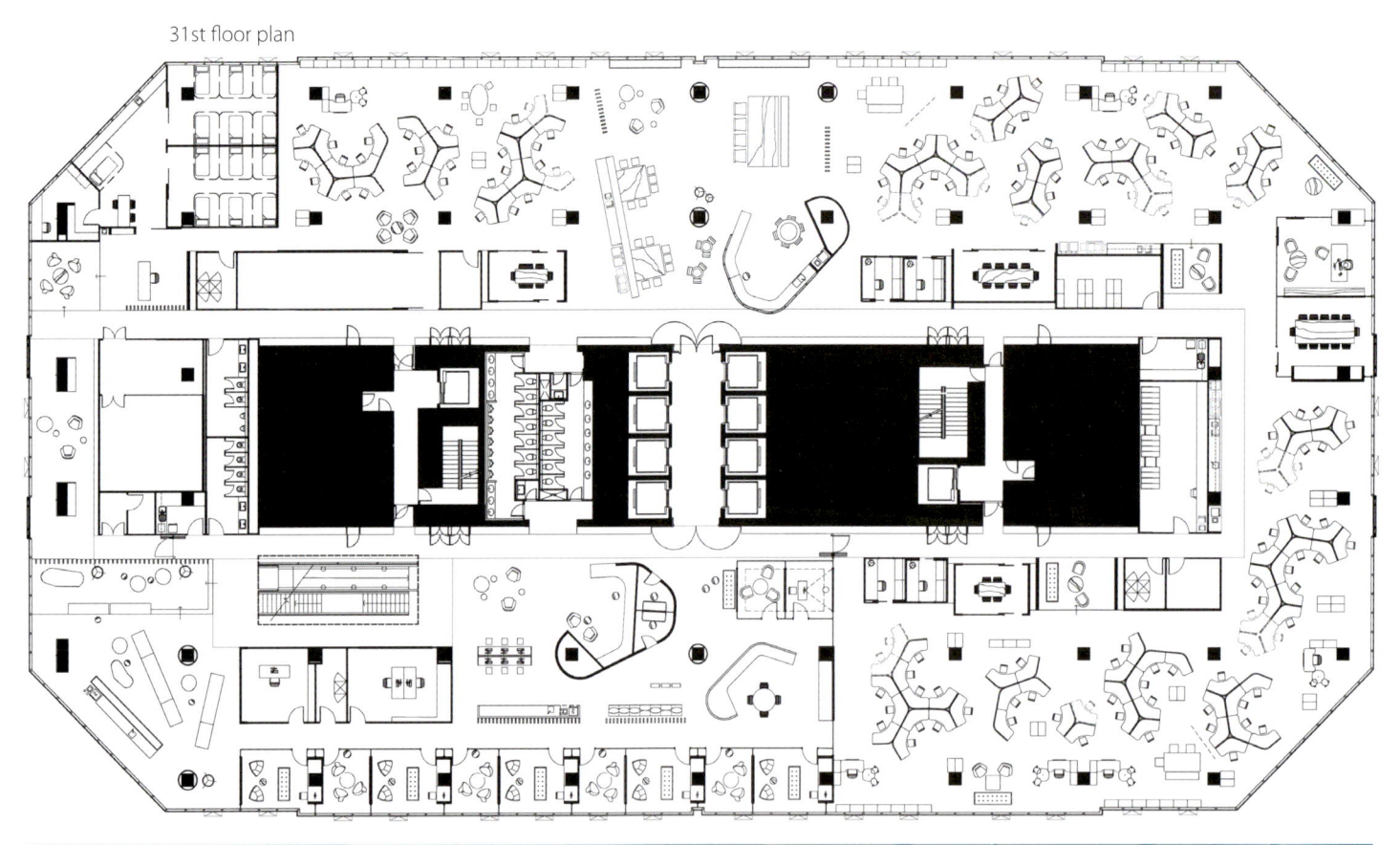

32nd floor plan

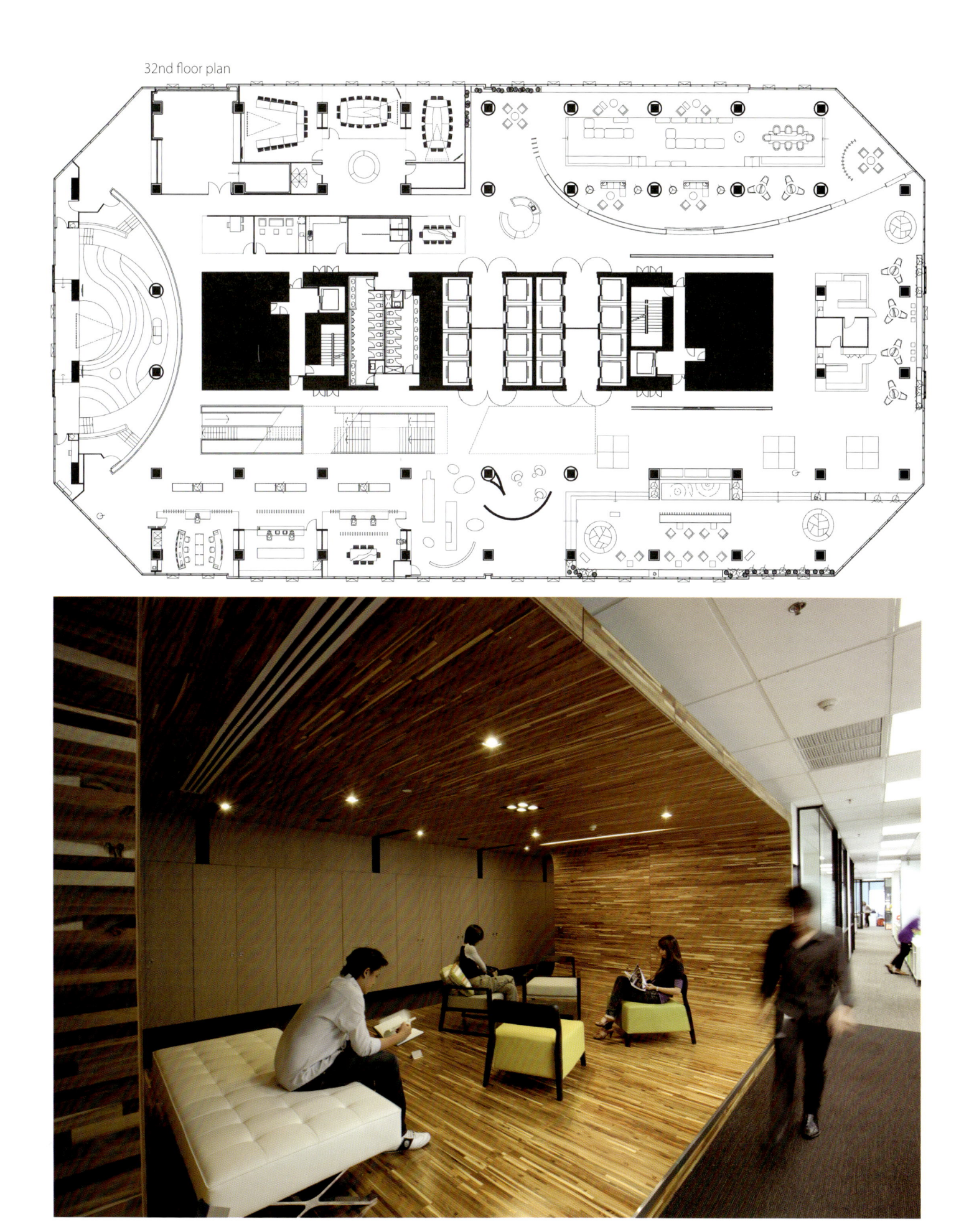

33rd floor plan

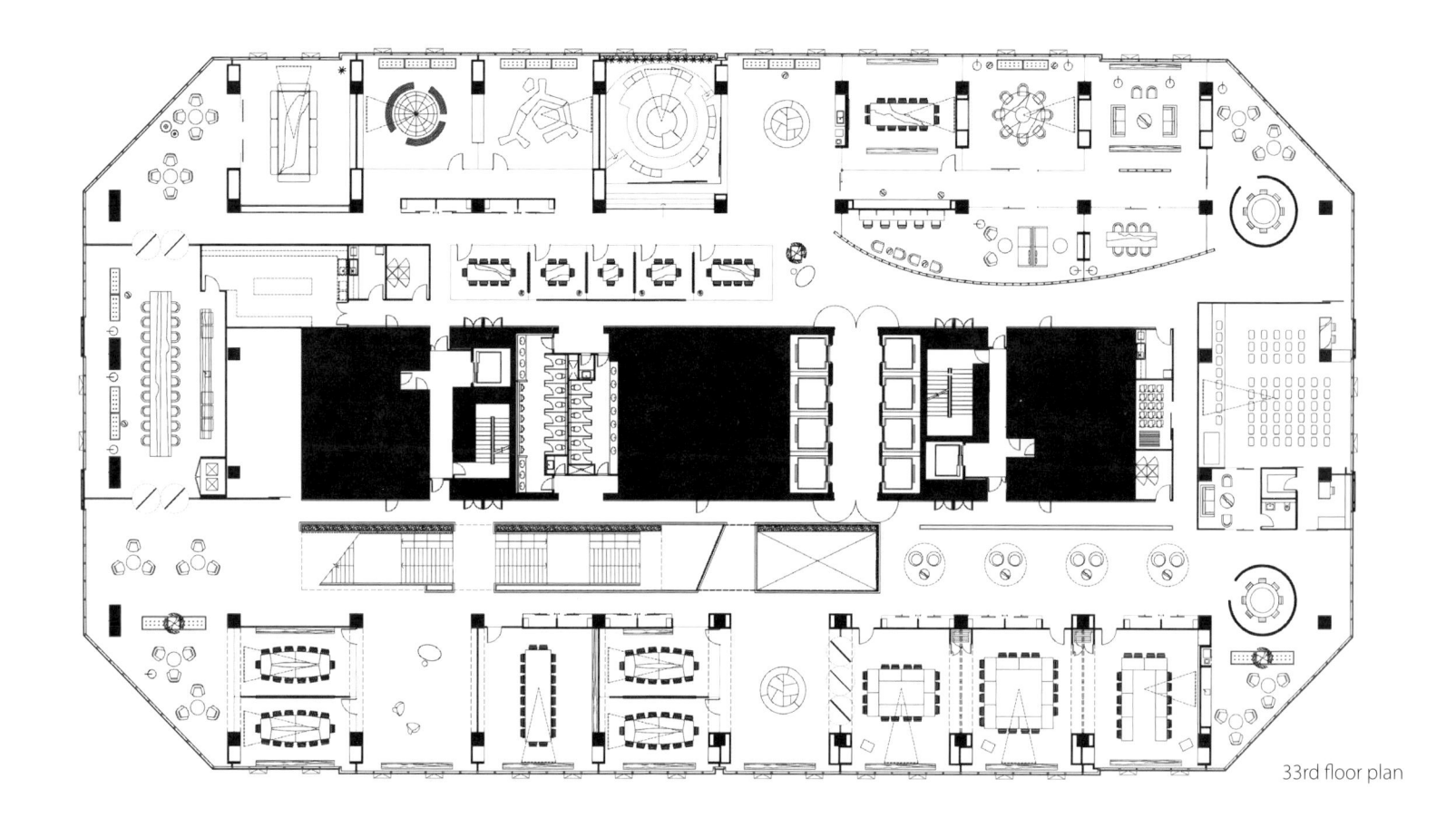

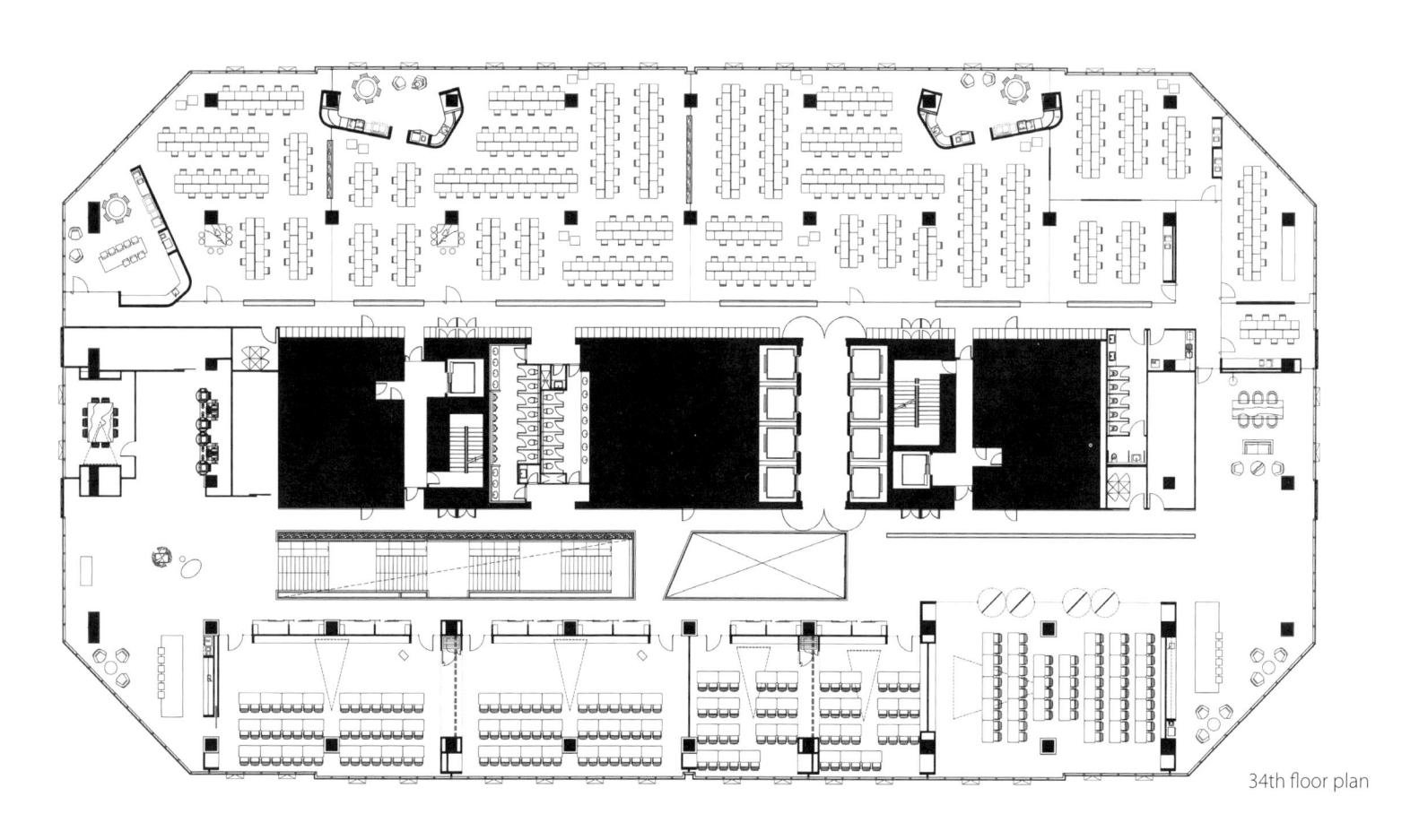

34th floor plan

37th floor plan

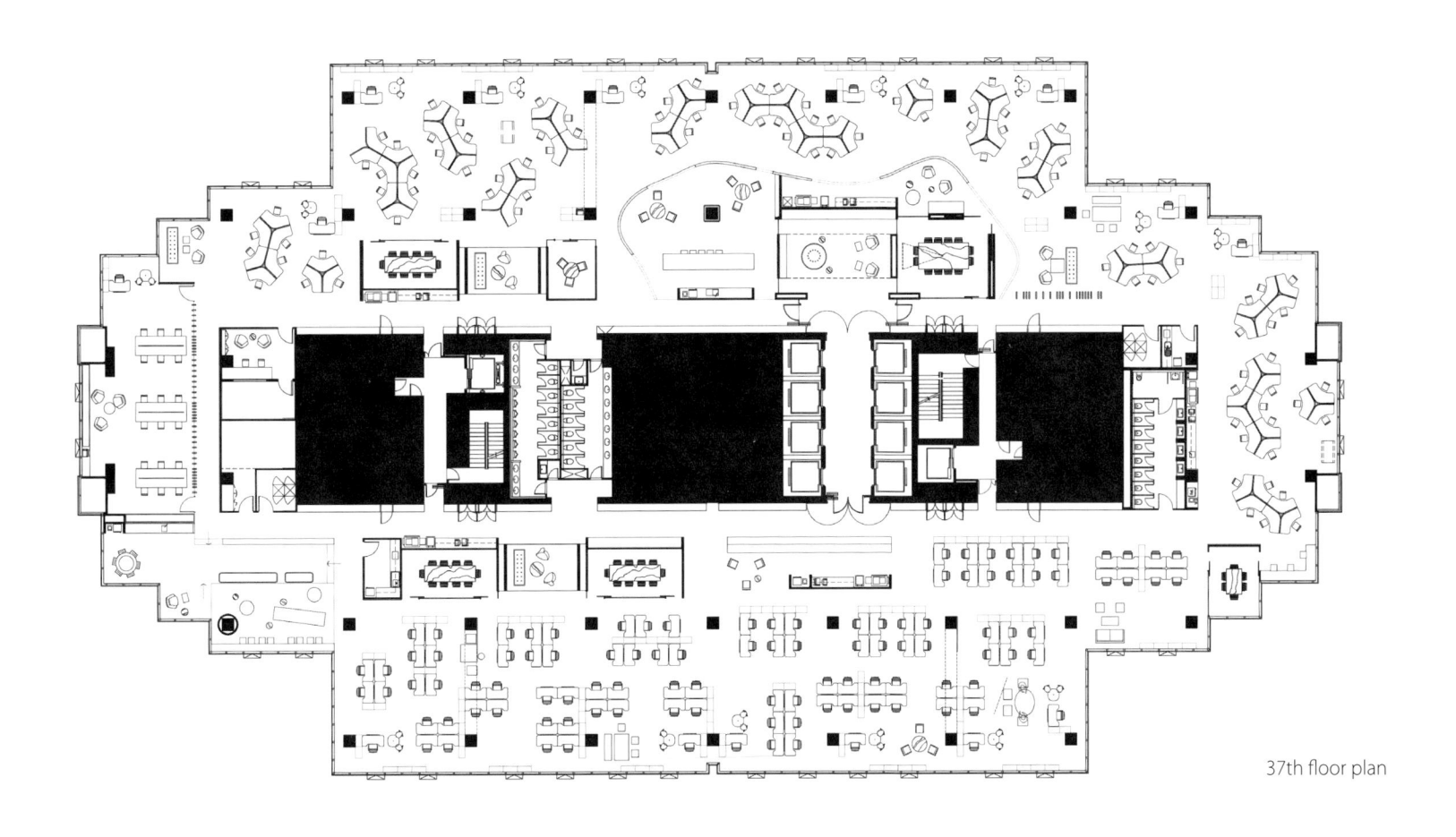

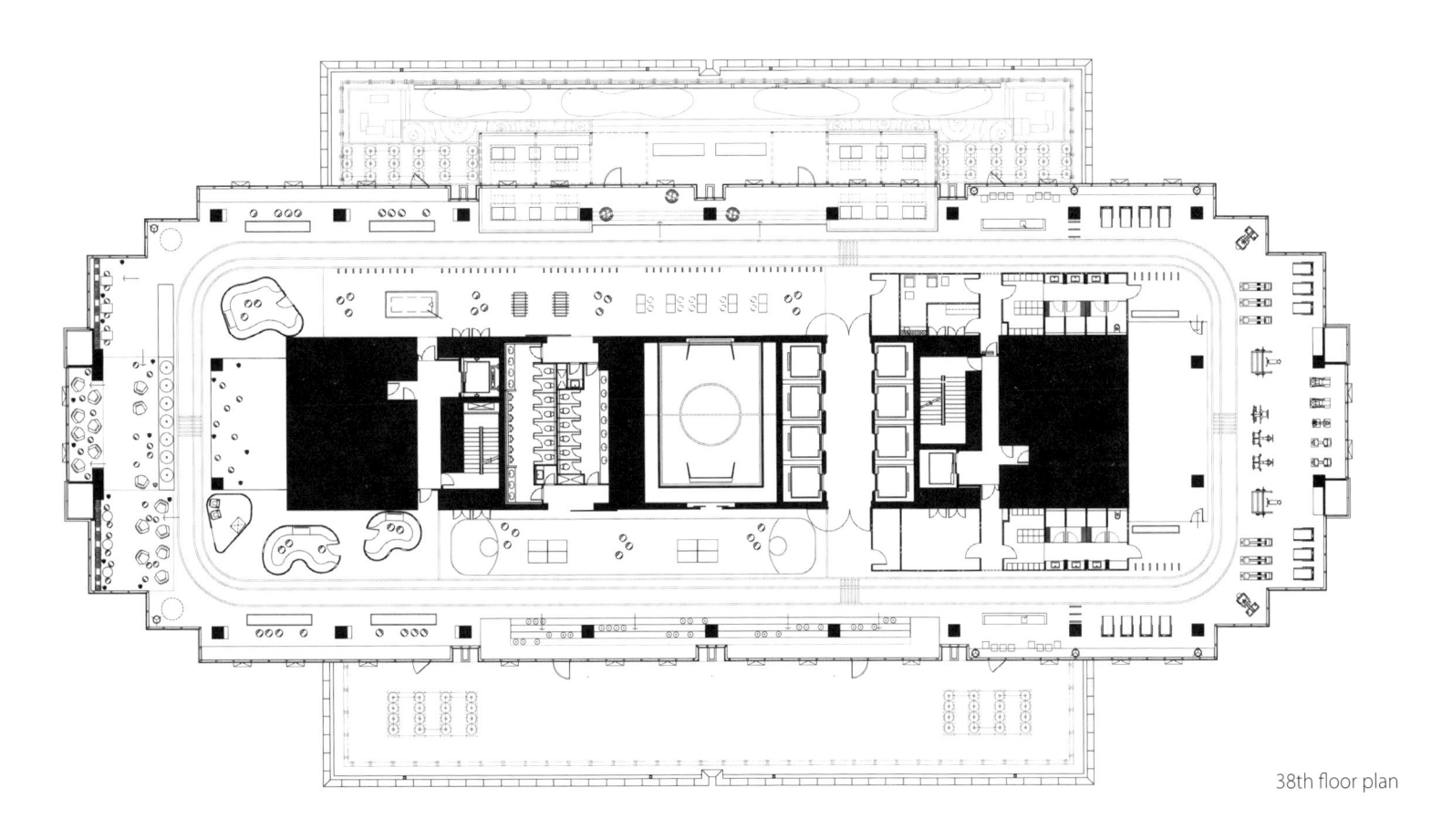

38th floor plan

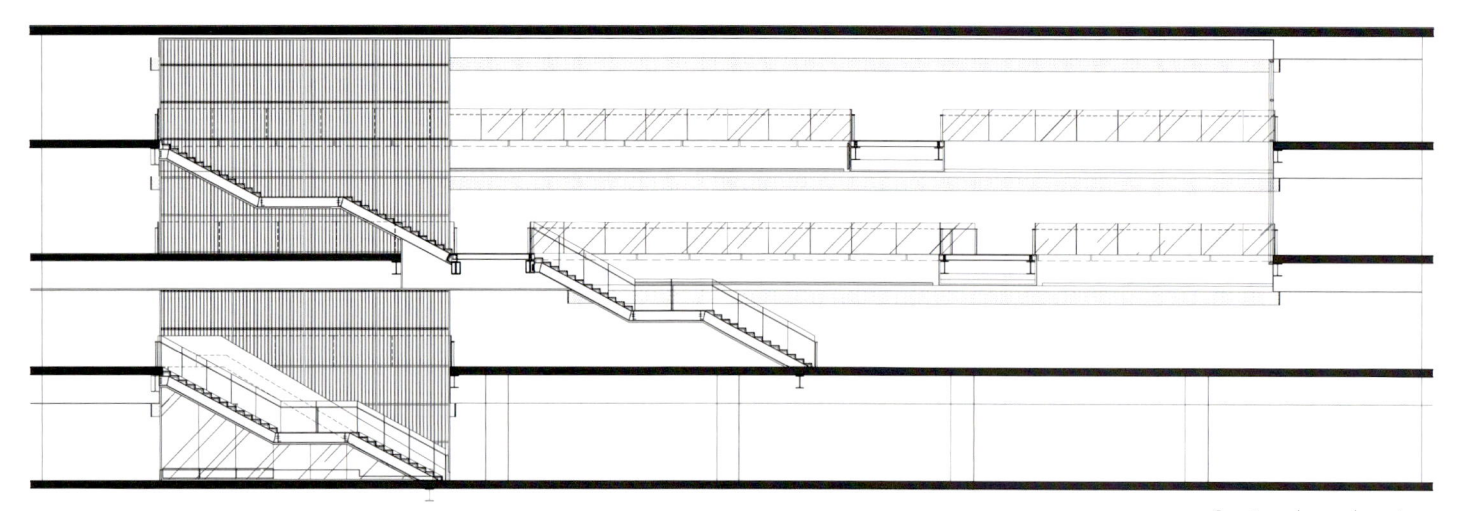

Section through staircase

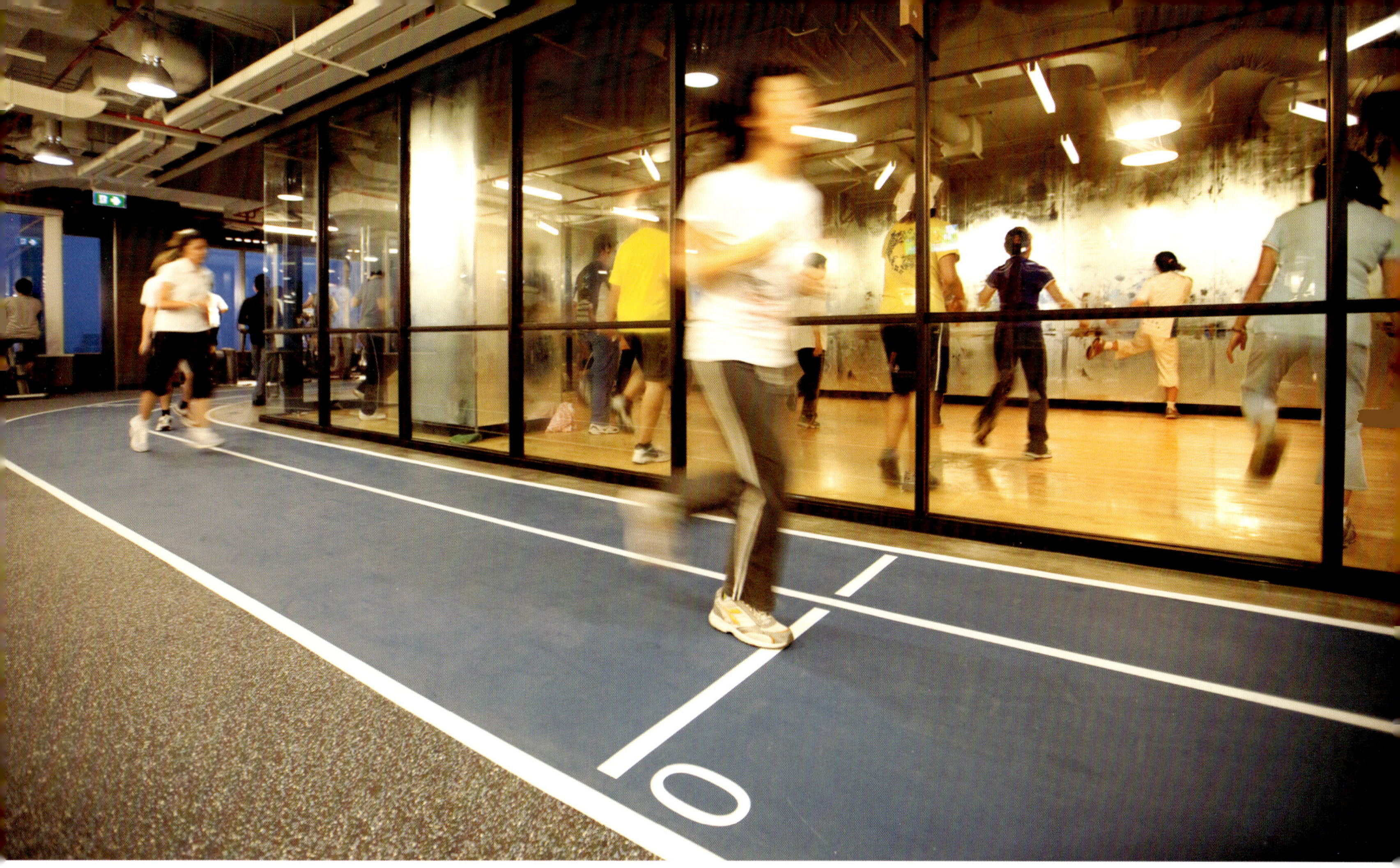

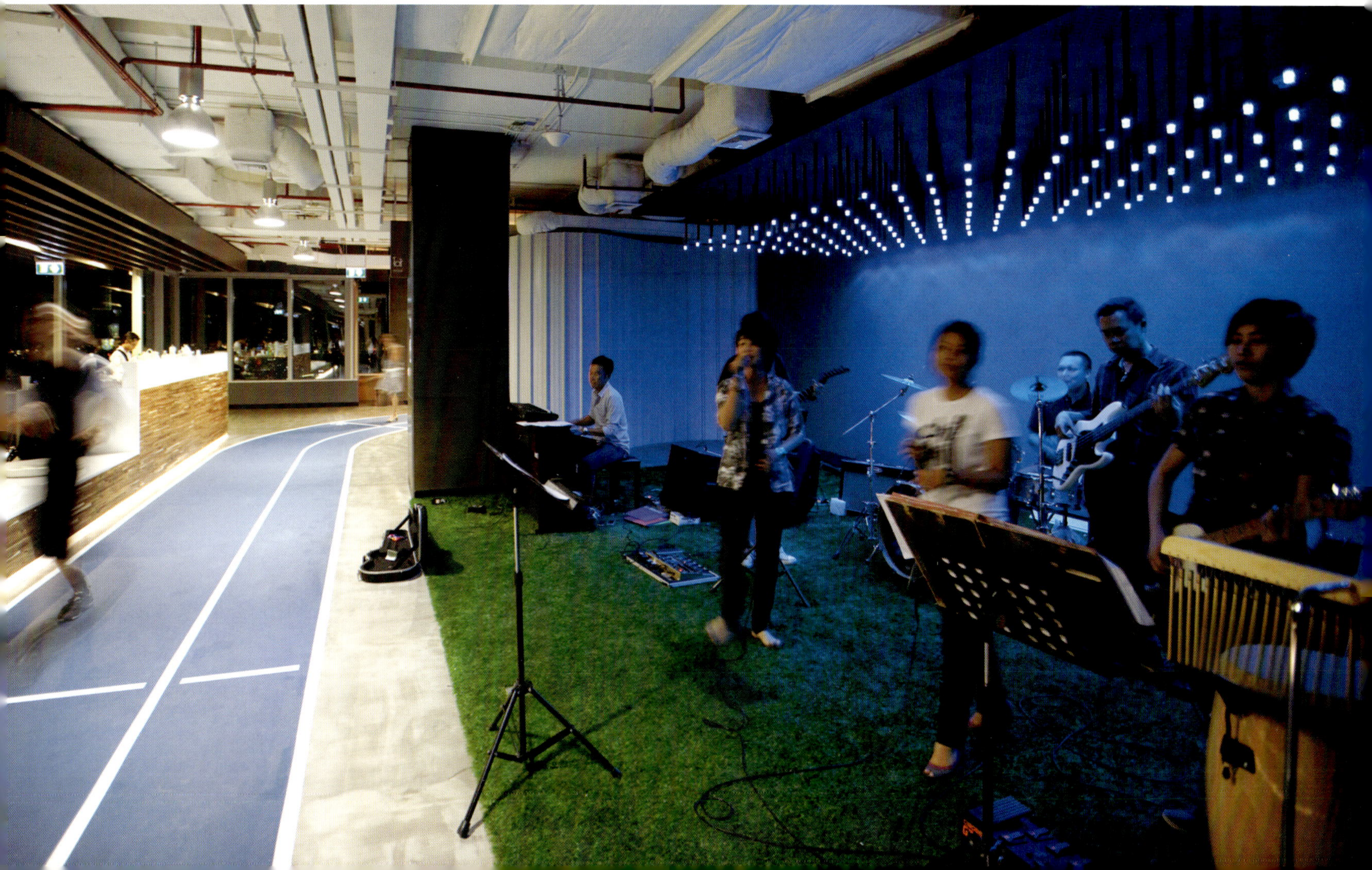

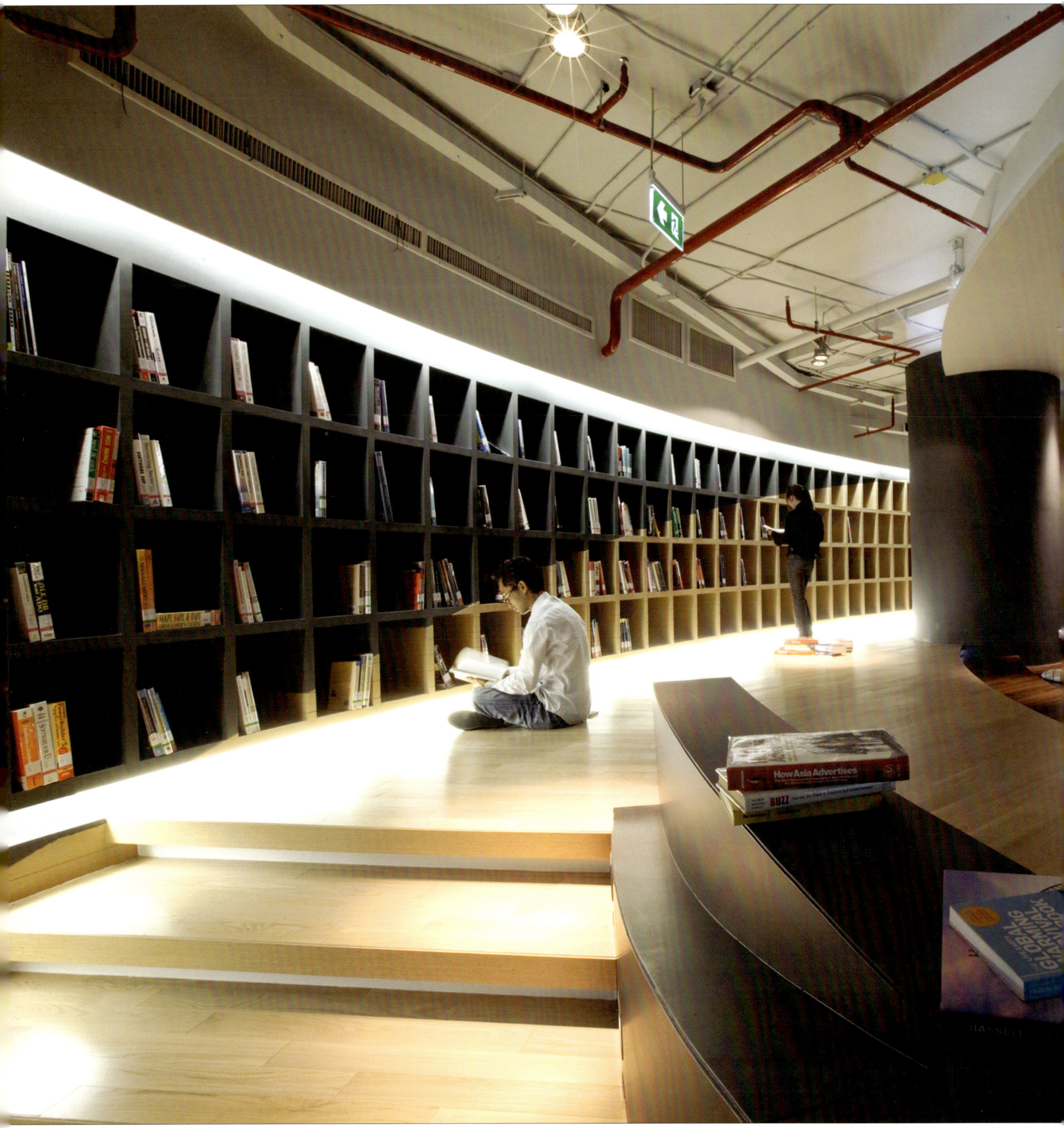
How Asia Advertises

The HASSELL design enables many areas to be defined as volumes, rather than through their function. An example is the extensive three-level open front-of-house space linked by a feature stairway that provides adaptable space to support different promotional activities and host a wide variety of client and staff events.

RA-DA

72andsunny

Los Angeles, California, USA

Photographs: Ralf Strathmann

The clients started their practice in a small space in el Segundo, with one long table that everyone sat around. As the firm grew, the partners needed more privacy, but the egalitarian attitude and the long communal work tables were kept. The architects understood their attitude, having worked with the clients on the expansion of their first space. After visiting several sites, a warehouse on the edge of Playa Vista was seen to fit the requirements of the energetic work environment.

A limited budget and raw design aesthetic drove the pursuit of simplicity, affecting the warehouse space in a minimal manner: the original concrete floor and wood joist ceiling were appropriate containers for the openness of the client's philosophy and work. In early concept studies, color emerged as an important element and became a key aspect of the design.

Striving to combine their goals and the separate functions they needed for an efficient office, it became clear that the square footage was insufficient for their future expansion needs. To solve this, three architectural devices were implemented:

1. The folding 'leaf' to delineate space
2. The blue solid to enclose space
3. The white wall to activate space

The 'leaf' starts on the east side of the space at the partners' room, turns up and across to create a small canopy marking the thresholds of the conference rooms, turns down to become a platform at the entry. It wraps up again to create the backdrop for the reception desk, passing over to the west side of the space to create the grand backdrop-wall to the open work area. It then folds under to become the floor plate of an added mezzanine and unfolds in the form of a wide stairway, leading back to the ground floor. Enclosed areas, such as the editing suite and the restrooms, were wrapped in bold 72andsunny blue, supporting the design's strong graphic character.

Architecture:
RA-DA
Project architect:
Rania Alomar
Project team:
Rania Alomar, Design Principal
Carolyn Telgard, Senior Designer
Jesse Madrid, Designer
Adelia Halim, Designer
Total surface area:
9,000 sqft (836 sqm)

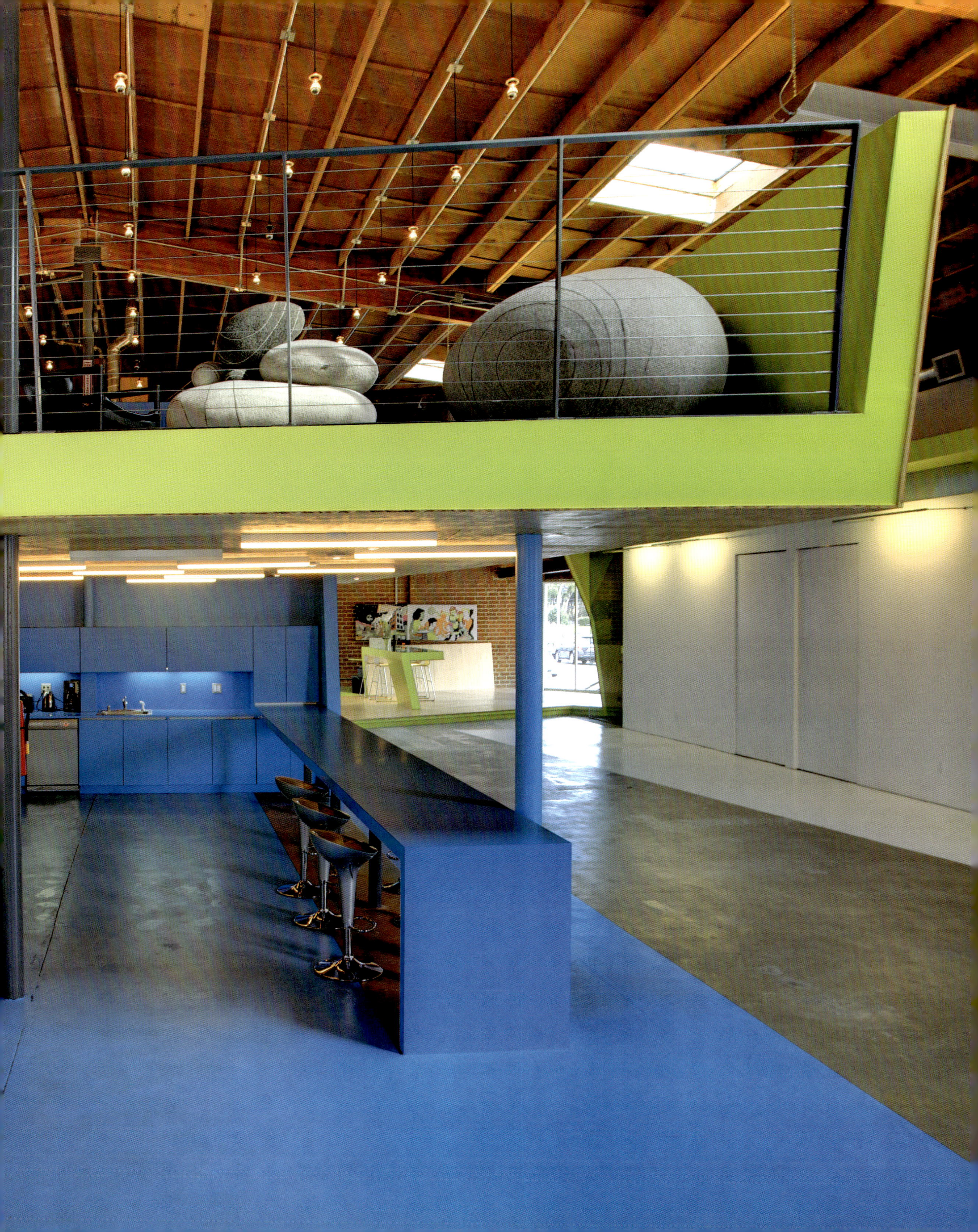

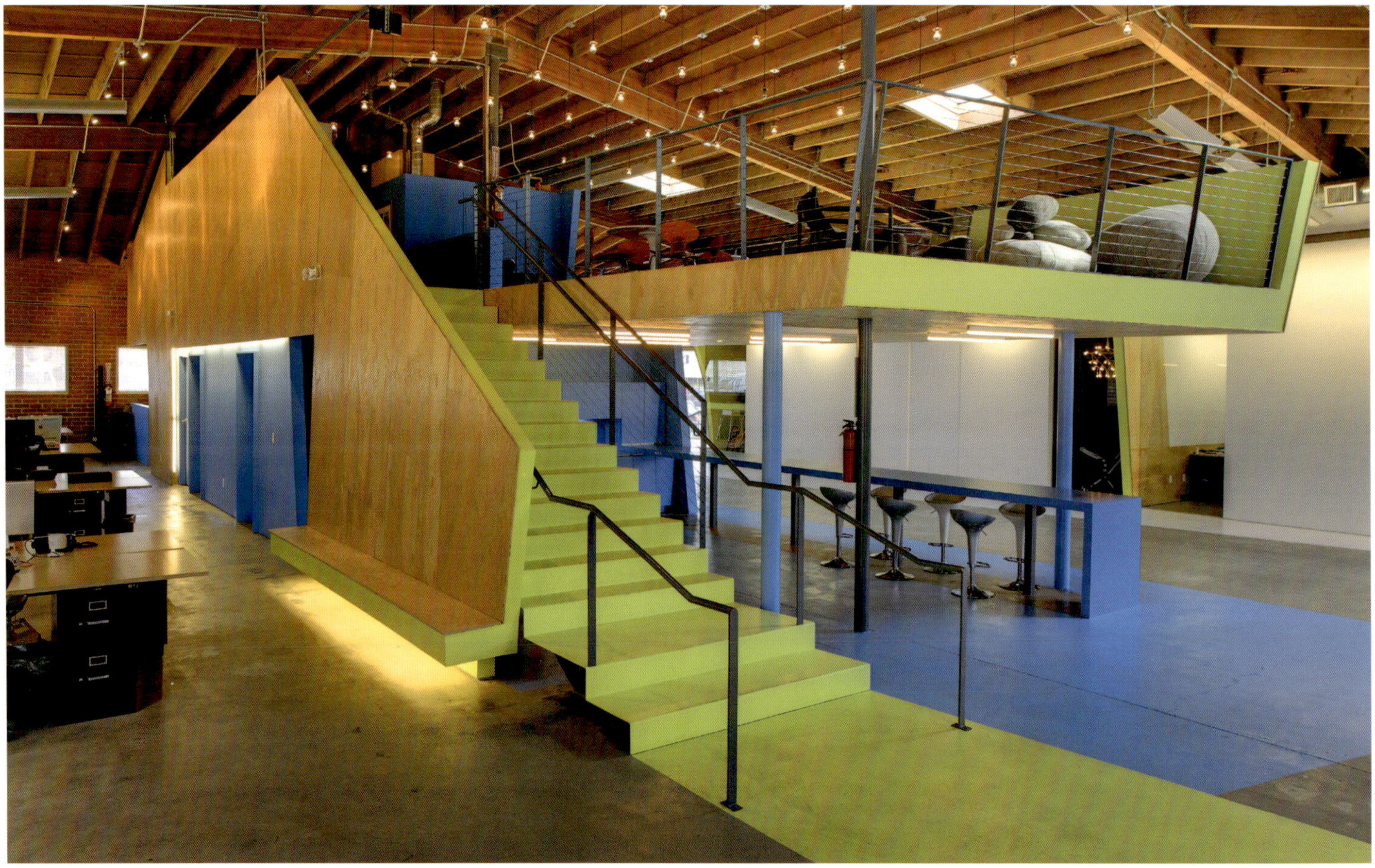

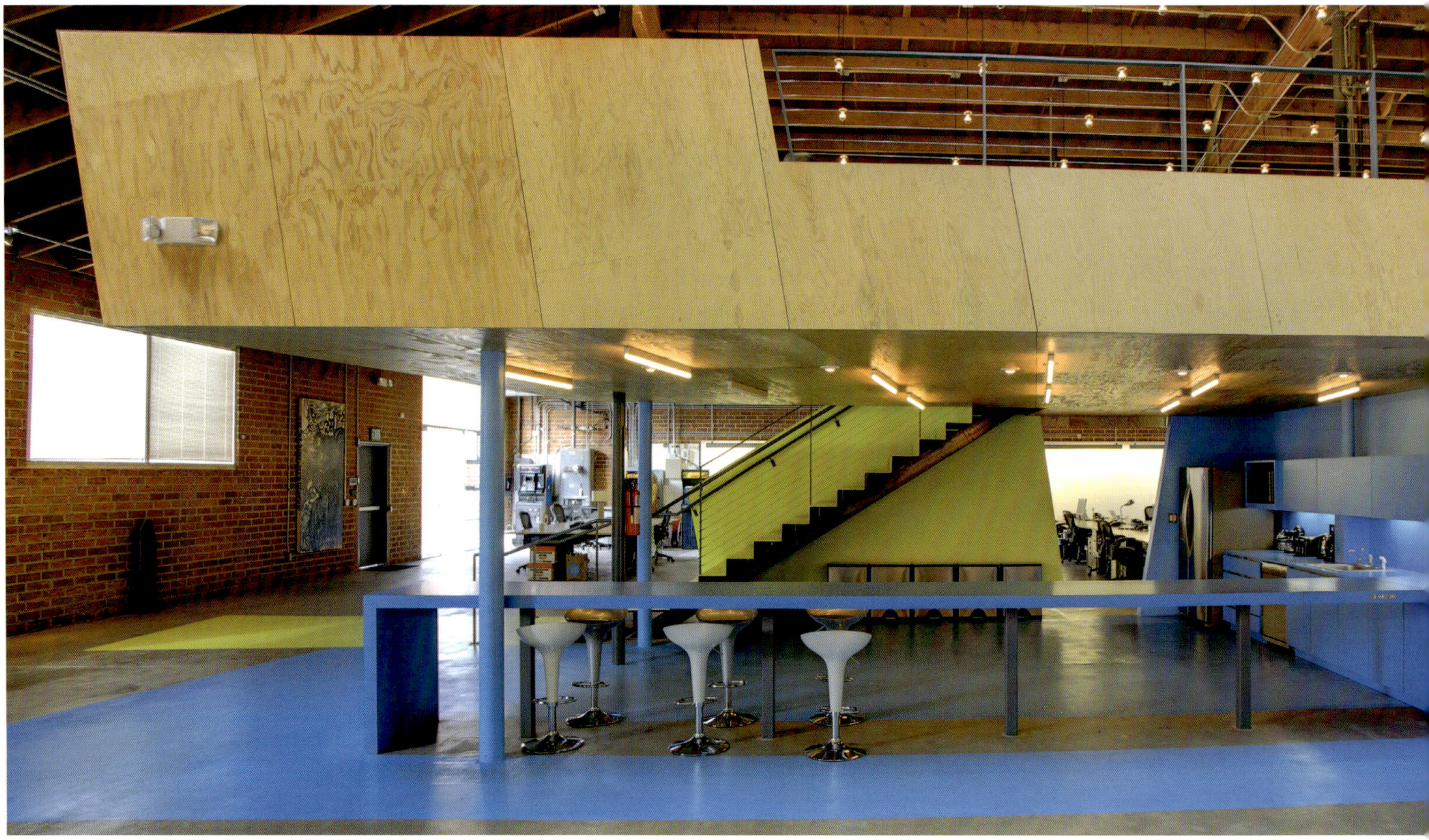

207

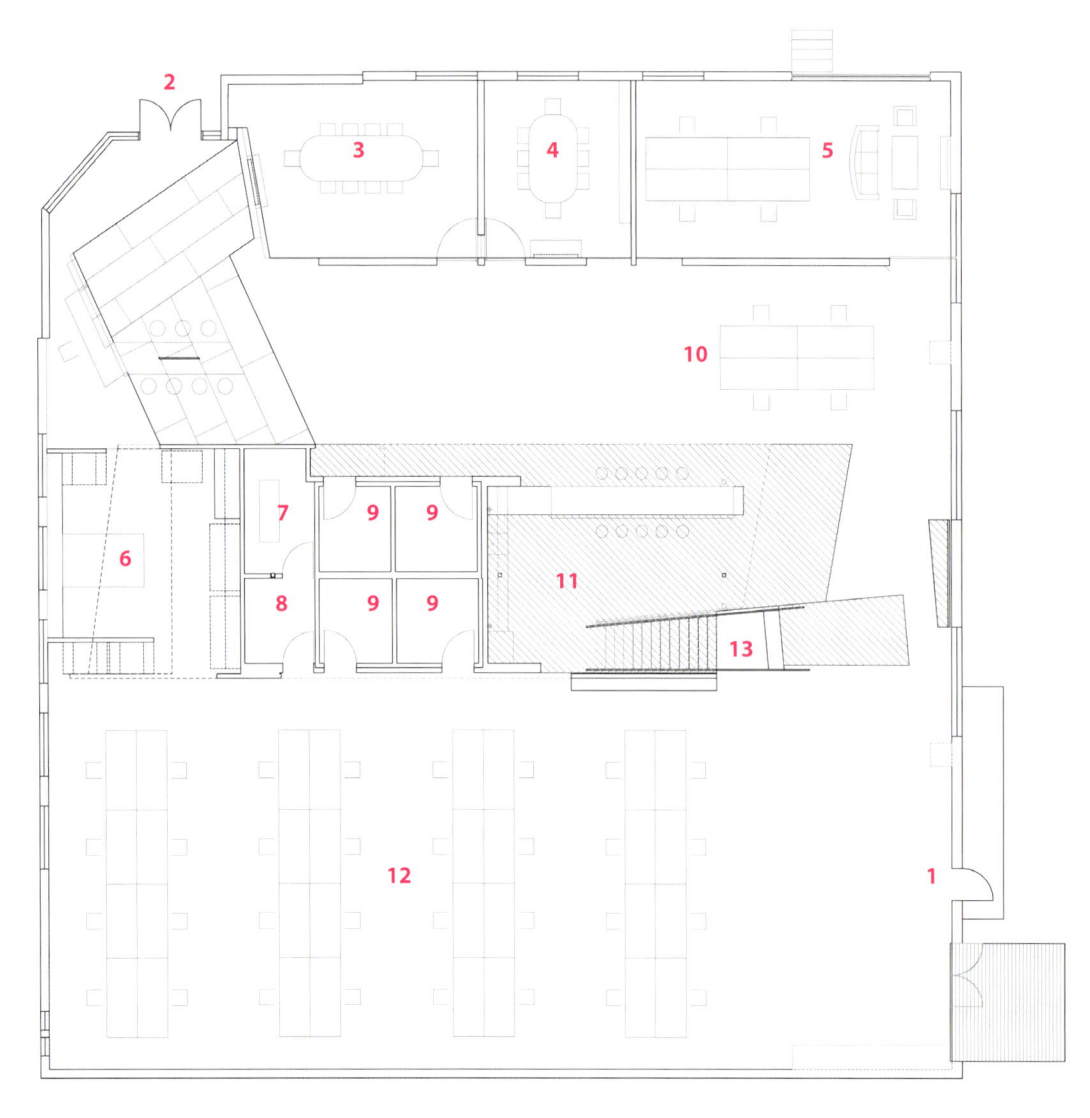

GROUND FLOOR PLAN

1. Entry 1
2. Entry 2
3. Conference room 1
4. Conference 02
5. Partners' room
6. Print room
7. Server room
8. IT room
9. Restroom
10. East workspace
11. Pantry
12. West workspace
13. Stairs up

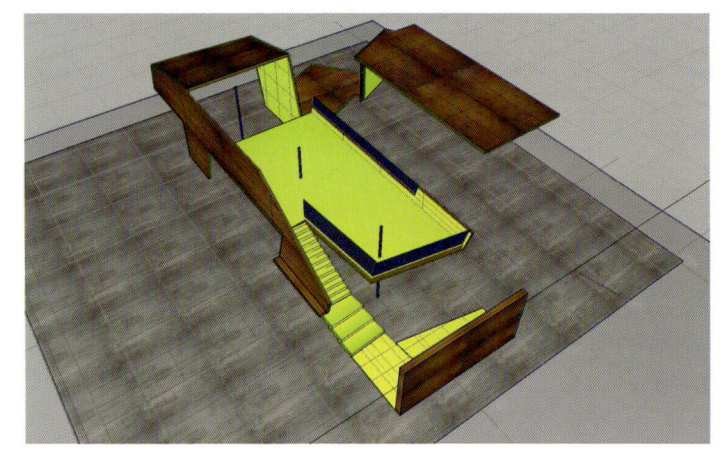

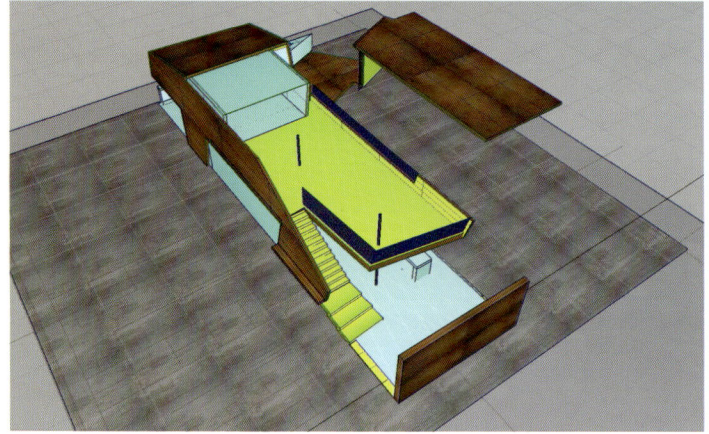

208

A single 'leaf' or 'plane' folds and turns through the space defining different areas. With raw construction-grade plywood on one side and the 72and-sunny green on the other, the leaf is a graphic element that moves from floor to wall to ceiling; it flips from plywood to green and back again, expressing which side of the leaf we are on.

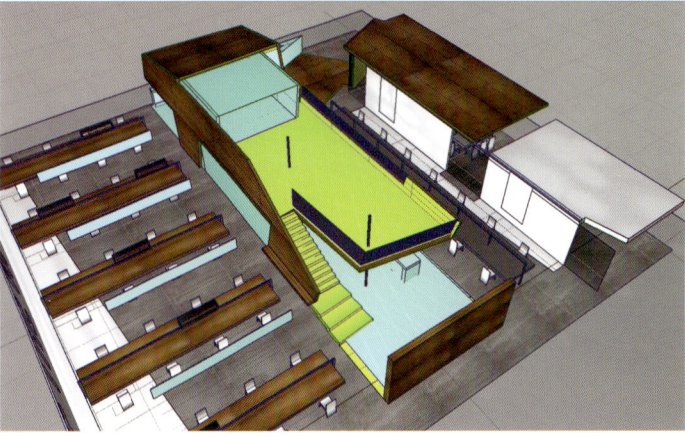

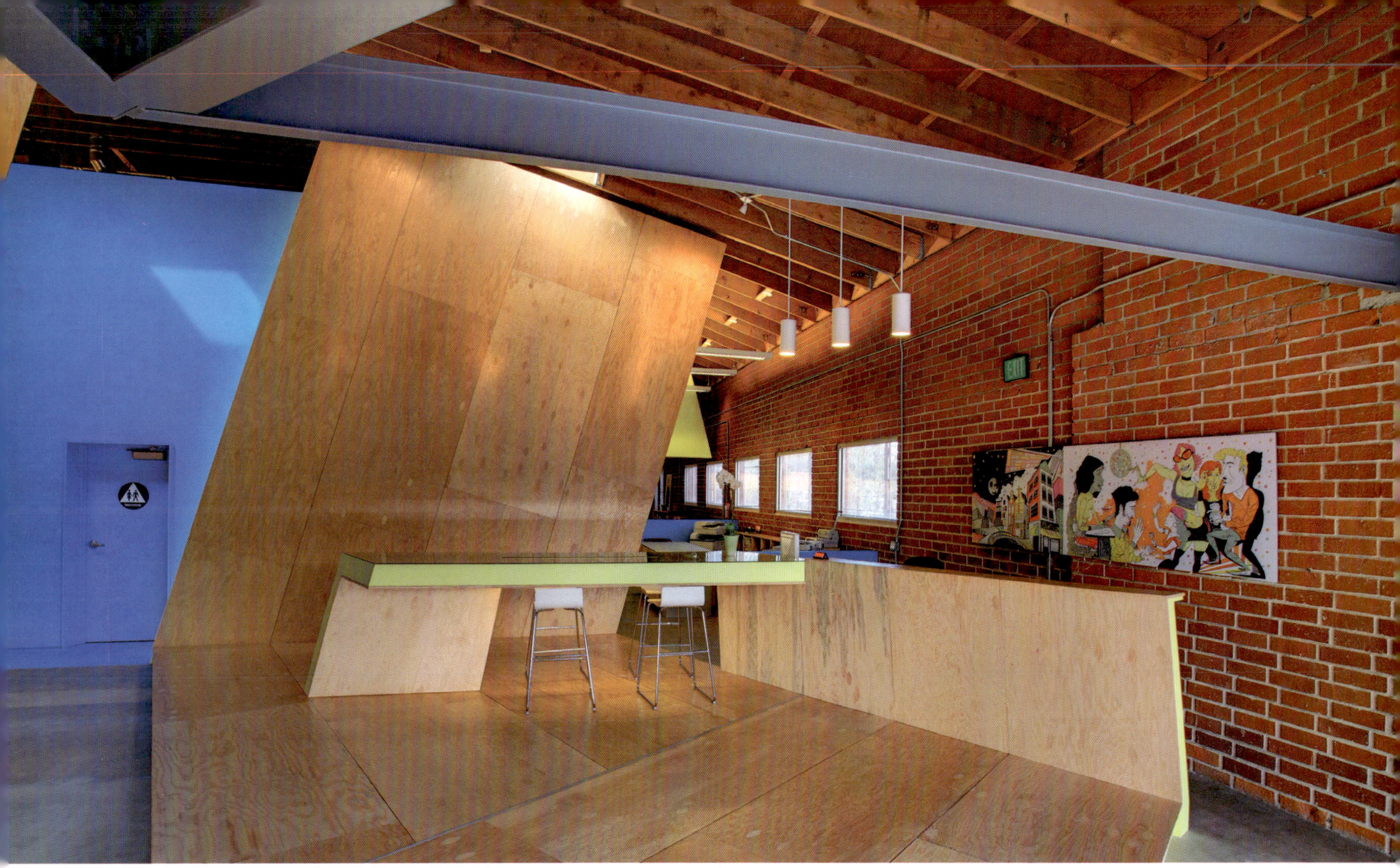

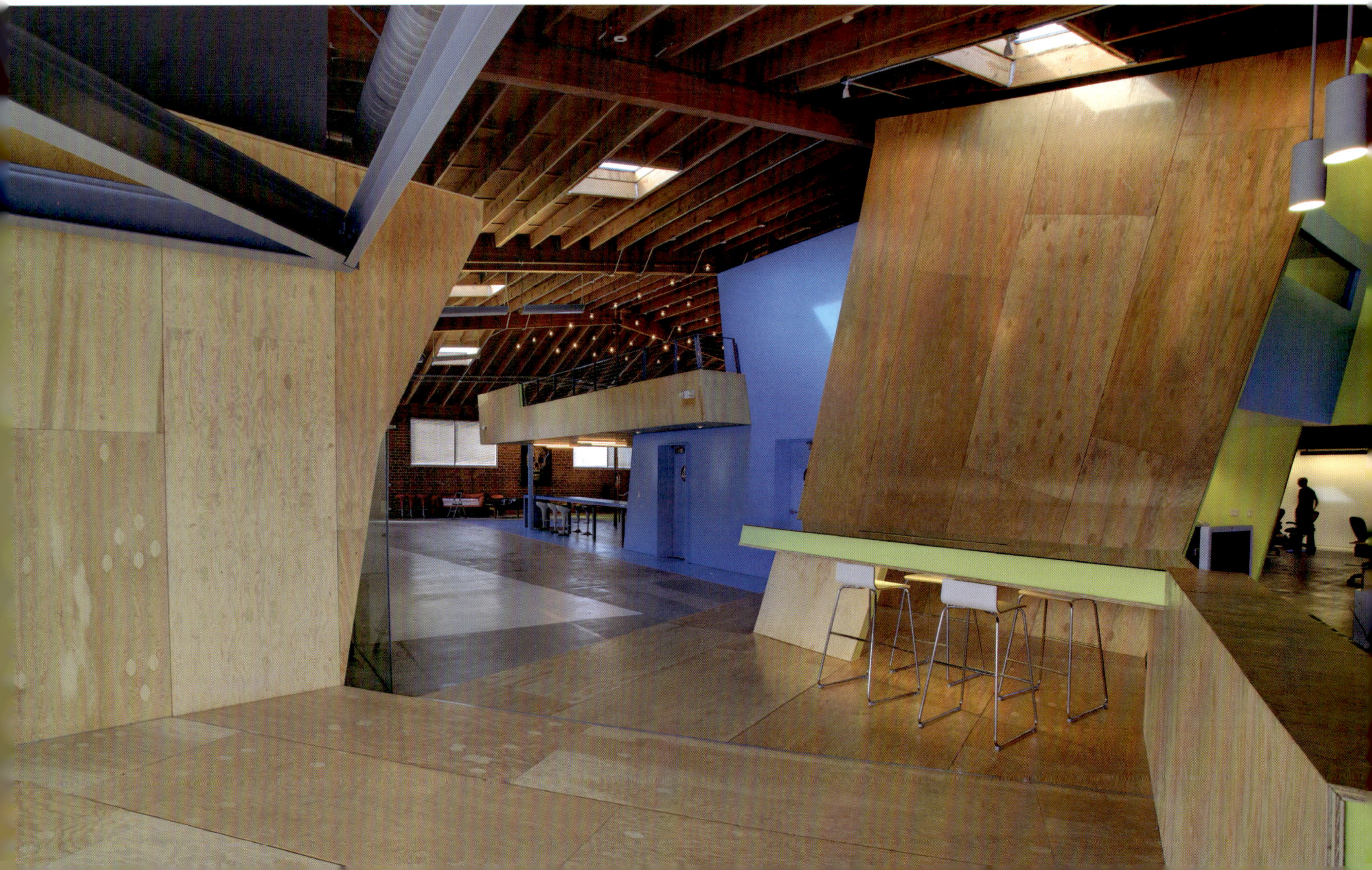

211

xarchitekten

Ecomplexx Office

Wels, Austria **Photographs: Max Nirnberger**

The web service provider Ecomplexx offers a wide range of internet services to its customers and has grown continuously since it was founded ten years ago. The key to its success is intensive networking within its own projects as well as with those neighboring companies. In 2008 they decided to upgrade to a new location.

They rented a 575 sqm (6190 sqft) industrial loft behind the brick façade of a former hat factory from the last century. As it is a listed building there were limitations to what could be done with it but with its open structure the space offered ideal conditions for the development of new ideas.

Terms and concepts that vertebrate how the Ecomplexx network functions such as "Plug in" or "Backbone" were to play an important role in the company's future architecture to support and develop its own identity. No changes were made that would affect the attractive windows in order to retain the impressive generosity of the "loft feeling". The corridor and operating space follow a façade that is suffused with light. The concept of the central "Backbone" tries to focus all the changes into this connecting core area which has the potential for many different uses. Numerous workstations are connected to the "Backbone", which creates an open and communicative office structure.

The entire expanse of the loft's historic window façade can exert its full effect, while the multifunctional Backbone offers all the essentials, such as stacking, archives, coat room, seating areas for relaxation and the bar, as well as the entire technical installation. The Backbone was built in the manner of serial shelf-like furniture, as a mega structure of untreated chipboard to comply with the extremely low budget.

This innovative office facility provides a communicative atmosphere for 38 workstations. The historic shell and the new additions interact smoothly through lightweight design. This has been combined with careful consideration of the spatial divisions.

Architecture:
xarchitekten
Floor space:
6190 sqft (575 sqm)

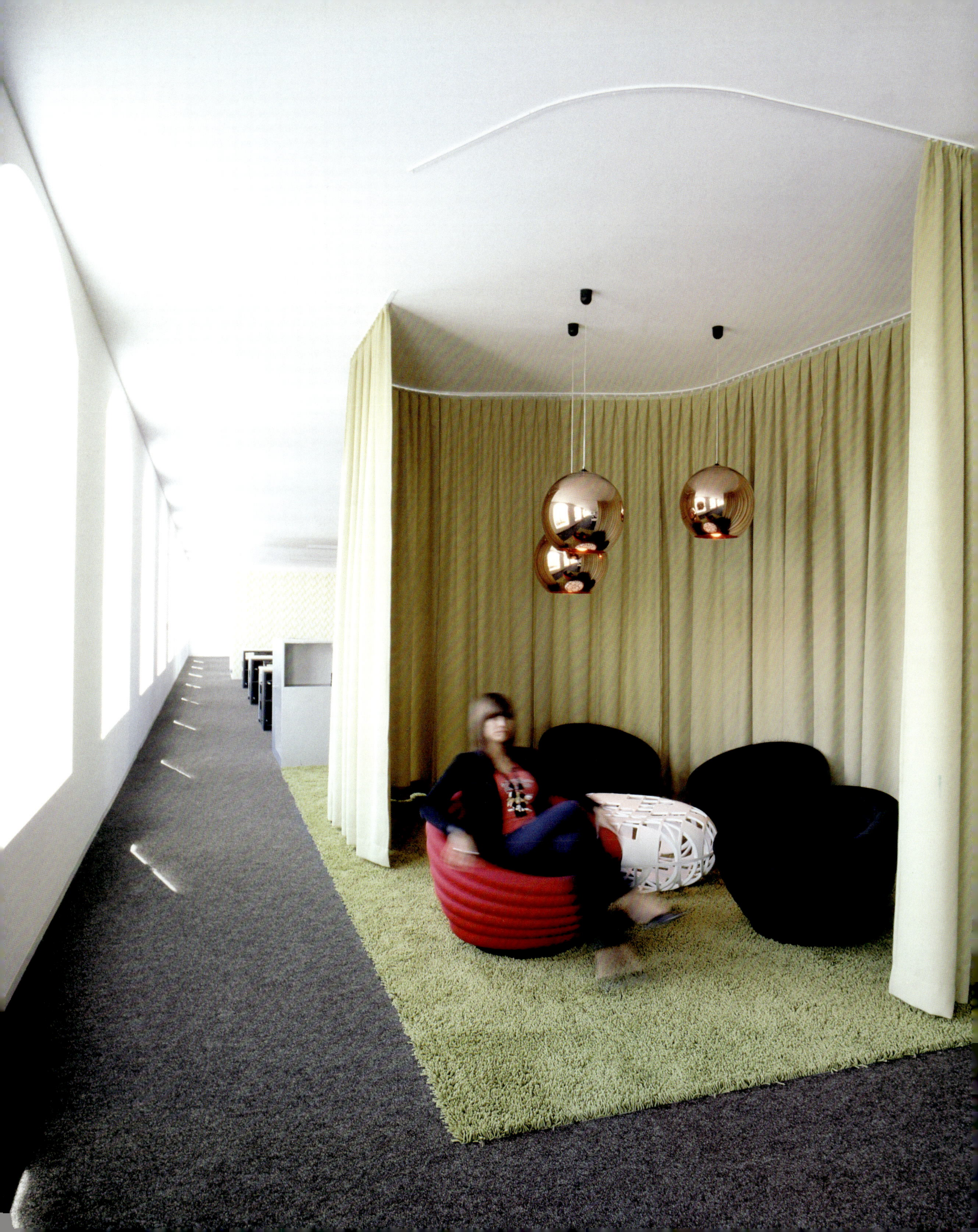

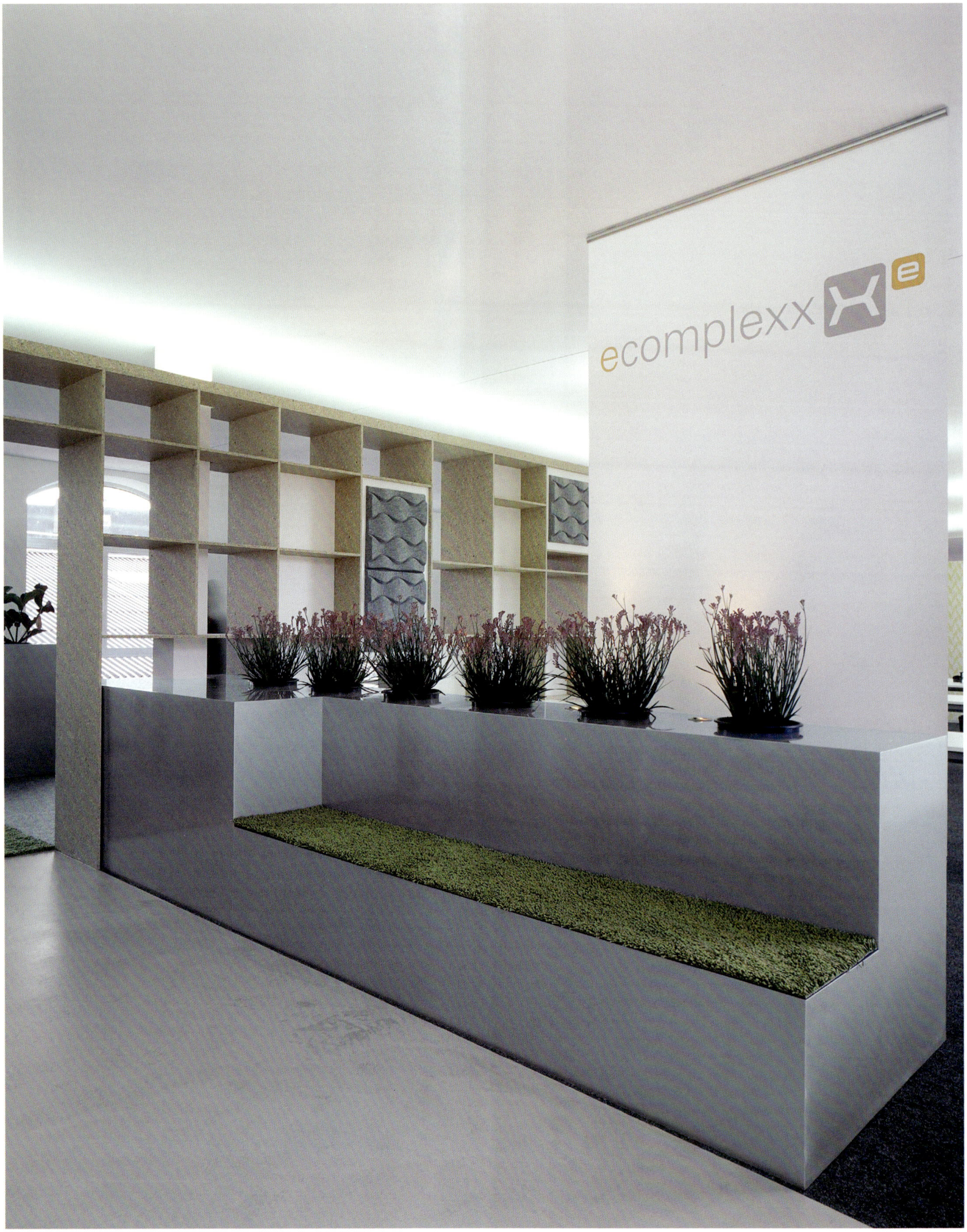
ecomplexx

Floor plan

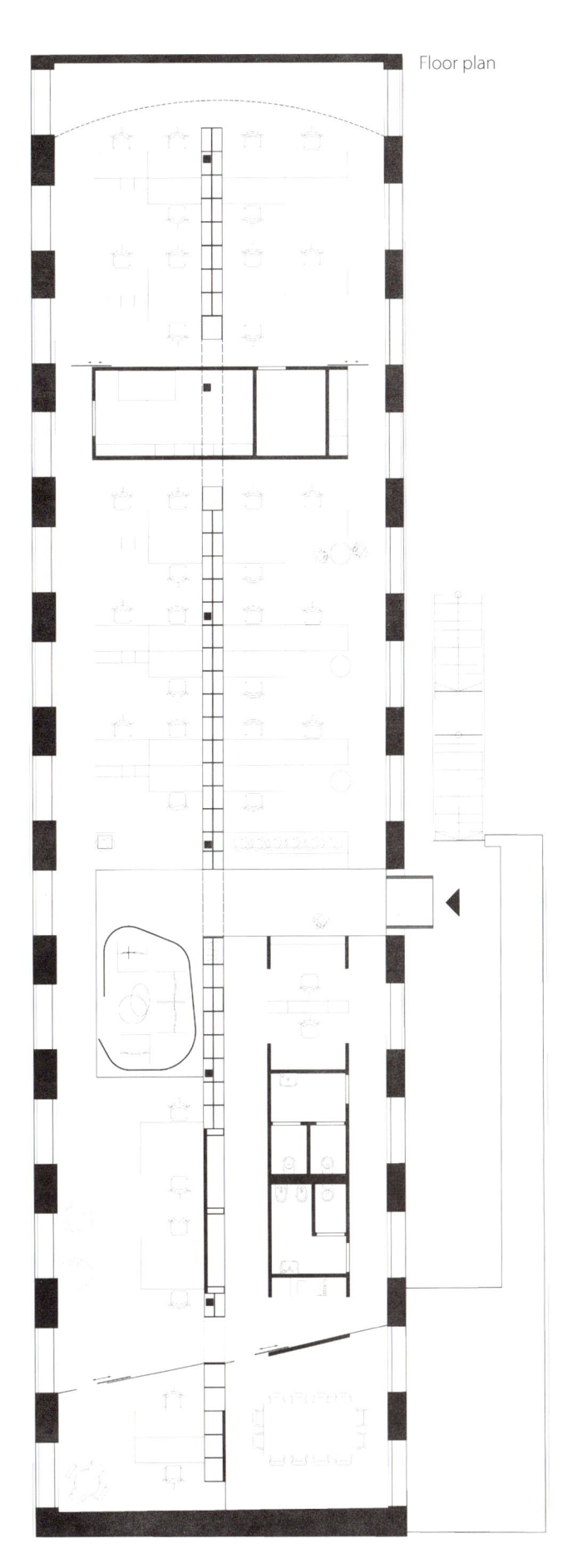

215

Longitudinal section

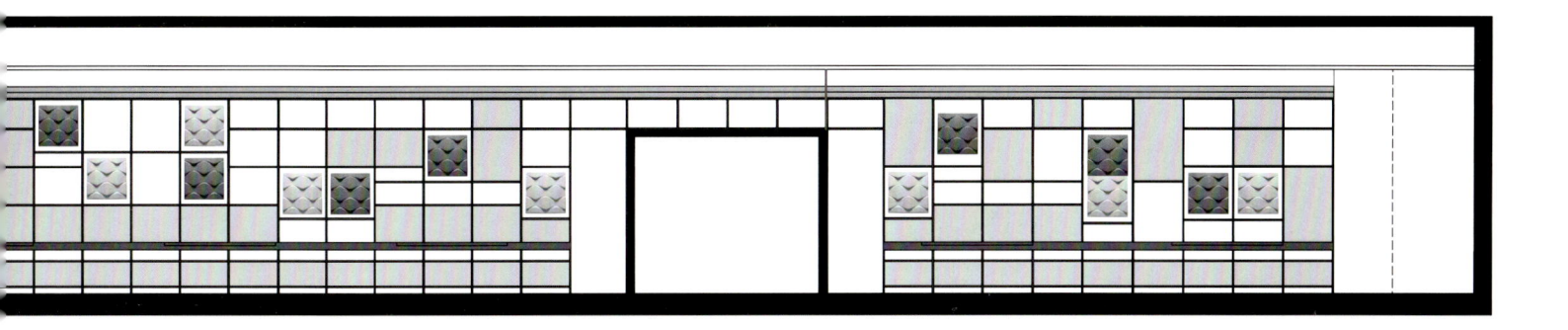

Special materials have been used for individual shelves to ensure appropriate acoustics. Soft seating and lounge-like meeting areas have been provided, surrounded by soft curtains. Glass walls complete the noise protection.

Studio Ramin Visch

Ogilvy Offices

Amsterdam, the Netherlands **Photographs: Jeroen Musch**

These premises for Ogilvy, a branch of the British advertising group WPP, in Amsterdam, project a strong sense of creativity and originality; a valuable message to transmit to potential clients for any advertising agency. The agency has set up office in the former factory hall of a bicycle manufacturers' located on an industrial site. The entire staff occupies a single colossal open space of 115 x 50 m (377 x 164 ft). Under the high shed roofs, interior partitions and offices are noticeably absent. The only interruption in this enormous workspace consists of four large patios.

To make the former factory halls suitable for housing a publicity firm, architect Georg Witteveen and interior designer Ramin Visch devised a strategy of 'light urbanism'. In other words, there was to be no fixed distribution of the interior space with a permanent infrastructure of corridors and services; instead a more or less provisional exploration of the floor area was adopted using detachable elements.

The strategy has been implemented before, but rarely on such a scale and with such an architectural design. In many regards the Ogilvy office has the character of a covered exterior space. Little pavilion-type buildings can be seen here and there between the long rows of work tables. There are two glass boxes on pillars for meeting rooms that are reminiscent of the famous glass houses of Mies van der Rohe and Philip Johnson in their design and detailing. And there are four black boxes of untreated steel, with raised work floors, which are built on 'cocoons' containing small offices. Two wooden sheds with red boards form an entrance portal and company kitchen respectively.

The pavilions are exceptionally neat and minimalist in their detailing. They are not placed free-standing under the roof, but have good solid foundations underneath the concrete floor, which is located 35 cm (14 in) above the original factory floor to provide room for invisible floor insulation, services and cable ducts. Reverberation is reduced by applying a strong sound-absorbent layer on the underside of the shed roofs.

Architecture:
Studio Ramin Visch
Client:
Ogilvy Group Nederland bv
Project team:
George Witteveen, Ramin Visch,
Bas van Mierlo, Simon Jongma,
Peter van de Geer
Floor area:
67,800 sqft (6,300 sqm)

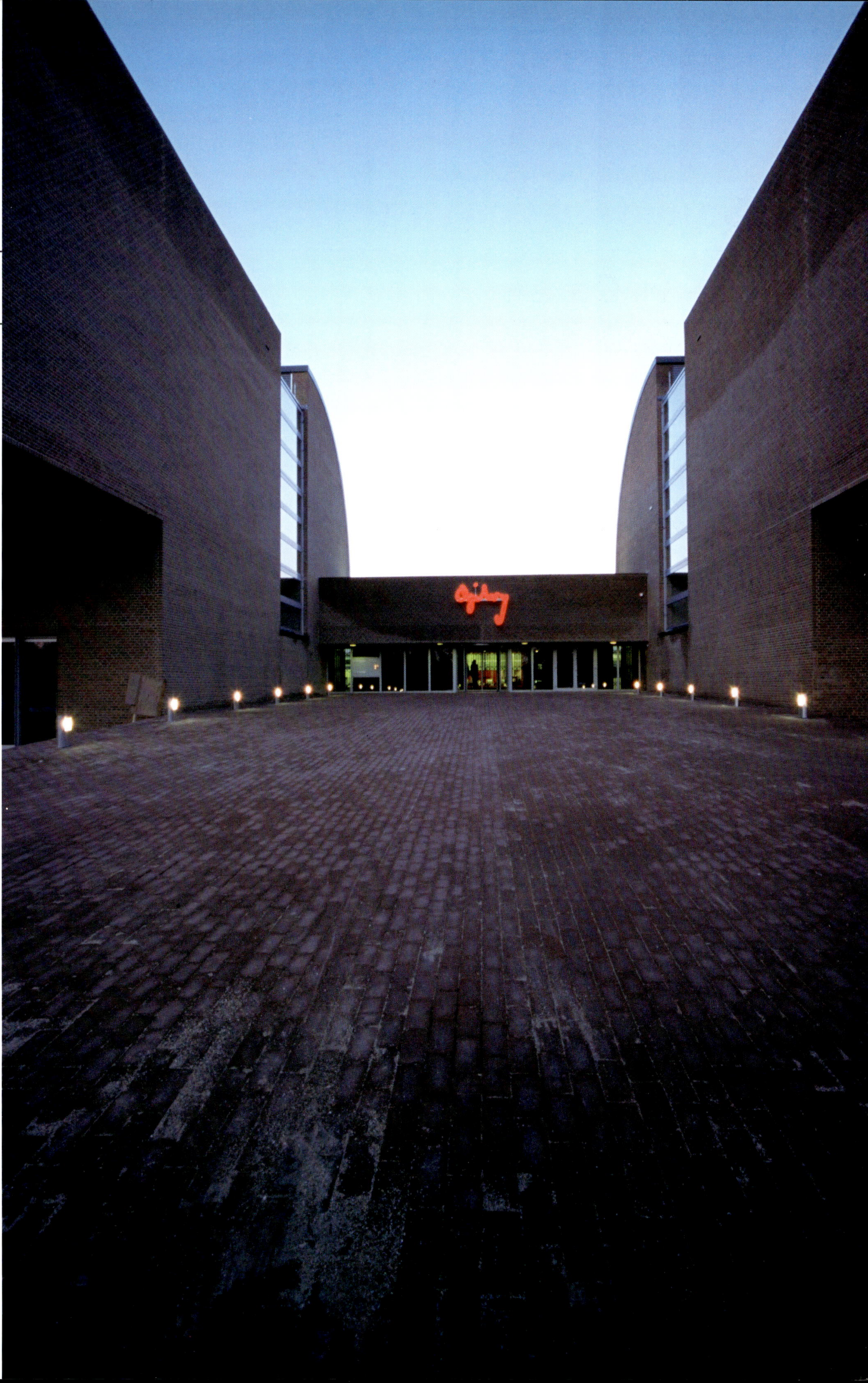

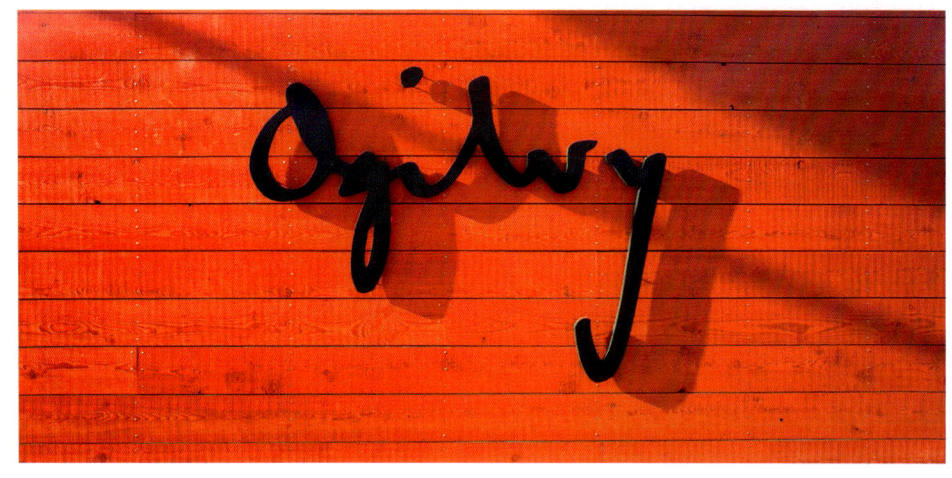

The agency has set up office in the former factory hall of a cycle manufacturers, located on an industrial site.

To make the former factory halls of the cycle factory suitable for housing a publicity firm, architect Georg Witteveen and interior designer Ramin Visch devised a strategy of 'light urbanism'.

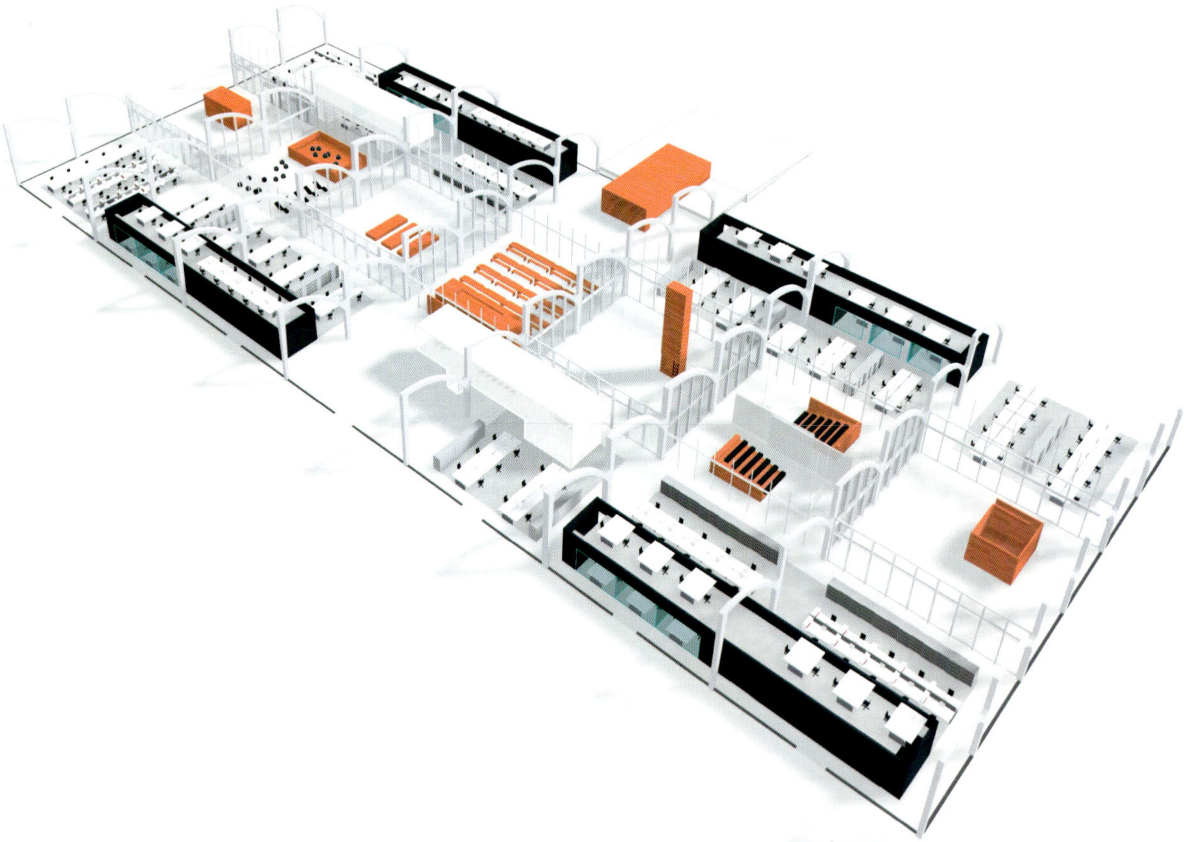

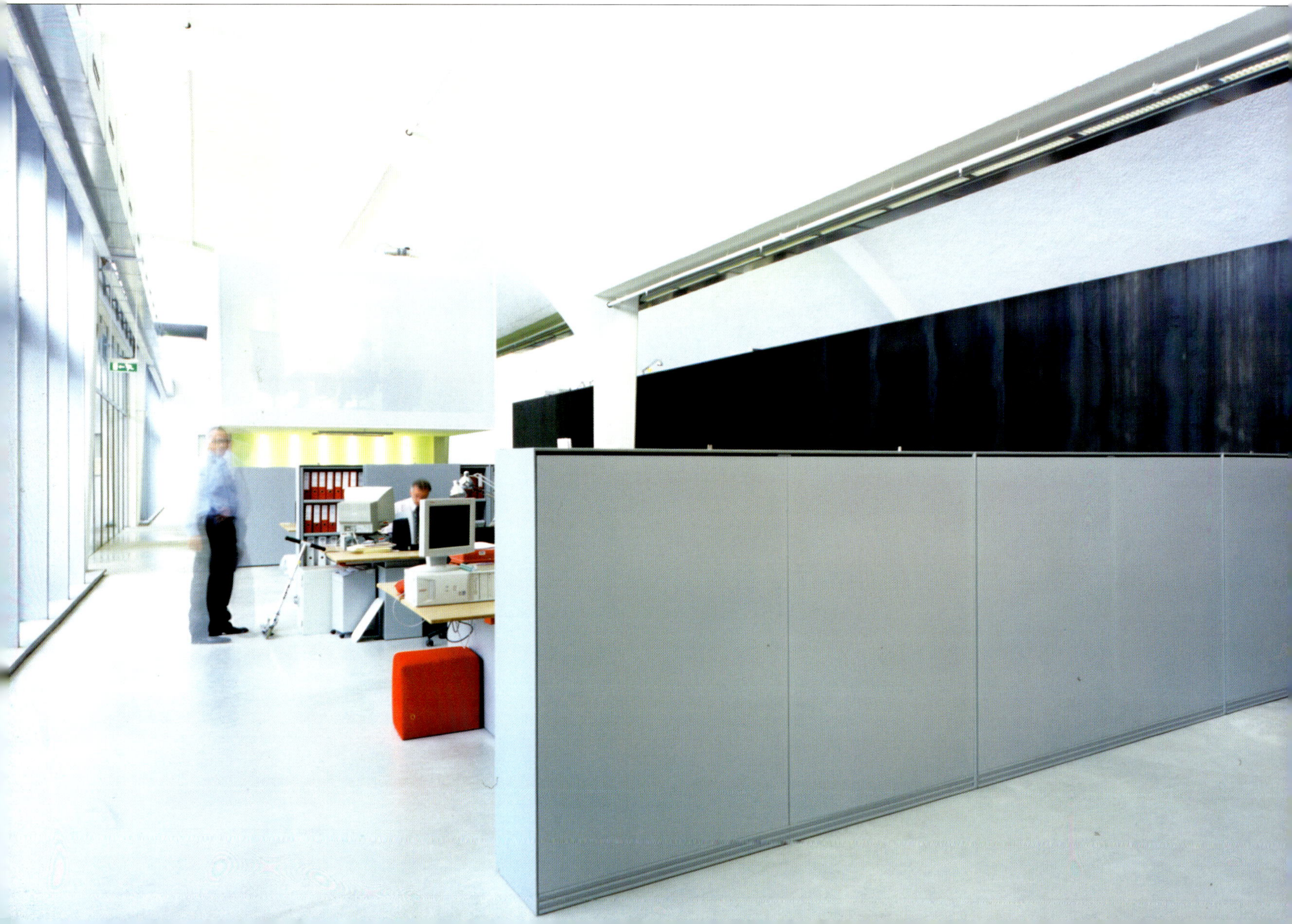

There are four black boxes of untreated steel with raised work floors, which are built on cocoons containing small offices.

Two wooden sheds with red boards form an entrance portal and company kitchen respectively.

Floor plan

Section AA

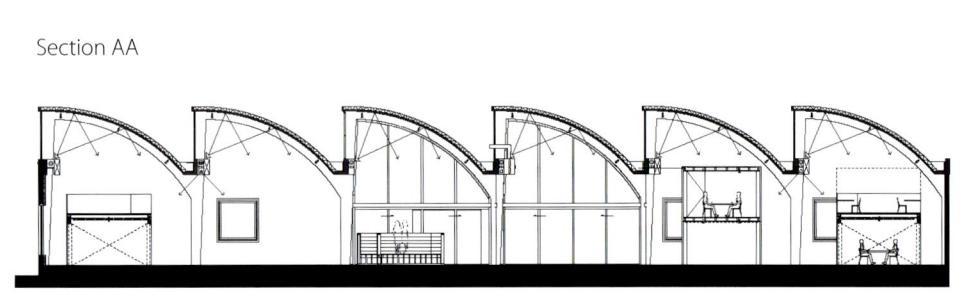

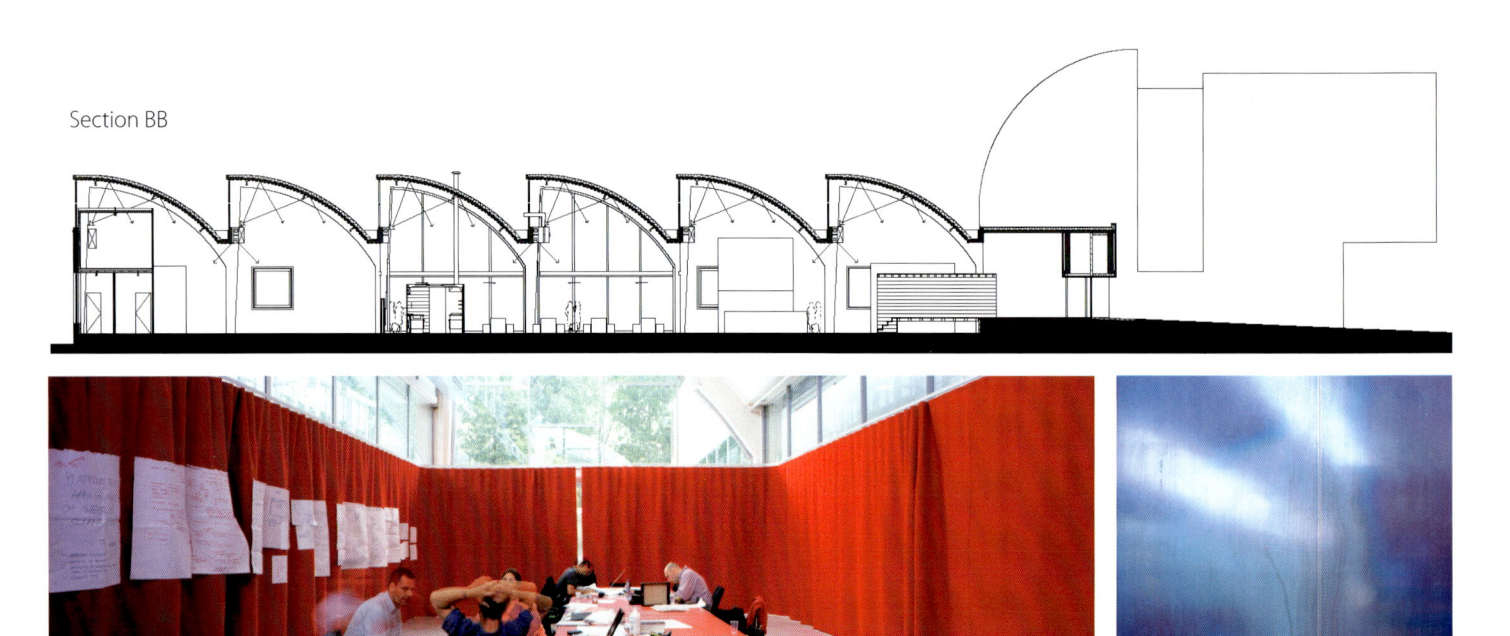

Section BB

227

El Dorado Architects

Hodgdon Powder Company

Herington, Kansas, USA **Photographs: Mike Sinclair**

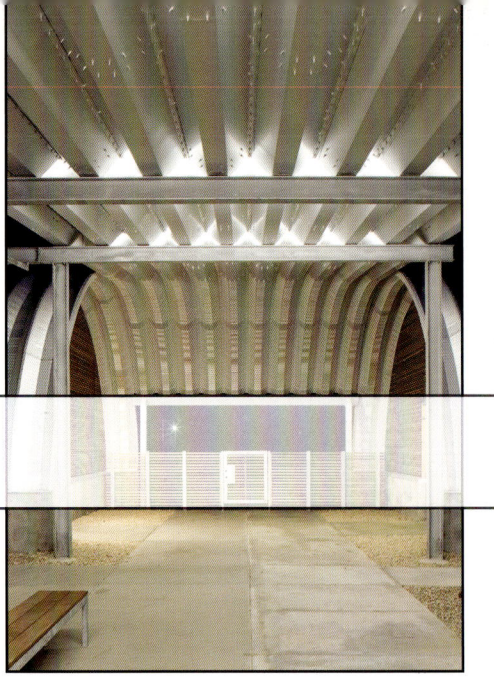

Rather than build yet another building for powder, the client, a gunpowder manufacturer, specified that it wanted to build an innovative building specifically for people.

The program for the company's new 790 sqm office was in part responsive to the hazardous nature of gunpowder manufacturing. Employees needed a changing facility with plumbing specifically designed to process lead residue from work clothing. Many employees smoke cigarettes, and a designated smoking area was required which was clearly separated from the manufacturing plant. Additionally, a dining hall large enough for all 50 employees was necessary. The CEO, impressed with research he had recently undertaken about open-office environments, asked El Dorado Inc. to create a combination of private offices and open workstations which would promote a sense of teamwork amongst employees.

Rather than design a singular structure, El Dorado proposed a series of Quonset Hut structures, all connected by an overhead canopy. Intimate courtyard spaces were developed as an integral part of the design, allowing the opportunity for outdoor dining, as well as creating a strong connection to the surrounding landscape. Additionally, these exterior spaces serve to buffer and organize varying aspects of the design program.

Due to the remote location of the office facility, the architects ultimately conceived the Hodgdon "campus" as a community center of sorts, capable of hosting casual BBQ's, employee birthday parties, and family-related events. At night, careful attention to lighting allows the sequence of indoor and outdoor spaces to remain animated and in tact.

El Dorado also designed and fabricated all office furniture for the facility, including custom outdoor and indoor dining tables. The project was completed for a modest $130 per square foot.

Architecture:
El Dorado Architects
Client:
Hodgdon Powder Company
Principal in charge:
Josh Shelton
Project architect:
Saen Slattery
Furniture design and fabrication:
Brady Neely
Structural engineer:
Genesis Structures
Metal building engineering:
Steelmaster USA
Landscaping:
El Dorado Inc.
General contractor:
Kelley Construction Company
Lighting design:
Derek Porter Studio
Floor area:
8,500 sqft (790 sqm)

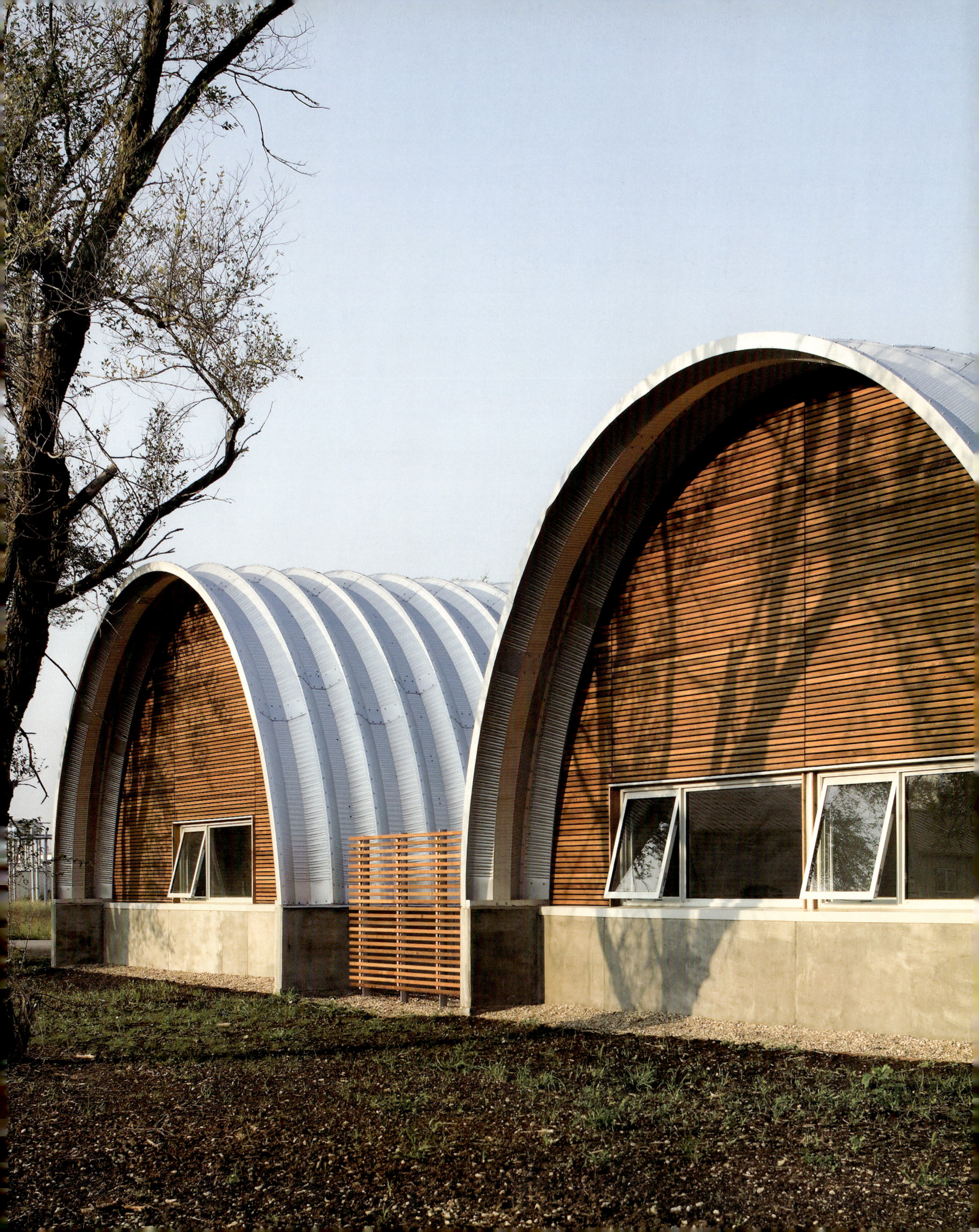

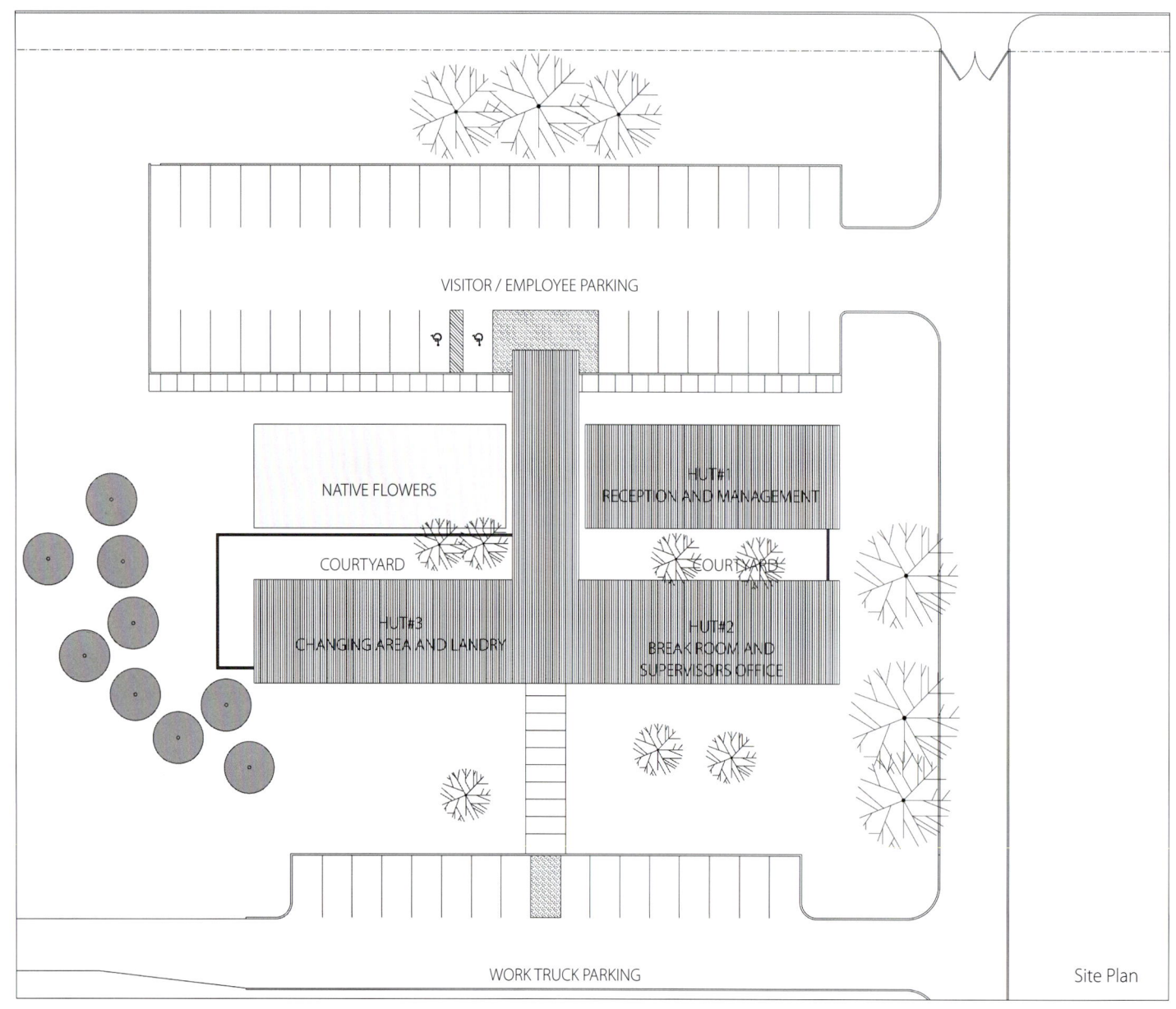

VISITOR / EMPLOYEE PARKING

NATIVE FLOWERS

HUT #1
RECEPTION AND MANAGEMENT

COURTYARD

COURTYARD

HUT #3
CHANGING AREA AND LANDRY

HUT #2
BREAK ROOM AND
SUPERVISORS OFFICE

WORK TRUCK PARKING

Site Plan

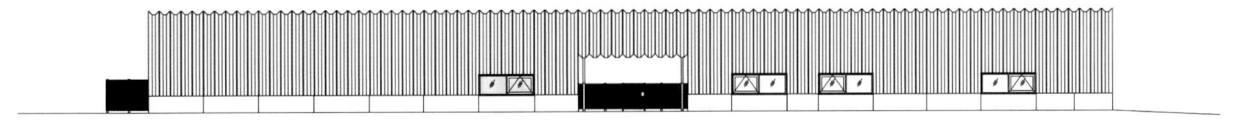

South elevation - Huts # 2 and #3

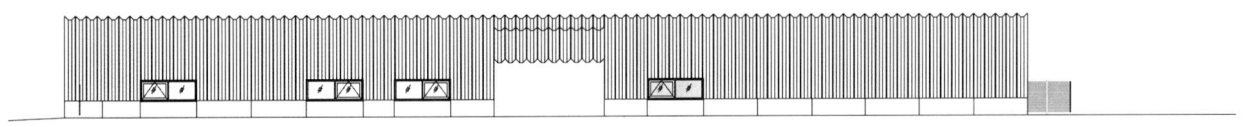

North elevation - Huts # 2 and #3

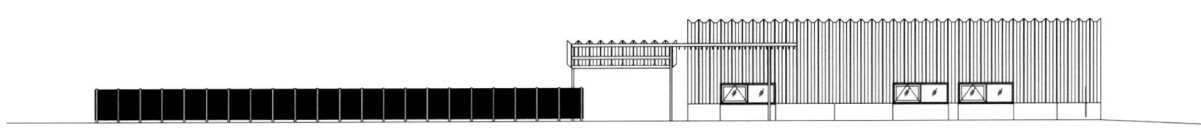

South elevation - Hut # 1

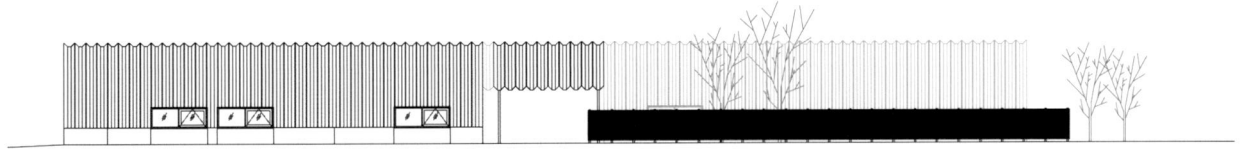

North elevation - Hut # 1

East elevation

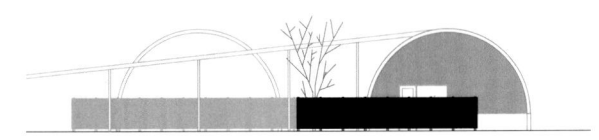

West elevation

West elevation

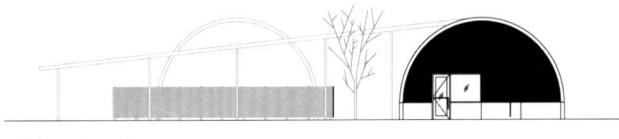

Elevations present the simplicity of a self-spanning corrugated structural skin system. The end walls are sheathed in cedar slats, an indigenous wood species abundant throughout Kansas.

Floor plan

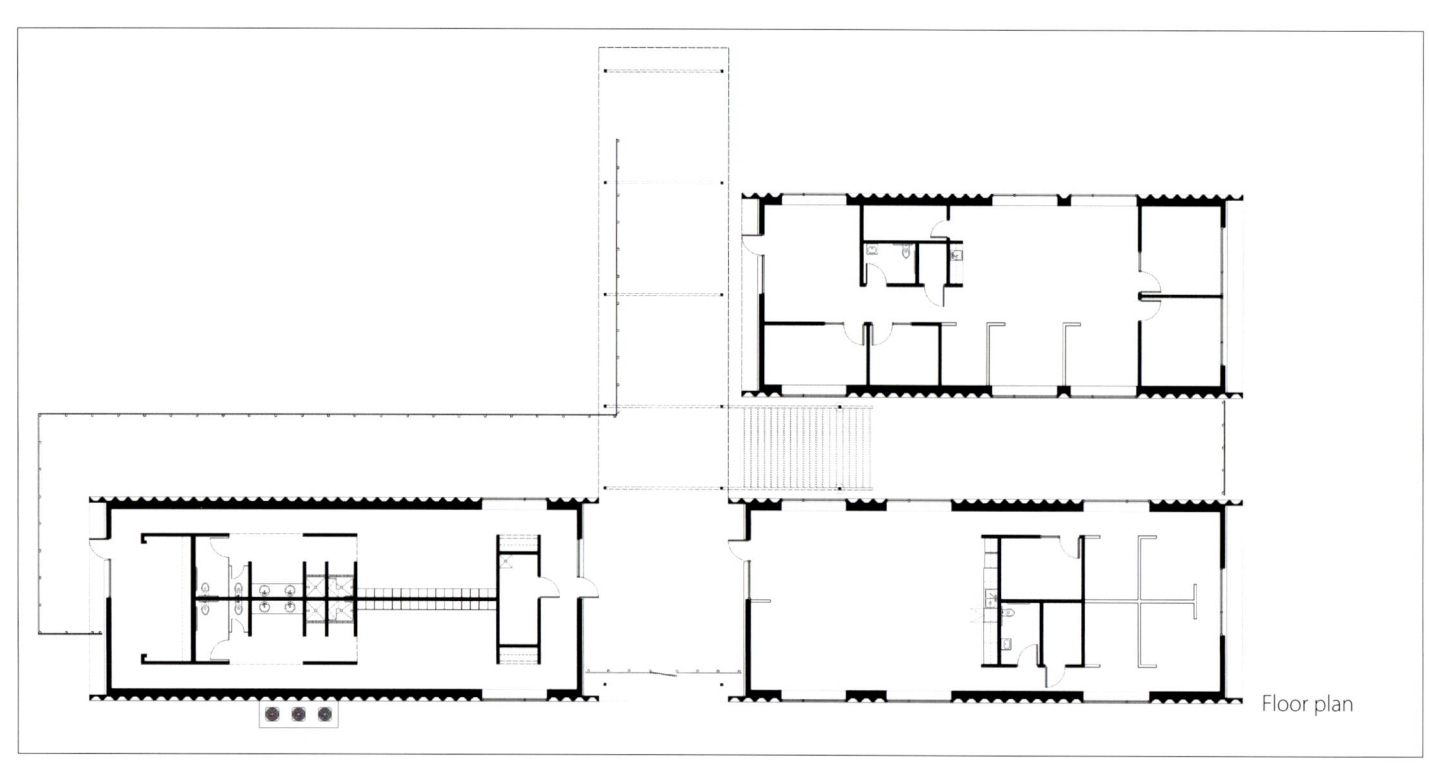

The building site is located within the Flint Hills of Central Kansas, a rolling terrain of indigenous prairie grasses and wildflowers. The building is a small office complex serving the employees of the gunpowder manufacturing plant. The plant is directly adjacent to a rural airport, which was once a military air base used for servicing WW2 bombers.

Informed by the surrounding rural vernacular, and guided by a tight budget (only $130 per square foot, including interior build-out), the architect proposed that a series of Quonset huts serve the function for a relatively simple office program.

Wall sections

235

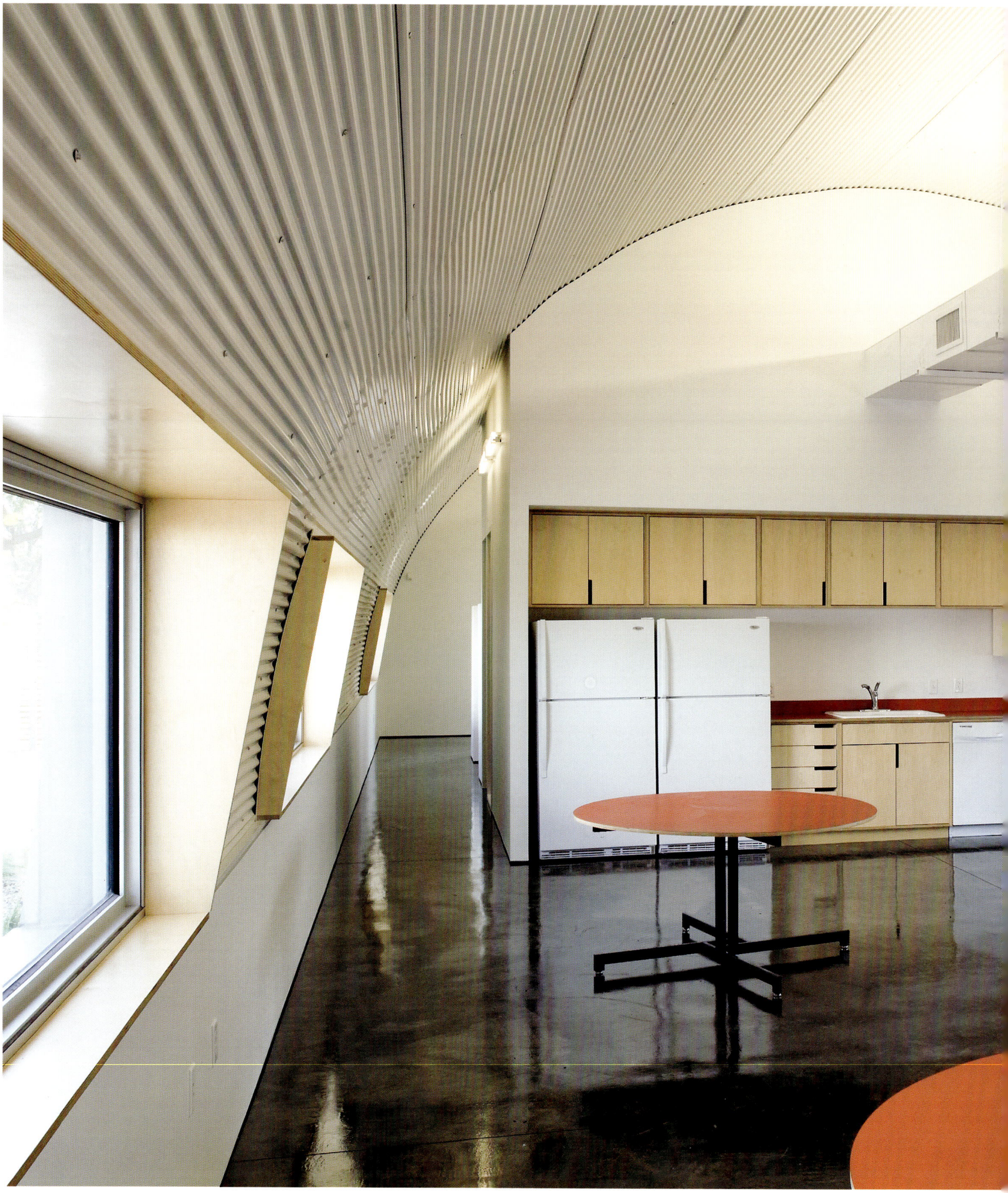

237

CL3

K-Boxing Headquarters

Shanghai, China   **Photographs: Nirut Benjabanpot**

K-Boxing is a Chinese fashion brand that relocated its headquarters in 2009 to Shanghai. The sleekly designed offices occupy a brand new seven-storey office building that houses the company's administration, sales and design activities.

The new headquarters are organized in a vertical manner, with the main reception area and conference center located on levels one and two. The sales department and general office space are found on levels three to five, while the executive offices are on level six. Finally, up above the rest, the design and workshop space, along with an outdoor deck, is on level seven.

In order to unite all of these disparate activities, which take place on different levels, the architects decided to visually connect the volume of spaces by way of a series of openings through the floors. This open connection is further reinforced by the visual transparency between the front office space and back office space, which are divided by glass partitions. The result is a dynamic and energetic environment ideally suited to both work and social activities.

Sleek, minimalist design, including powerful graphic displays and the use of a visually strong corporate color, further emphasize the identity of this corporation.

Architecture:
CL3
Floor area:
50,700 sqft (4,712 sqm)

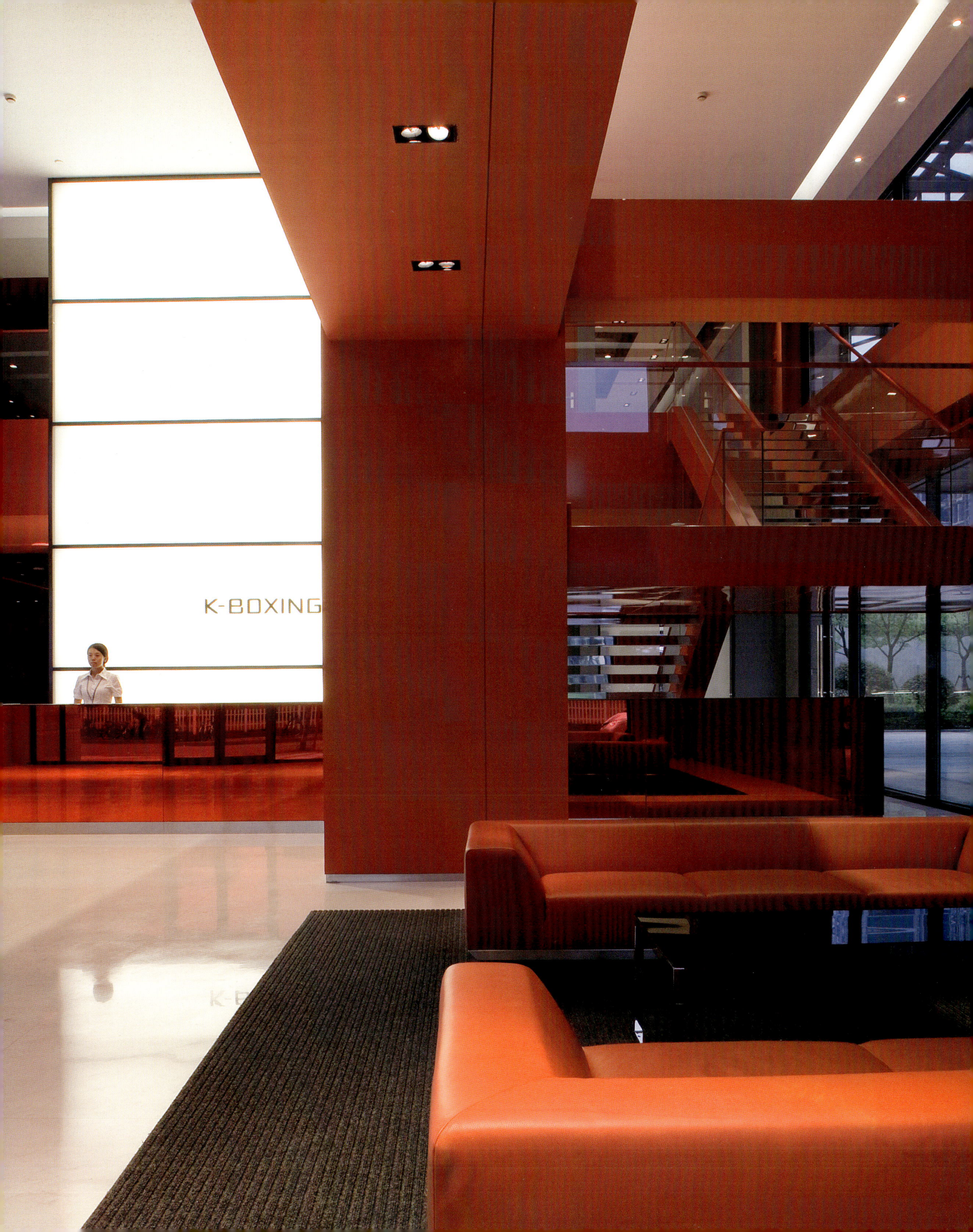
K-BOXING

A sign of China's rising corporate power, the sleek new headquarters of the K-Boxing fashion brand make use of minimalist lines, strong graphics and ubiquitous touches of red.

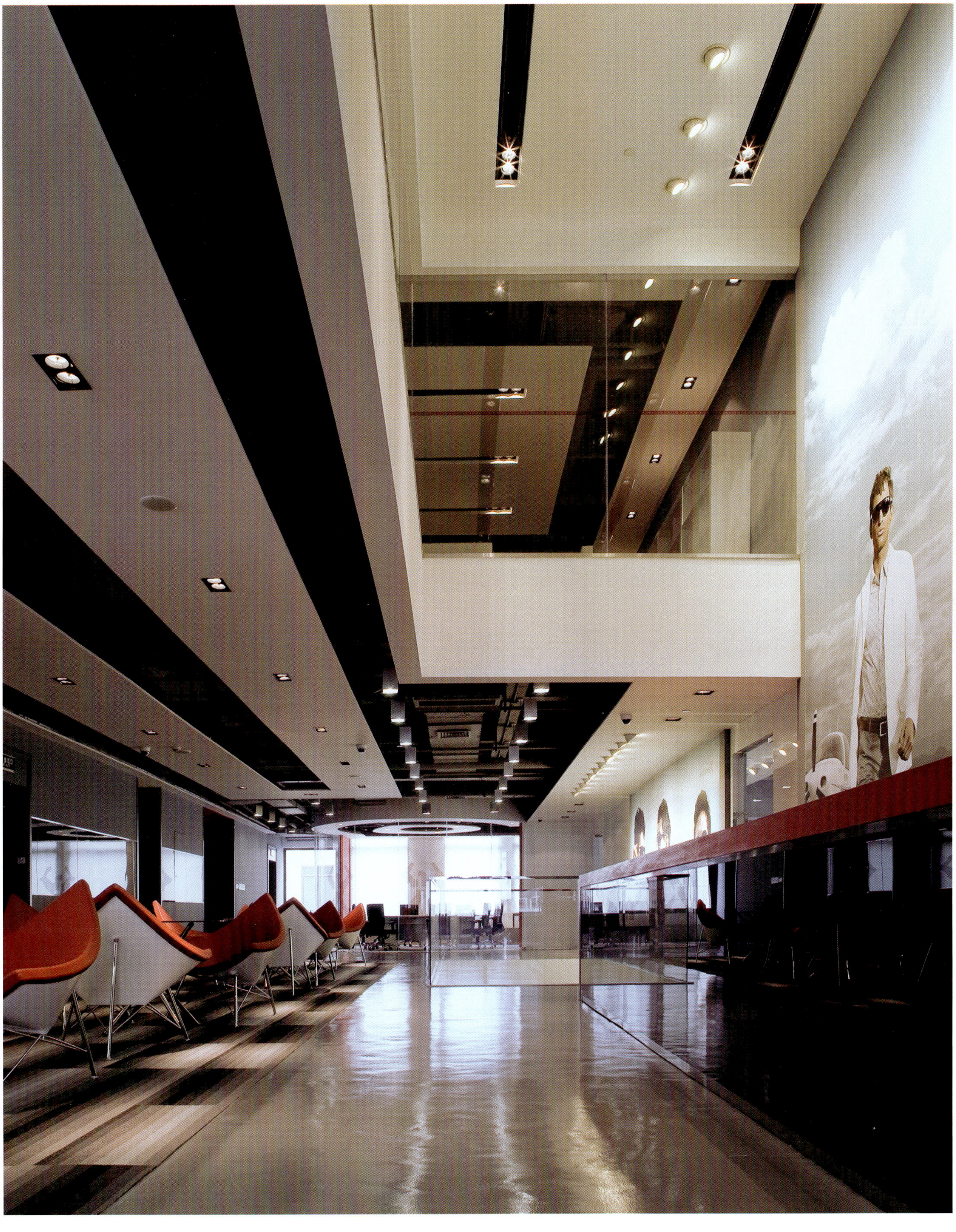

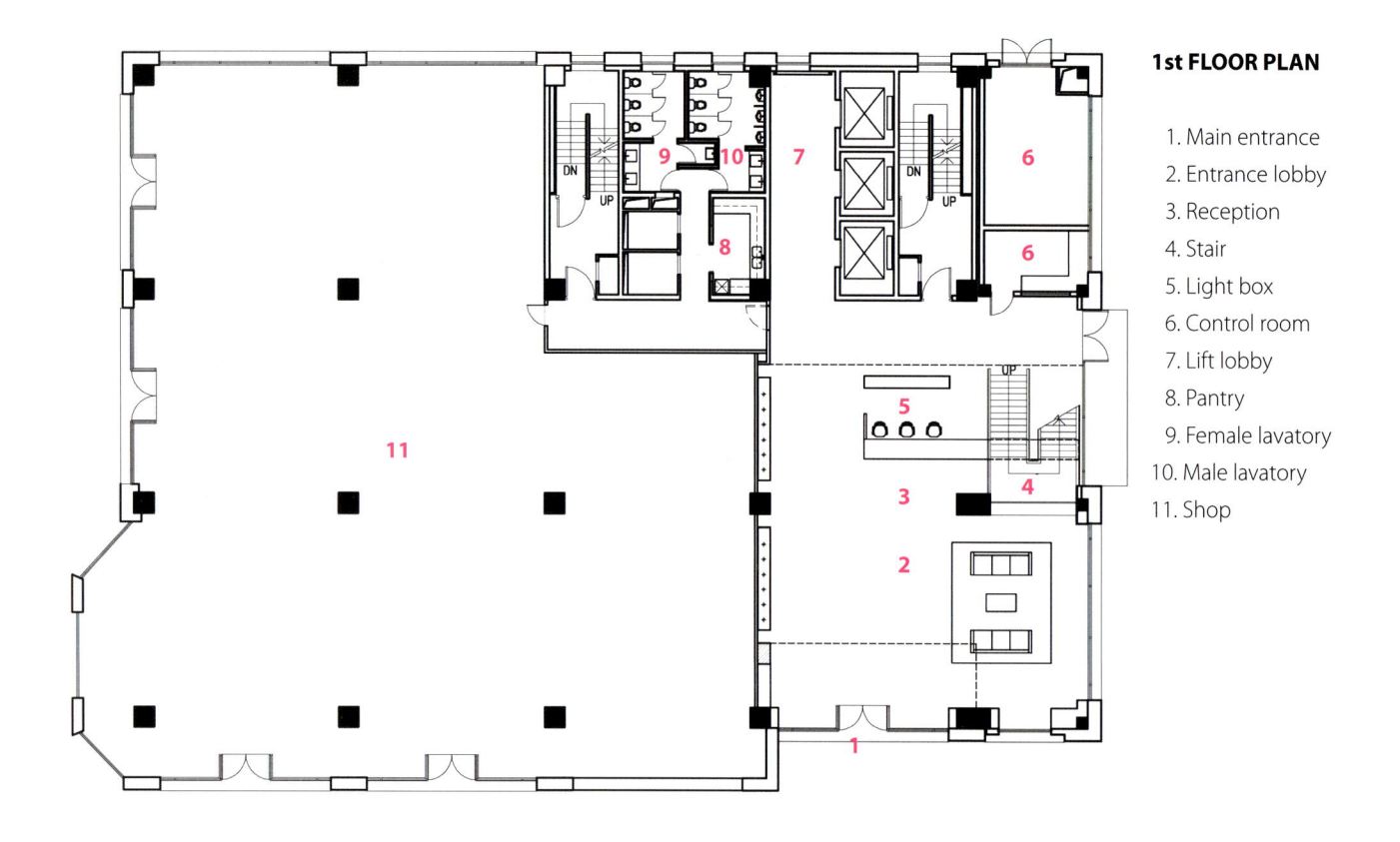

1st FLOOR PLAN

1. Main entrance
2. Entrance lobby
3. Reception
4. Stair
5. Light box
6. Control room
7. Lift lobby
8. Pantry
9. Female lavatory
10. Male lavatory
11. Shop

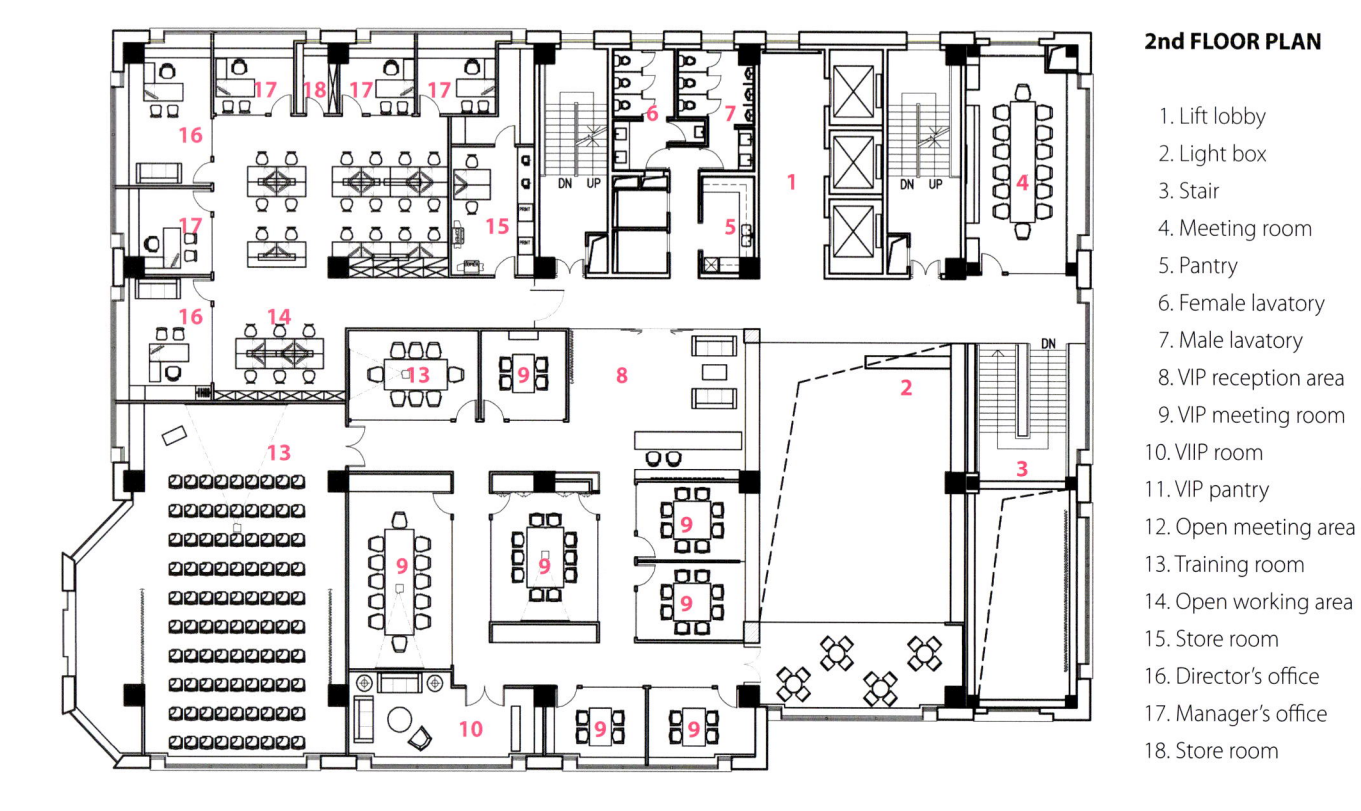

2nd FLOOR PLAN

1. Lift lobby
2. Light box
3. Stair
4. Meeting room
5. Pantry
6. Female lavatory
7. Male lavatory
8. VIP reception area
9. VIP meeting room
10. VIIP room
11. VIP pantry
12. Open meeting area
13. Training room
14. Open working area
15. Store room
16. Director's office
17. Manager's office
18. Store room

3rd FLOOR PLAN

1. Lift lobby
2. Pantry
3. Female lavatory
4. Male lavatory
5. Lounge
6. Meeting room
7. Open working area
8. Manager's office
9. Director's office
10. General manager's office
11. Store room
12. Computer room
13. IT department

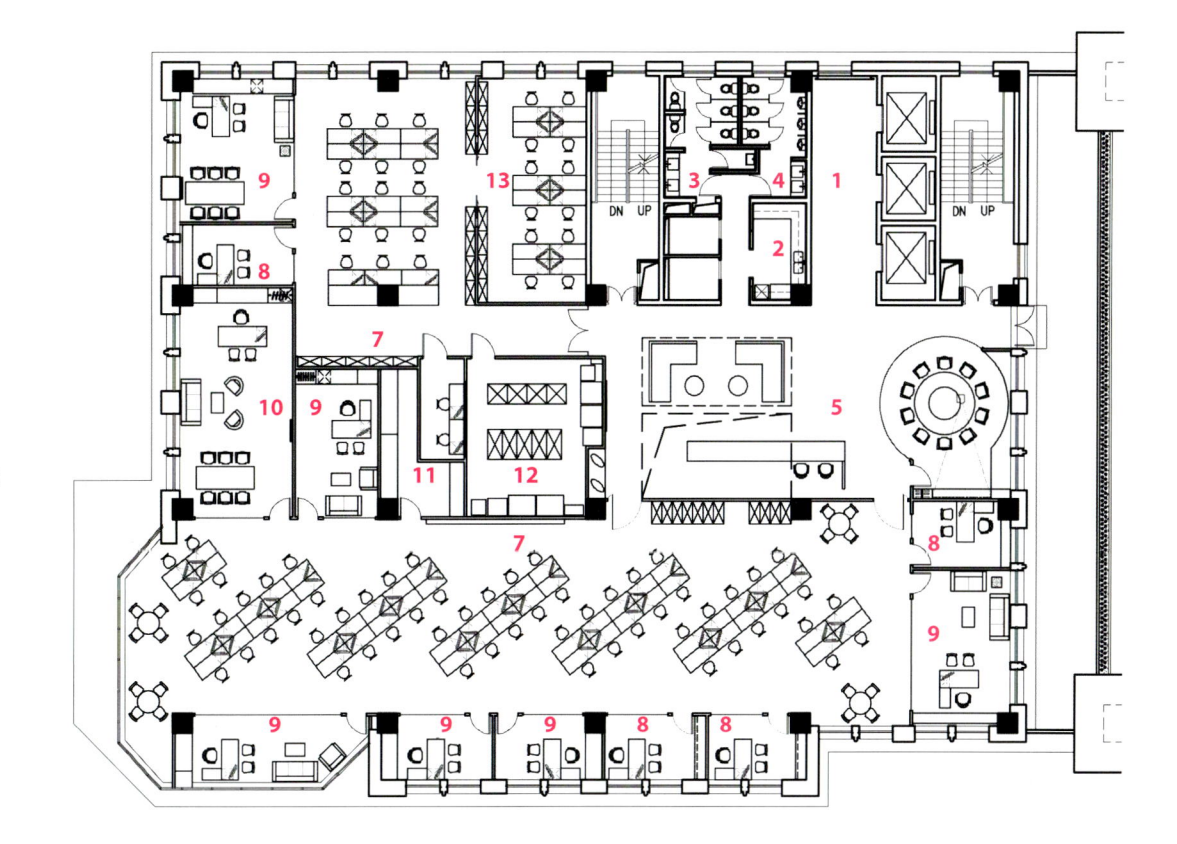

4th FLOOR PLAN

1. Lift lobby
2. Pantry
3. Female lavatory
4. Male lavatory
5. Open meeting area
6. Leisure bar
7. Meeting room
8. Manager's office
9. Director's office
10. Open working area
11. Image promotion
12. General manager's office

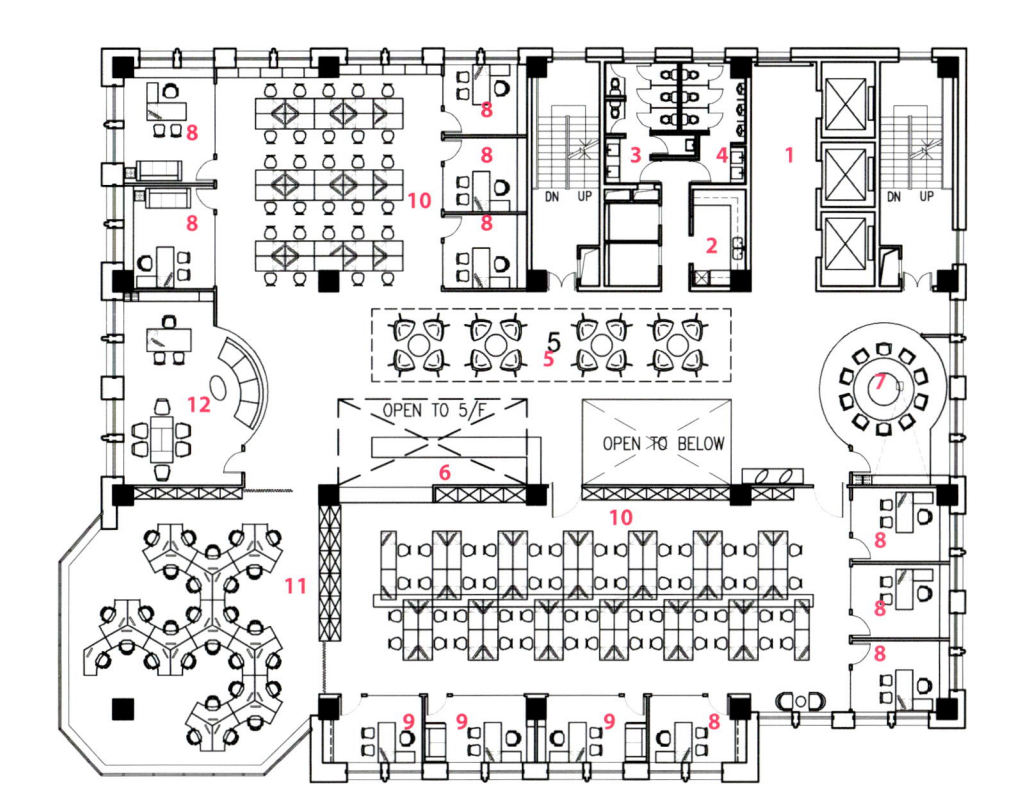

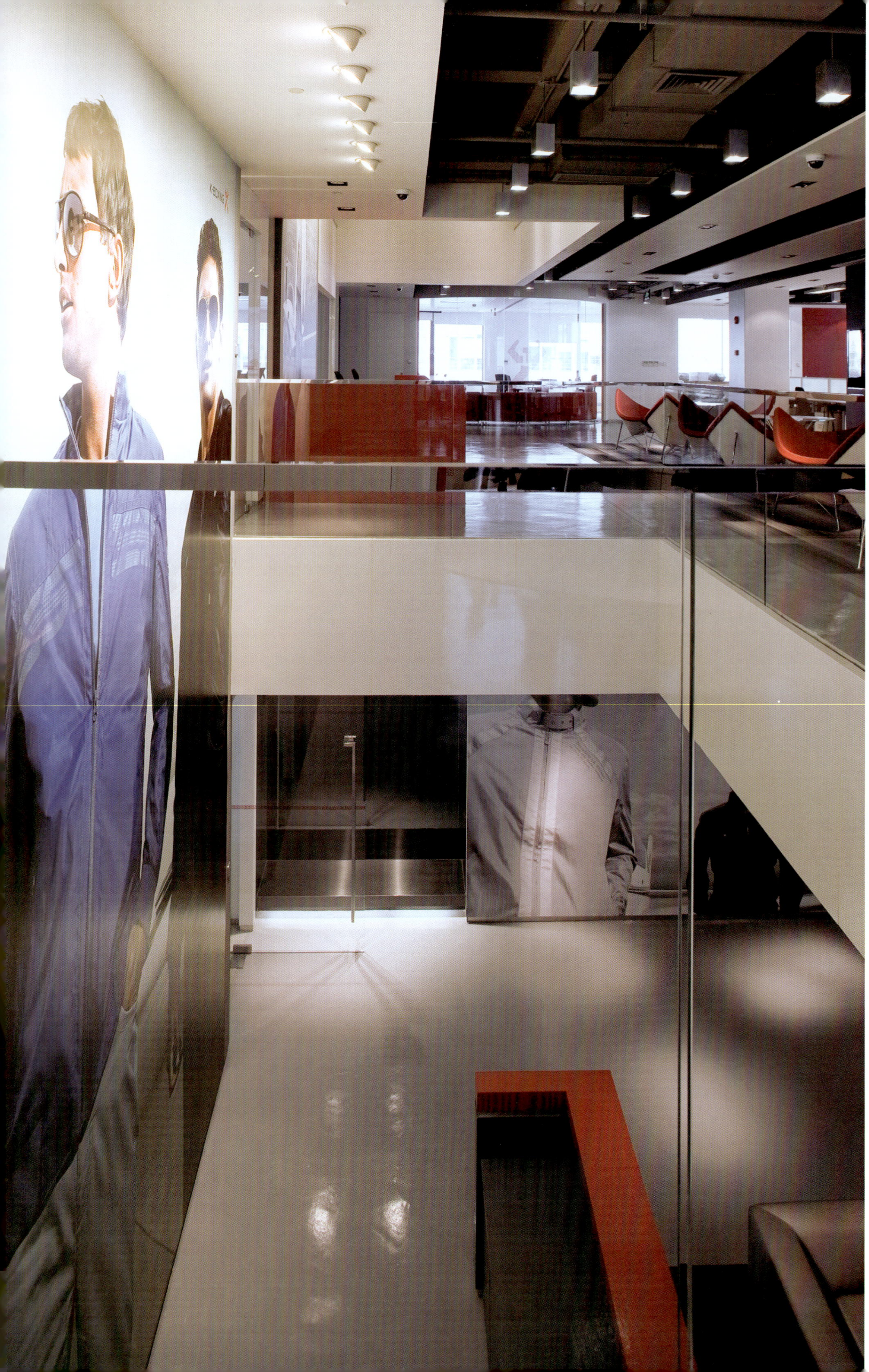

5th FLOOR PLAN

1. Lift lobby
2. Pantry
3. Female lavatory
4. Male lavatory
5. Library
6. Open working area
7. Store room
8. Manager's office
9. Director's office
10. Showroom

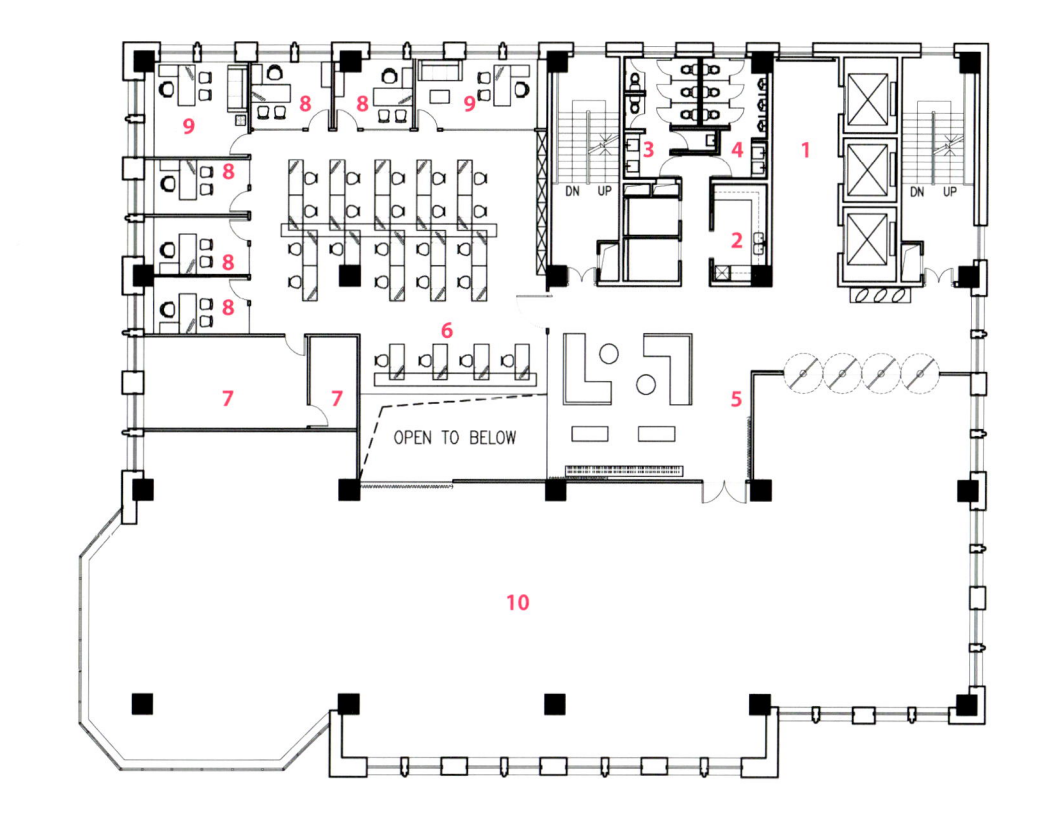

6th FLOOR PLAN

1. Lift lobby
2. Pantry
3. Female lavatory
4. Male lavatory
5. Reception area
6. Filing room
7. Waiting area
8. President's secretary
9. President's meeting room
10. President's office
11. President's study room
12. Private washroom
13. Senior vice president
14. Store room
15. VIP guest room
16. Chairman's office
17. Secretary area
18. Meeting room
19. Assistant president's office

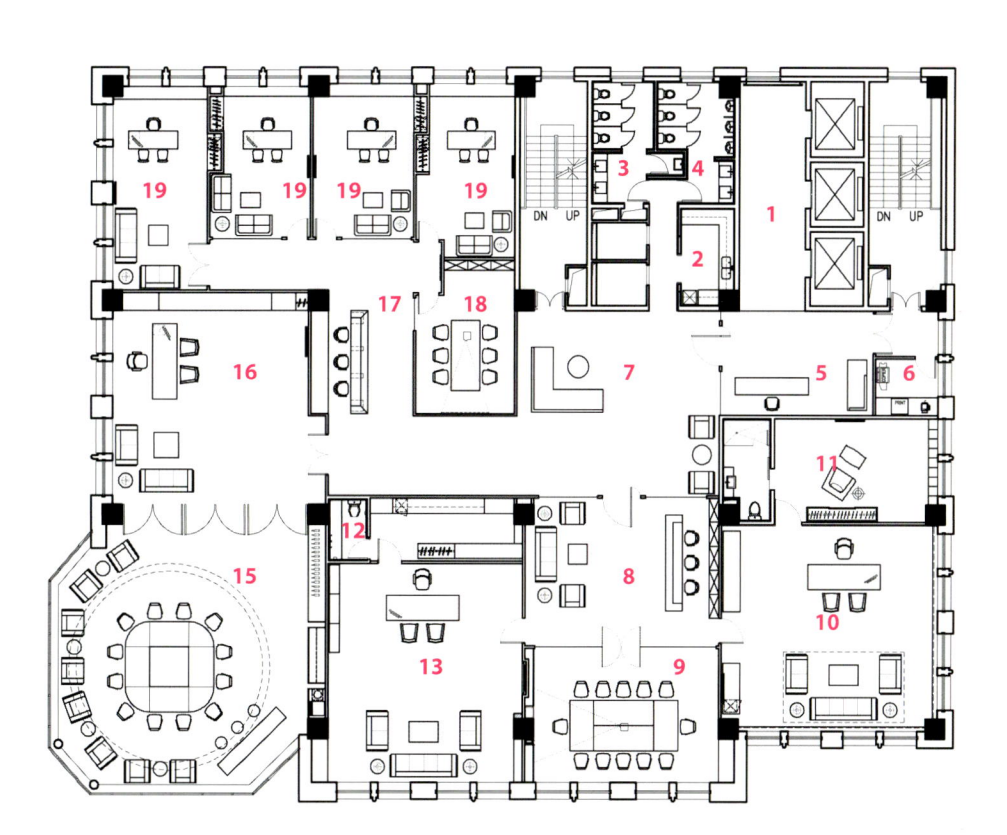

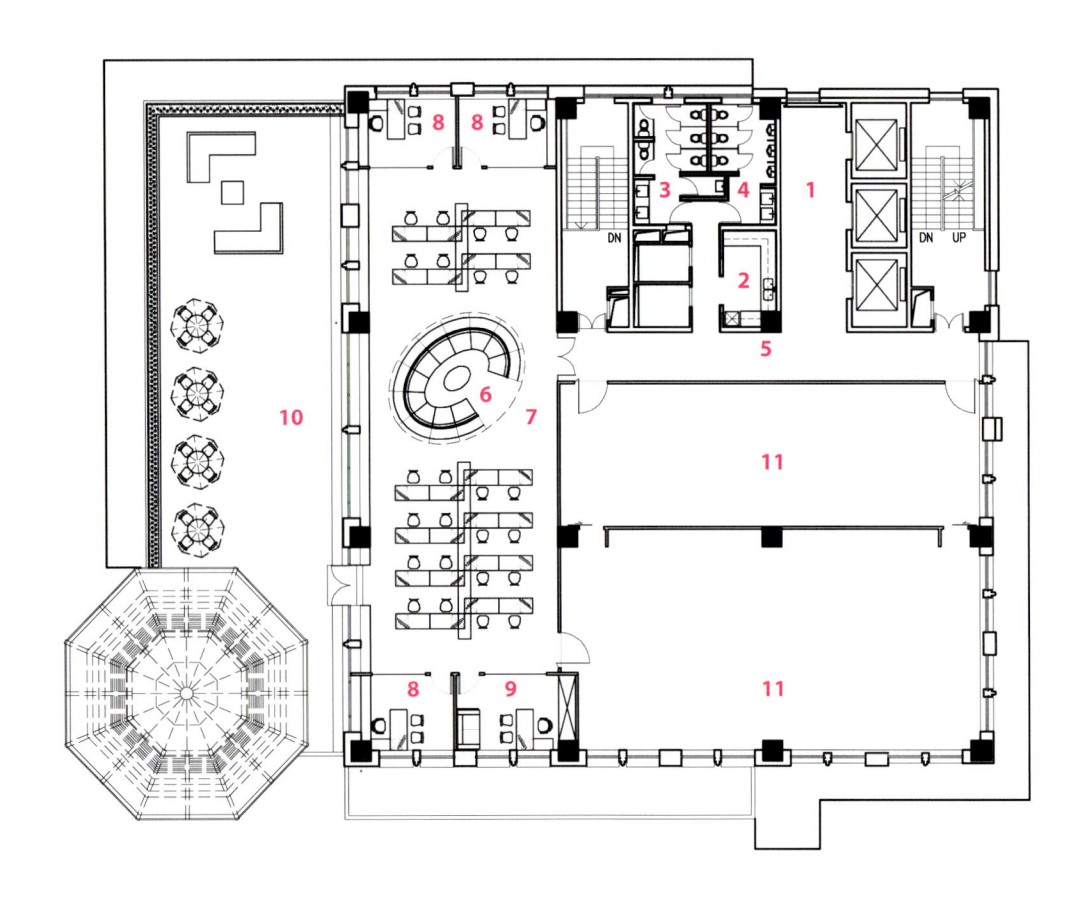

7th FLOOR PLAN

1. Lift lobby
2. Pantry
3. Female lavatory
4. Male lavatory
5. Corridor
6. Meeting room
7. Open working area
8. Manager's office
9. Director's office
10. Roof garden
11. Workshop

Sleek, minimalist design, including powerful graphic displays and the use of a visually strong corporate color, further emphasize the identity of this corporation.

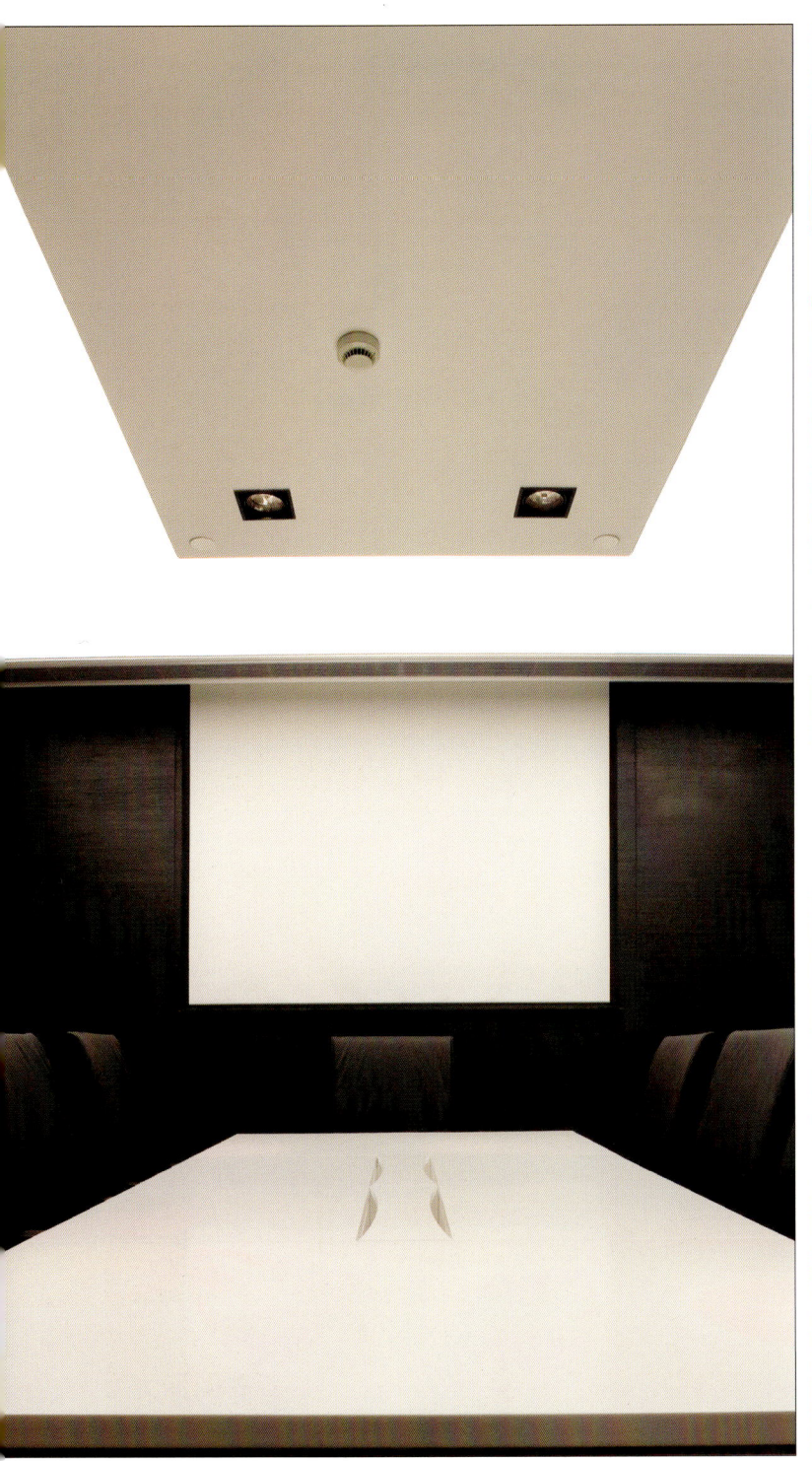

Giorgio Borruso Design

Fornari Group Headquarters

Milan, Italy   Photographs: Alberto Ferrero

For the Fornari Group Headquarters on Via Morimondo in the Navigli area of Milan, a conversion of the famous historic porcelain workshops of Richard Ginori, the intention was to create a 35,000 sqft (3250 sqm) flexible space, with industrial concrete floors and exposed steel structures throughout, to house the showrooms, as well as executive offices, storage, and areas to be utilized for exhibitions and events for the various brands that comprise the Fornari Group.

To take advantage of this sequence of large open spaces in a severe orthogonal grid, the architects inserted a central spine that penetrates the entire volume, not only connecting the different levels in a fluid and organic way, but also forming a pathway to guide traffic inside the expansive volume of the building. As you step through the main entrance door from Via Morimondo, illuminated by color-changing LEDs, there is a sort of corridor that becomes a reception area. This continues to penetrate directly into the showroom area. The geometrical construction is based on a series of thoughtfully controlled curves that are carved into the wall, ceiling and floors. You can see the process in three dimensions as seamless stainless steel pipes diverge and converge along the outlines of these curves, disengaging from the various volumes to become distinct lines, fulfilling additional functions as handrails or hanging space for the displays. The illusion created is that there is no gravitational force; that one can walk on any surface; that the entire system can be rotated ninety degrees and still work.

Architecture:
Giorgio Borruso Design
Area:
35,000 sqft (3250 sqm)

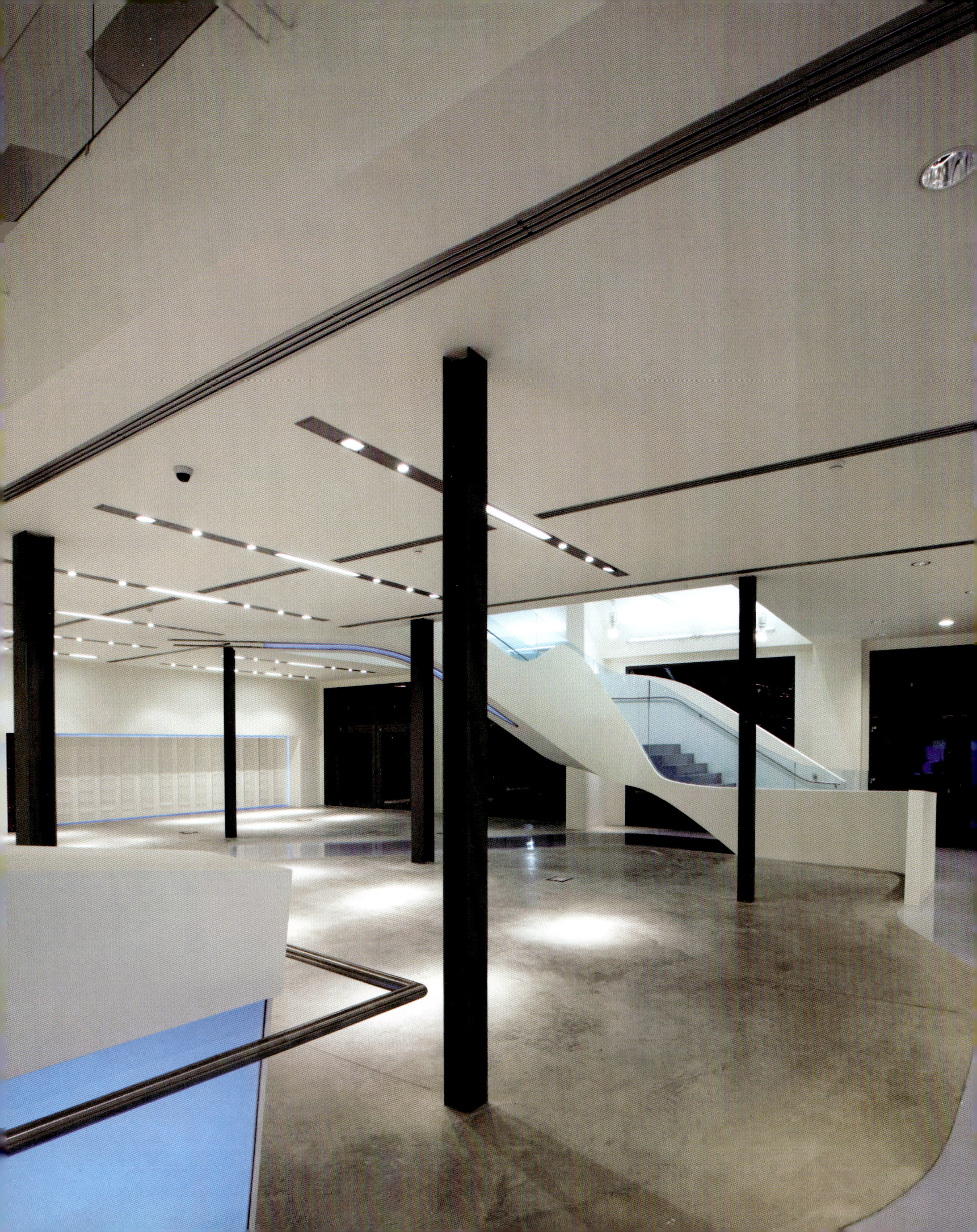

250

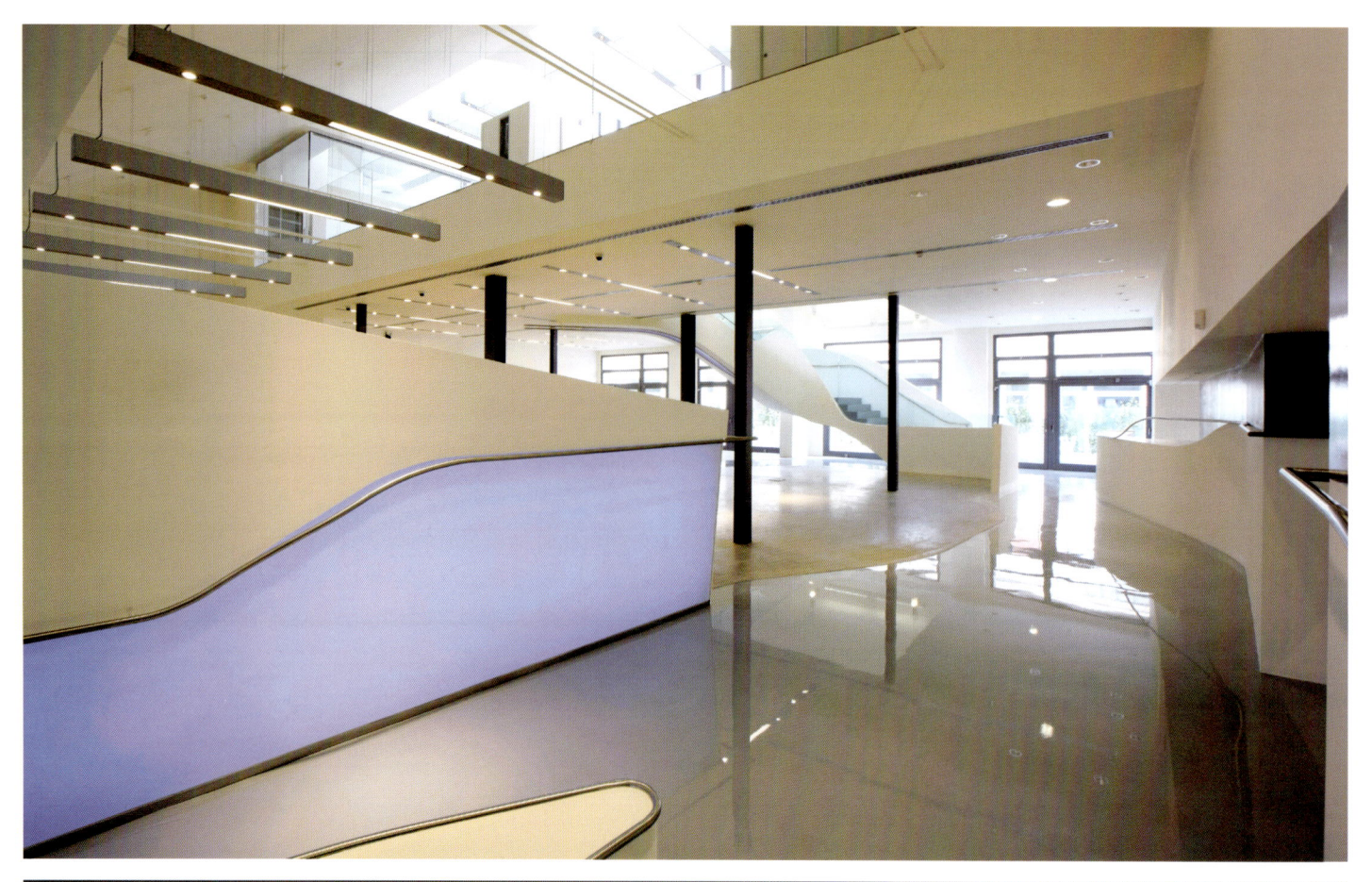

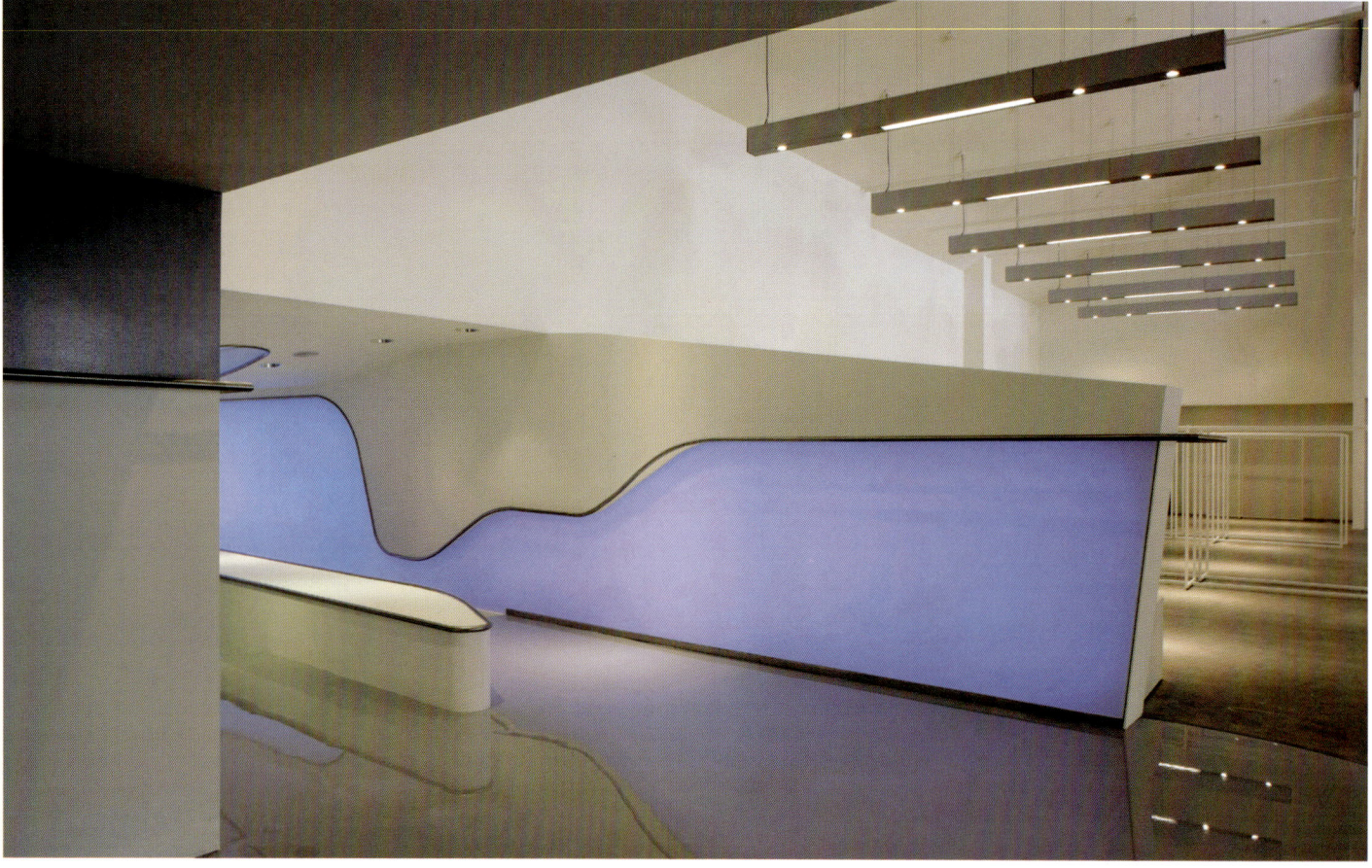

Ground floor plan

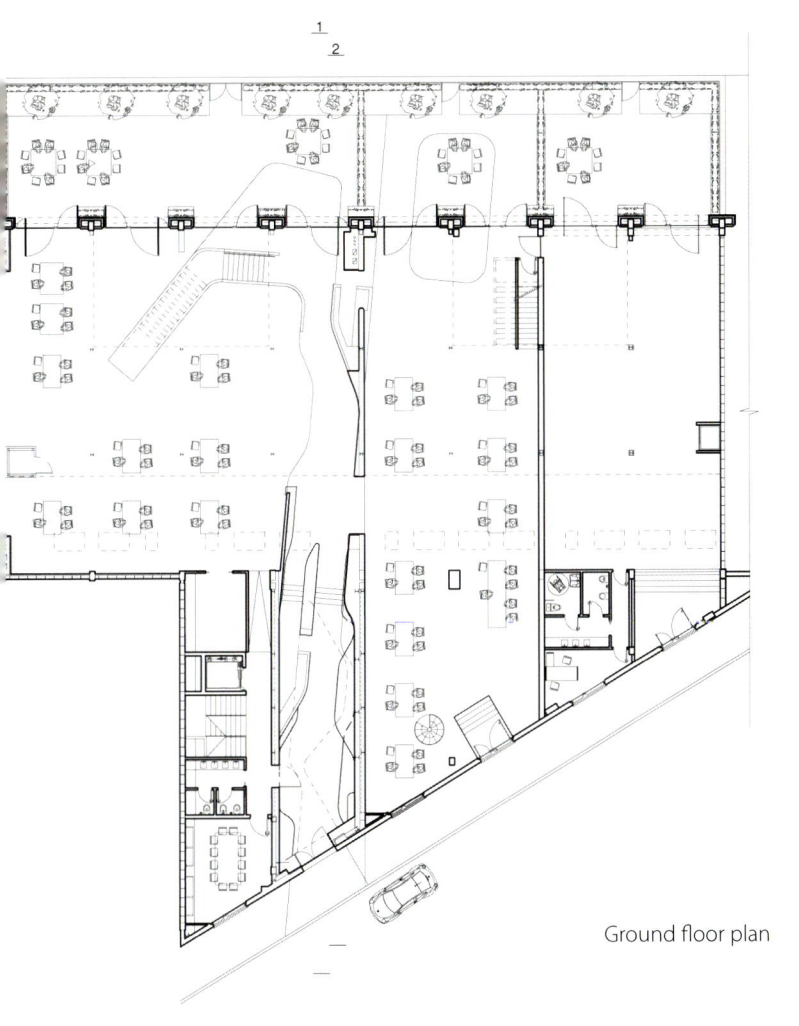

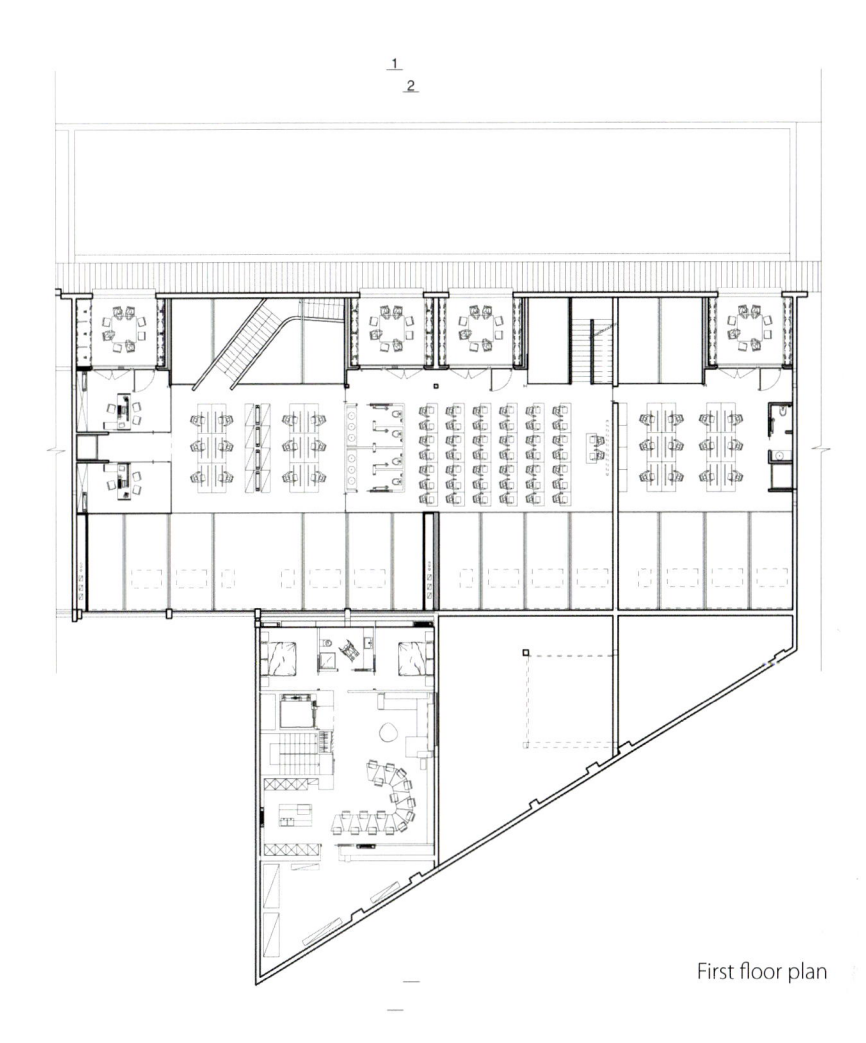

First floor plan

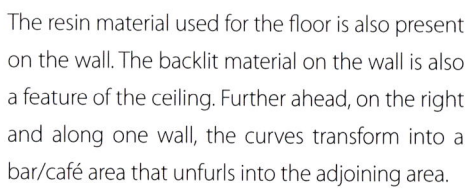

The resin material used for the floor is also present on the wall. The backlit material on the wall is also a feature of the ceiling. Further ahead, on the right and along one wall, the curves transform into a bar/café area that unfurls into the adjoining area.

Further forward still, on the left, the curves eventually take the shape of a staircase that leads up to the second level. The space beneath the staircase is defined by a projection of resin flooring that forms a sort of runway, used occasionally for product presentation. The illumination of the underside of the staircase echoes the lighting mood of the entrance area.

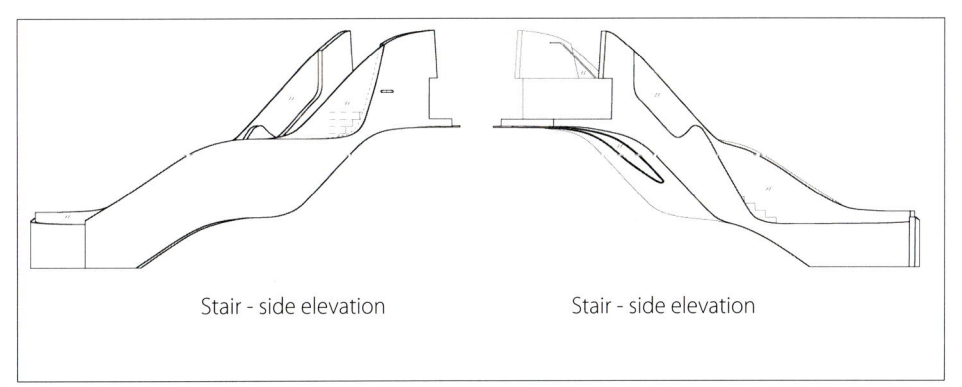

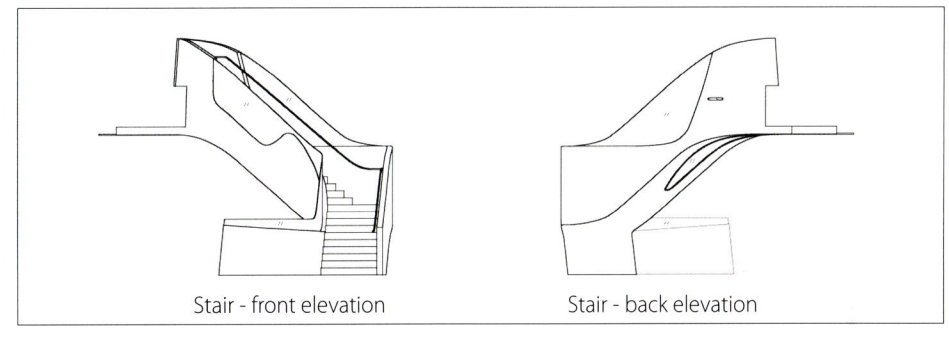

Stair - side elevation

Stair - side elevation

Stair - front elevation

Stair - back elevation

Section 1

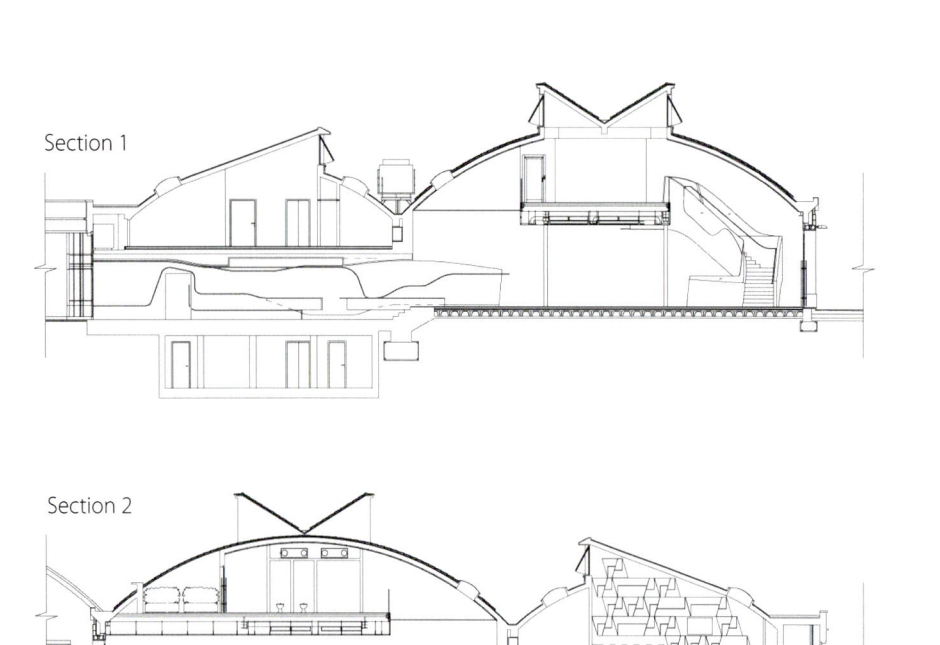

Section 2

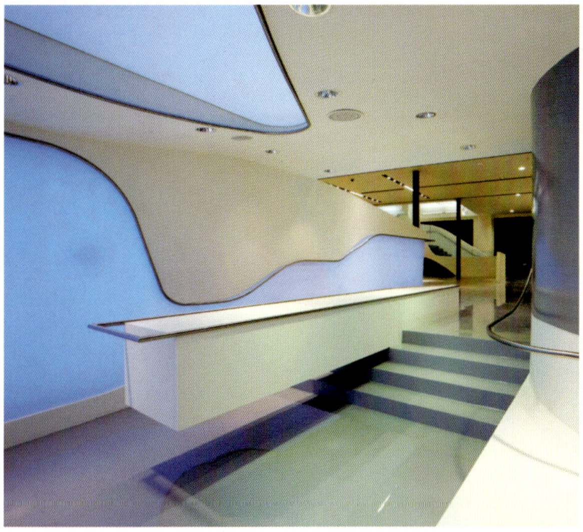
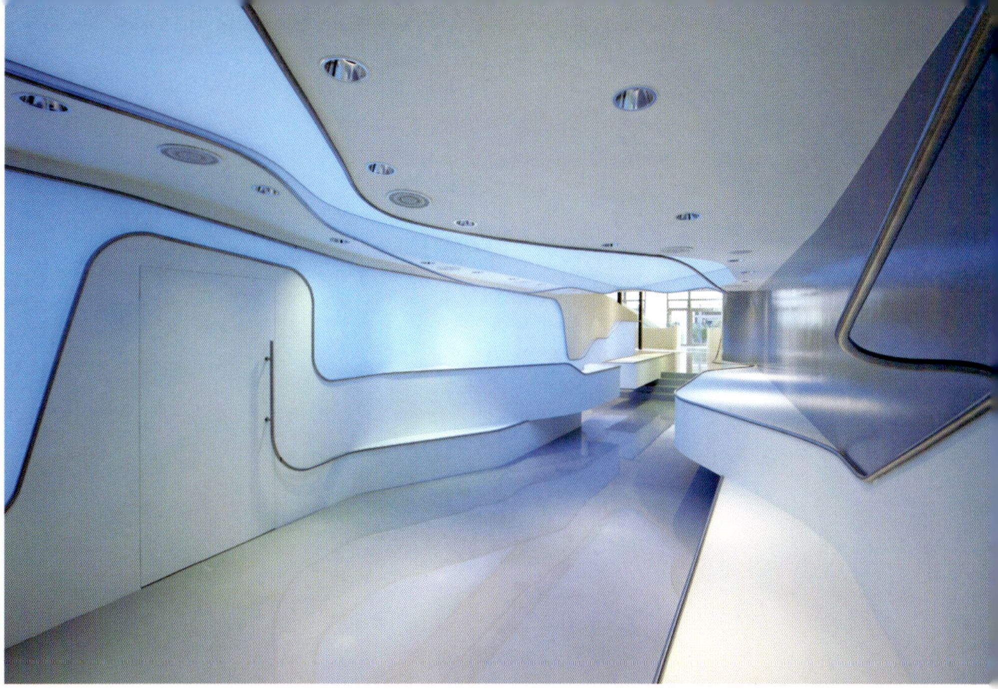
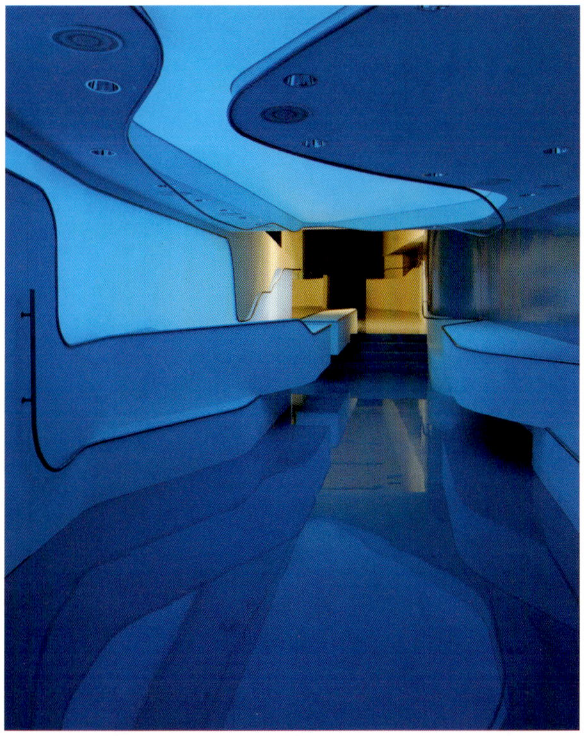
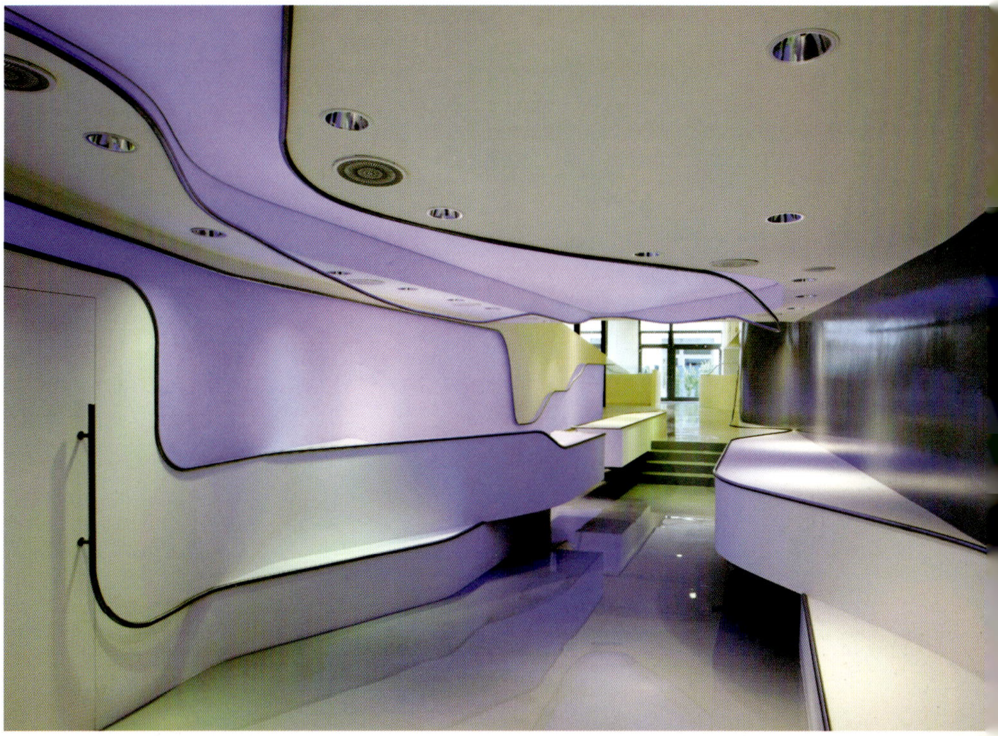
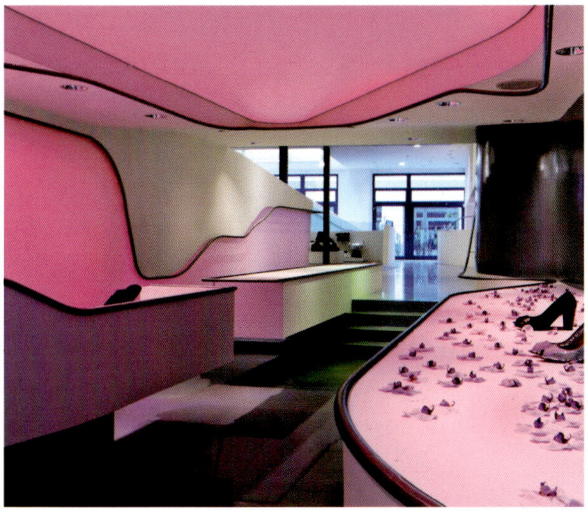
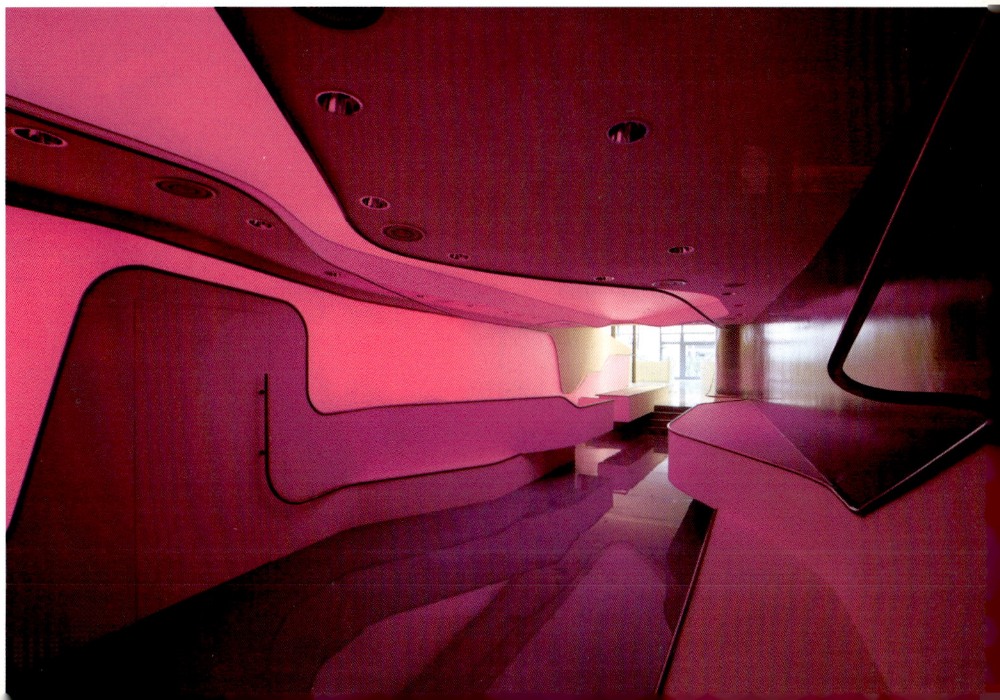

Featherstone Young Architects

Wieden + Kennedy London

London, UK **Photographs: Tim Brotherton**

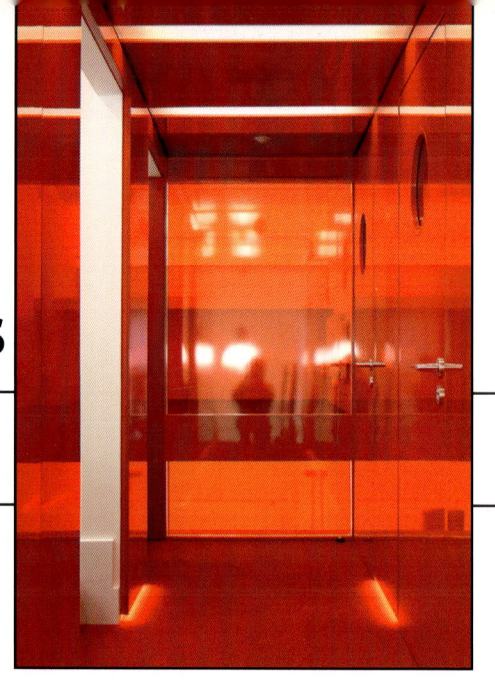

Architecture:
Featherstone Young Architects

In September 2008, Featherstone Young won the commission to refurbish and set up the offices for leading communications agency Wieden + Kennedy (W+K London). The new office -called "The Cole"- is situated in the old Truman Brewery, in London's Brick Lane area.

The new offices had to provide a dynamic workspace for the agency's staff and a multi-functional event-space to encourage collaborations with creative partners and their clients. The program included space for "Platform", the agency's new in-house school and craft-and-product development department. Platform is a floating space in the new offices, as students occupy different parts of both buildings adhoc, immersed in the work process. Platform gathers prominent figures from the arts, sciences, technology and education communities who offer lectures, workshops, debates and work swaps, participating in many different areas of W+K London Platform's programme.

Other facilities include editing suites, product development and research labs, flexible gallery space and a roof terrace. Featherstone Young designed all the spaces to be flexible and fun. The kitchen and dining area, where informal meetings can occur, has a 5 metre (16.40 feet) long island unit which doubles up as a meeting table and toast-making worktop.

A series of garage lock-ups with customised up-and-over doors can become private hideaways or extensions of the main space. The ability for W+K to customise and take ownership of their space was central to the architects' design. The architects commented: "It's great to see the garage doors personalised with slogans and graffiti, and the blackboard lining of the vintage toilets covered with the team's thoughts." Sam Brookes, Managing Director of Platform said, "We handed Featherstone Young a multi-purpose brief to suit many uses. How far beyond our expectations they went is reflected in the diversity of events taking place since "The Cole" opened.

Featherstone Young offers a distinctive and innovative approach to residential, urban regeneration, education and arts and leisure projects, combined with the boldness and expertise to make them happen, working with informed clients to ensure that design brings value in the widest sense - socially, culturally and economically.

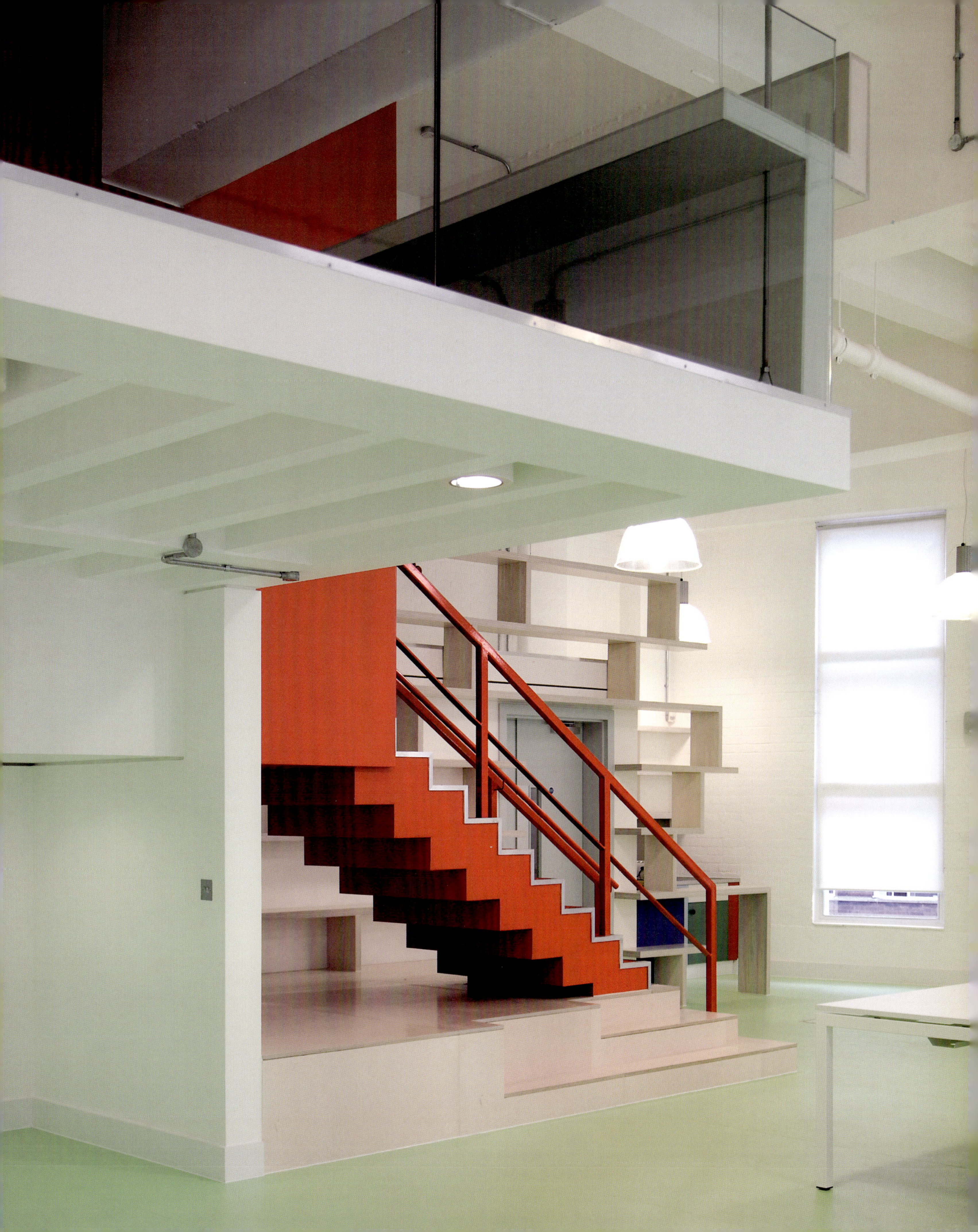

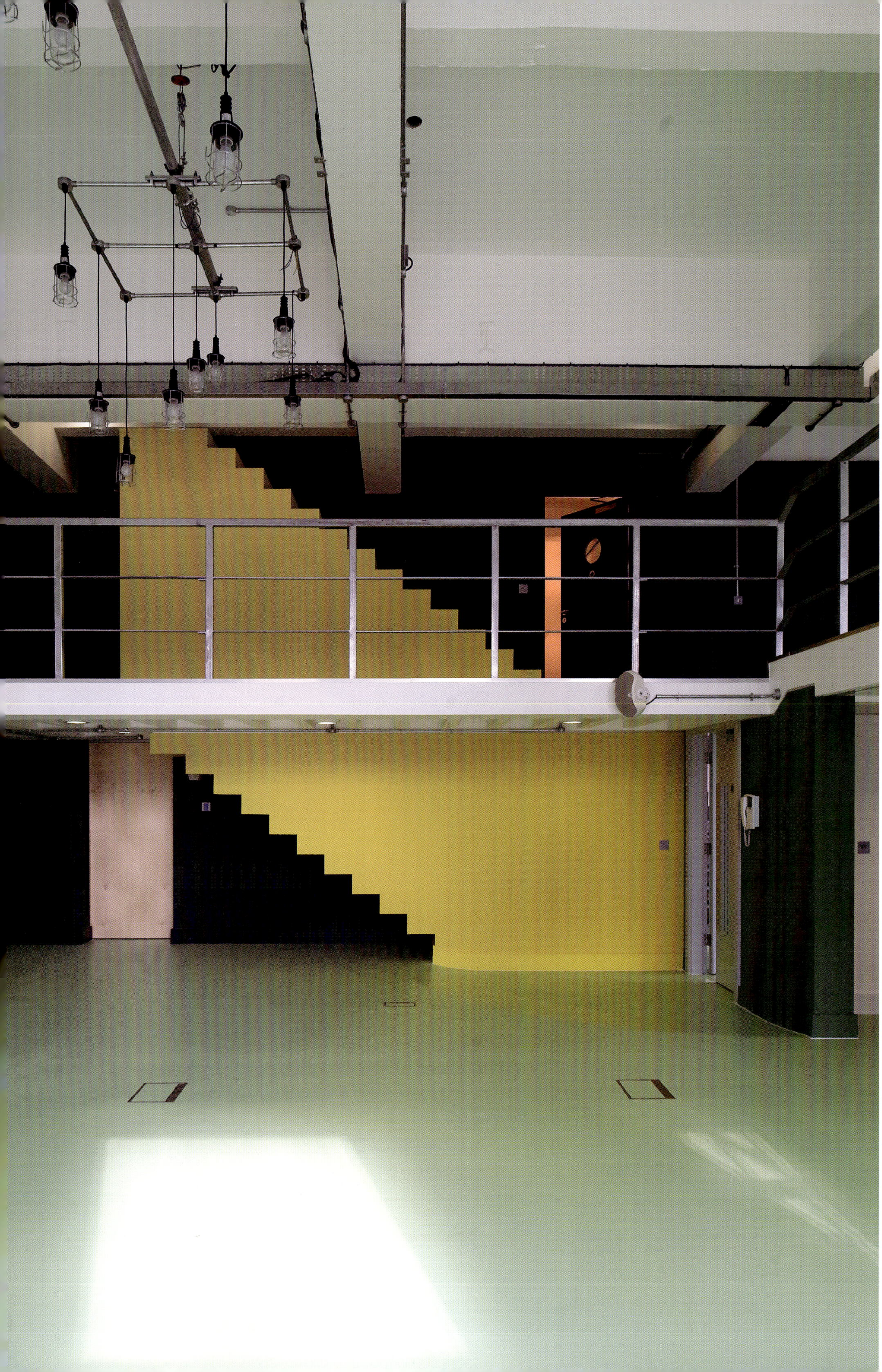

259

First floor plan

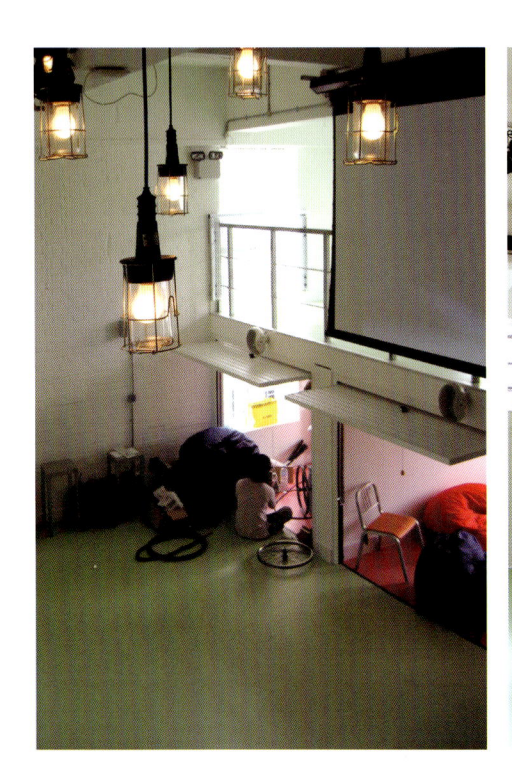

First floor plan - mezzanine

KEY TO PLANS

1. Workstations
2. Pin-up space
3. Informal meeting
4. Pitch/meeting room
5. Tea point
6. Lobby
7. Lockers
8. Main stairwell
9. Library "Crows-Nest"
10. Editing suite
11. Data comms
12. Storage
13. Flexible event space
14. Social space
15. Garage lock-up
16. Terrace
17. Gallery
18. Void

Second floor plan

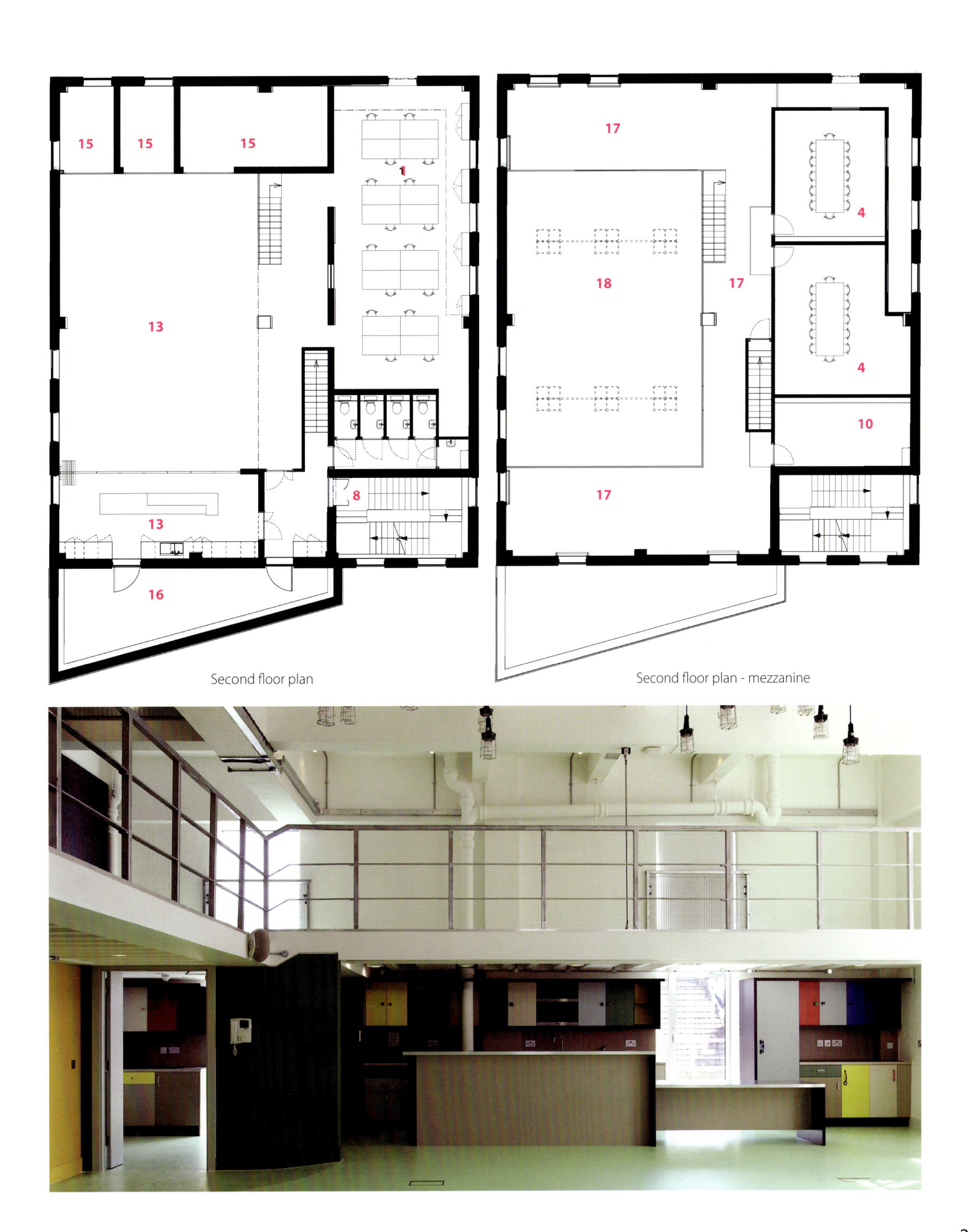

Second floor plan - mezzanine

Features designed to guide people round the space, such as a "stairway to heaven" and the red-tunnelled corridor conceived as "a mouth with its tongue sticking out" inject an element of humour.

Cross section

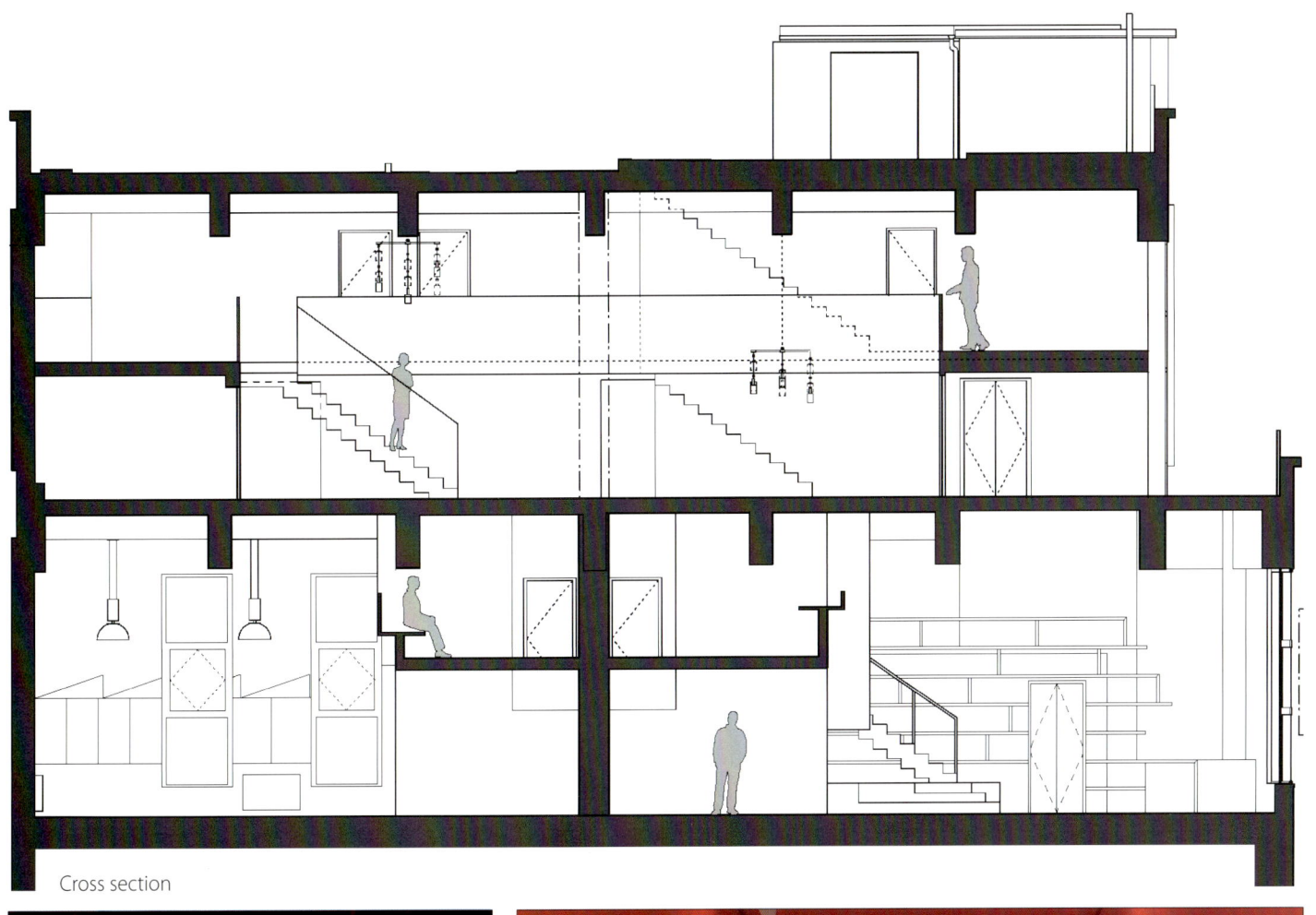

Dive Architects

Electric Works

Sheffield, UK   Photographs: Ake E:son Lindman

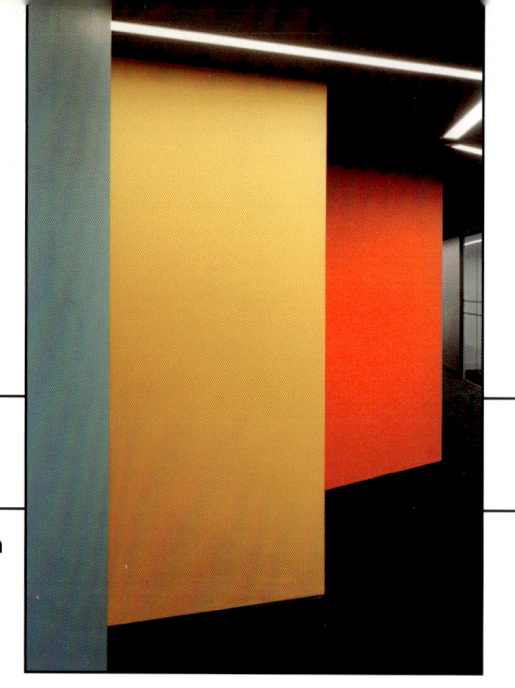

In May 2007 Sheffield Council held an invited competition to design the interior for a new company called Electric Works. This new office building on the recently created Sheffield Digital Business Campus is a close collaboration between the Sheffield Council and Creative Space Management, who will manage the building. Electric Works provides four floors of flexible office space aimed specifically at digital, creative and media businesses between 1-75 people. A conference area, meeting rooms and social areas, such as "the club", allow tenants and members to use the facilities 24 hours a day.

The original building, an anonymous four-floor speculative office building aimed at larger corporate companies, still under construction when Dive was appointed, enabled the architects to intervene on elements they considered important. Solid balustrades were constructed through the atrium instead of chrome and glass screens. The mechanical and electrical installation was more difficult as the building was not envisaged divided into eighty offices. The task was to create an inspiring and fun work space, where office modules and corridors designed unconventionally.

The division of office spaces became a much more intricate task than creating the open communal areas on the ground floor of the building. The architects were very conscious of having to avoid a prison like series of small cells connected by a linear itinerary. Initially the circulation plan was based on the patterns of electrical circuitry and cable diagrams, which developed over time into the corridors, which, in turn, began to define a footprint and graphic network that unfolds throughout the building. Shaping the design of the communal areas generated the purpose made features such as the reception desk, bar bench and storage.

Architecture:
Dive Architects
Design team:
Ia Hjärre, Andy Nettleton, Jasmin Meier
Client:
Sheffield City Council/
Creative Space Management

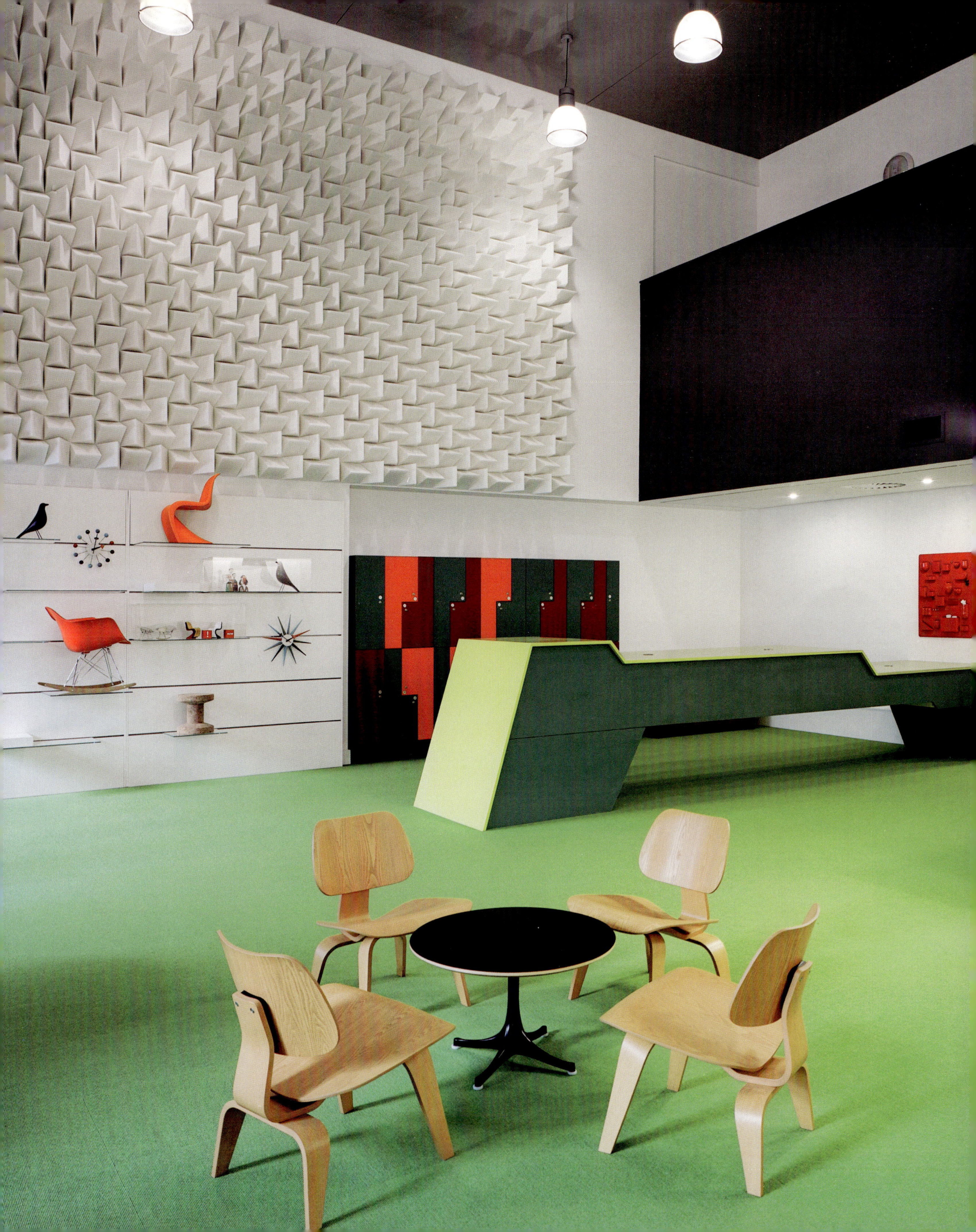

At ground floor level the reception is located in a tall, narrow atrium. Part of the client's brief was to install a slide within this area, permits a rapid and amusing exit from third floor to ground in about 7 seconds.

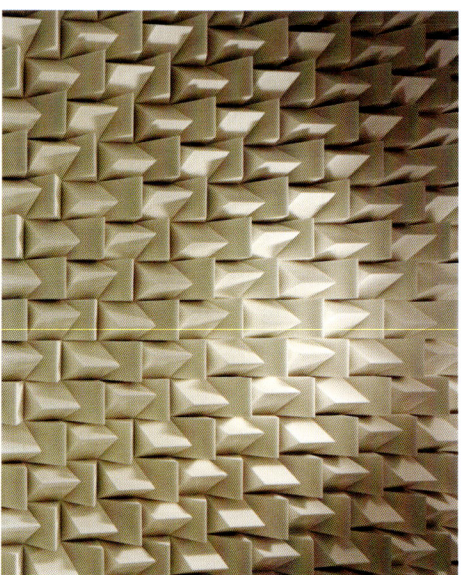

General floor plan

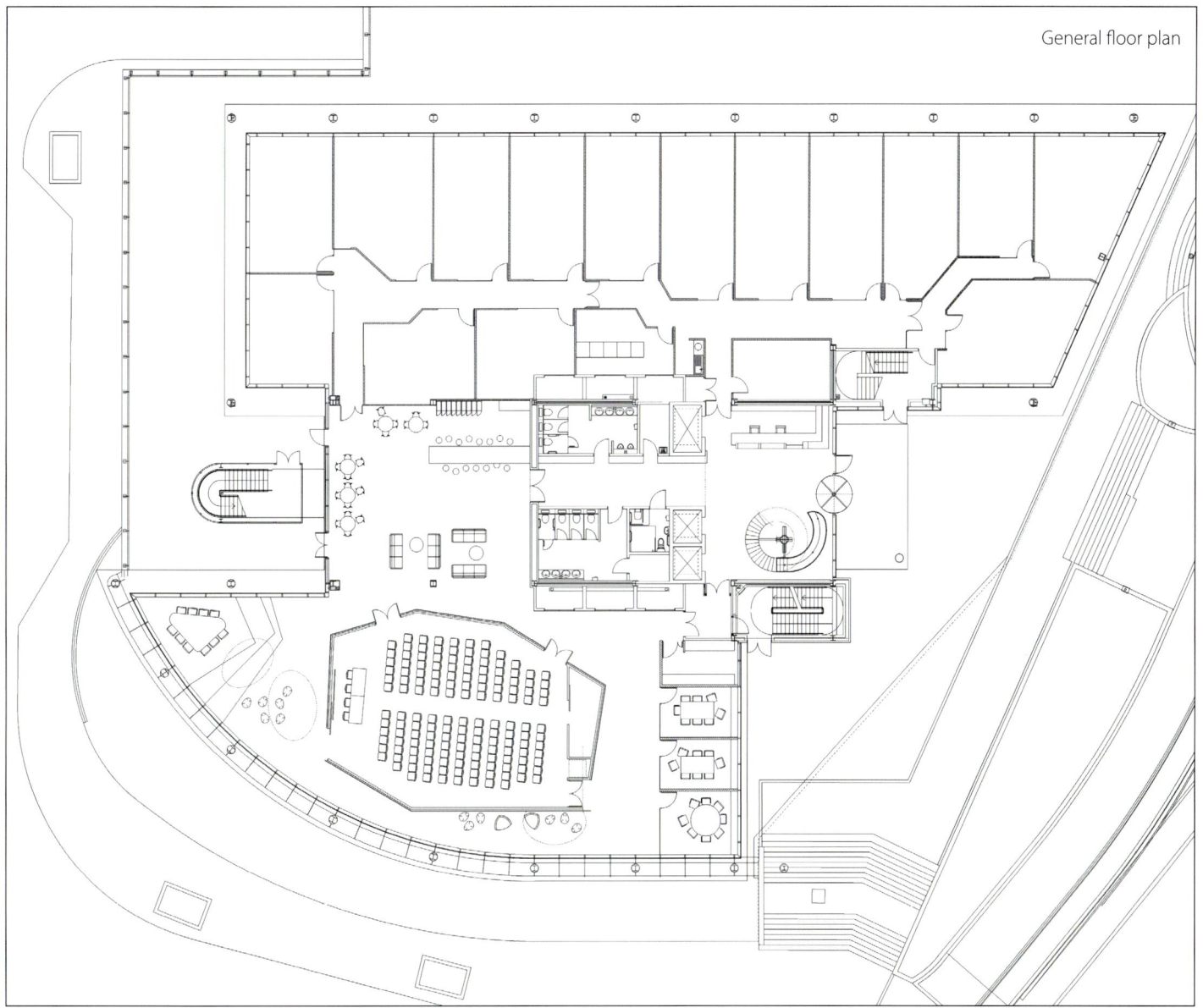

267

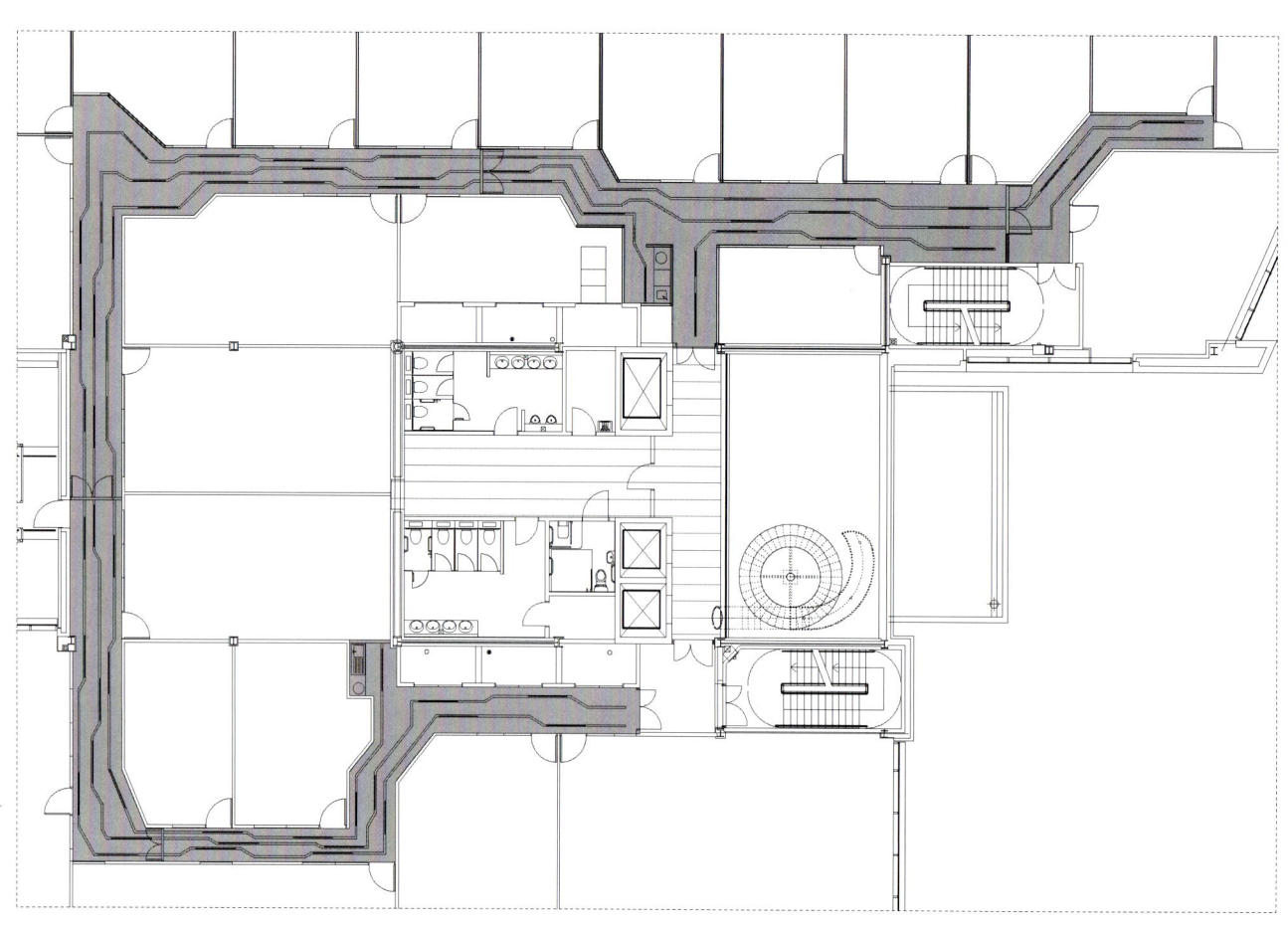

Corridor floor plan

corridor - details

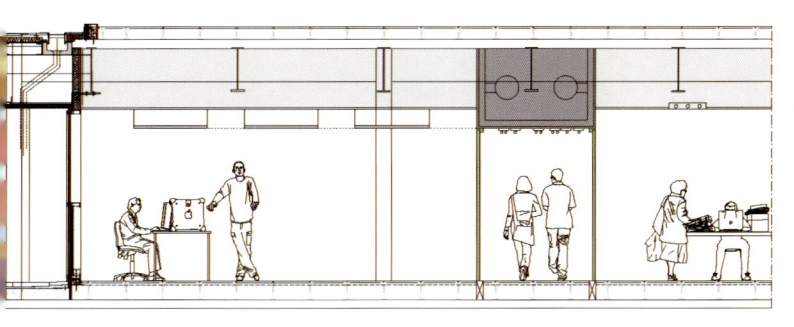

The architects chose to condense the circulation space by lowering the already low ceiling and use a backdrop of dark grey surfaces contrasted with strong colours, giving the offices a lighter, more spacious feel. All have glazed screens looking onto the corridor with circulation diagrams used as the manifestation.

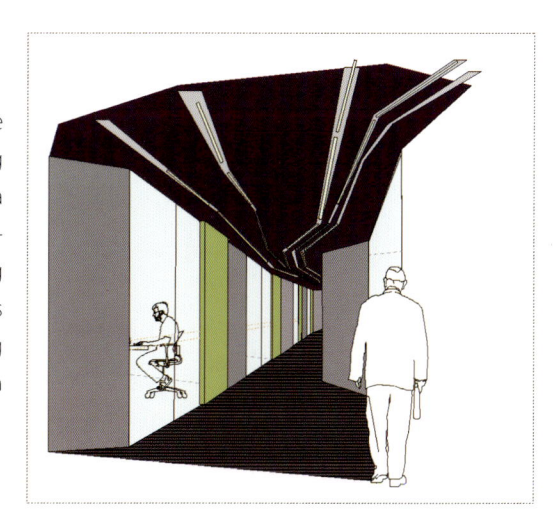

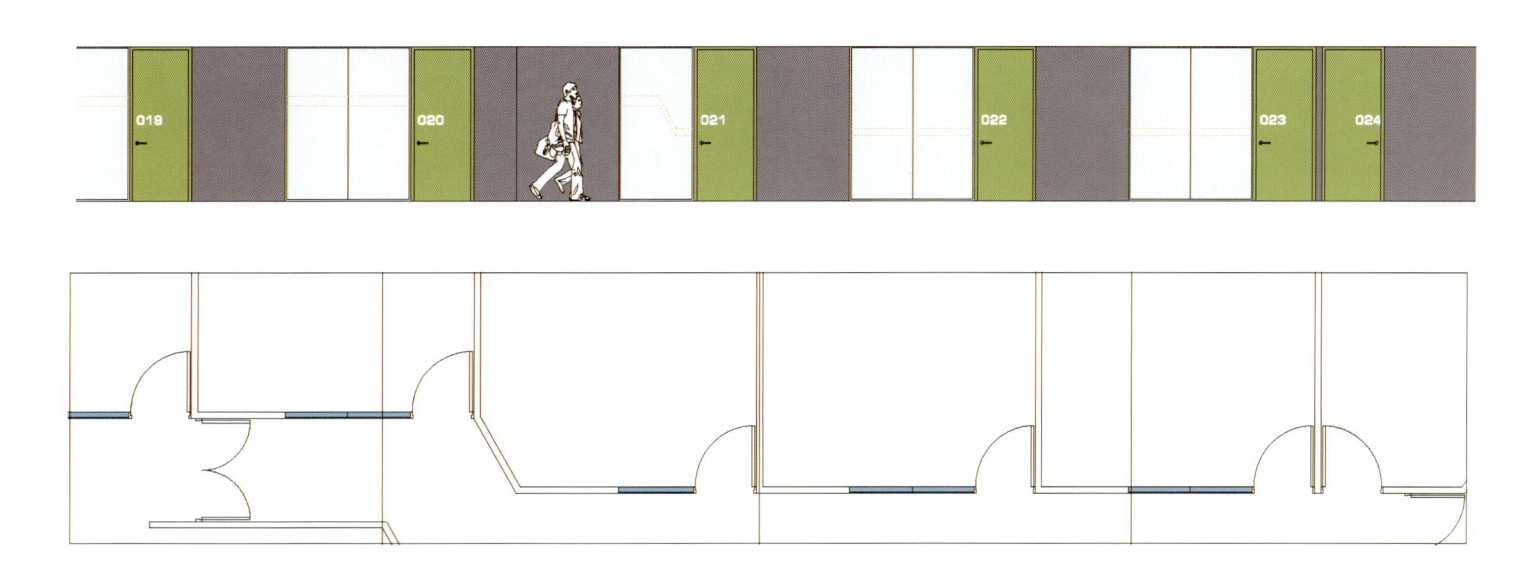

Conference room - details

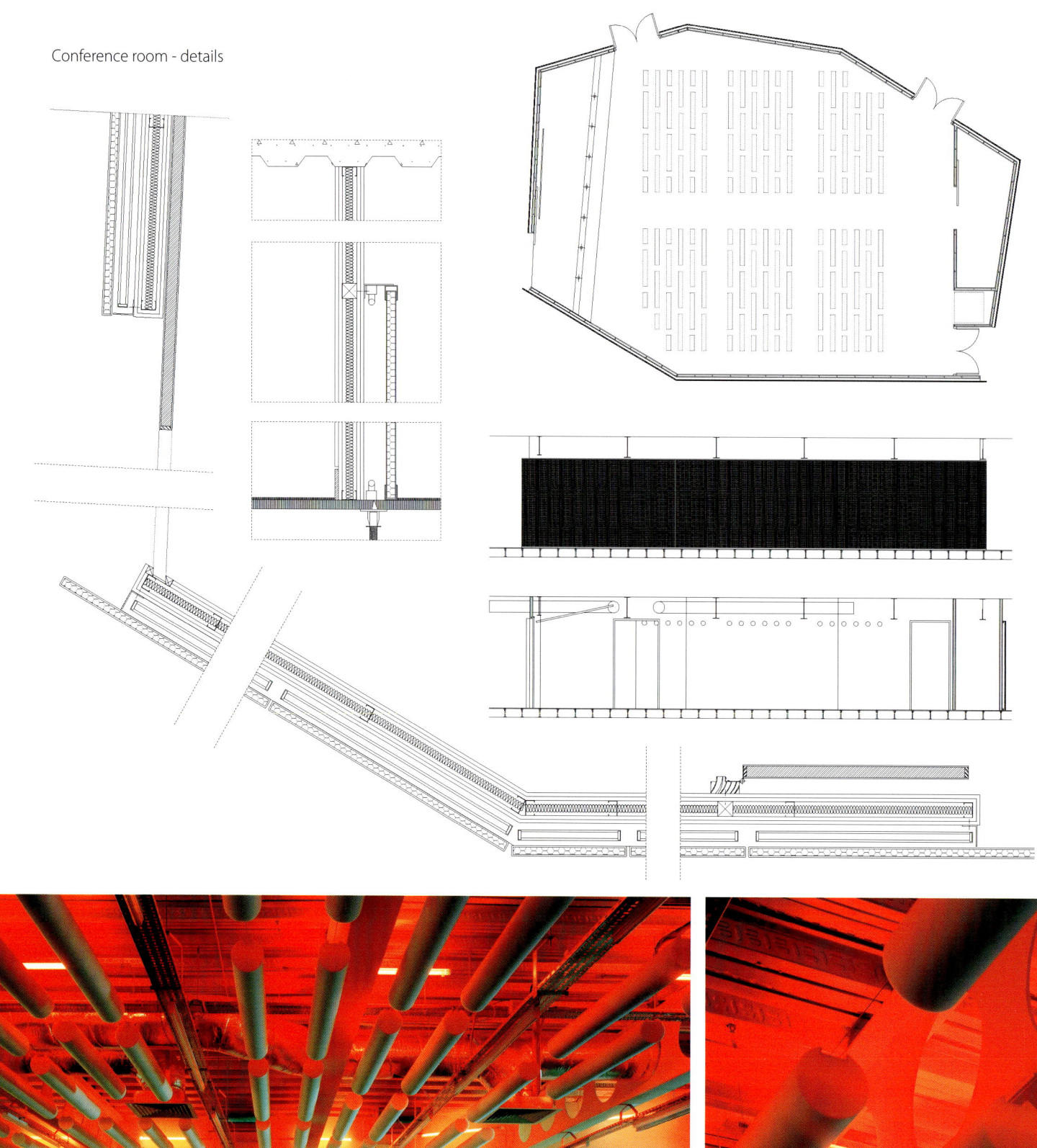

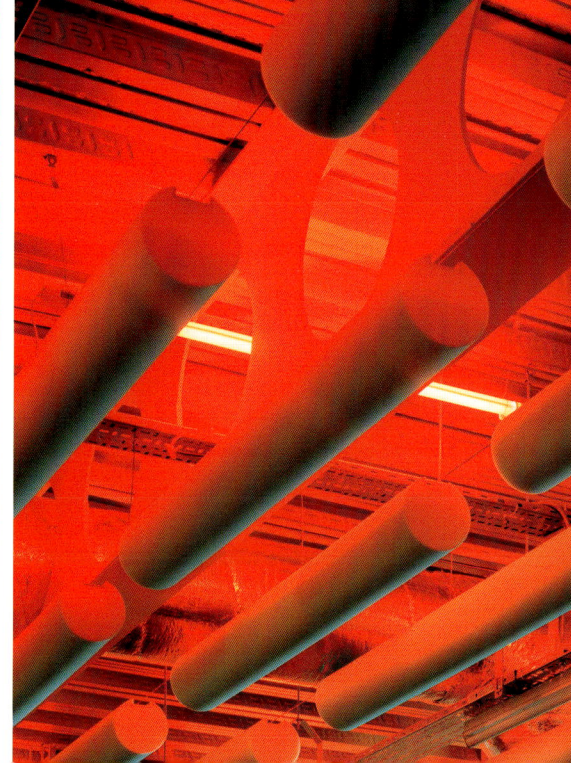

Longitudinal section

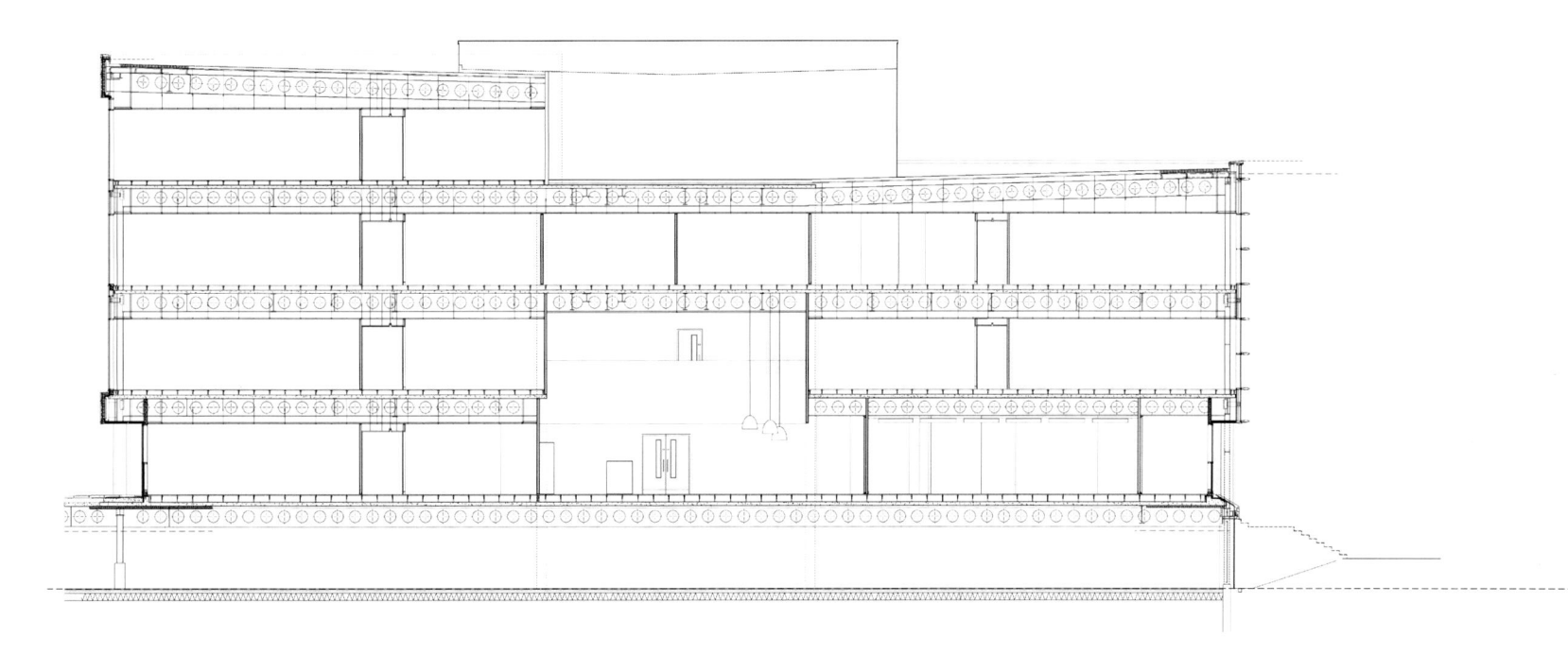

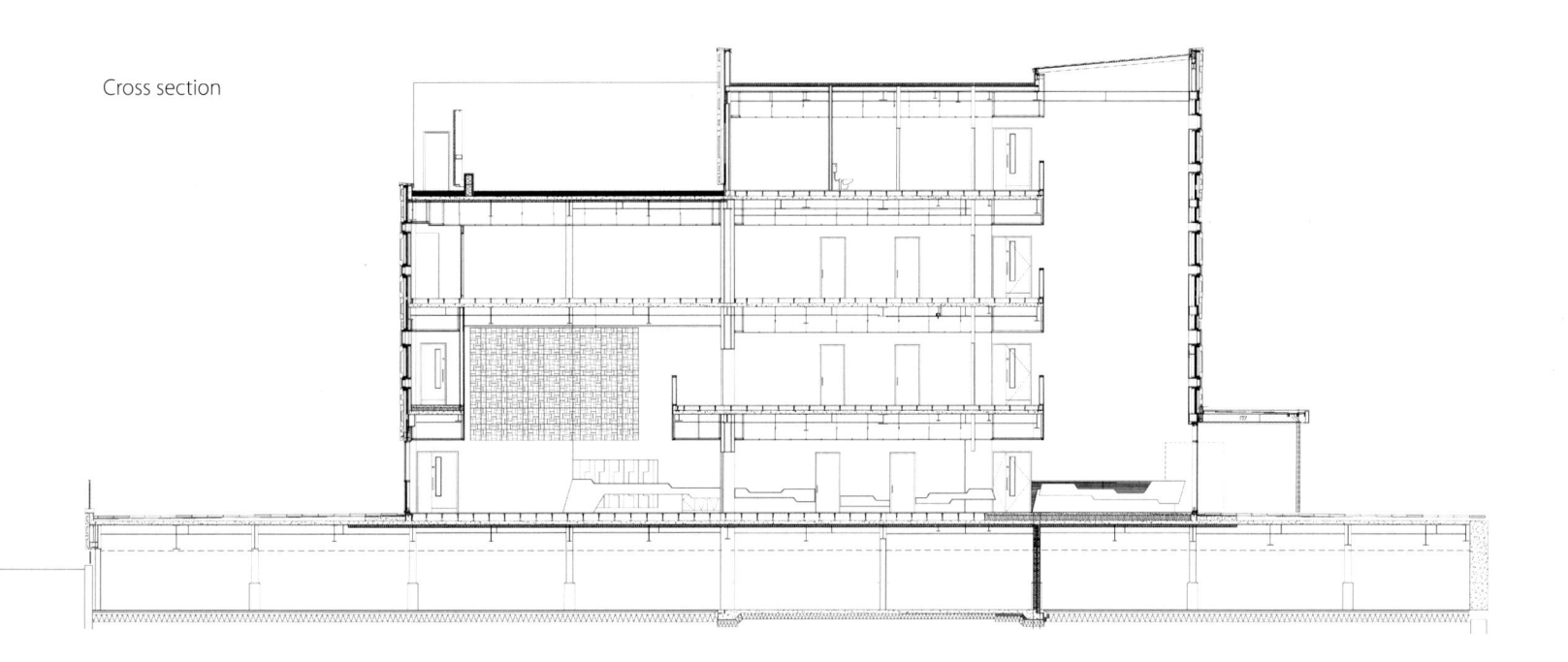

Cross section

271

272

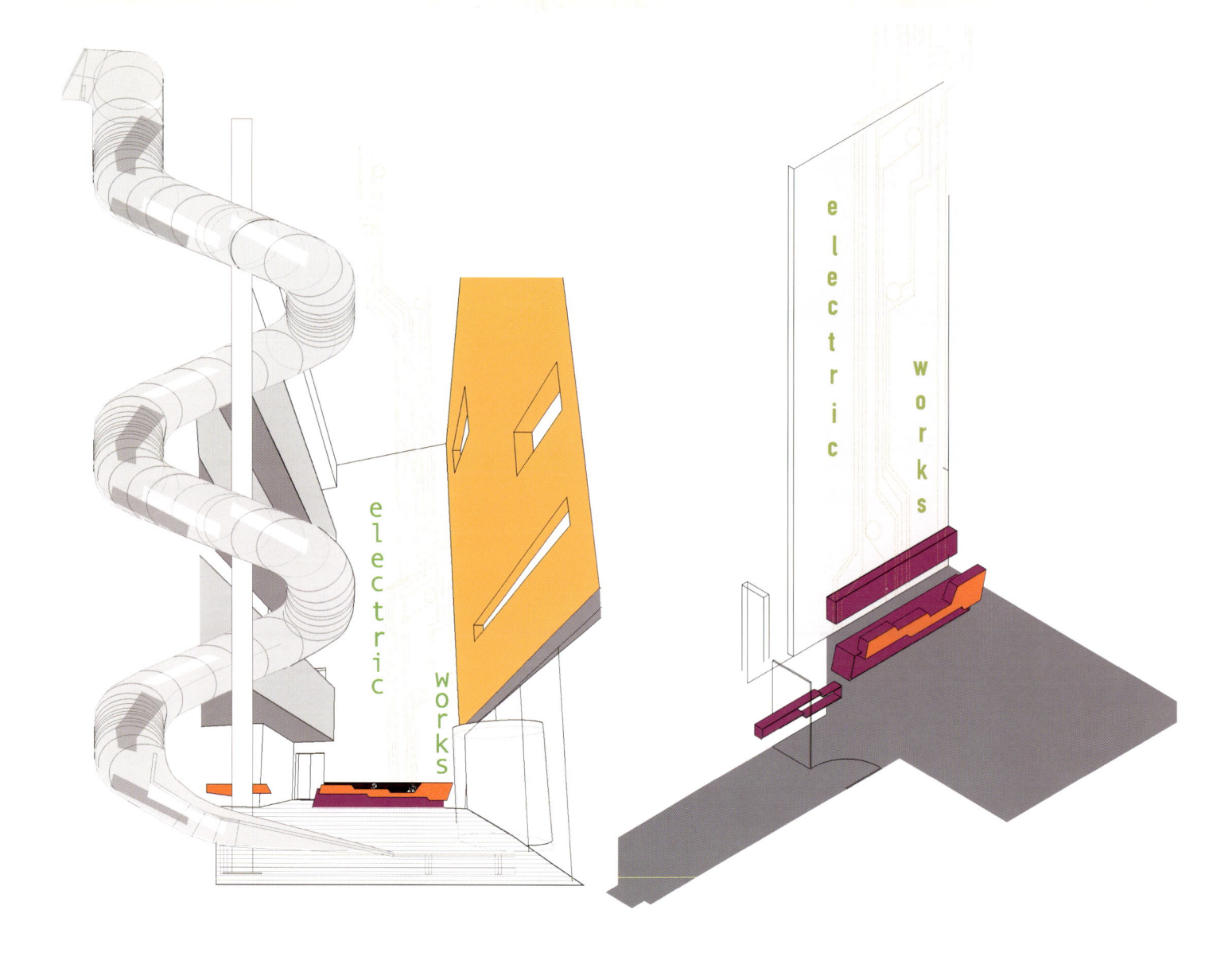

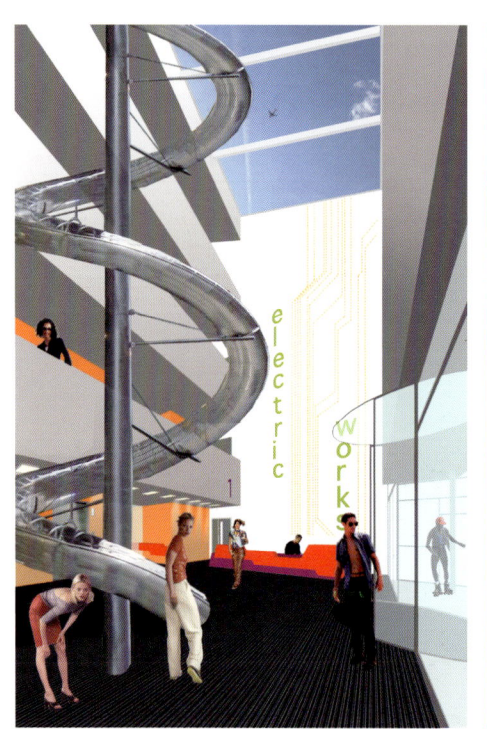

electricworks

HASSELL
National Foods

Melbourne, Victoria, Australia **Photographs: Shannon McGrath**

National Foods' 12,000 sqm workplace in Melbourne's Docklands is designed to unify their various offices into a single building able to accommodate the needs of National Foods on a long term basis – through expansion or contraction. National Foods wanted the new workplace to underline its leading market position and the vitality of its brands and to stress National Foods' philosophy of making foods based on natural ingredients, in touch with the land and with people who create food. Understanding that a traditional corporate environment would not achieve this, they commissioned HASSELL to reflect what makes National Foods different from others. The designers took a non-traditional approach that acknowledges food's journey from farm to factory. The design celebrates National Foods' commitment to food's primary producers and manufacturers.

With two levels at the base of the building for car parking, lobby and retail space, National Foods' offices are on levels 3 to 8. Level 3 is a general work environment with a central staff hub connected to a landscaped terrace. This social space, for staff or events, reinforces the firm's commitment to health and outdoor living. The terrace consists of interconnected timber platforms inspired in aerial views of a farming landscape.

On level 4, National Foods' public face covers some 400 sqm of the 1,800 sqm floor plate. The reception space is visually connected to the testing kitchen, where visitors can watch foods being made and tested. Glazed meeting rooms flanking the space suggest a 'nothing to hide' attitude.

Besides desks, level 5 has a boardroom and a private client meeting room, for entertaining and running the more strategic aspects of the business. Views of the city and exposed ceilings reiterate the open approach.

Levels 6 to 8 contain a more typical approach to the workplace that envelops the central core with an open desking-layout connected to the facade and suffused with natural light. Materials were selected to reiterate the design aspiration.

Interiors:
HASSELL
HASSELL team:
Scott Walker, Meredith Nettleton, Rob Ryan, Bronwyn Pratt, Jayson Deadman, Jaclyn Iles, Rhian Barker, Robin Archer, Robert Harper, Madeleine Joyce
Client:
National Foods Ltd
Floor area:
129,000 sqft (12,000 sqm)

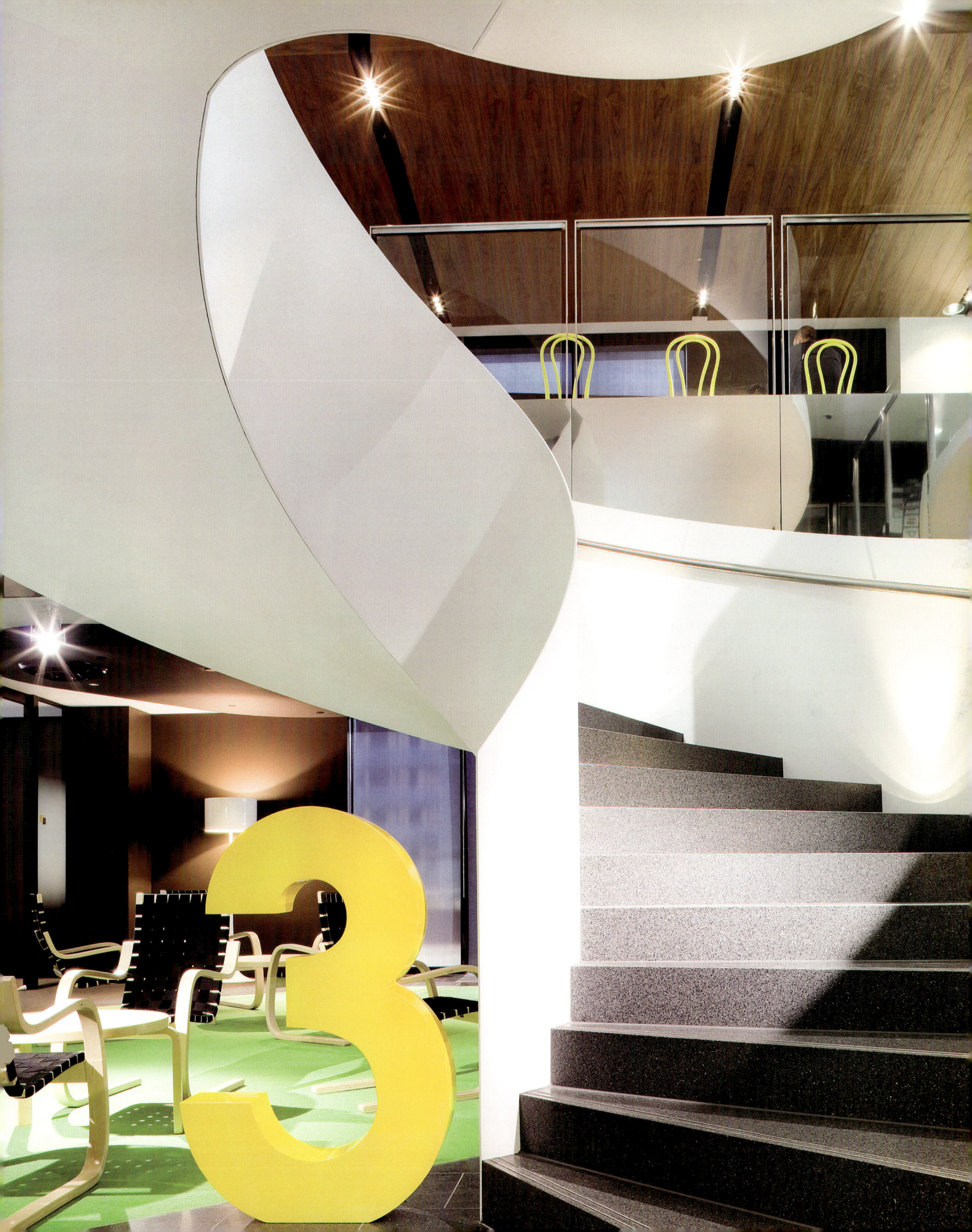

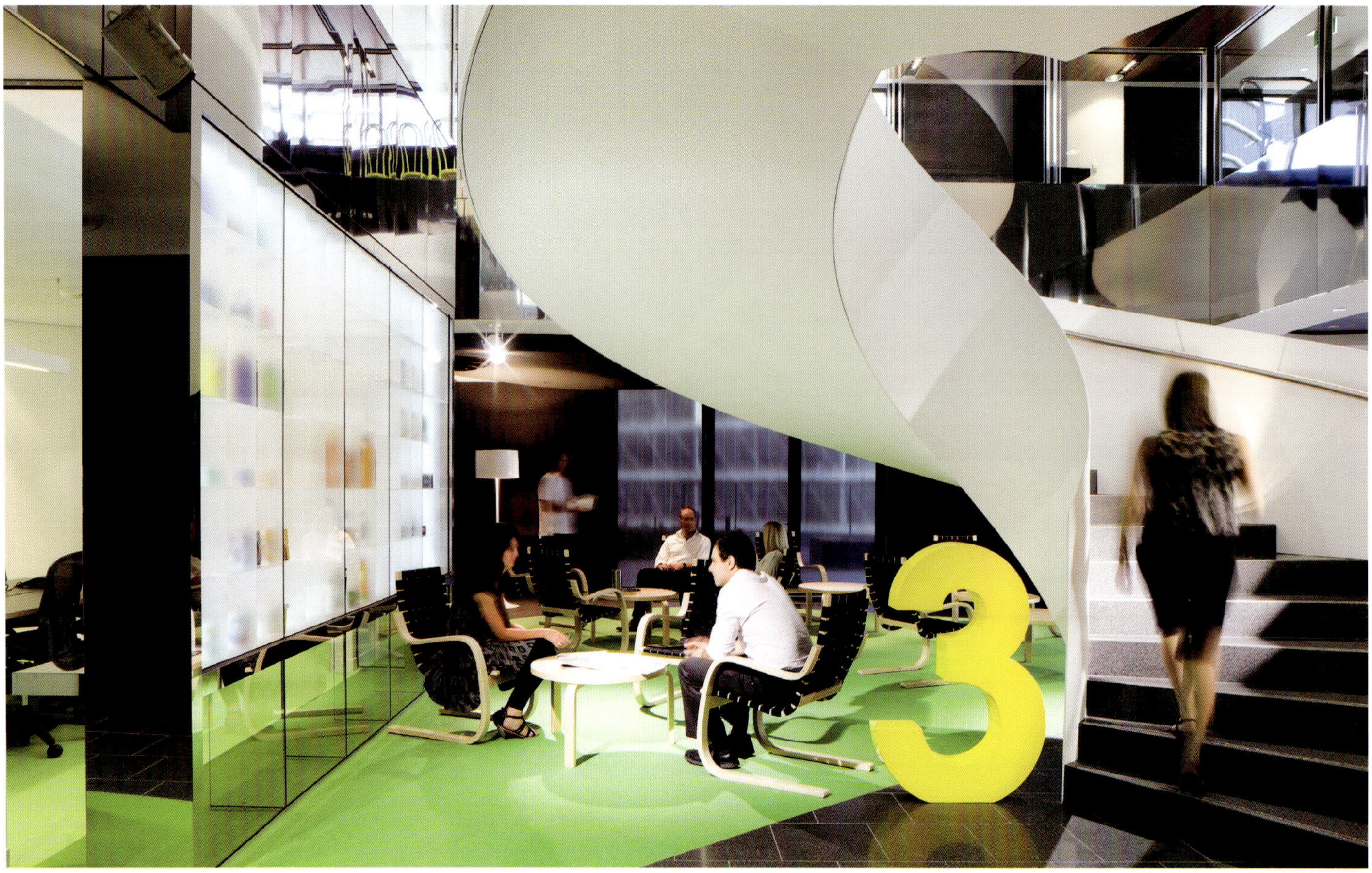

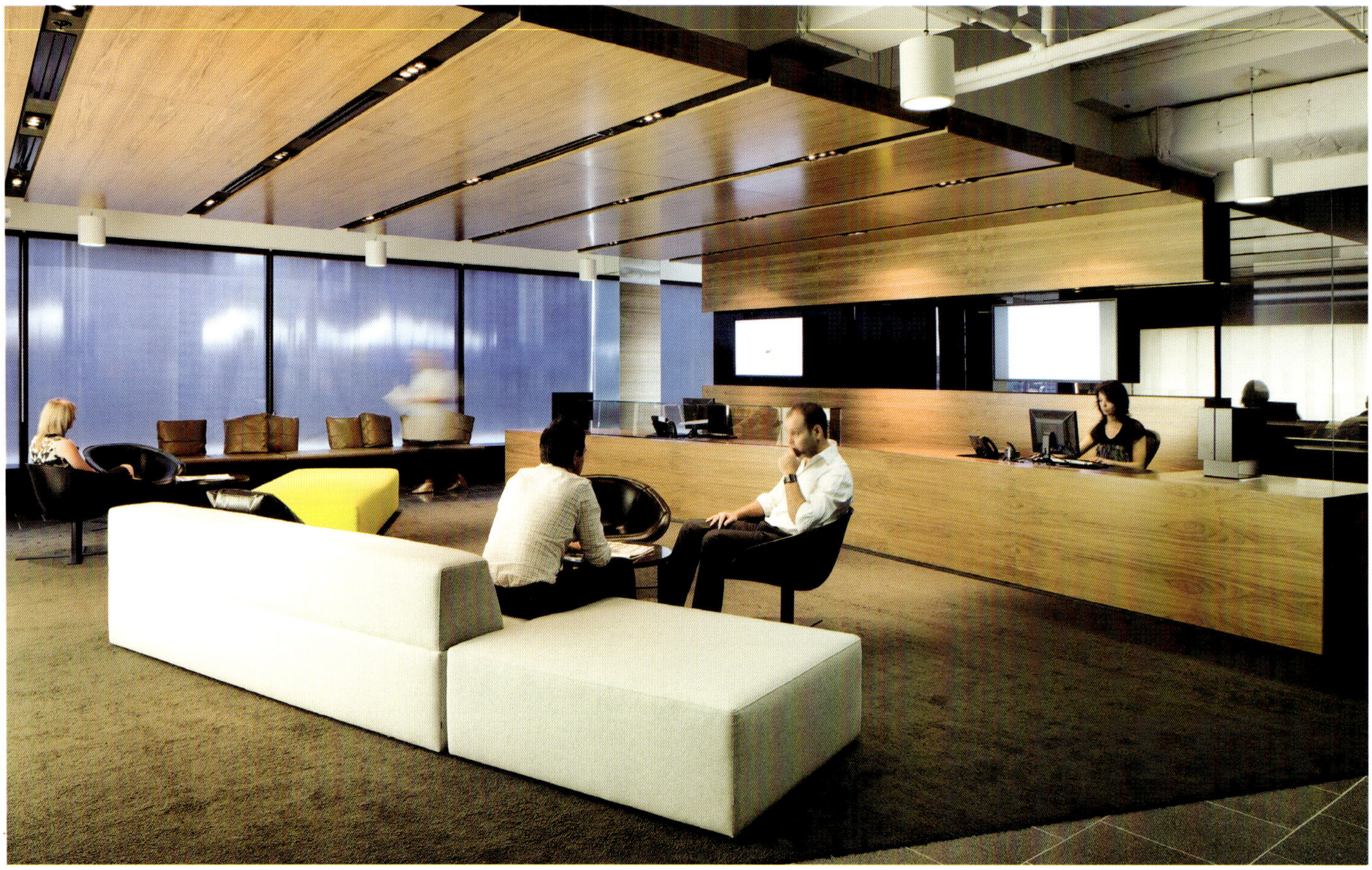

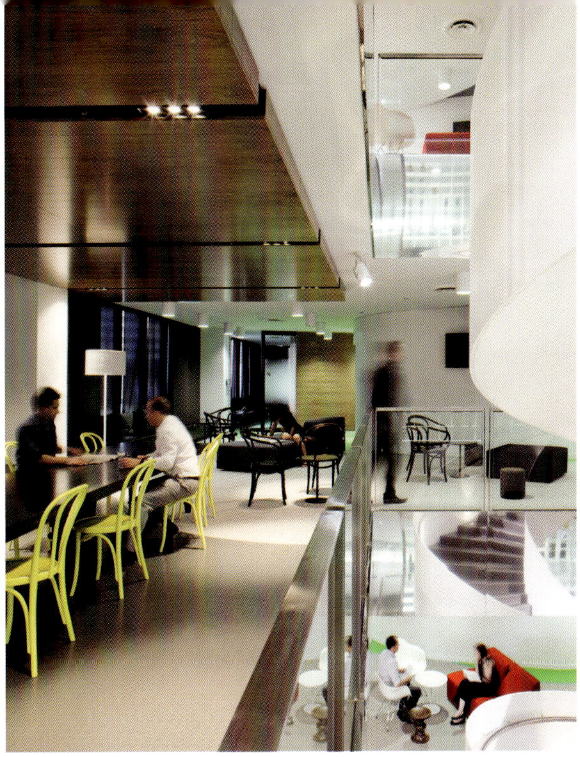
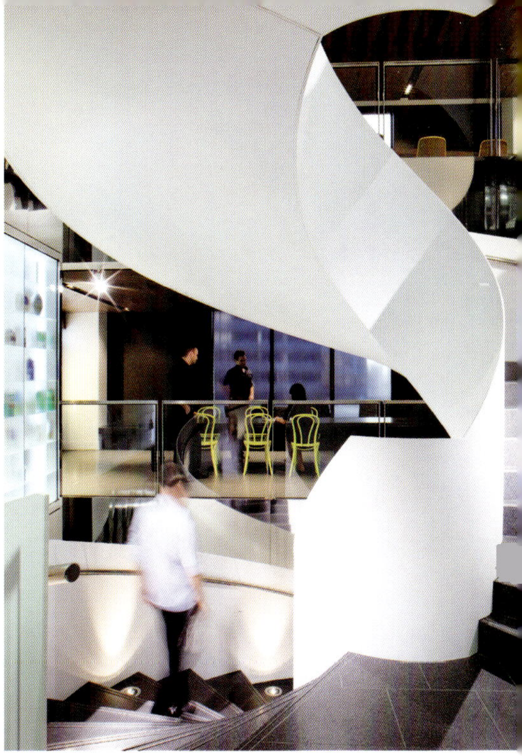
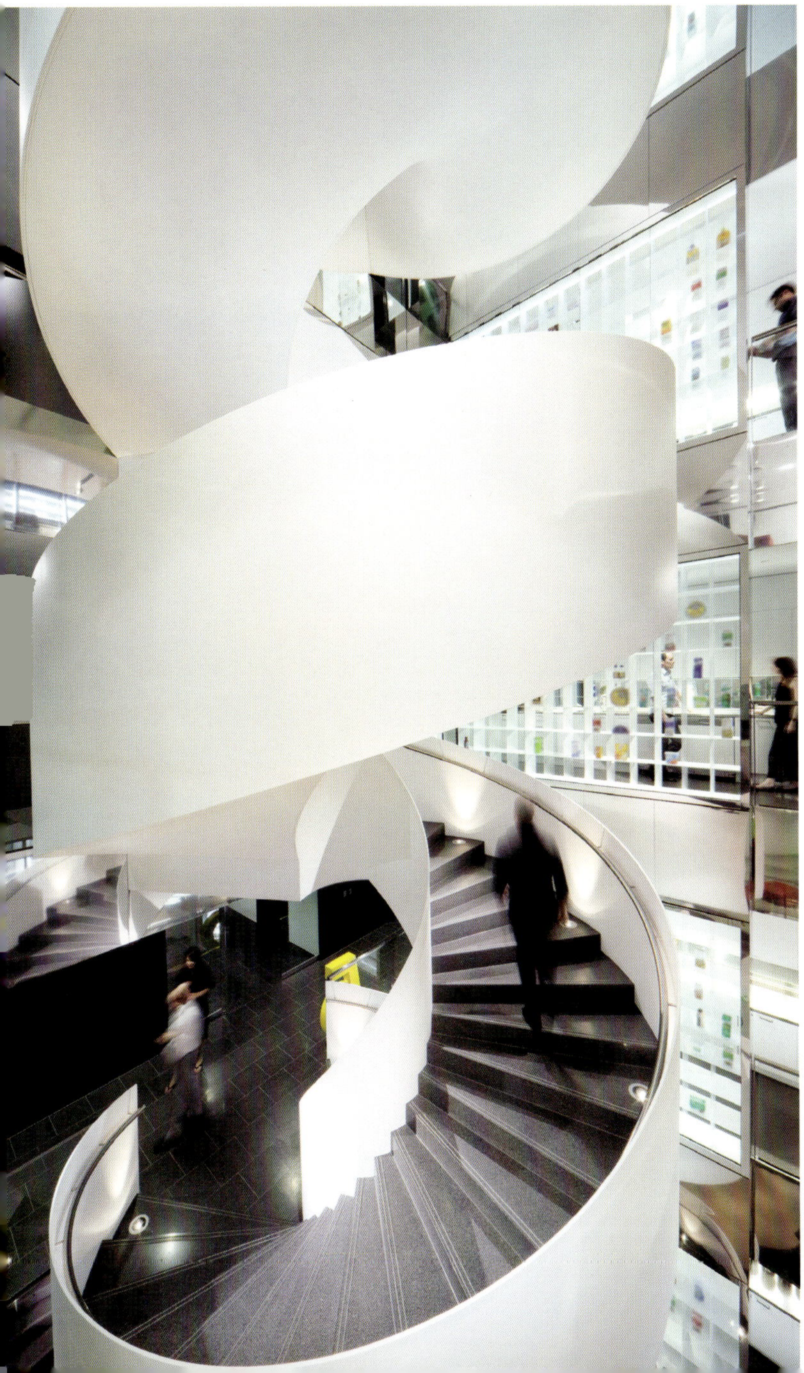
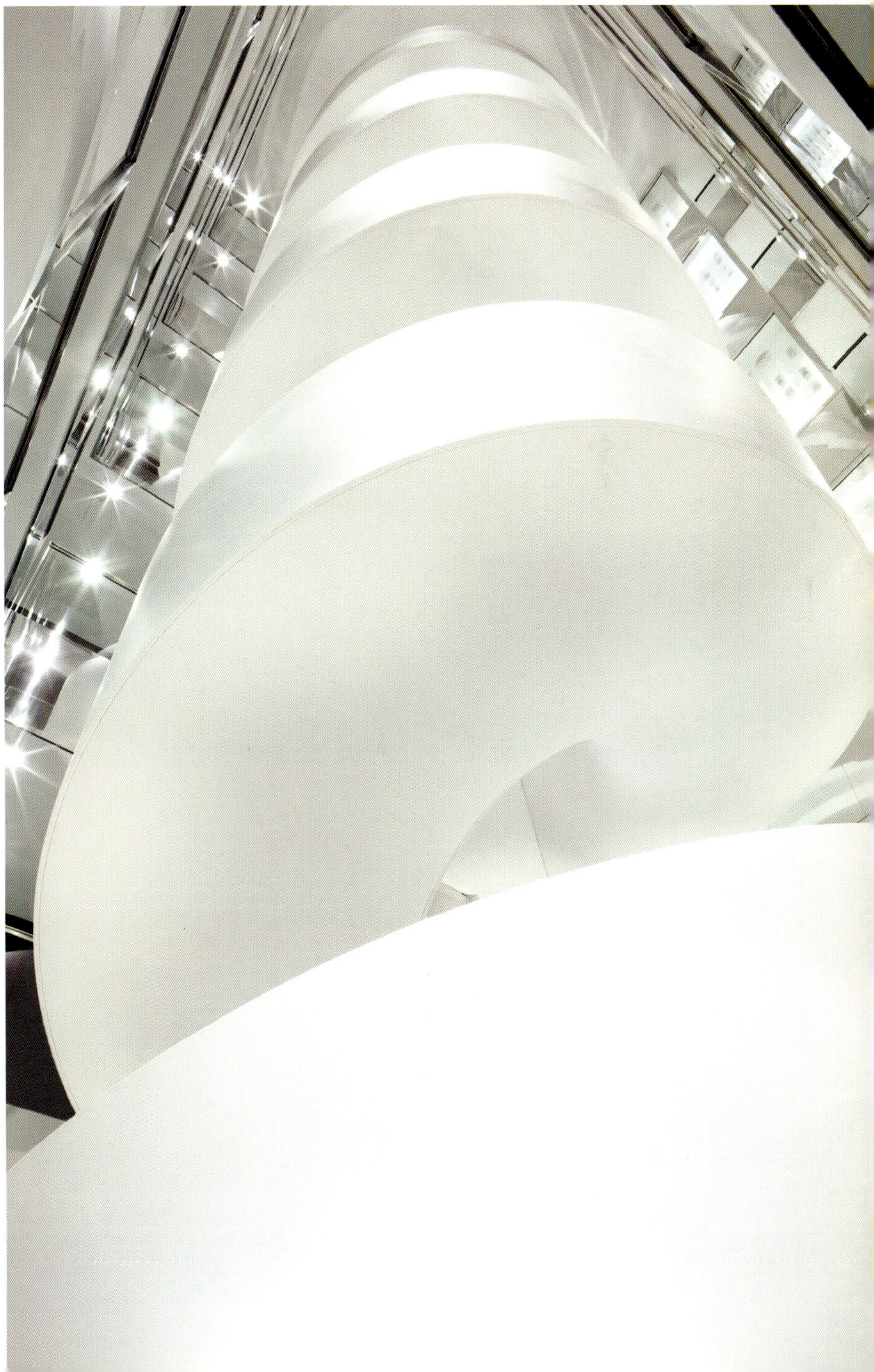

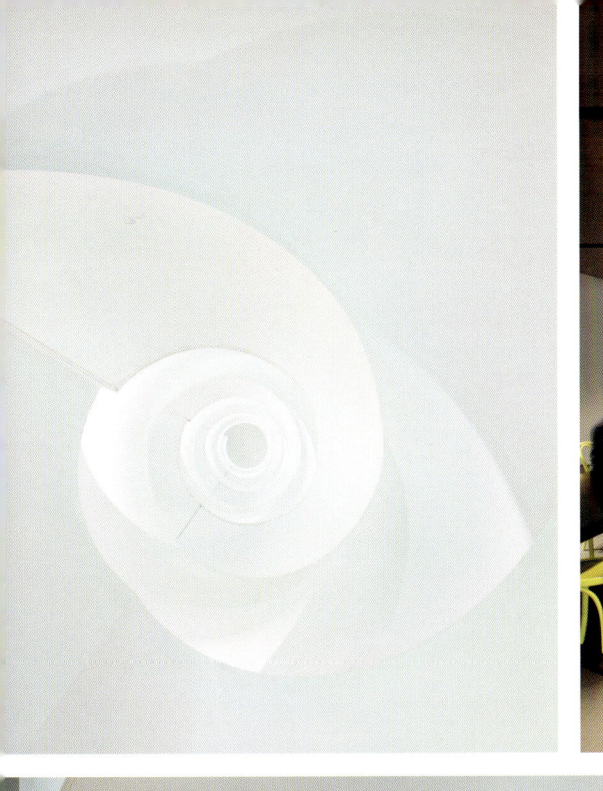

Typical floor plan

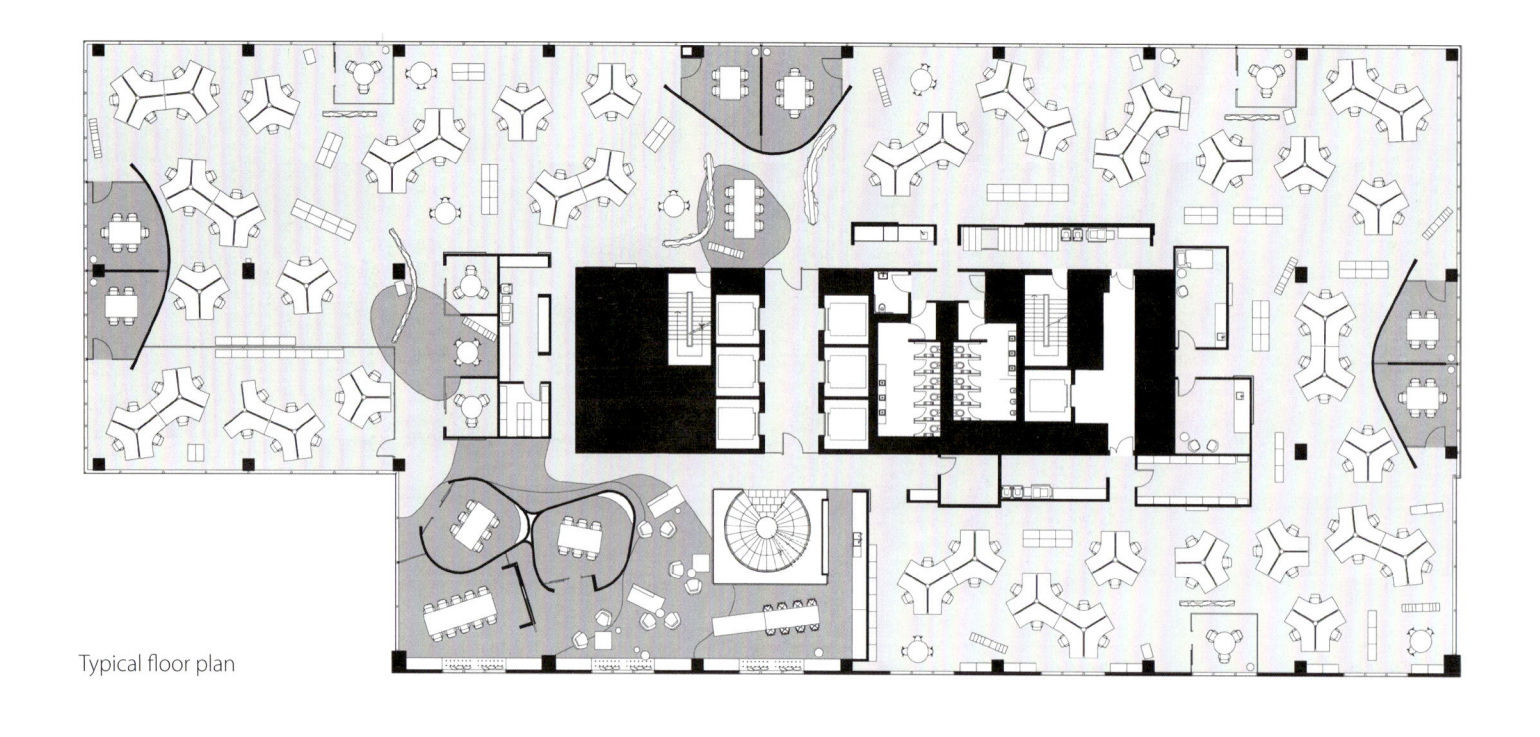

278

Floor plan

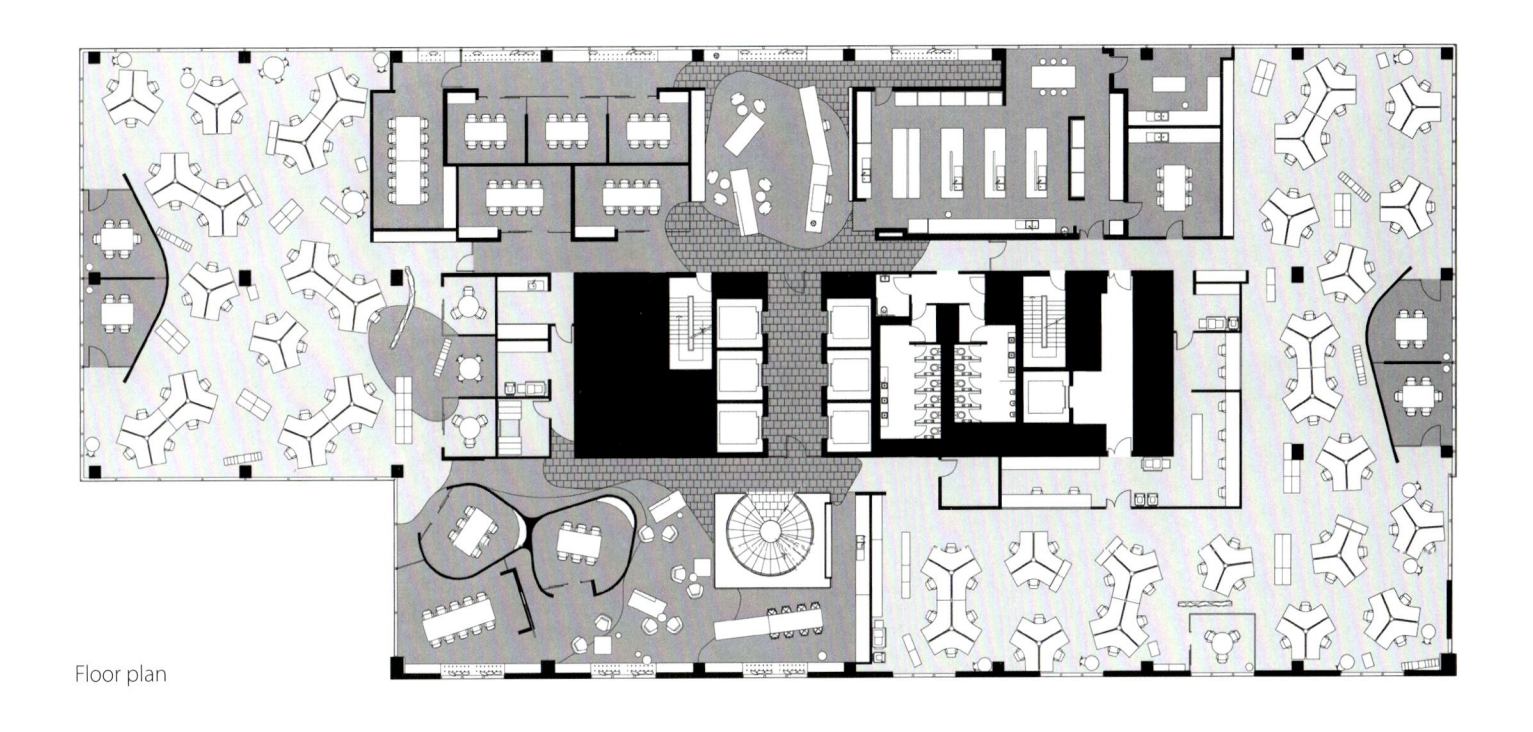

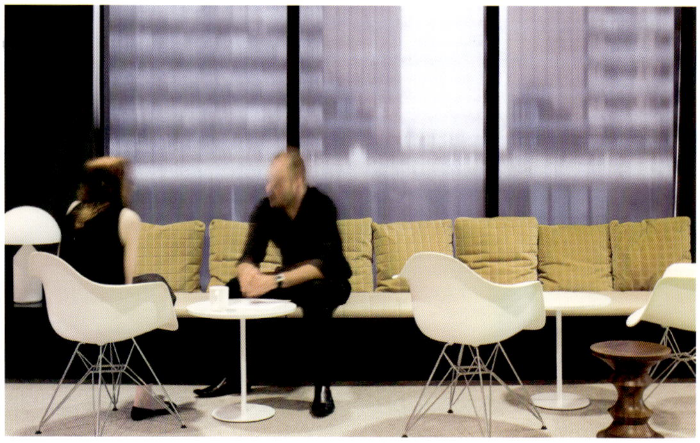

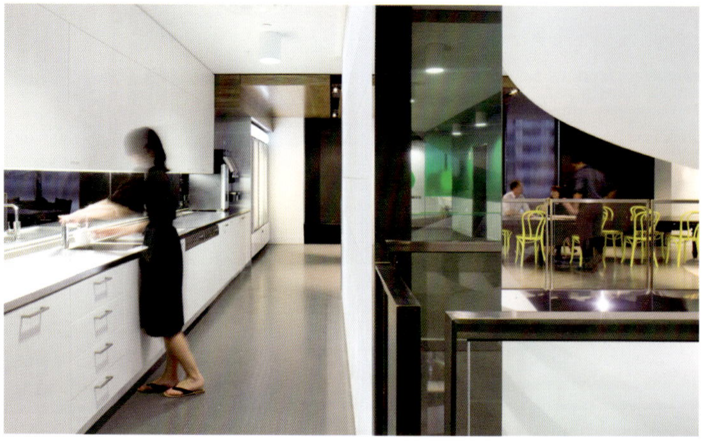

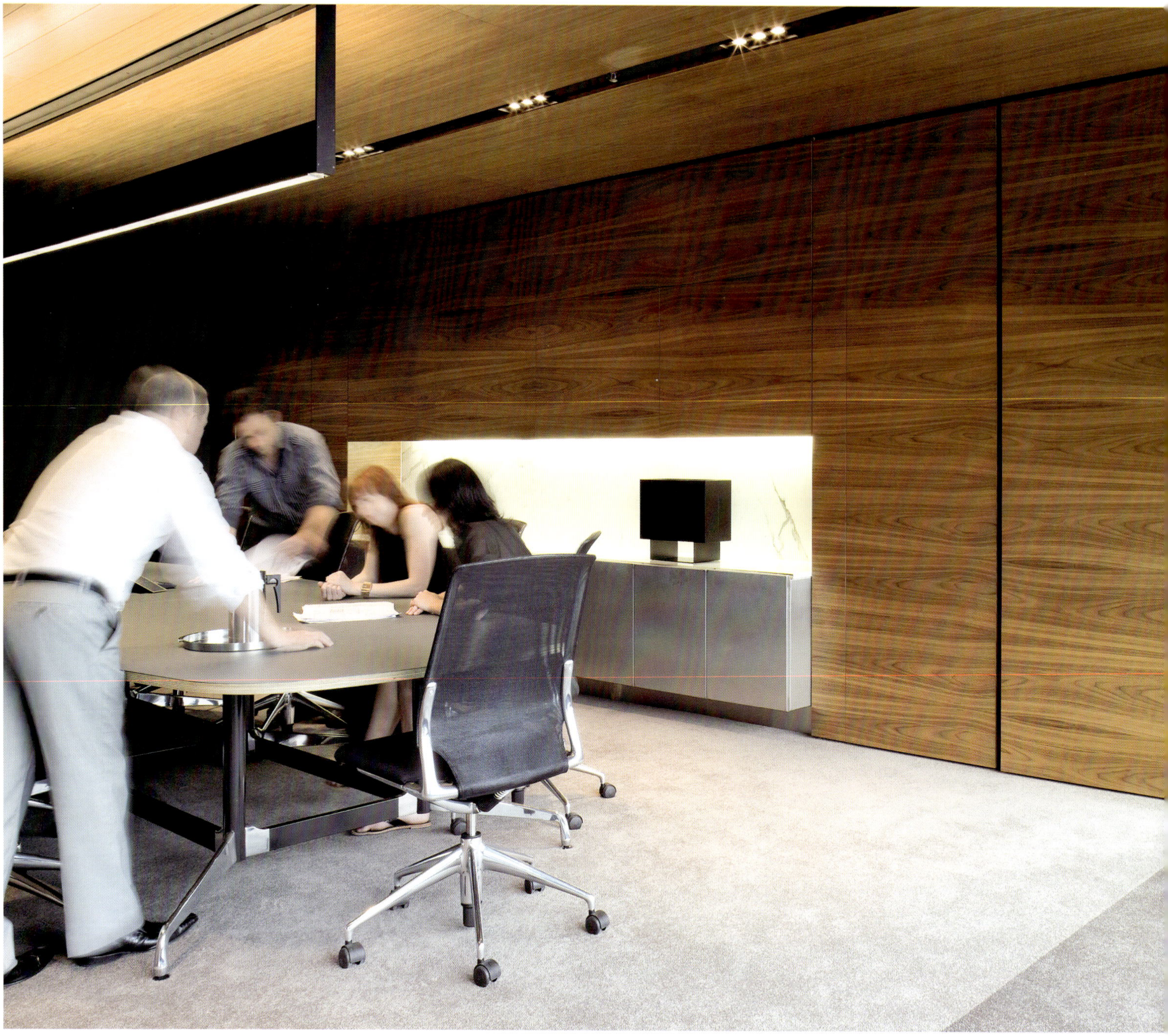

The main staff hub, a place to bring the entire staff together in a cafeteria atmosphere, anchors the foot of a spiral stairway that connects the entire office. An expressive use of timber is set off by glazed partitions and polished chrome; primary colours add vibrancy. Curved plant screens improve air quality and evoke the land the enterprise is based on.

Camenzind Evolution

Google Zurich

Zurich, Switzerland Photographs: contributed by Camenzind Evolution

Google's offices in Zurich, Switzerland, transmit the message that this is not a conventional company through a design that cultivates an energized and inspiring work environment that is relaxed but focused, and buzzing with activities.

The Google building is a contemporary seven-story shell and core office block offering 12,000 sqm (130,000 sqft) floor area for up to 800 staff members. The challenge for the architects here was to set up a tailor-made design and construction process, which would meet the tight time and budget constraints whilst endorsing a very broad participatory design methodology.

Google celebrates individuality, creativity and innovative business practice within a high-energy environment and emphasizes the importance of the individual and maintaining a small-company ambience. A key element in the design approach was that the Googlers in Zurich (known as Zooglers) should participate in the design process to create their own local identity. A diverse team of local Zooglers was formed as the steering committee to represent the entire office.

The office areas are organized along a central core and are a mixture of open-plan workspaces for 6-10 people and enclosed offices for 4-6 people. All office enclosures are constructed using a glass partition system, which maintains transparency and optimizes daylight while reducing noise and achieving the required degree of privacy for working teams.

There are a large number of small to medium-size meeting rooms situated throughout the office space. Apart from the standard meeting rooms, there are also many informal meeting areas, which have a more relaxed atmosphere for teams to have creative discussions around whiteboards. Some of them also incorporate the theme in the floor materials, like the Igloo Satellite Cabins with penguins on the blue floor.

Camenzind Evolution also developed themed communal areas associated with sport and leisure, for example, an aquarium water lounge for relaxation and a games room to play billiards, table football and interactive video games. Most spaces contain 'micro kitchens' offering the Zooglers a variety of drinks and snacks throughout the day.

Architecture:
Camenzind Evolution
Site management:
Quadras Baumanagement Ltd.
Building engineering:
Amstein + Walthert Ltd.
Area:
130,000 sqft (12,000 sqm)

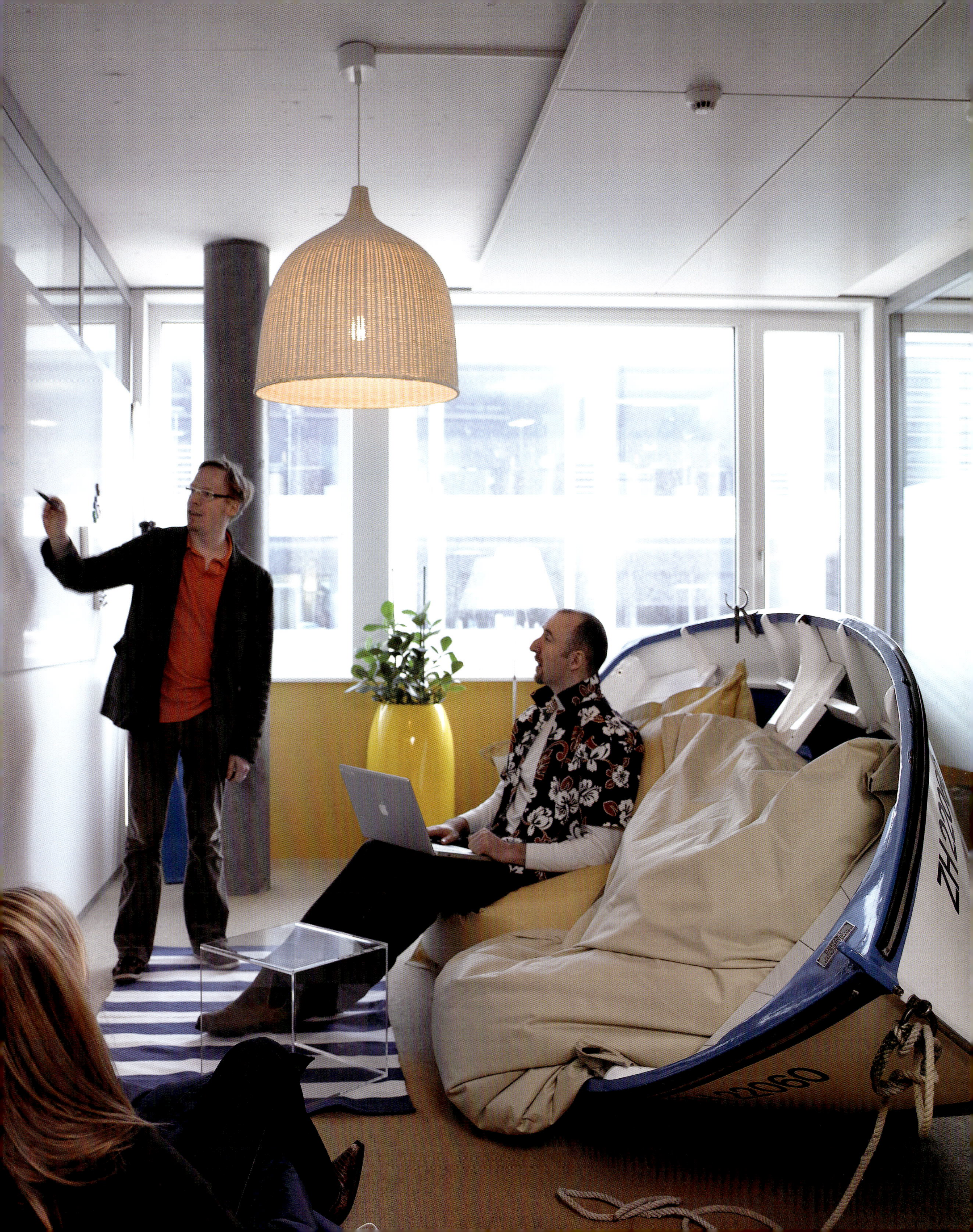
22060

284

An in-house survey revealed that the optimal working environment needed to be diverse, harmonious and a fun and enjoyable place to work in. Personal workspace needed to be functional and neutral, while communal areas had to offer strong visual and entertaining qualities to stimulate creativity, innovation and collaboration.

LEVEL 1

- ▢ Office area
- ▢ Meeting rooms
- ▢ Informal meeting rooms
- ▢ Communal and special area

1. Lift
2. Massage room
3. Lounge
4. Games room
5. Quick connection
6. Training 1
7. Training 2

LEVEL 1

- ▢ Office area
- ▢ Meeting rooms
- ▢ Informal meeting rooms
- ▢ Communal and special area

1. Lift
2. Water lounge
3. Quick connections
4. Tech stop

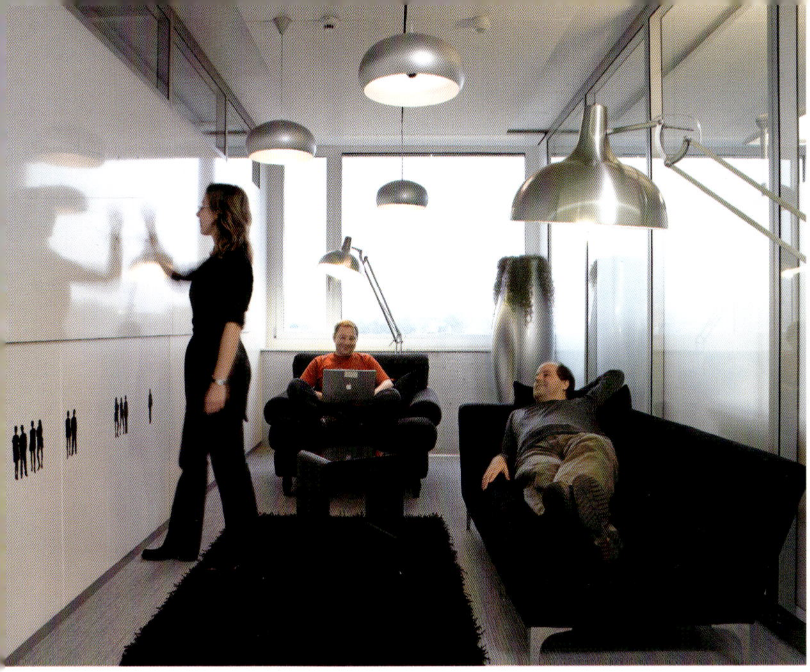
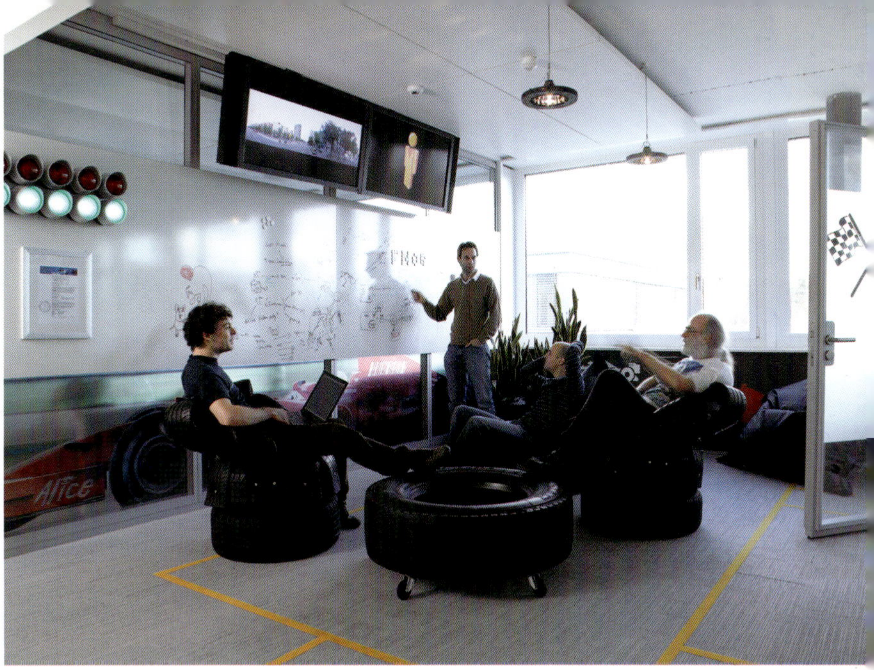
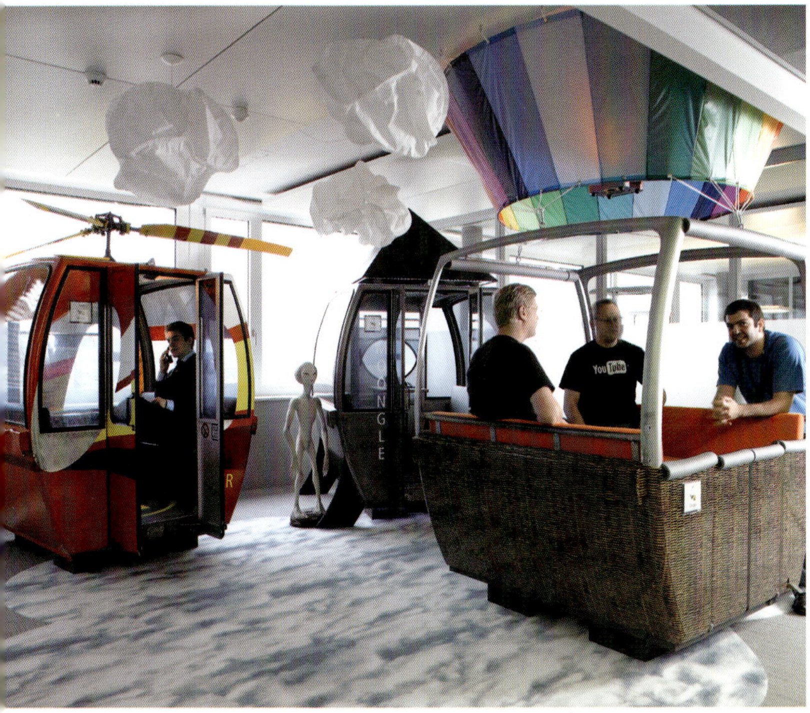
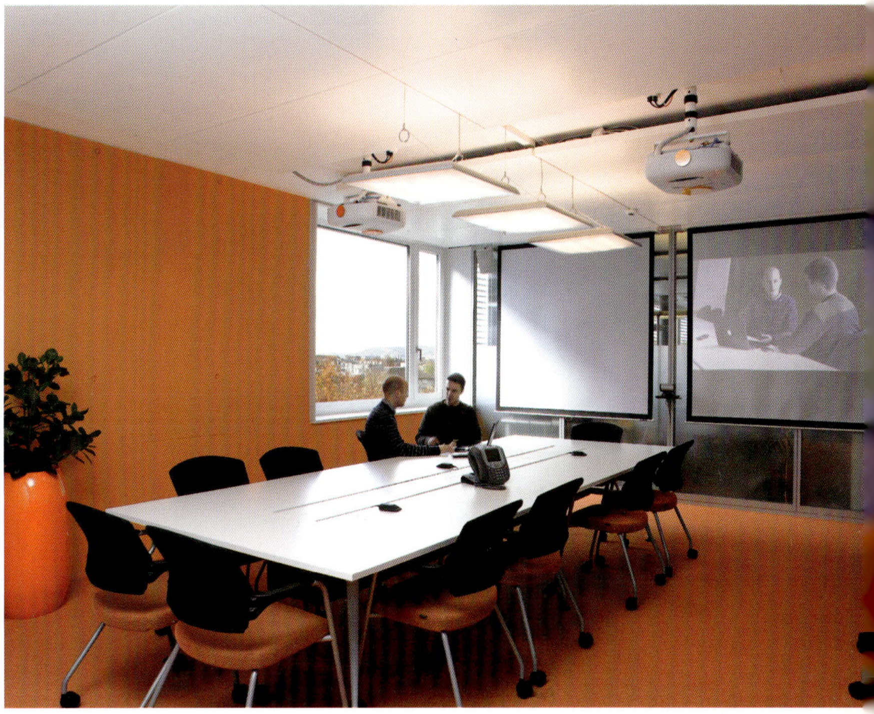
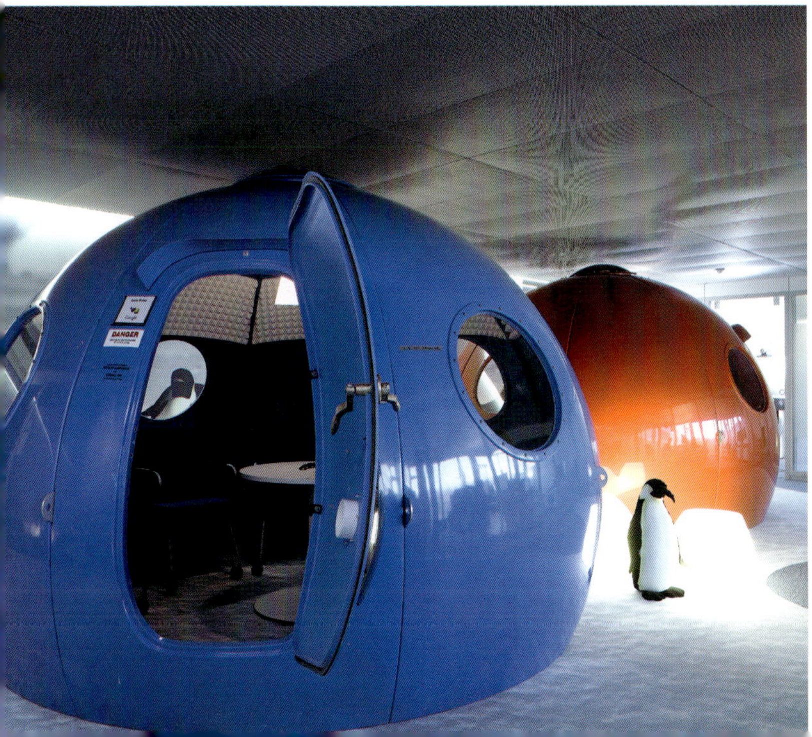
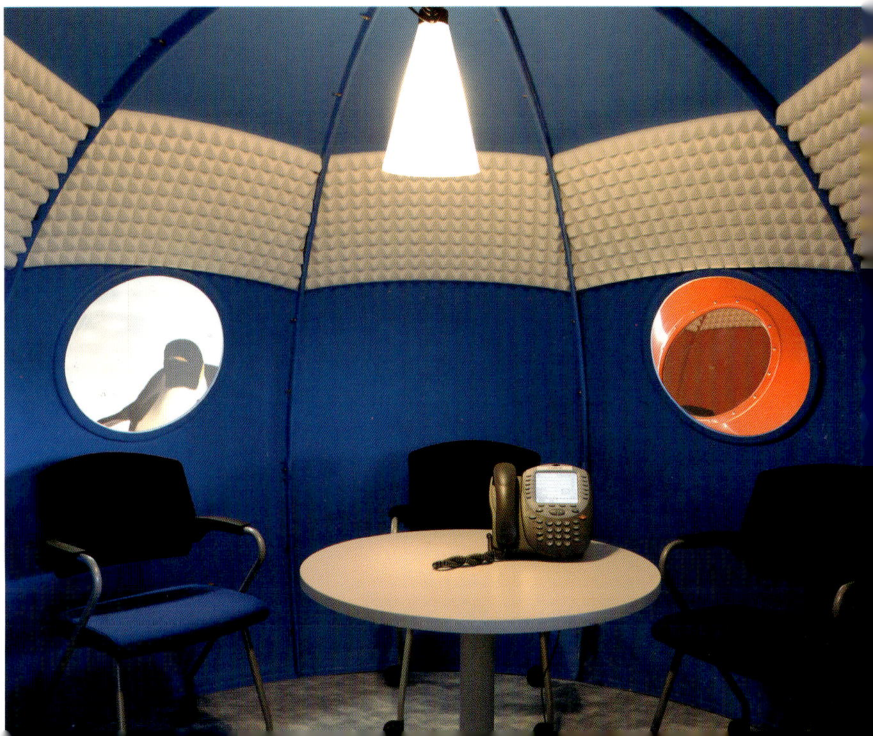

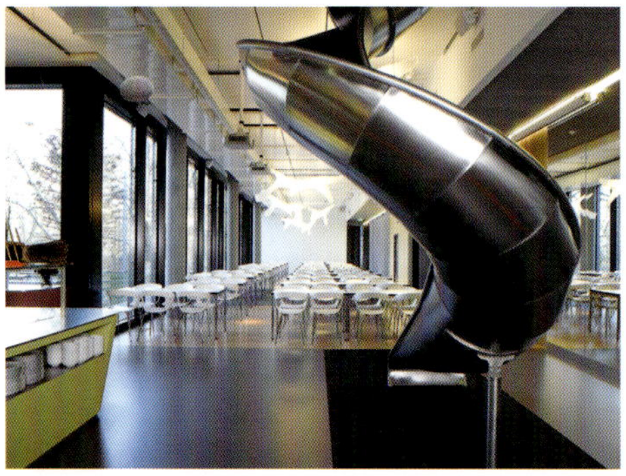
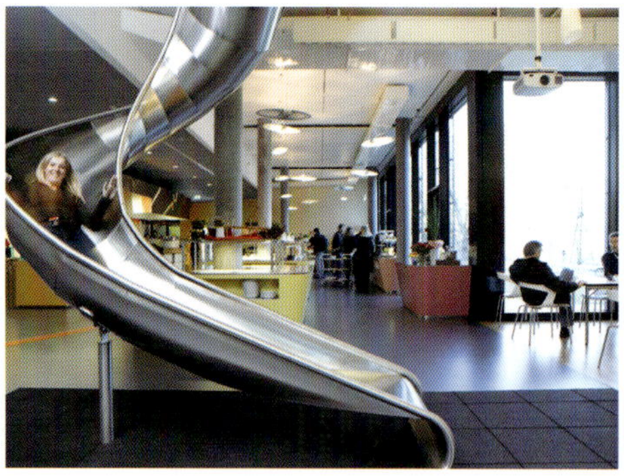
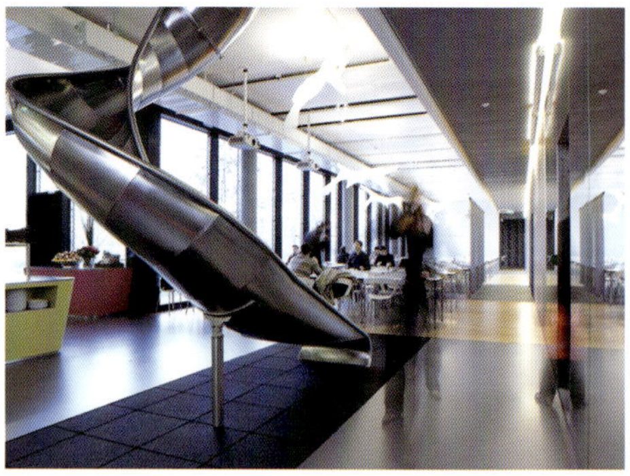
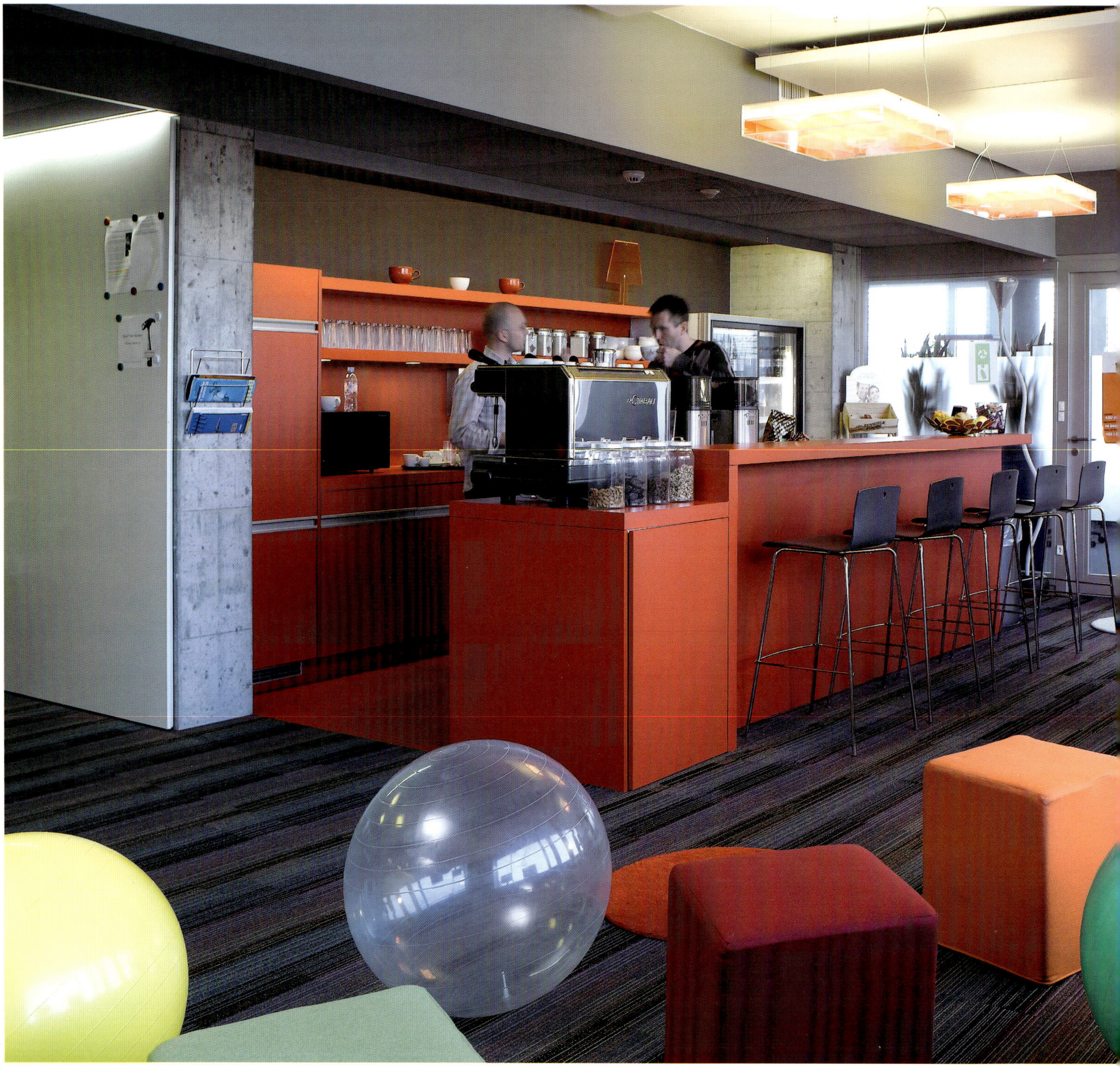

The communal areas are intentionally dispersed throughout the building to encourage Zooglers to circulate throughout the seven floors to enhance communication between the different working groups and teams. In this way the building has evolved into a Google city with easy reference points for Zooglers and visitors to navigate the building.

290

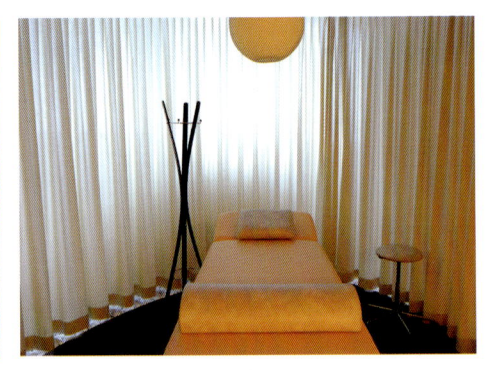

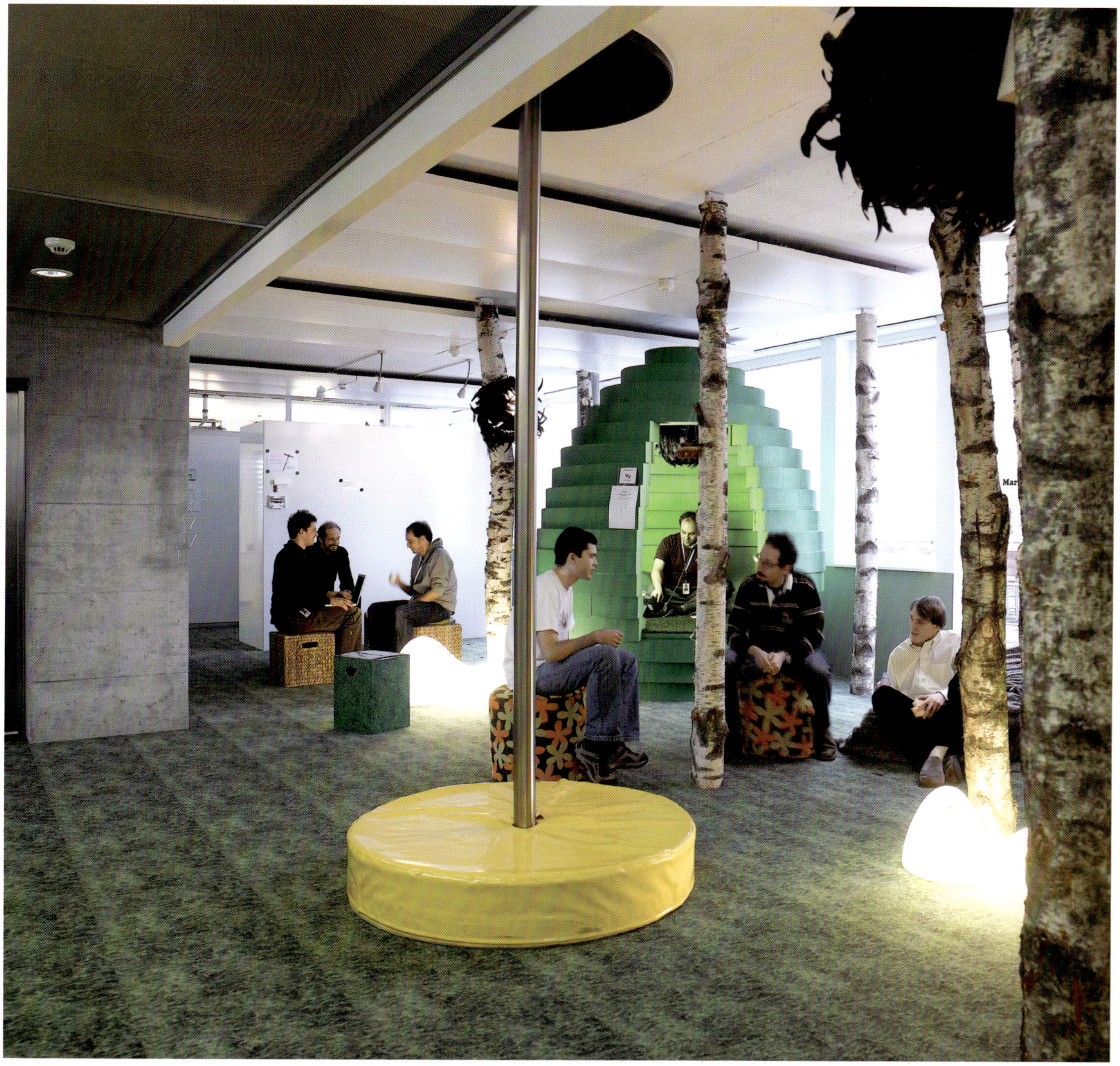

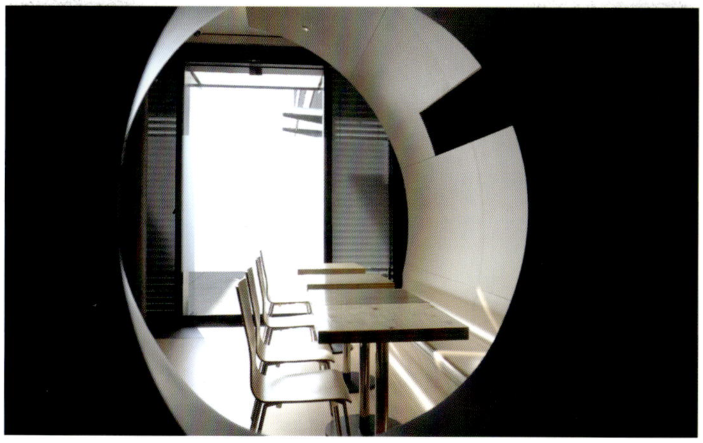

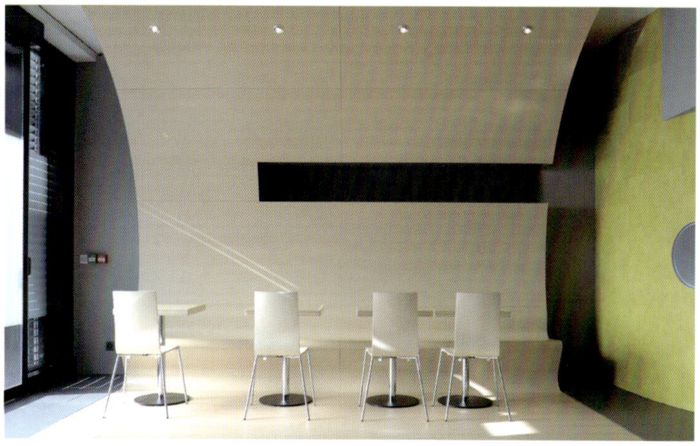

Clive Wilkinson Architects

The Disney Store Headquarters

Pasadena, California, USA **Photographs: Benny Chan / Fotoworks**

Clive Wilkinson Architects along with the workplace strategists DEGW conceived and designed The Disney Store's West Coast headquarters. The company decided to relocate its operations to the historically significant Royal Laundry Building (a former laundry built in 1927) in downtown Pasadena, California.

The design solution for the 7,525 sqm space evolved from the desire to create a functional yet playful environment that befits the Disney image. Equally significant was the company's desire for an open, flexible and collaborative work environment for 230 employees.

The original building is wooden-framed and composed of three parts. The front portion is a 16ft(4.9 m) high space with large timber trusses. The large rear portion is a double height wooden-framed atrium space with a saw-tooth roof that results in dramatic clerestory lighting spanning the width of the space. These two portions are connected by a long interstitial brick walled structure, which inspired the creation of brick-like elements for the interior. These modular elements allude to the playful block building habits of children and remind the staff of their role in creating products for the world of children.

The two major portions of the building are anchored by two main conference rooms. The first, known as the Block Conference Room, is formed on two sides by removable foam block walls. When these foam modules are disassembled for 200 person company-wide meetings, they become the seating system. On most days, they are vertically stacked in a brick pattern to form the walls for a 20 person meeting room.

The second main conference room, formed by a unique modular honeycomb structure, is located in the atrium portion of the building. Originally conceived as a flexible means of managing the Disney sample product display, it became the centerpiece of the space.

Approximately 500 modular honeycombs units, 24" (61 cm) wide by 17" (43 cm) deep and fabricated in rotation-molded plastic, form a dramatic two-story open conference room. The organic configuration of the undulating honeycomb units captures the light from the clerestory windows creating a warm glow in the room as well as in the surrounding space.

Architecture:
Clive Wilkinson Architects
Client:
The Children's Place
Workplace strategists:
DEGW
Floor area:
81,000 sqft (7,525 sqm)

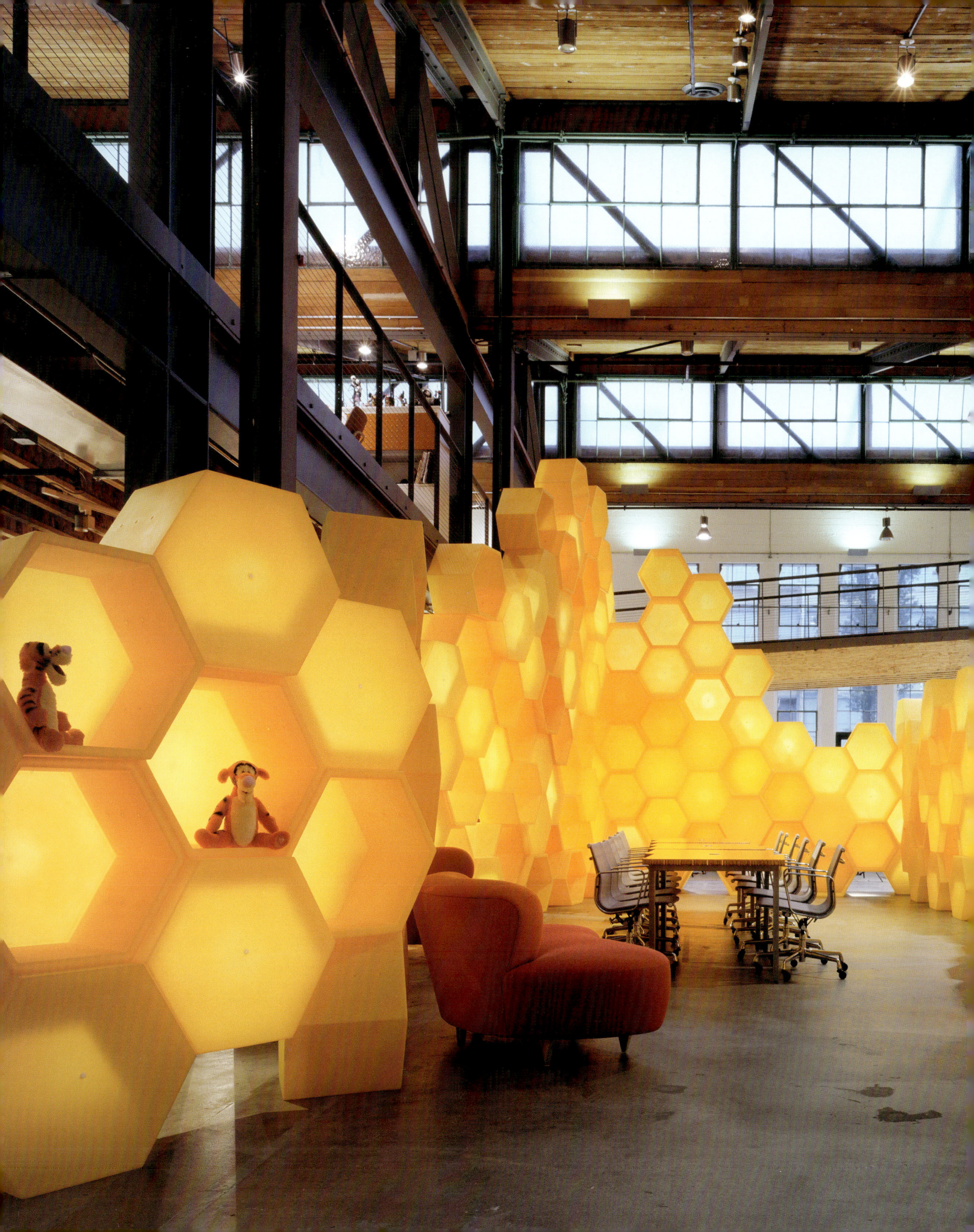

An ivy topiary of the Mickey Mouse ears is located at the front entrance.

First floor plan

Ground floor plan

A - Exterior courtyard
B - Reception
C - Block conference room
D - Mock store
E - Cafeteria
F - Pantry
G - Exterior lightwell
H - Workrooms
I - Brainstorming room
J - Training room
K - Informal lounge
L - Honeycomb conference room
M - Mail room
N - Library
O - Trend room
P - Executive conference room
Q - Executive offices
R - Executive reception
S - Garage

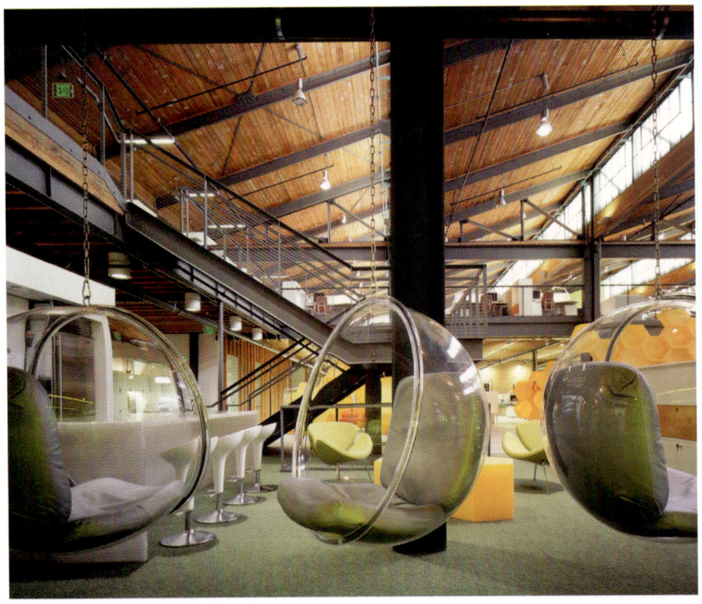

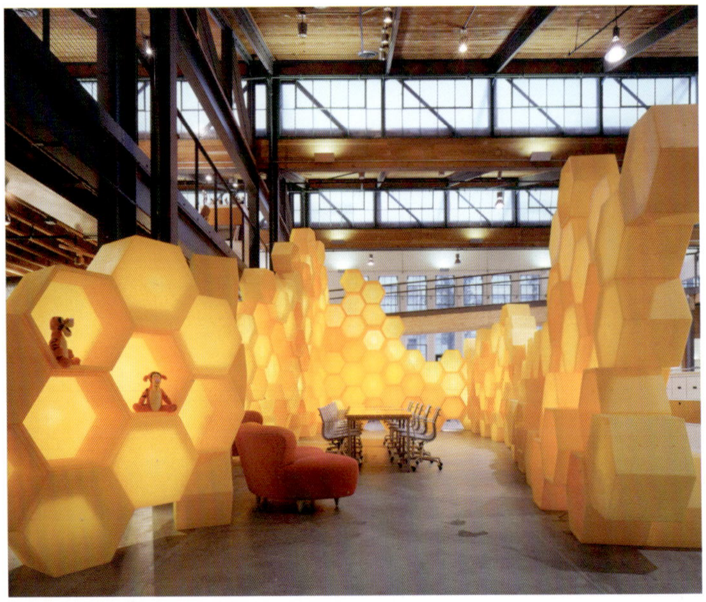

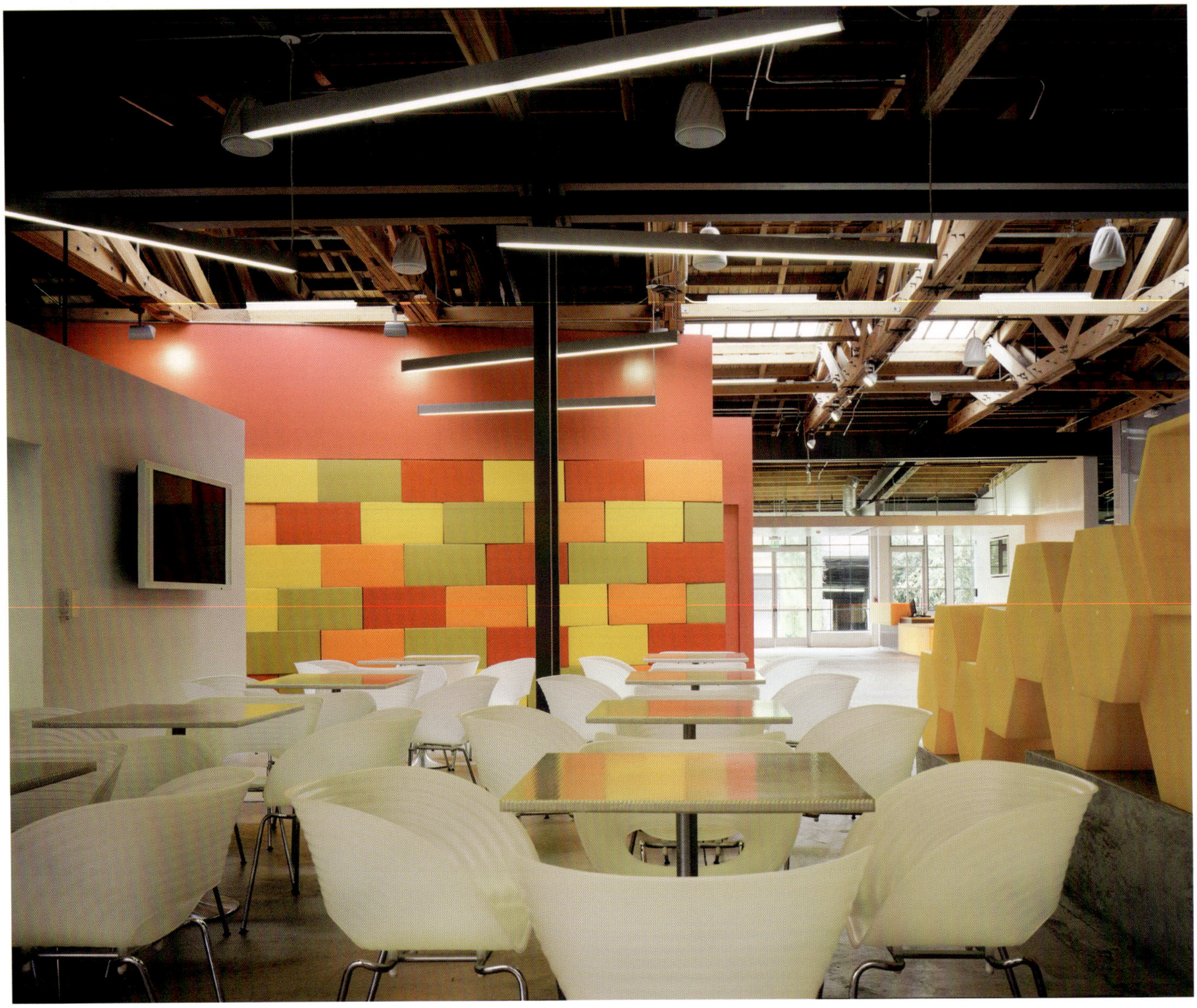

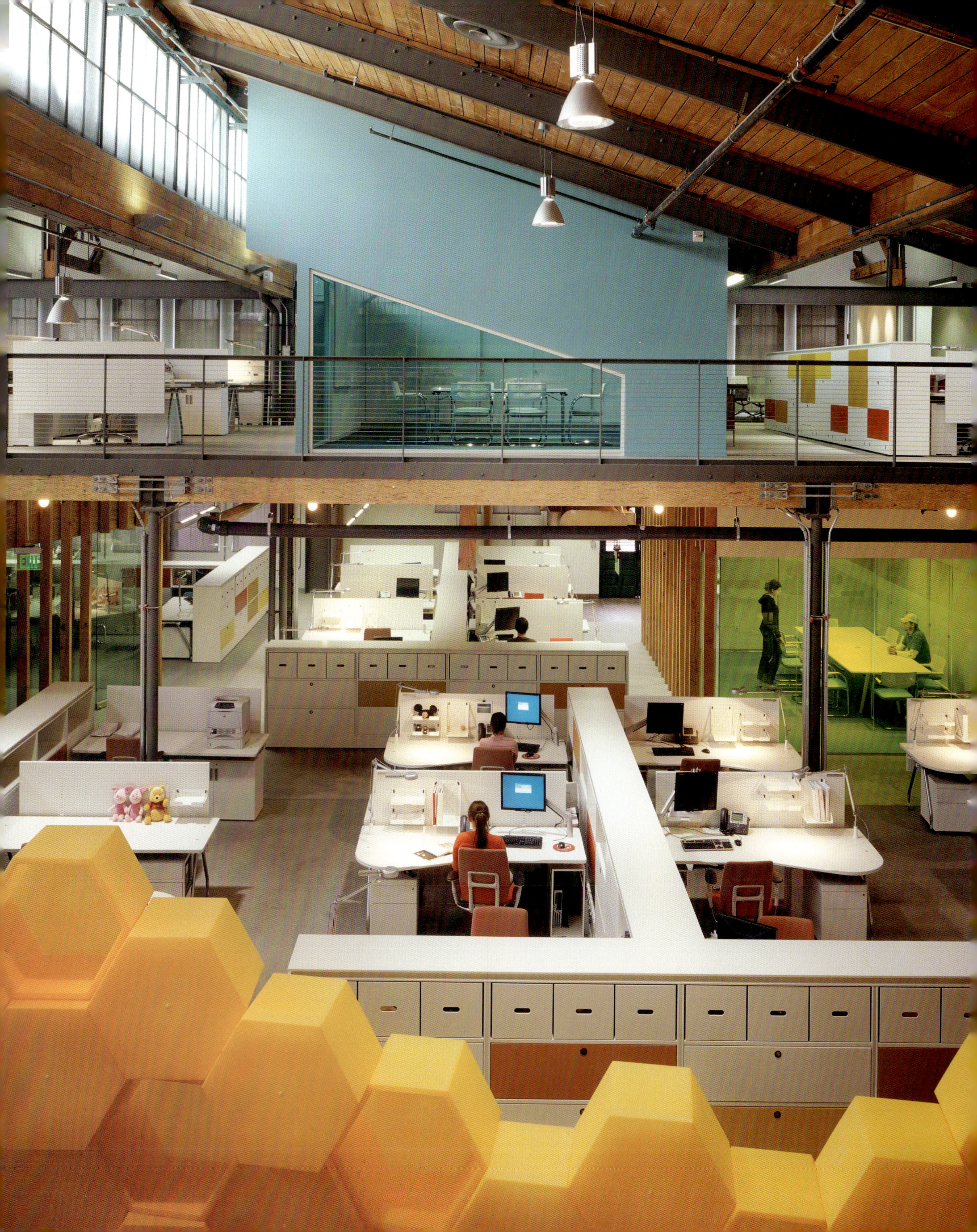

298

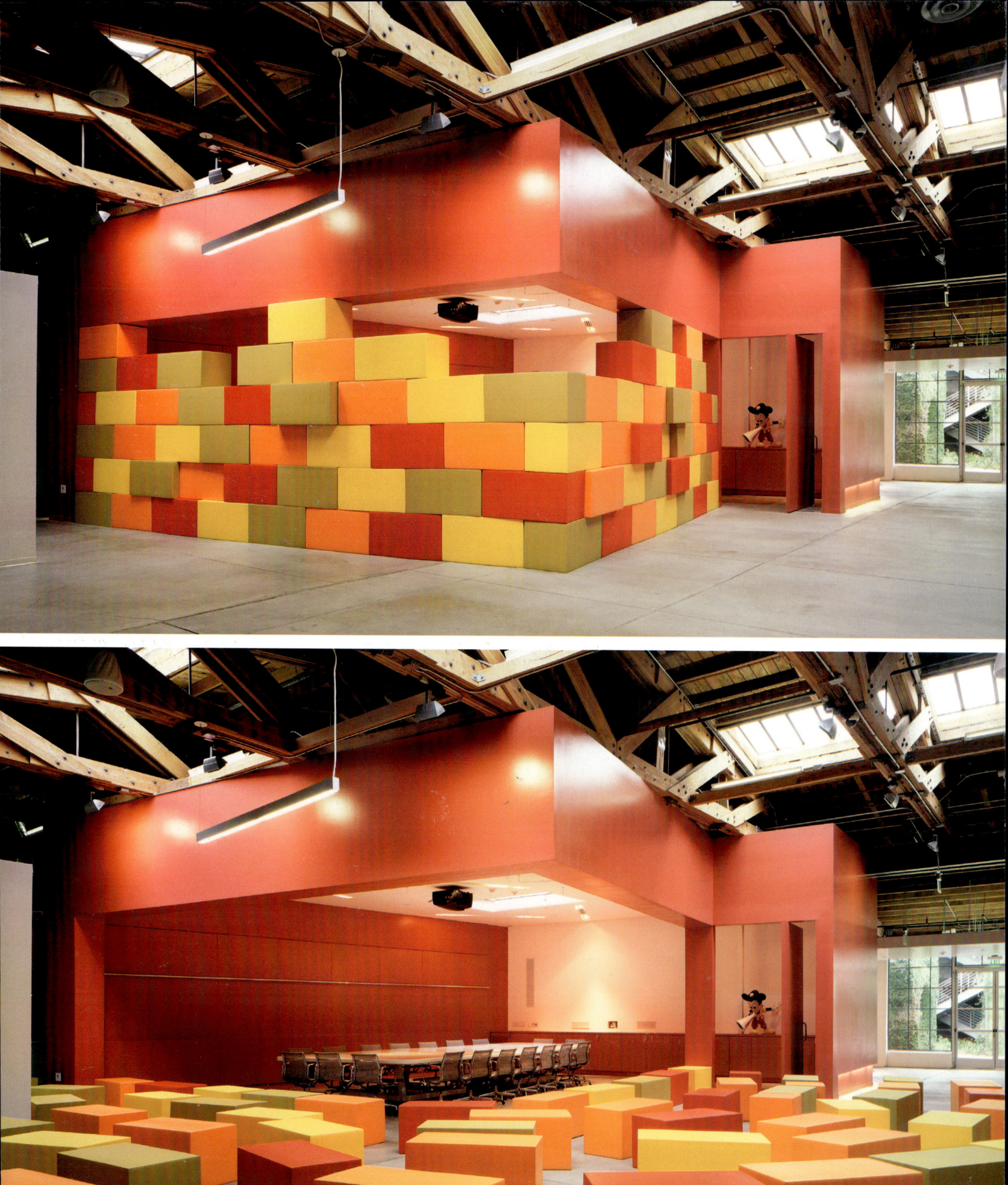